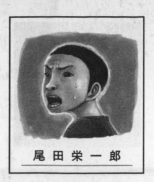

尾田栄一郎

Timing is important. George really has to fart.
But right now the classroom is really quiet. So he
thinks about it. If he shouts at the same time he
farts, he can cover up the sound. Ready...set...
"Aaaaaaaaaaargh!!!"
"What the heck?" *Murmur murmur!!*
Silence...
BRRRRAP!!!
All right, let's begin volume 43!!

  -Eiichiro Oda, 2006

E iichiro Oda began his manga career at the age of
17, when his one-shot cowboy manga **Wanted!**
won second place in the coveted Tezuka manga
awards. Oda went on to work as an assistant to
some of the biggest manga artists in the industry,
including Nobuhiro Watsuki, before winning the
Hop Step Award for new artists. His pirate
adventure **One Piece**, which debuted in
Weekly Shonen Jump in 1997, quickly became
one of the most popular manga in Japan.

ONE PIECE VOL. 43
WATER SEVEN PART 12

SHONEN JUMP Manga Edition

STORY AND ART BY EIICHIRO ODA

English Adaptation/Jake Forbes
Translation/John Werry
Touch-up Art & Lettering/Hudson Yards
Design/Sean Lee
Supervising Editor/Yuki Murashige
Editor/Yuki Takagaki

VP, Production/Alvin Lu
VP, Sales & Product Marketing/Gonzalo Ferreyra
VP, Creative/Linda Espinosa
Publisher/Hyoe Narita

Printed in the U.S.A.

Published by VIZ Media, LLC
P.O. Box 77010
San Francisco, CA 94107

10 9 8 7 6 5 4 3 2 1
First printing, April 2010

www.viz.com

THE WORLD'S
MOST POPULAR MANGA

www.shonenjump.com

WATER SEVEN

Vol. 43
Legend of a Hero

CONTENTS

THE STORY OF ONE PIECE

Volume 43

Monkey D. Luffy started out as just a kid with a dream—to become the greatest pirate in history! Stirred by the tales of pirate "Red-Haired" Shanks, Luffy vowed to become a pirate himself. That was before the enchanted Devil Fruit gave Luffy the power to stretch like rubber, at the cost of being unable to swim—a serious handicap for an aspiring sea dog. Undeterred, Luffy set out to sea and recruited some crewmates—master swordsman Zolo; treasure-hunting thief Nami; lying sharpshooter Usopp; the high-kicking chef Sanji; Chopper, the walkin' talkin' reindeer doctor; and the mysterious archaeologist Robin.

After many adventures have left their ship, the *Merry Go*, in less than seaworthy condition, the Straw Hats crew set sail for the city of Water Seven in the hopes of finding a shipwright to join their crew. There they learn that the ship is beyond repair, so Luffy reluctantly decides to find a new ship. Usopp, however, is fiercely opposed to this decision and leaves the crew.

The covert government agency Cipher Pol No. 9 has also come to Water Seven, looking for the blueprints for the ancient weapon the Pluton. They capture Robin and the hot-headed ship dismantler Franky, both of whom are key to unlocking the Pluton's secrets. Luffy and the crew come to their rescue and succeed in rescuing Franky, but Robin is taken to the judicial island, Enies Lobby. As CP9's leader, Spandam, leads Robin to the Gates of Justice, he accidentally presses the button for a Buster Call which summons the Navy to annihilate Enies Lobby and everyone on it! The Straw Hats don't have a moment to lose if they want to get out alive!

The Franky Family

Professional ship dismantlers, they moonlight as bounty hunters.

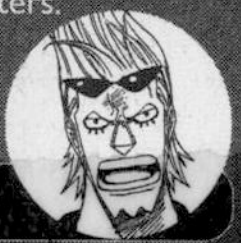

The master builder and an apprentice of Tom, the legendary shipwright.

Franky (Cutty Flam)

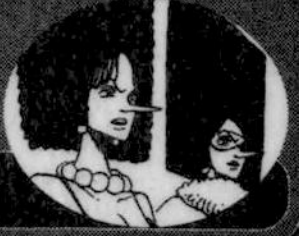

The Square Sisters

Kiwi & Mozu

Galley-La Company

A top shipbuilding company. They are purveyors to the World Government.

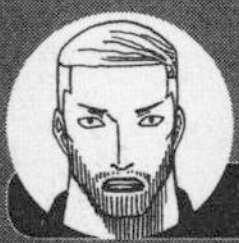

Mayor of Water Seven and president of Galley-La Company. Also one of Tom's apprentices.

Iceberg

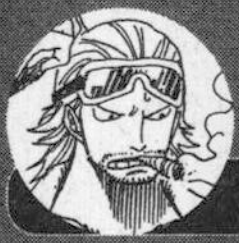

Rigging and Mast Foreman

Paulie

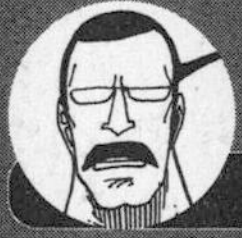

Pitch, Blacksmithing and Block-and-Tackle Foreman

Peepley Lulu

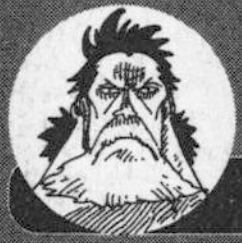

Cabinetry, Caulking and Flag-Making Foreman

Tilestone

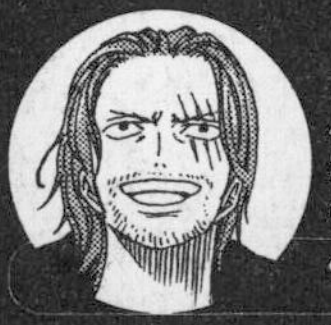

A pirate that Luffy idolizes. Shanks gave Luffy his trademark straw hat.

"Red-Haired" Shanks

Cipher Pol No. 9

A covert intelligence agency under the direct supervision of the World Government. They have been granted the license to kill uncooperative citizens.

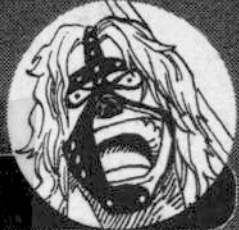

Director

Spandam

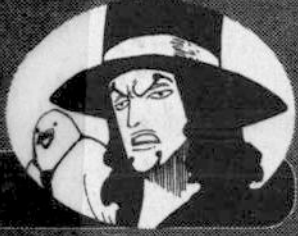

Rob Lucci & Hattori

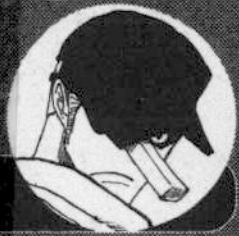

Kaku

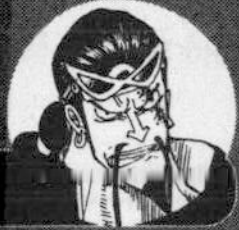

Jabra

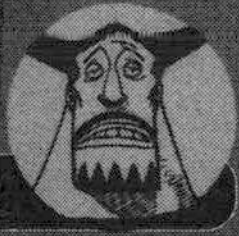

Blueno

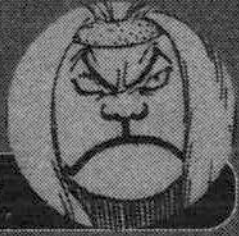

Kumadori

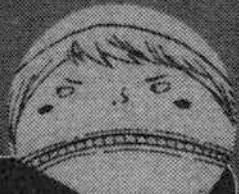

Fukurô

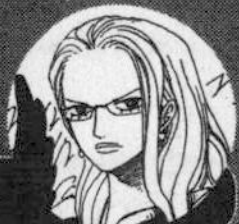

Kalifa

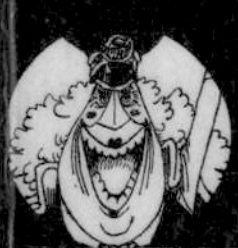

Formerly the beautiful secretary of Tom's workers. Currently operates the Sea Train. Stationmaster of Shift Station

Kokoro

The Straw Hats

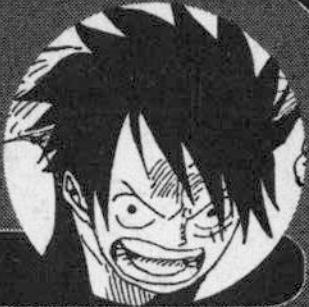

Boundlessly optimistic and able to stretch like rubber, he is determined to become King of the Pirates.

Monkey D. Luffy

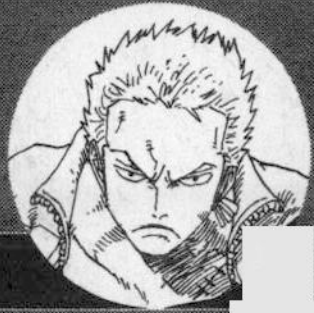

A former bounty hunter and master of the "three-sword" style. He aspires to be the world's greatest swordsman.

Roronoa Zolo

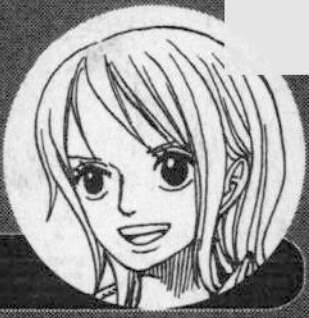

A thief who specializes in robbing pirates. Nami hates pirates, but Luffy convinced her to be his navigator.

Nami

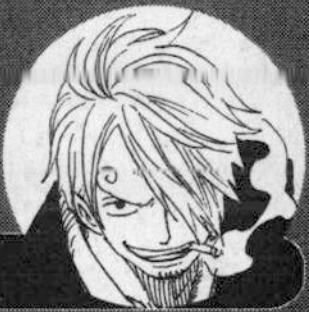

The bighearted cook (and ladies' man) whose dream is to find the legendary sea, the "All Blue."

Sanji

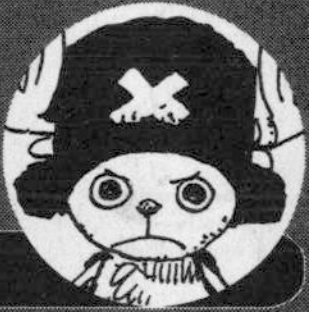

A blue-nosed man-reindeer and the ship's doctor.

Tony Tony Chopper

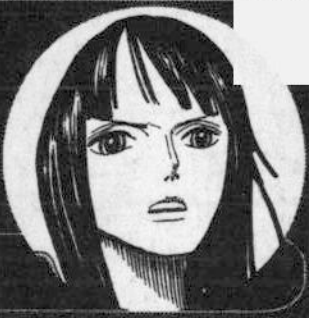

A mysterious woman in search of the Ponegliff on which true history is recorded.

Nico Robin

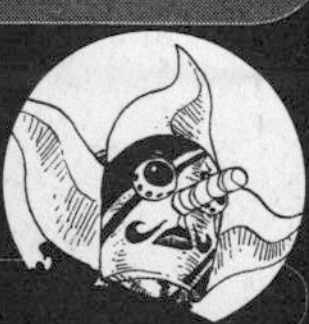

A "good friend" of former crewmate Usopp and a superhero who's come to save Luffy and crew... or at least that's what he says.

Sniper King

SHONEN JUMP MANGA

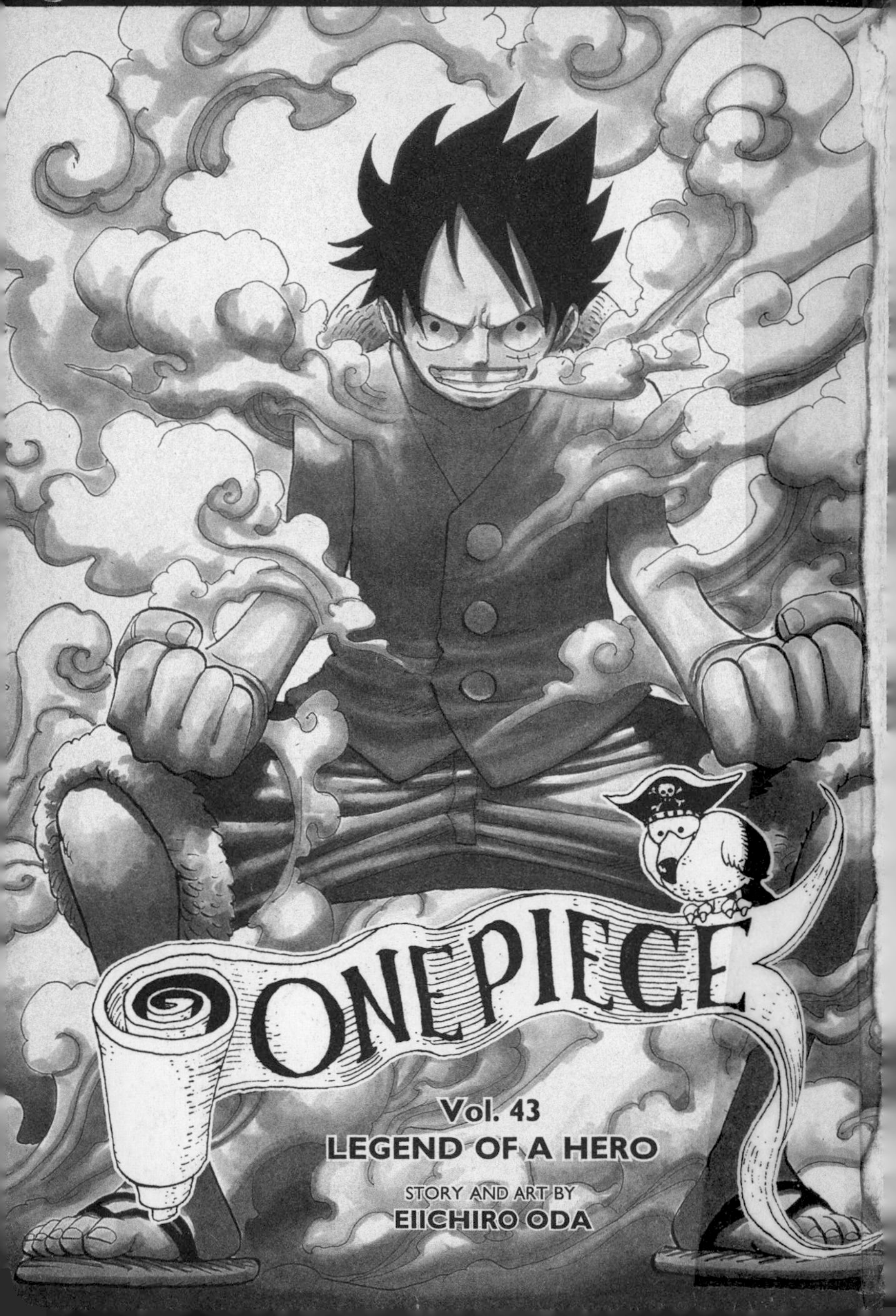

ONE PIECE

Vol. 43
LEGEND OF A HERO

STORY AND ART BY
EIICHIRO ODA

SUPER-SIZE NAMI

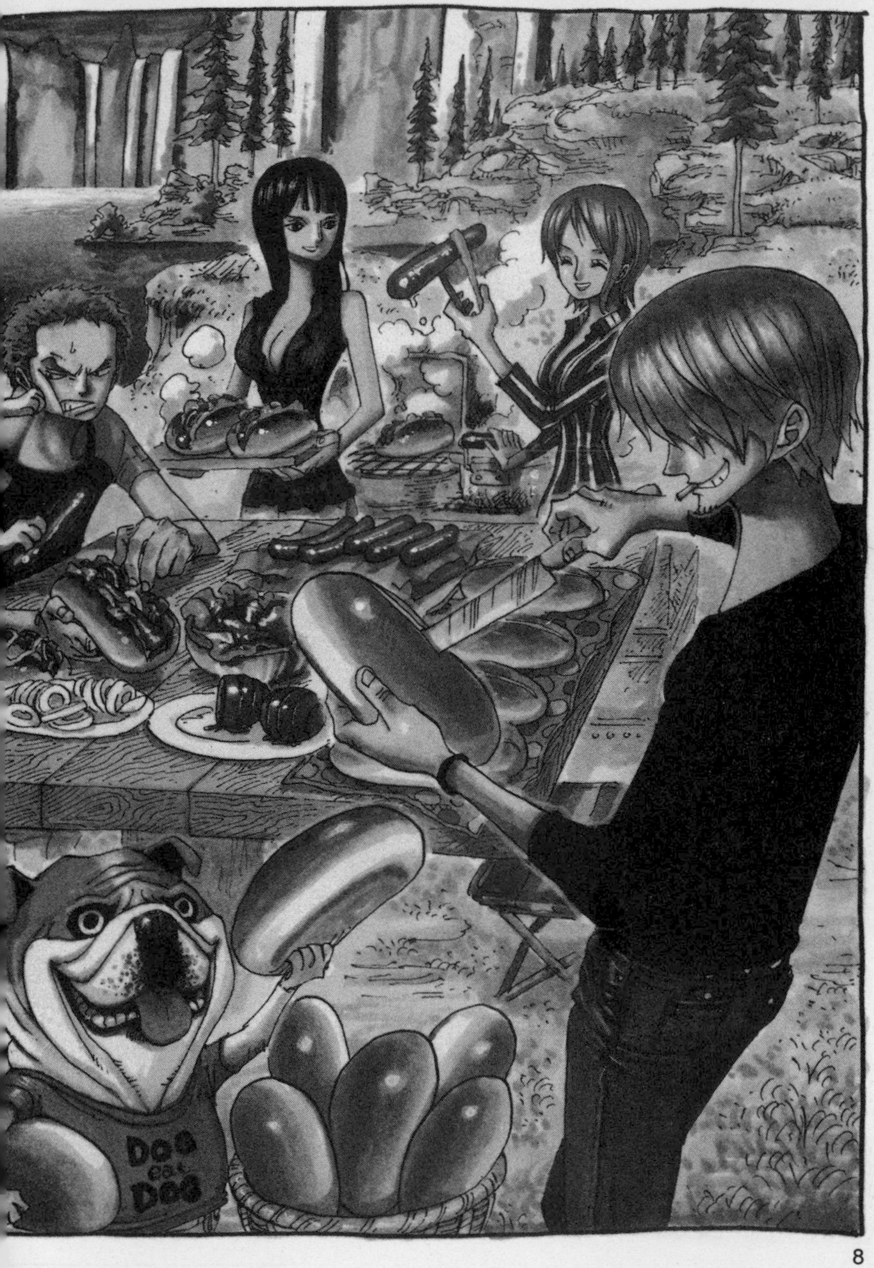
Dog eat Dog

Chapter 410:

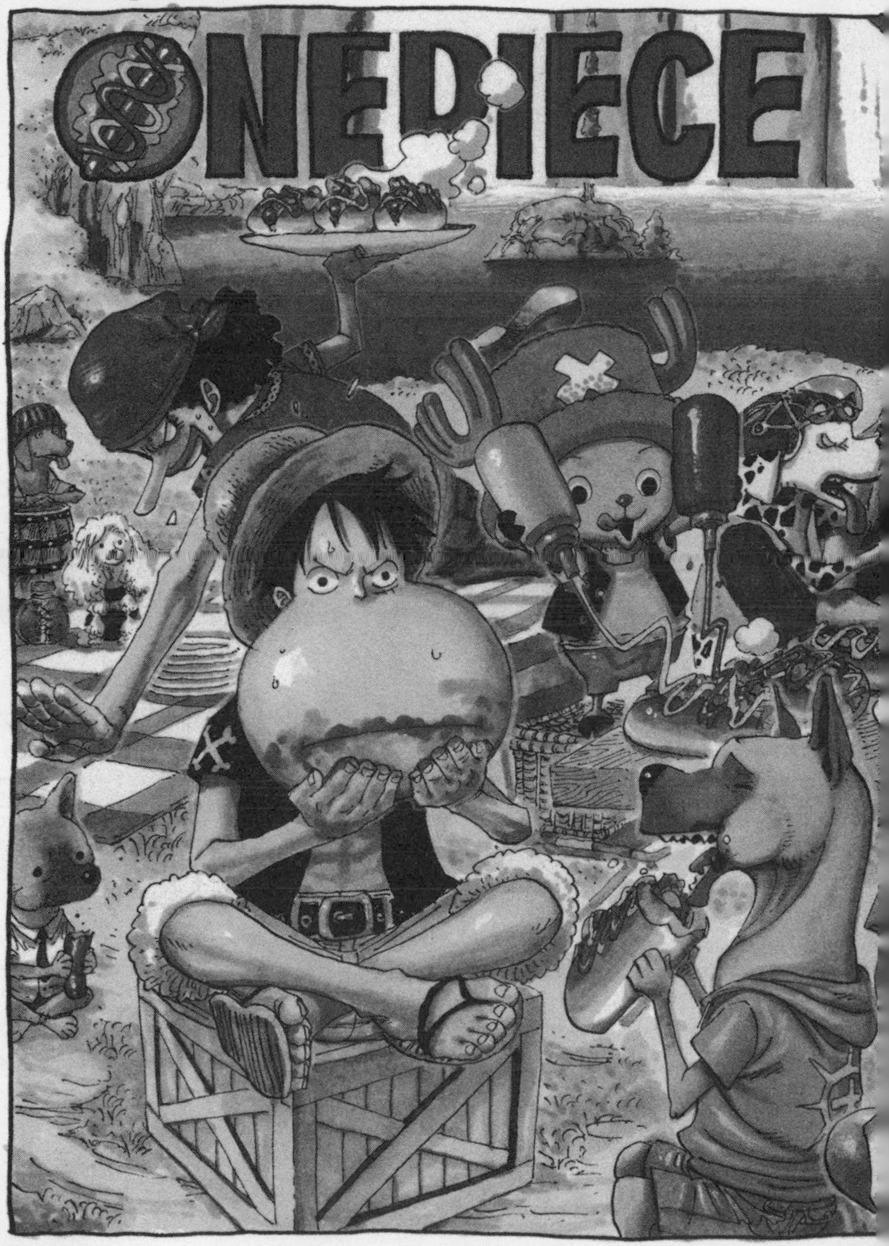
ONE PIECE

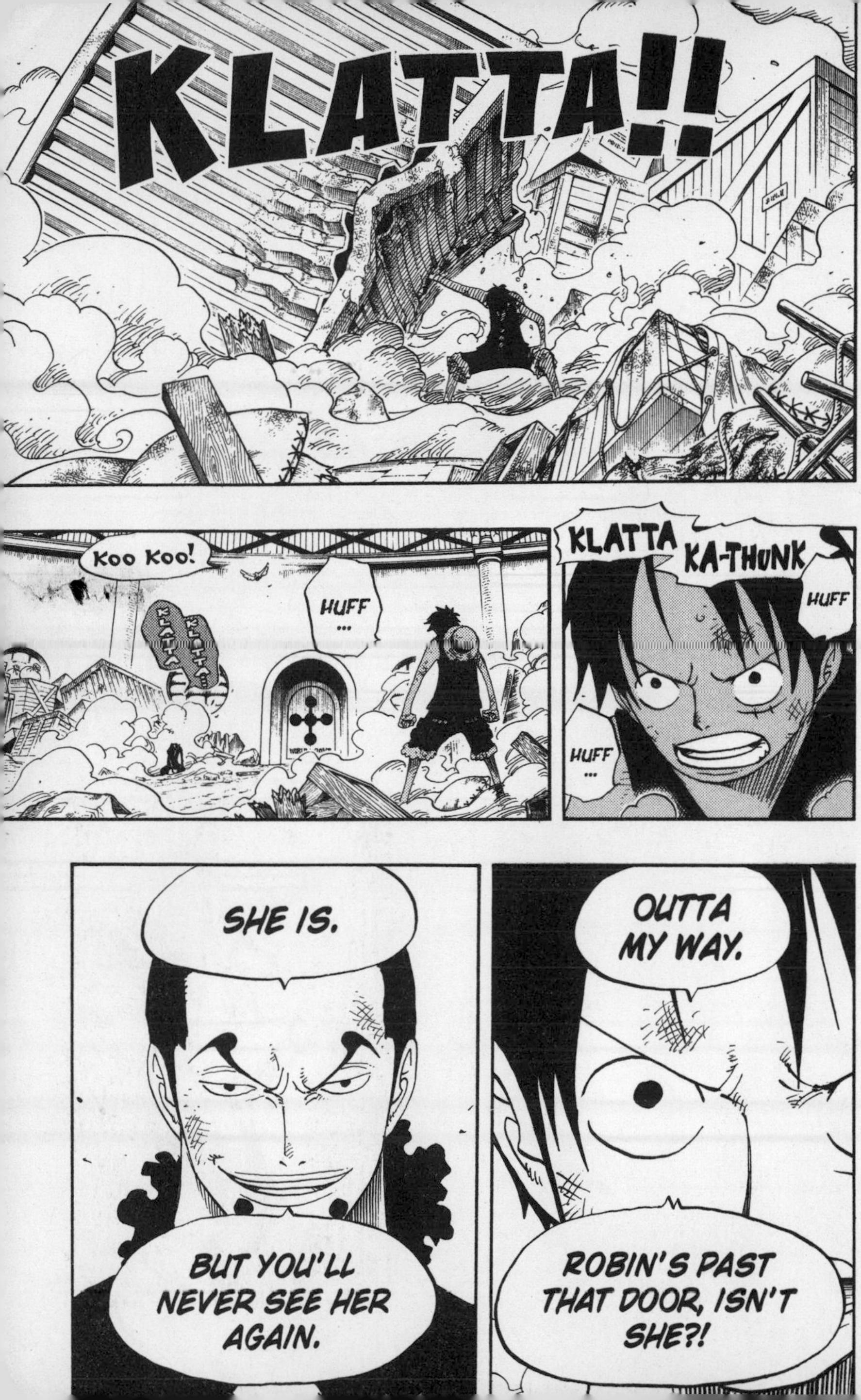
KLATTA!!
KLATTA
KA-THUNK
HUFF
HUFF ...
Koo Koo!
HUFF ...
KLATTA
KLATTA...
OUTTA MY WAY.
ROBIN'S PAST THAT DOOR, ISN'T SHE?!
SHE IS.
BUT YOU'LL NEVER SEE HER AGAIN.

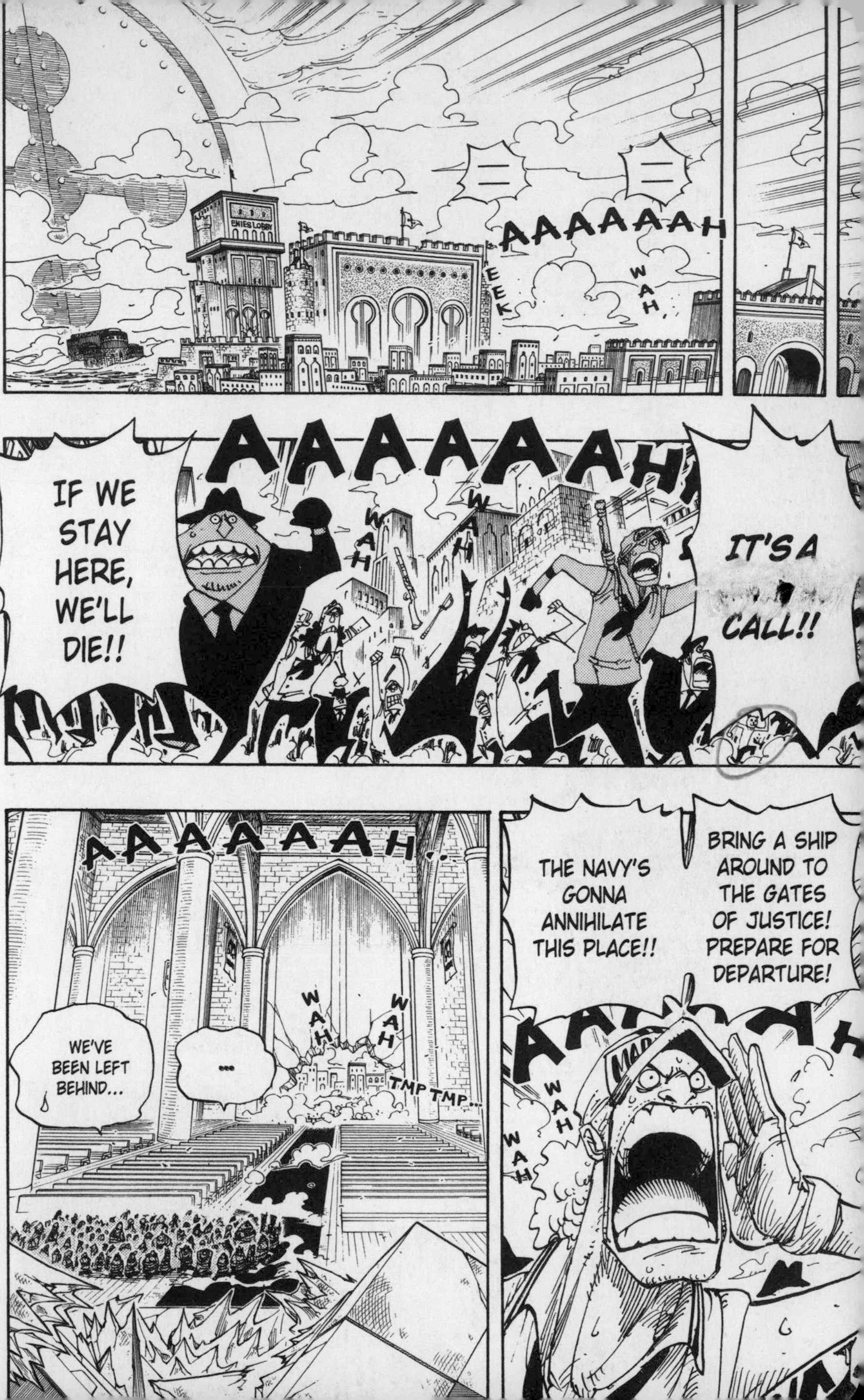

AAAAAAH
EEEK
WAH
IT'S A
CALL!!
AAAAAAH
WAH
WAH
IF WE STAY HERE, WE'LL DIE!!
BRING A SHIP AROUND TO THE GATES OF JUSTICE! PREPARE FOR DEPARTURE!
THE NAVY'S GONNA ANNIHILATE THIS PLACE!!
WAH
WAH
AAAAAAH
WAH
WAH
TMP TMP...
...
WE'VE BEEN LEFT BEHIND...

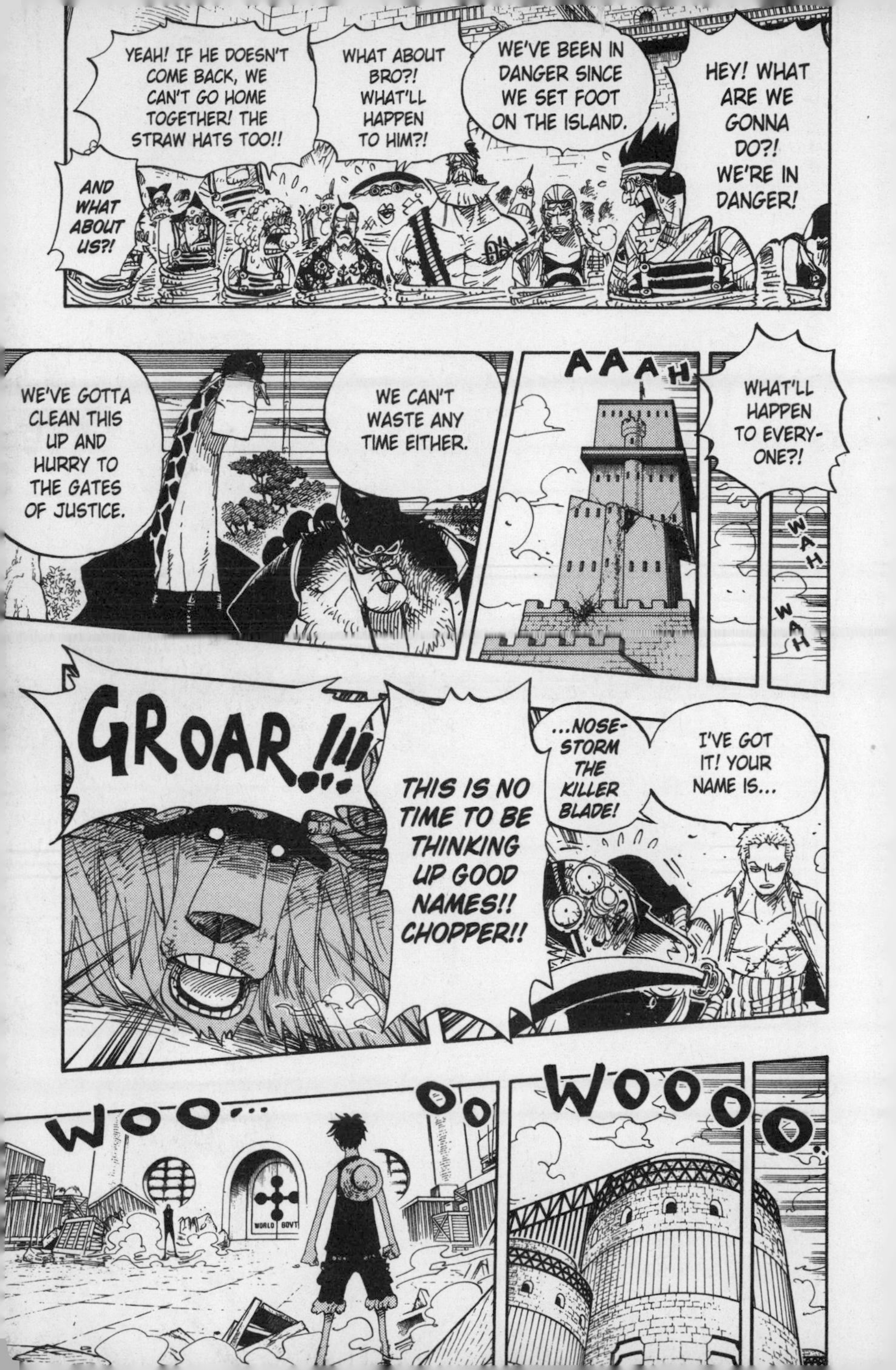

HEY! WHAT ARE WE GONNA DO?! WE'RE IN DANGER!
WE'VE BEEN IN DANGER SINCE WE SET FOOT ON THE ISLAND.
WHAT ABOUT BRO?! WHAT'LL HAPPEN TO HIM?!
YEAH! IF HE DOESN'T COME BACK, WE CAN'T GO HOME TOGETHER! THE STRAW HATS TOO!!
AND WHAT ABOUT US?!
WHAT'LL HAPPEN TO EVERY-ONE?!
WAH
WAH
AAAH
WE CAN'T WASTE ANY TIME EITHER.
WE'VE GOTTA CLEAN THIS UP AND HURRY TO THE GATES OF JUSTICE.
I'VE GOT IT! YOUR NAME IS...
...NOSE-STORM THE KILLER BLADE!
THIS IS NO TIME TO BE THINKING UP GOOD NAMES!! CHOPPER!!
GROAR!!!
WOOOO..
WORLD GOVT
WOO... OO

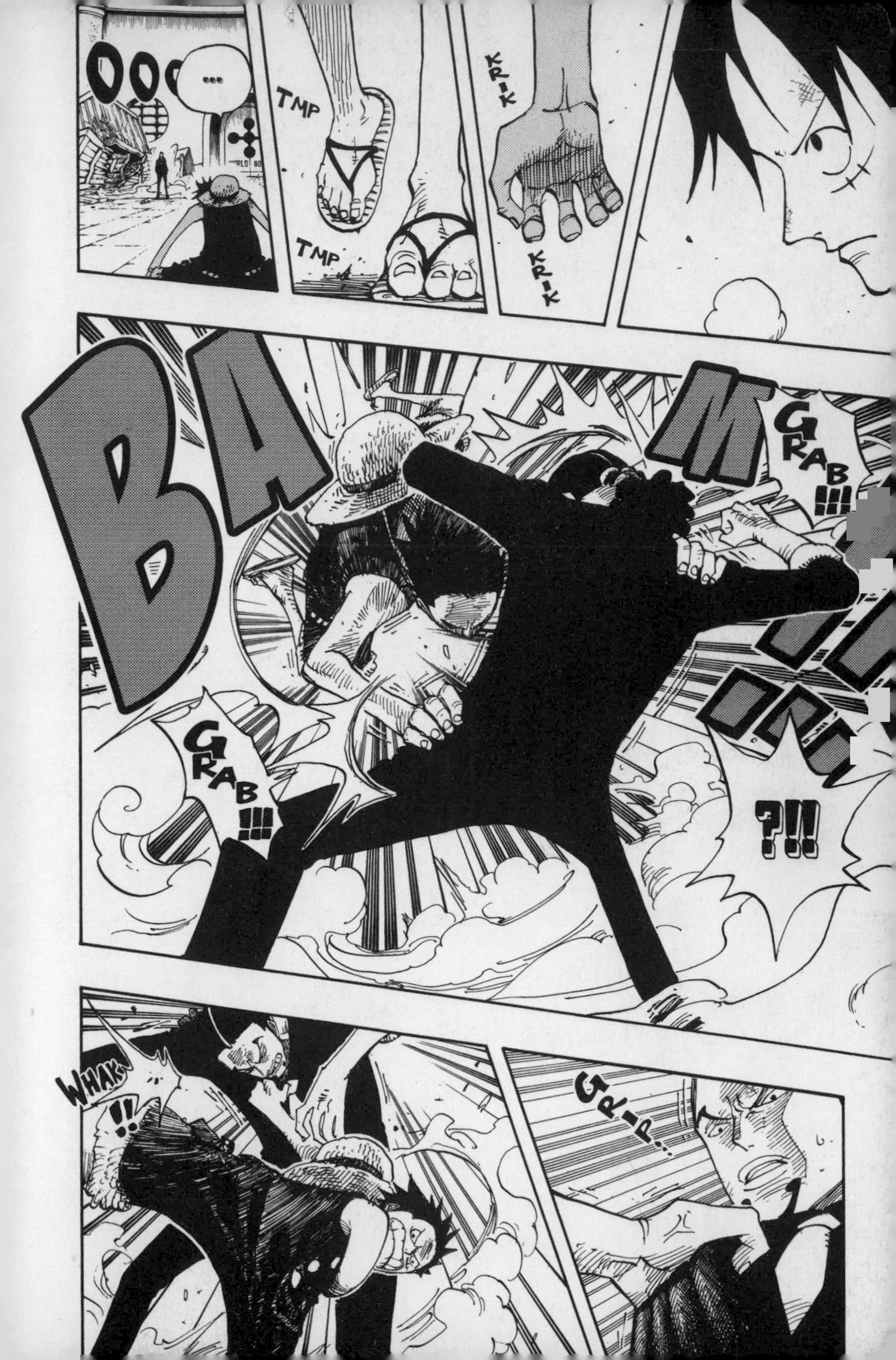
KRIK
KRIK
TMP
TMP
...
BAM
GRAB!!!
?!!
GRAB!!!
GR-P...
WHAK!!

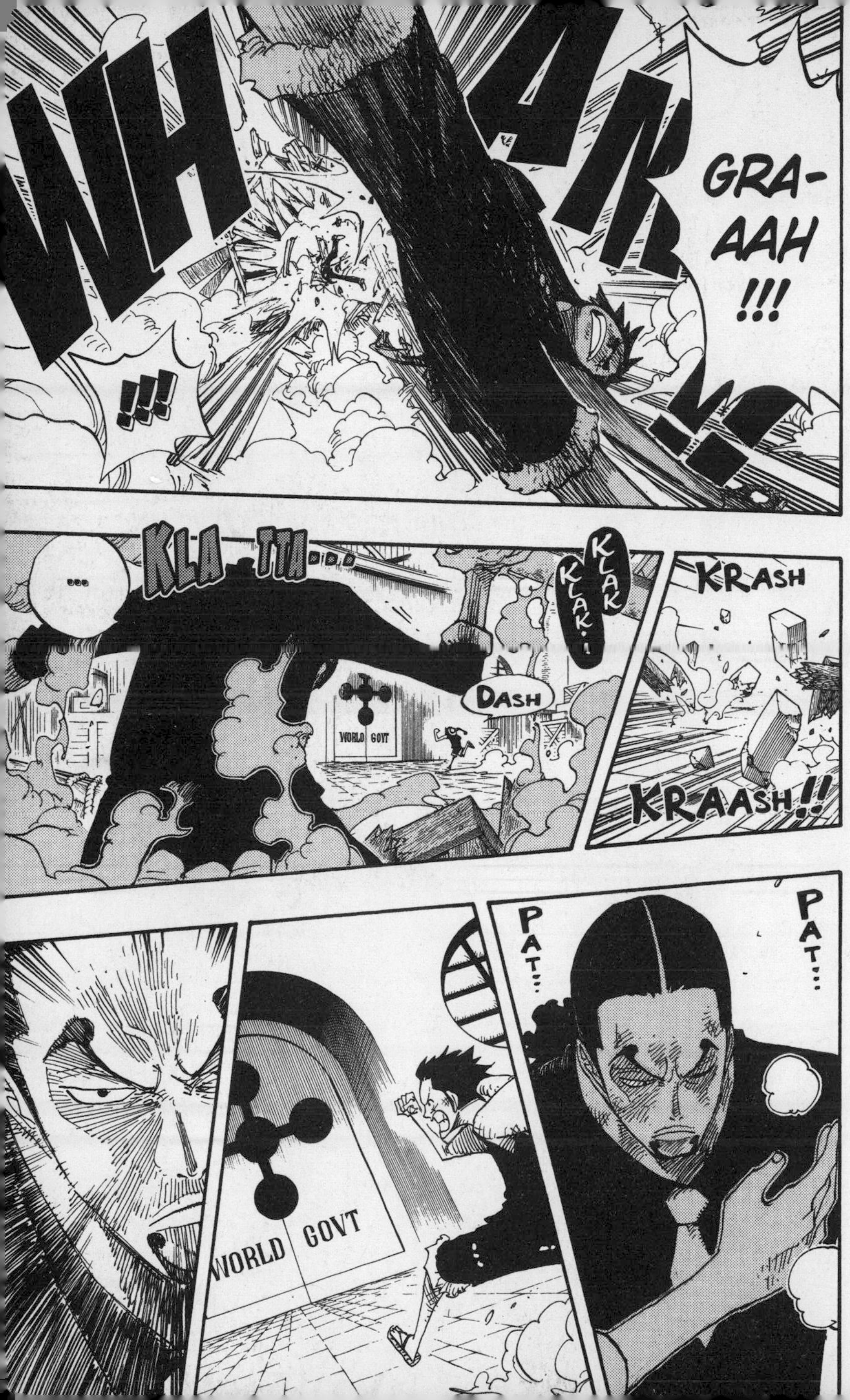
GRA-AAH!!!
WHAAM!!
!!!
KRASH
KRAASH!!
KLAK KLAK KLAK..!
DASH
WORLD GOVT
KLATTA...
...
PAT...
PAT...
WORLD GOVT

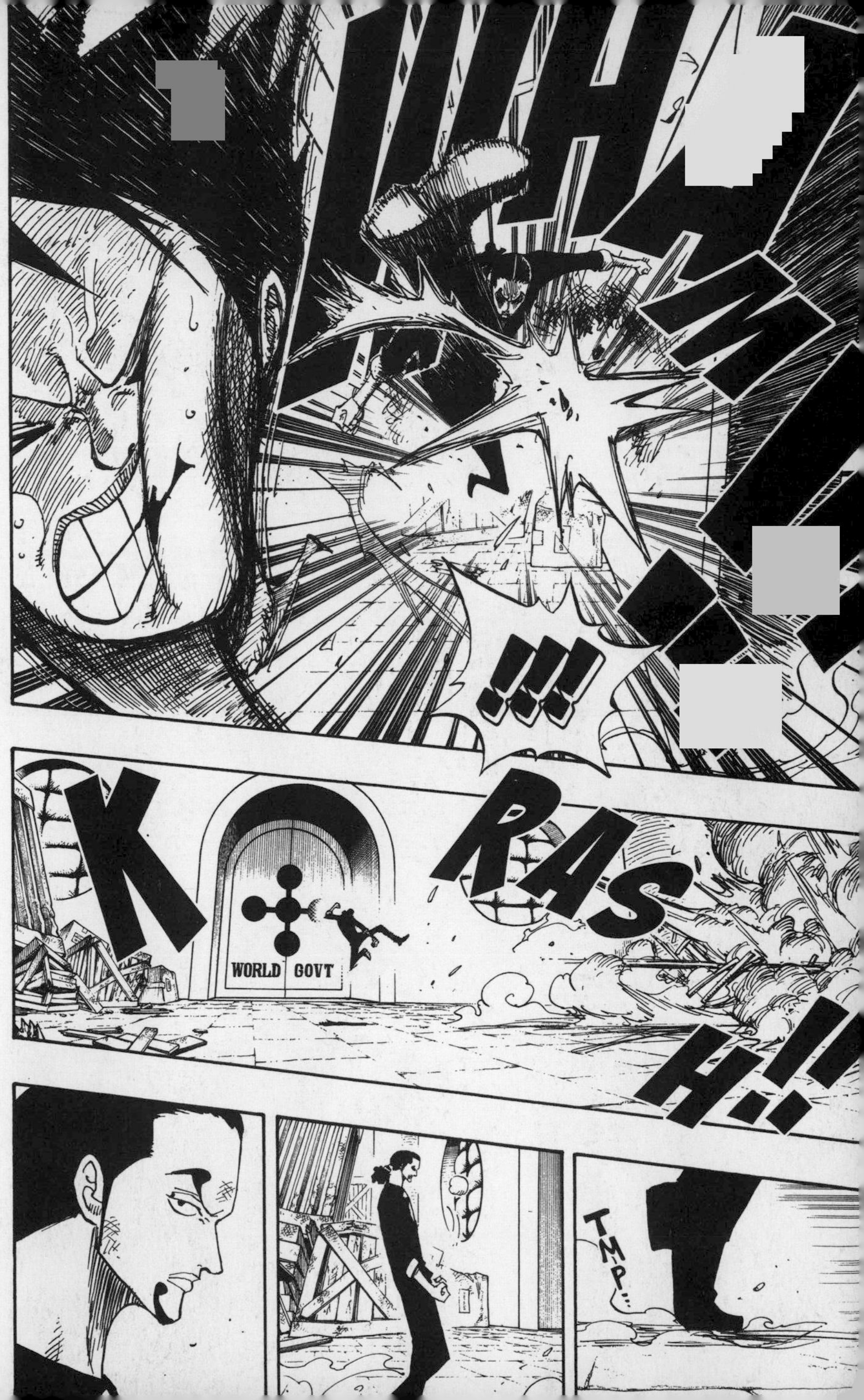
!!!
WORLD GOVT
KRASH!!
TMP...

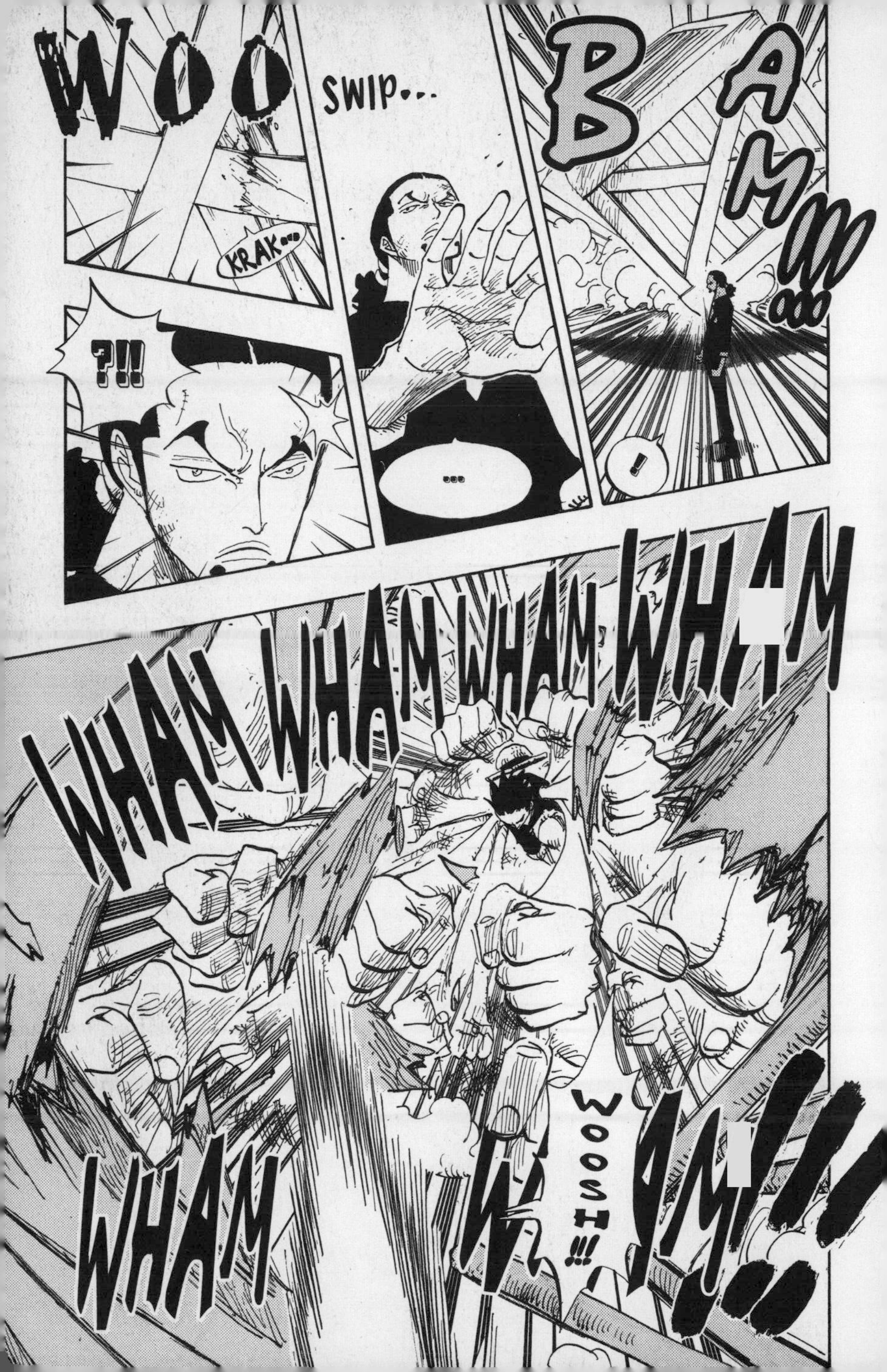
BAMM!!...
!
SWIP...
...
WOOO
KRAK...
?!!
WHAM WHAM WHAM WHAM
WOOSH!!!
WHAM!!...
WHAM

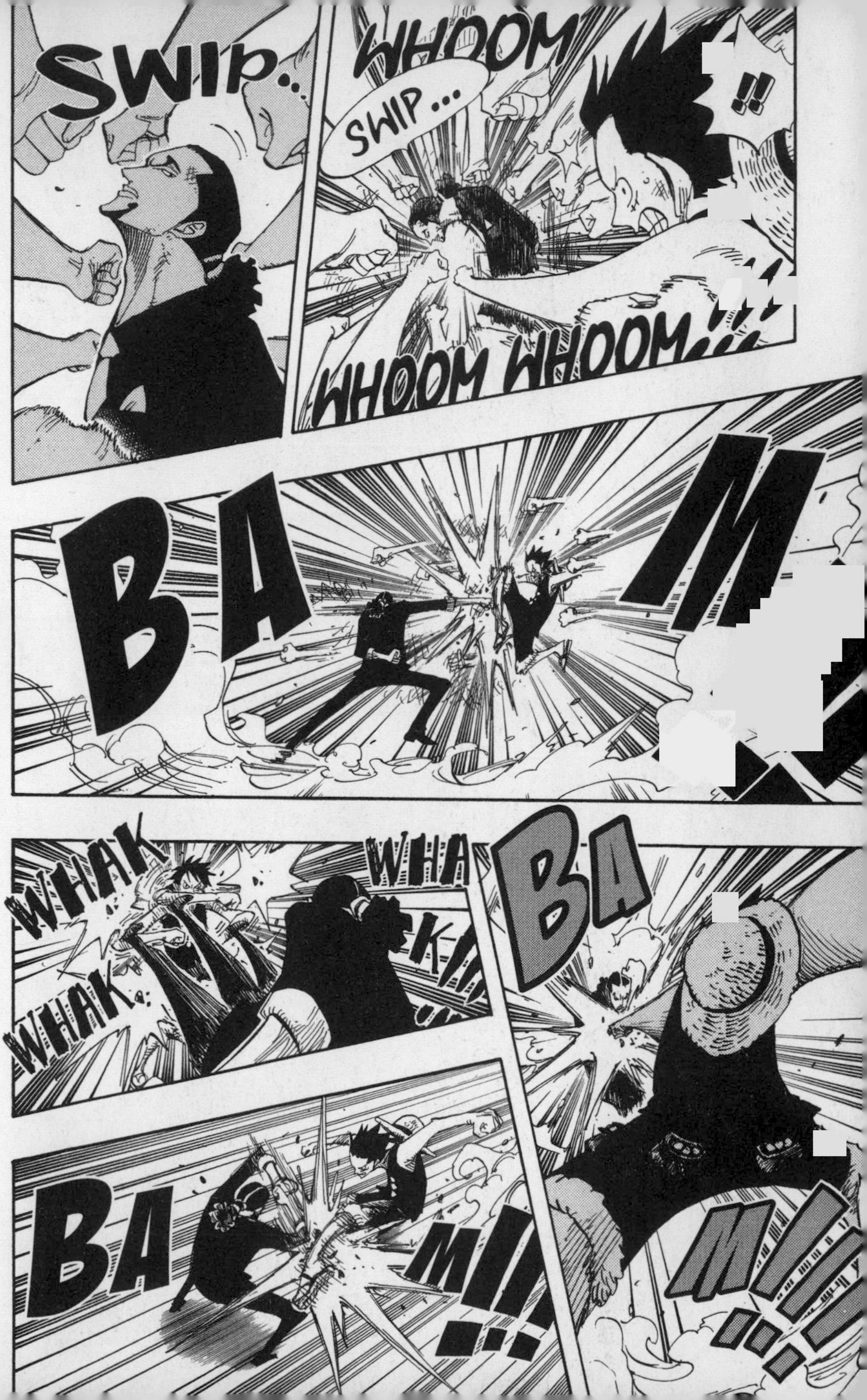
WHOOM
SWIP...
!!
WHOOM WHOOM...
SWIP...
BAM
BAM!!
WHAK
WHAK
WHAK!!
BAM!!

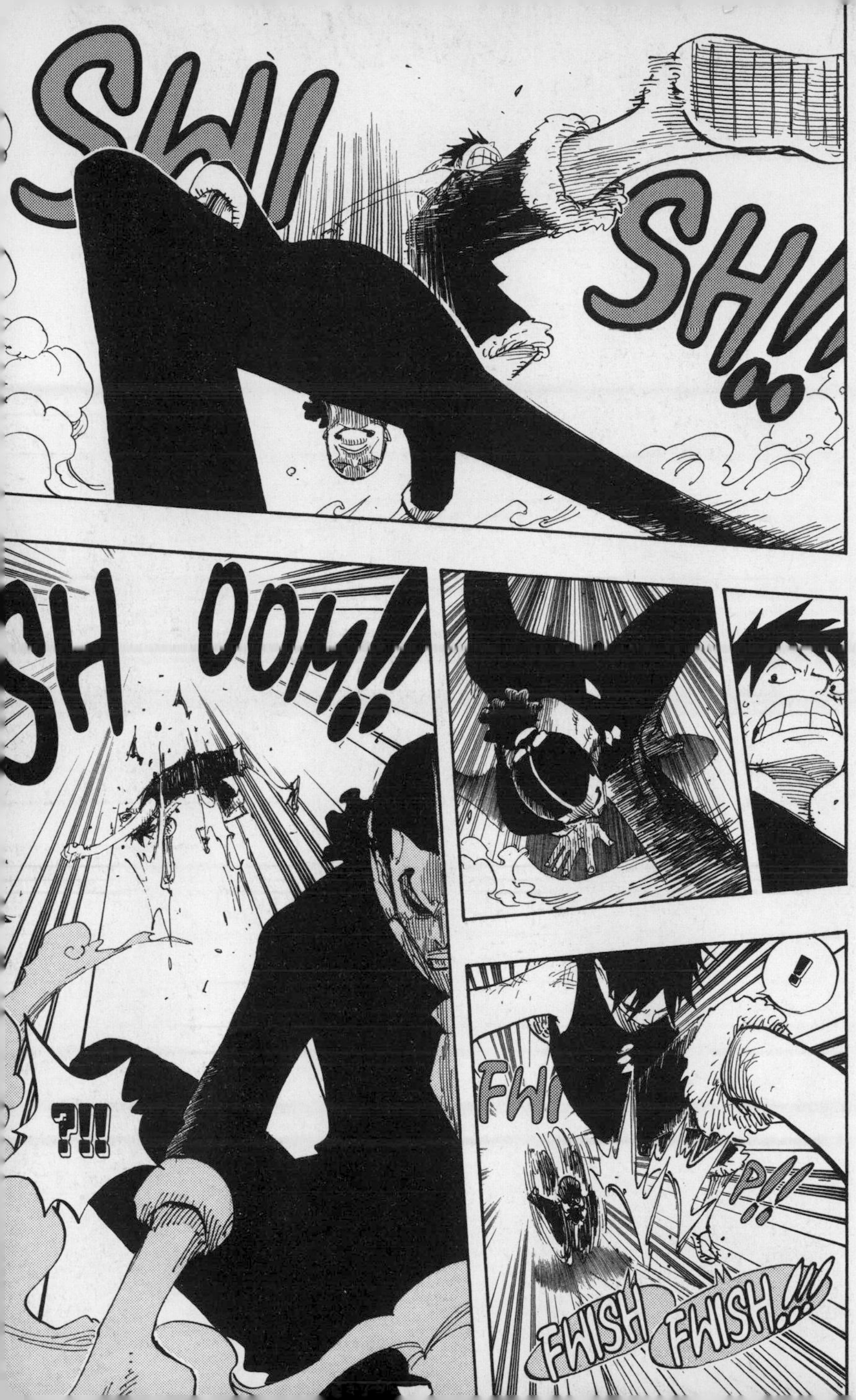
SHI..
SHI
!
FWI
P!!
FWISH FWISH...!!!
SH
OOM!!
?!!

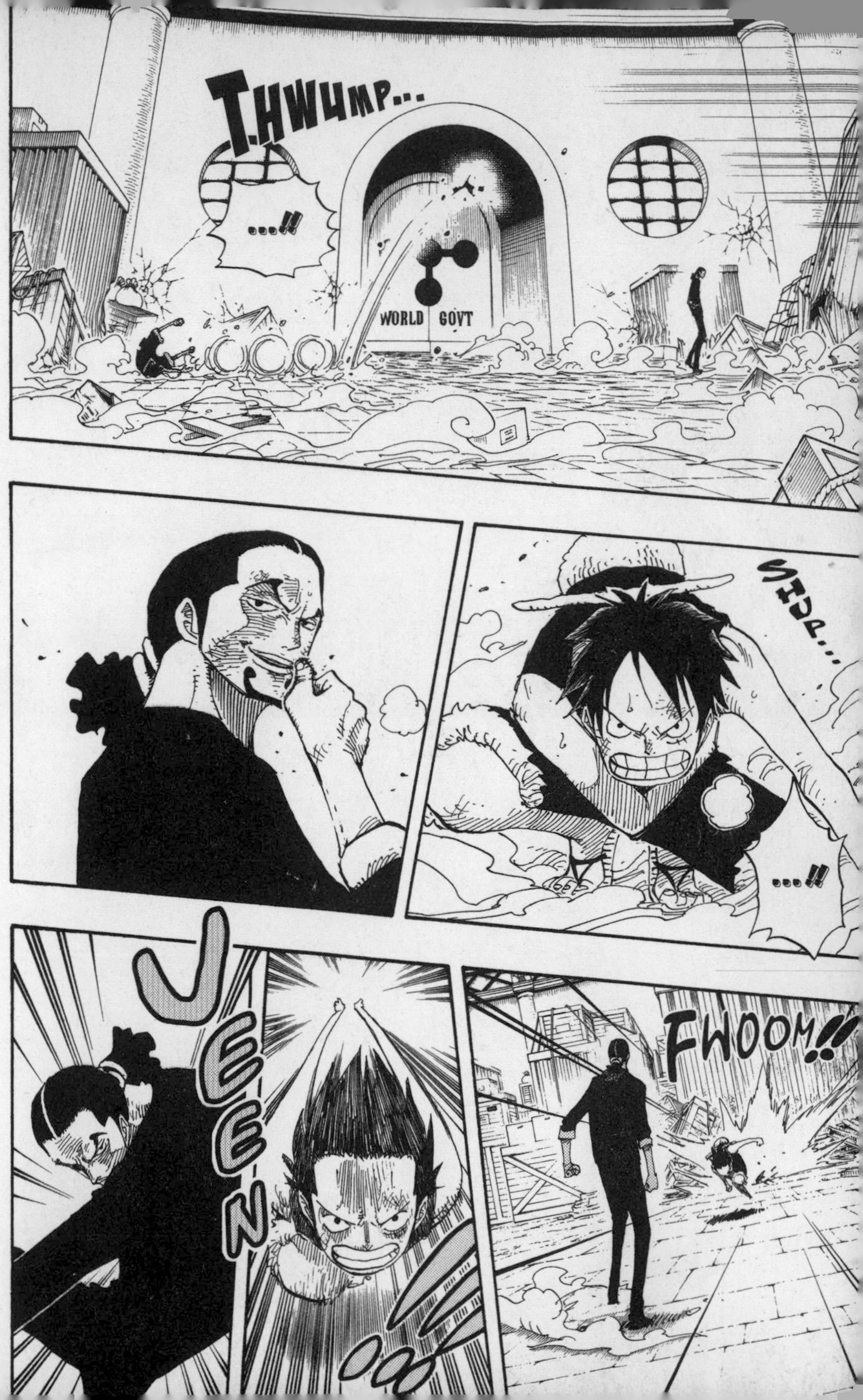

THWUMP...
...!!
WORLD GOVT
SHUP...
...!!
FWOOM!!
JEEN

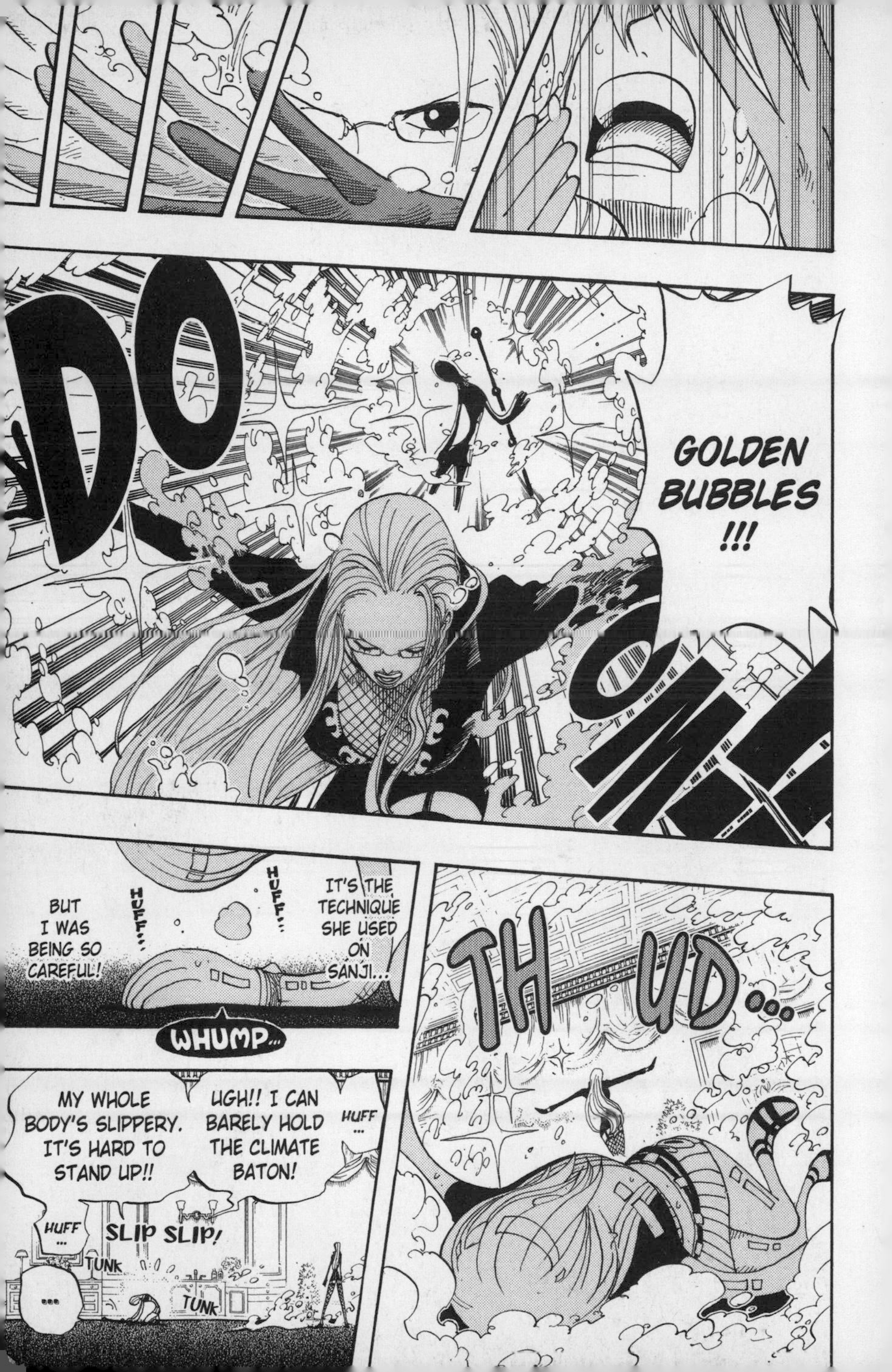

GOLDEN BUBBLES !!!
DO
TH UD...
IT'S THE TECHNIQUE SHE USED ON SANJI...
HUFF...
HUFF...
BUT I WAS BEING SO CAREFUL!
WHUMP...
HUFF ...
UGH!! I CAN BARELY HOLD THE CLIMATE BATON!
MY WHOLE BODY'S SLIPPERY. IT'S HARD TO STAND UP!!
SLIP SLIP!
HUFF ...
TUNK
TUNK
...

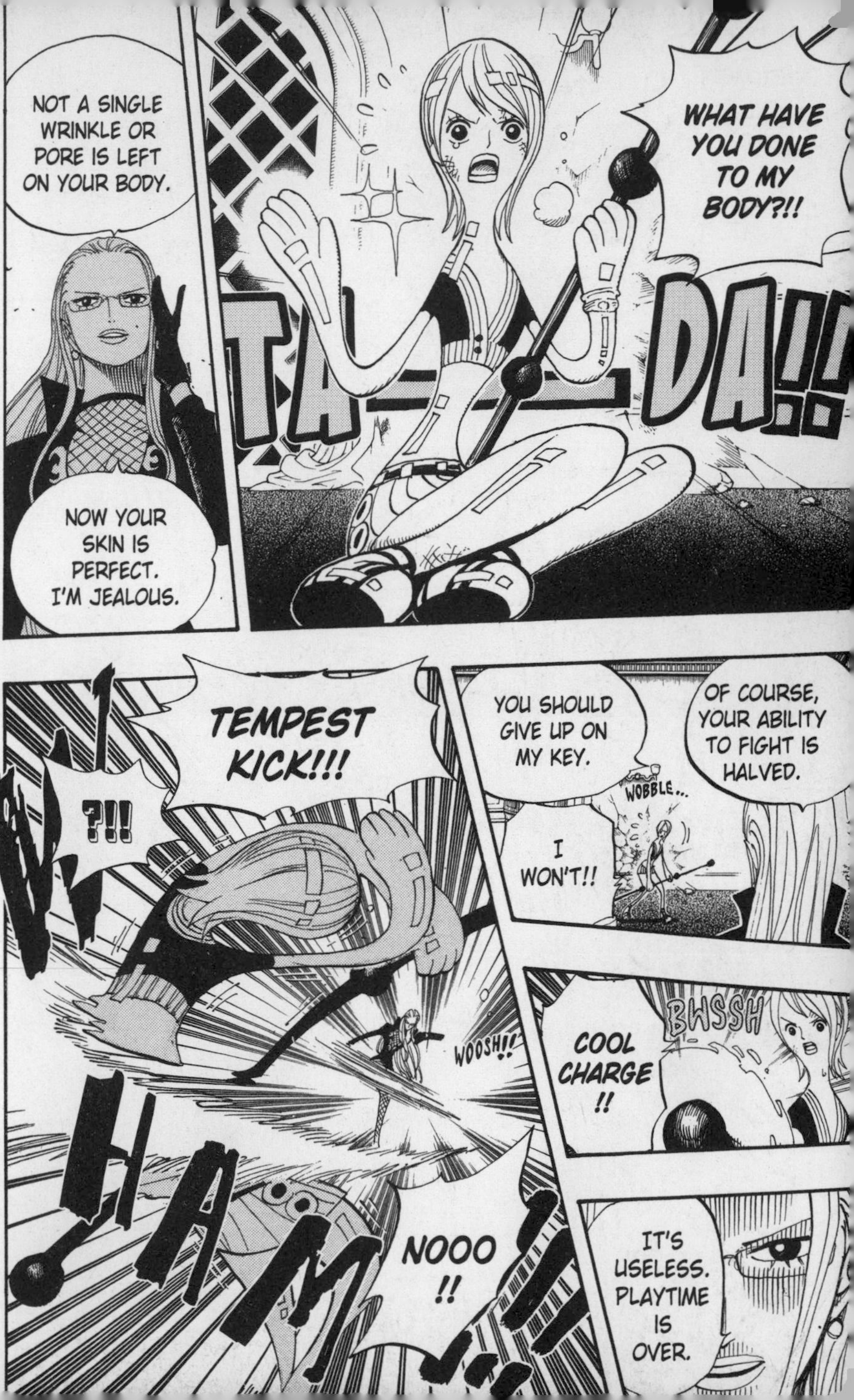
WHAT HAVE YOU DONE TO MY BODY?!!
TA-DA!!
NOT A SINGLE WRINKLE OR PORE IS LEFT ON YOUR BODY.
NOW YOUR SKIN IS PERFECT. I'M JEALOUS.
OF COURSE, YOUR ABILITY TO FIGHT IS HALVED.
YOU SHOULD GIVE UP ON MY KEY.
WOBBLE...
I WON'T!!
BWSSH
COOL CHARGE !!
IT'S USELESS. PLAYTIME IS OVER.
TEMPEST KICK!!!
?!!
WOOSH!!
WHAM!!
NOOO !!

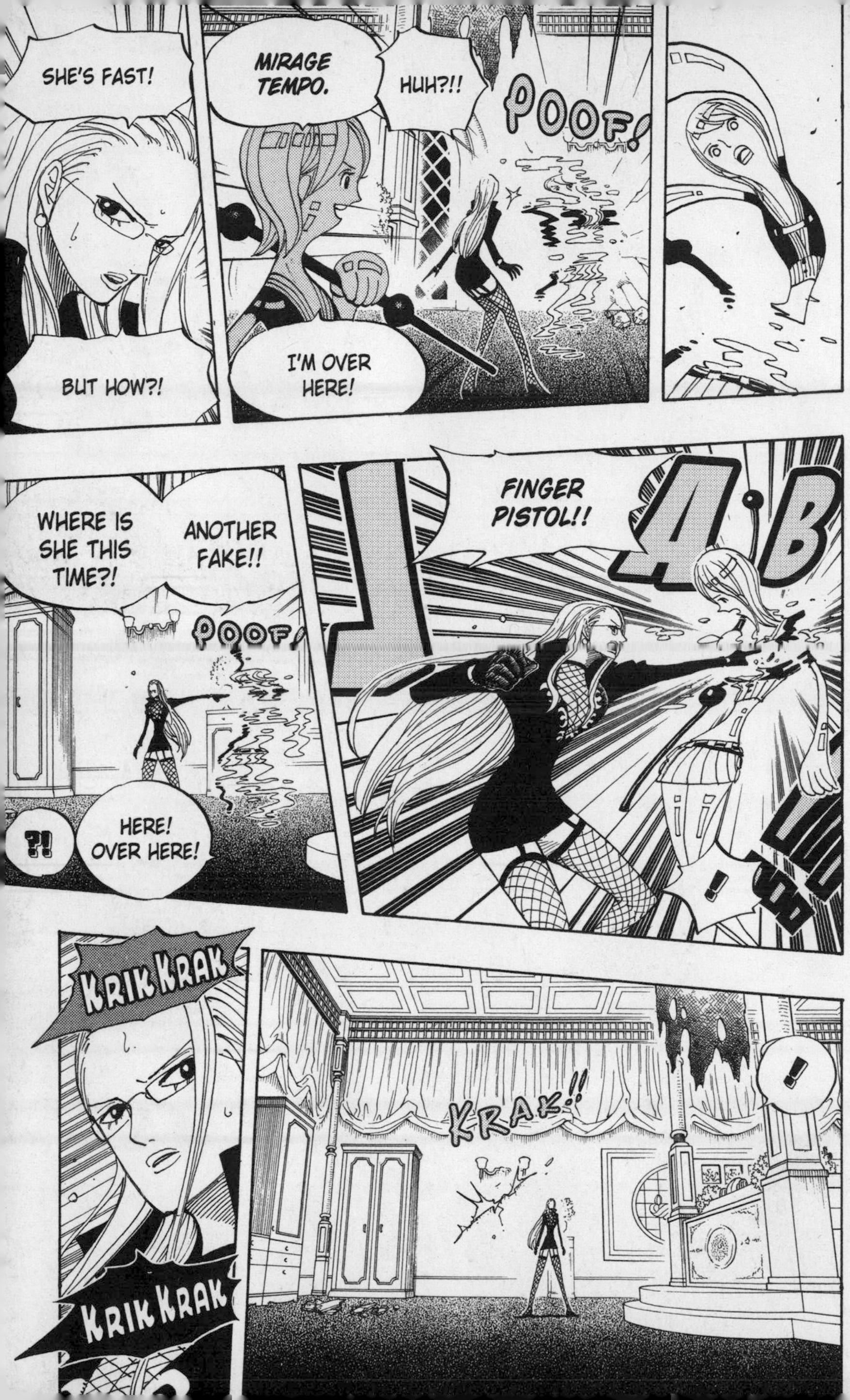
POOF!
HUH?!!
MIRAGE TEMPO.
I'M OVER HERE!
SHE'S FAST!
BUT HOW?!
FINGER PISTOL!!
!
ANOTHER FAKE!!
WHERE IS SHE THIS TIME?!
POOF
HERE! OVER HERE!
?!
!
KRAK!!
KRIK KRAK
KRIK KRAK

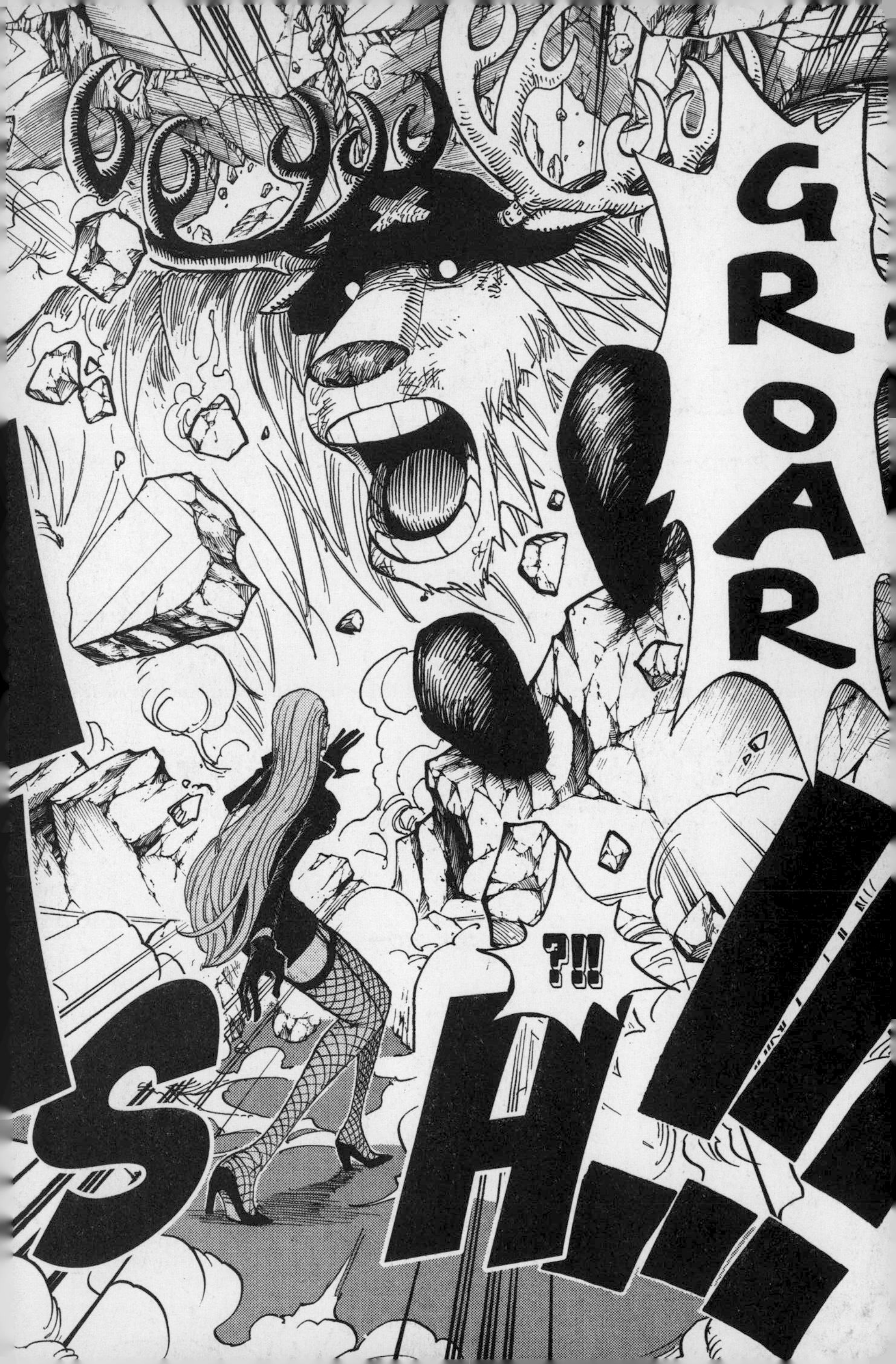
GROAR
?!!
SH

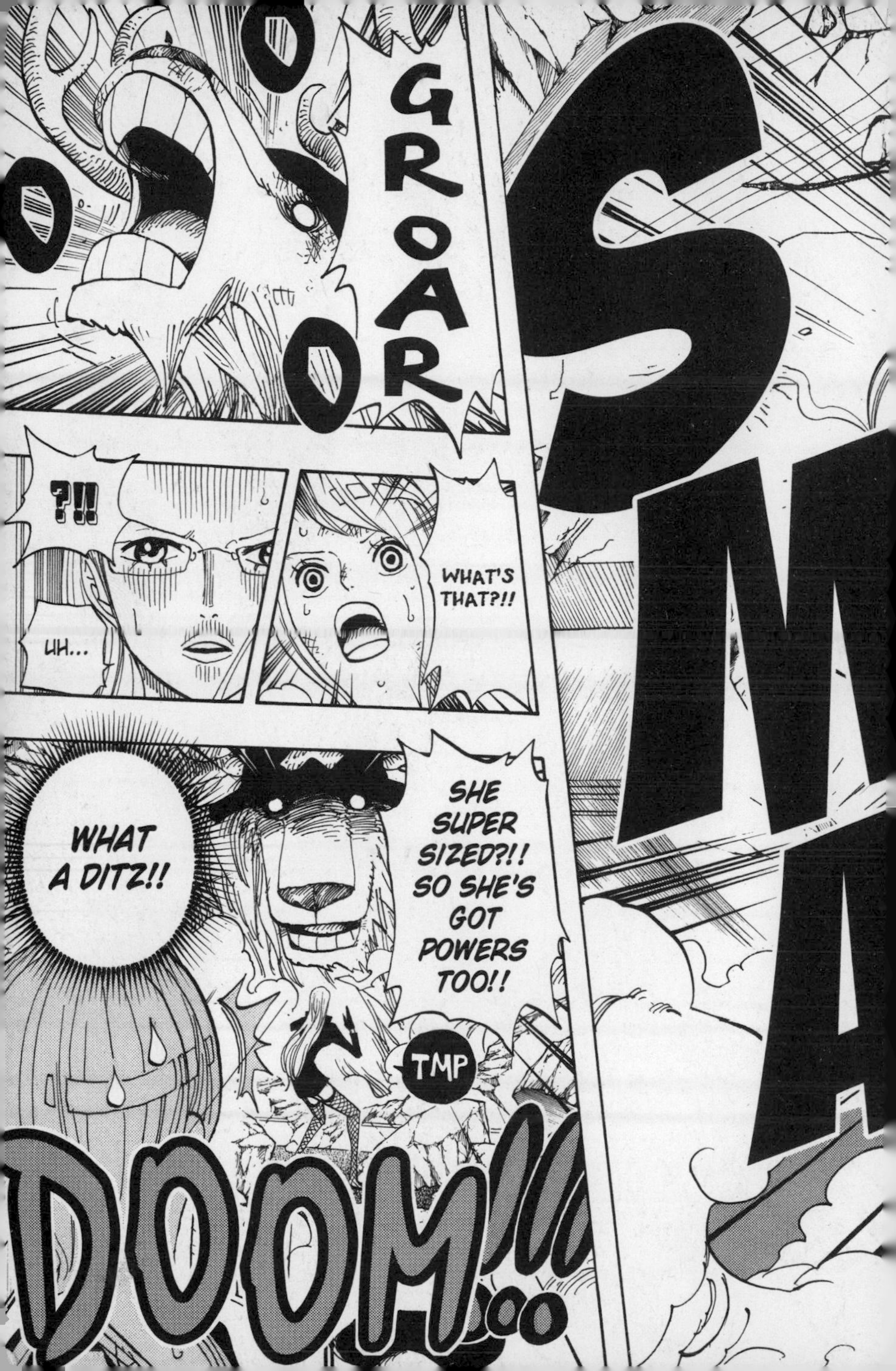
SMA
GROAR
OOO
WHAT'S THAT?!!
?!!
UH...
SHE SUPER SIZED?!! SO SHE'S GOT POWERS TOO!!
WHAT A DITZ!!
TMP
DOOM...

Question Corner
SBS

Reader: This is the news at noon. As a result of a CP9 meeting at eleven o'clock this morning, it appears that a Buster Call was made on manga creator Eiichiro Oda's house. Everyone who lives nearby--everyone except Eiichiro Oda--should evacuate immediately.

--Zolo's Wife

ISLAND, ENIES LOBBY.
AAH!

Oda: Whaat?! A Buster Call?! Uh-oh!! But I...!! I...!! I can't run away!! Because children all over the country are waiting for the Question Corner!!!

(↑Not really.)

Q: Dear Oda Sensei. This is about Robin's Cinco Fleurs. What language are Robin's attacks in? And how about a new attack called "Stinko Fleurs"?

--Heita

THWUP
THWUP
SWOOM
CINCO FLEURS!

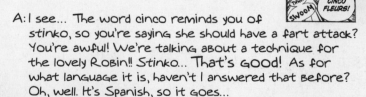

A: I see... The word cinco reminds you of stinko, so you're saying she should have a fart attack? You're awful! We're talking about a technique for the lovely Robin!! Stinko... That's good! As for what language it is, haven't I answered that before? Oh, well. It's Spanish, so it goes...

1	2	3	4	5	6	7	8	9	10
Uno	Dos	Tres	Cuatro	Cinco	Seis	Siete	Ocho	Nueve	Diez

...like that. You've heard some of these before, haven't you?

Chapter 411:
NAMI VS. KALIFA

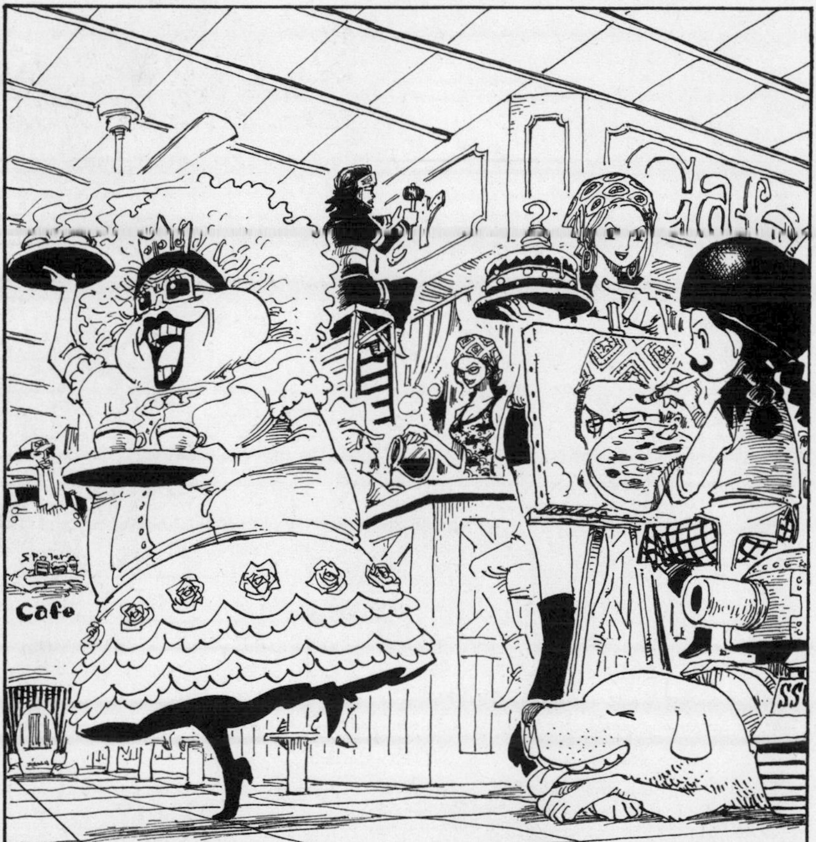
Cafe

MS. GOLDEN WEEK'S BIG PLAN, A BAROQUE REUNION, VOL. 40:
"EVERYONE'S HERE TO OPEN NEW SPIDERS CAFÉ"

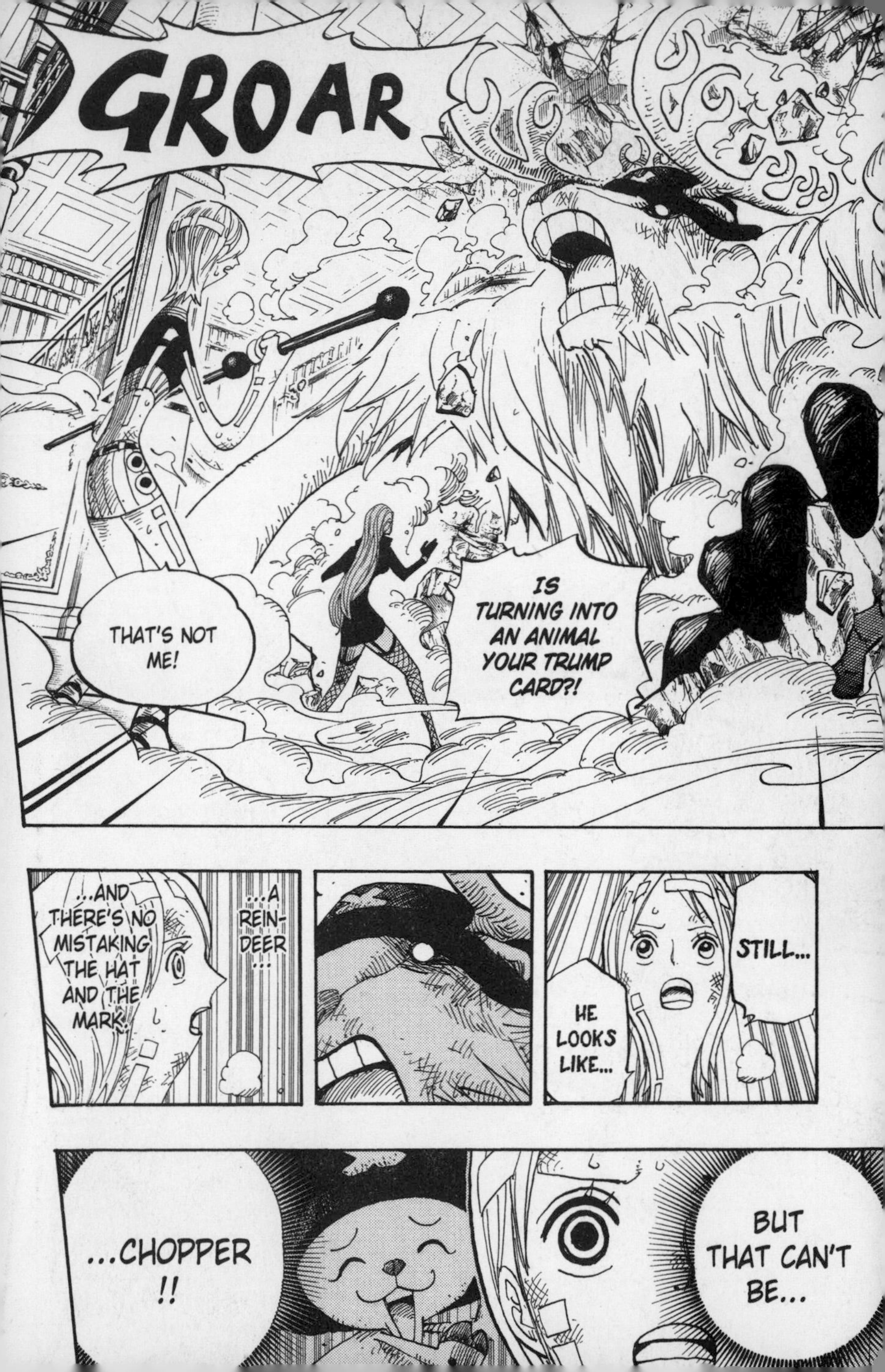
GROAR
IS TURNING INTO AN ANIMAL YOUR TRUMP CARD?!
THAT'S NOT ME!
STILL...
HE LOOKS LIKE...
...A REIN-DEER...
...AND THERE'S NO MISTAKING THE HAT AND THE MARK.
BUT THAT CAN'T BE...
...CHOPPER !!

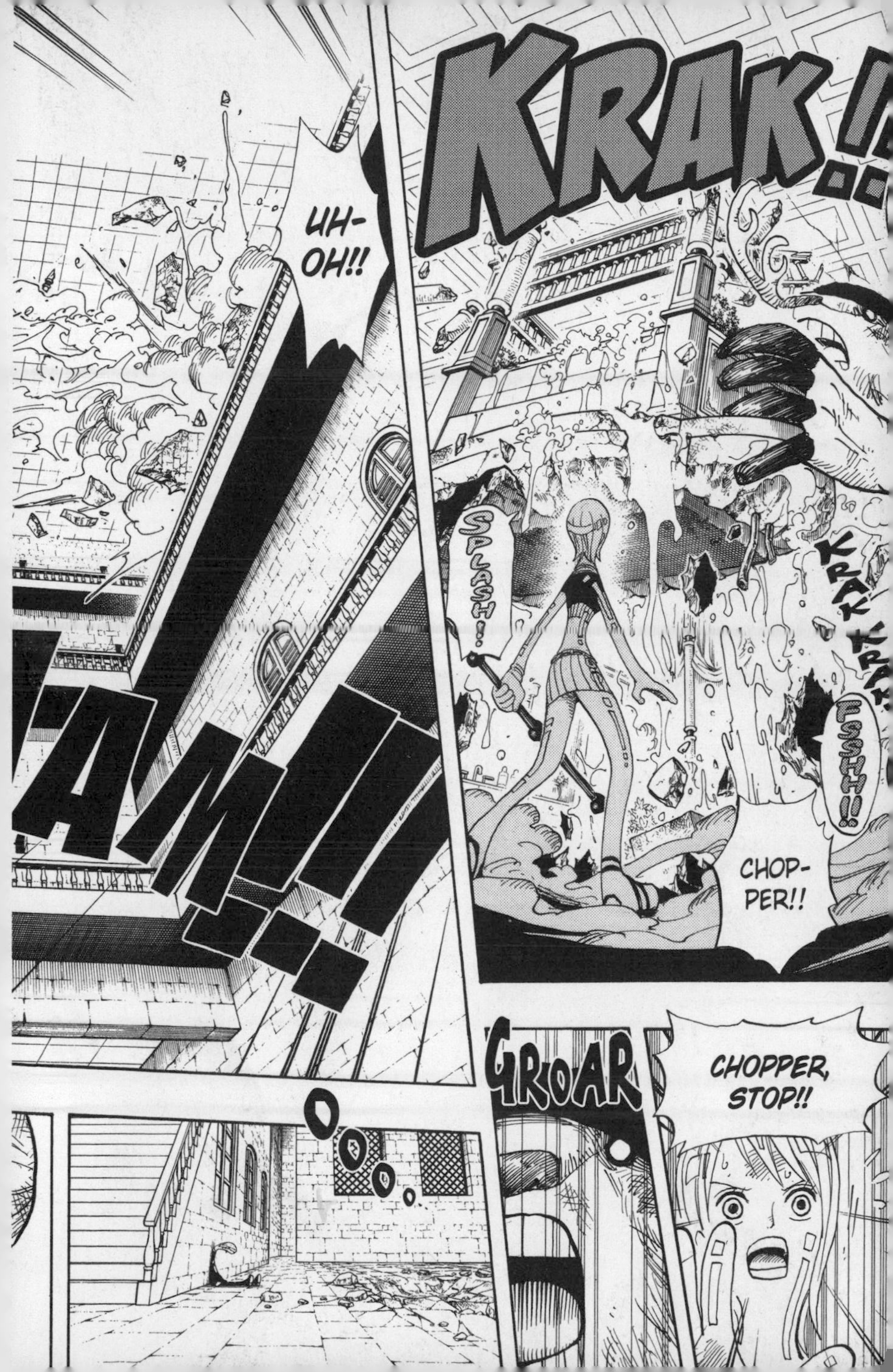
KRAK!!
SPLASH!
KRAK KRAK
FSSHH!!
CHOPPER!!
UH-OH!!
AM!!
CHOPPER, STOP!!
GROAR

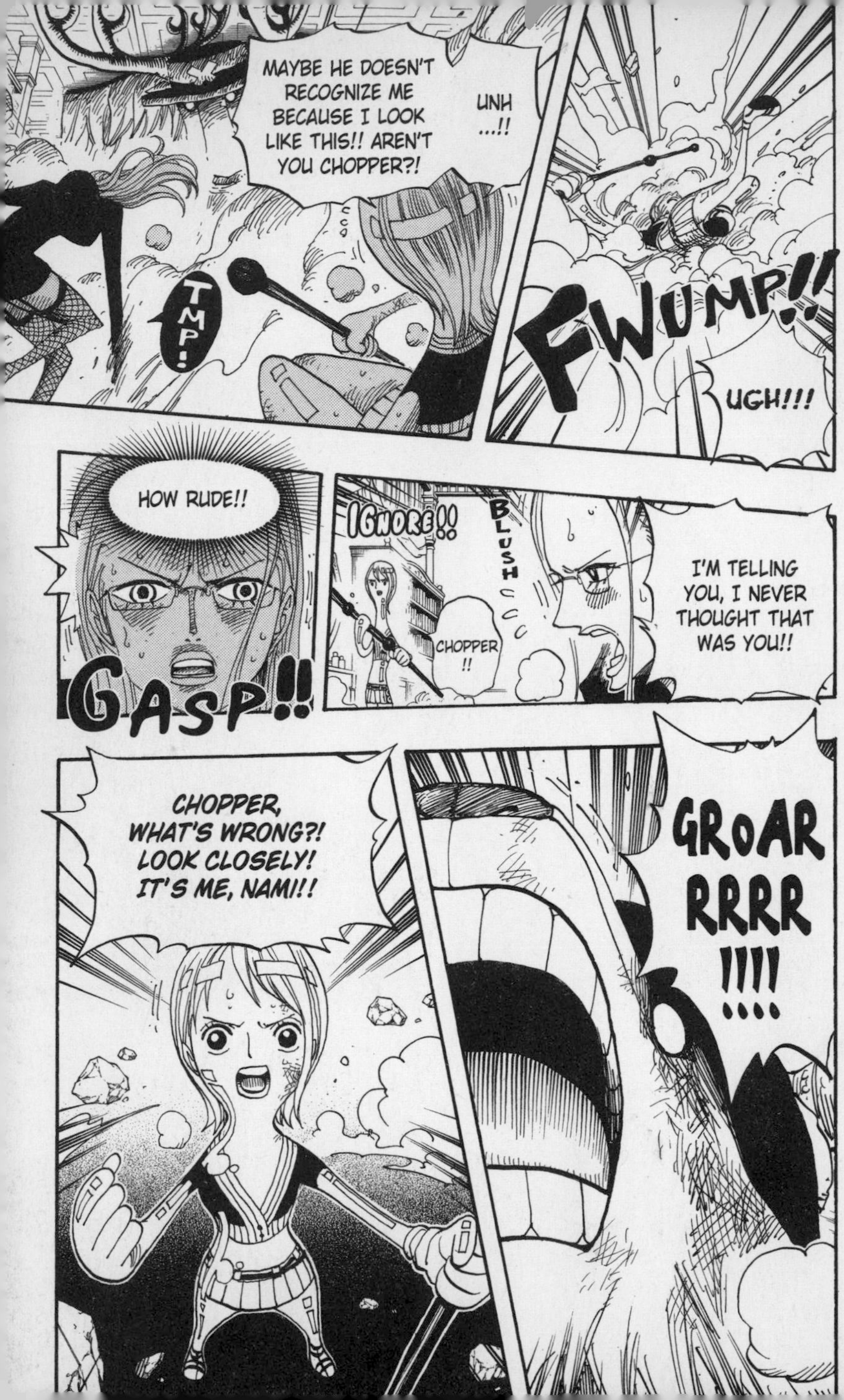
FWUMP!!
UGH!!!
MAYBE HE DOESN'T RECOGNIZE ME BECAUSE I LOOK LIKE THIS!! AREN'T YOU CHOPPER?!
UNH ...!!
TMP!
I'M TELLING YOU, I NEVER THOUGHT THAT WAS YOU!!
BLUSH
IGNORE!!
CHOPPER !!
HOW RUDE!!
GASP!!
GROAR RRRR !!!! ....
CHOPPER, WHAT'S WRONG?! LOOK CLOSELY! IT'S ME, NAMI!!

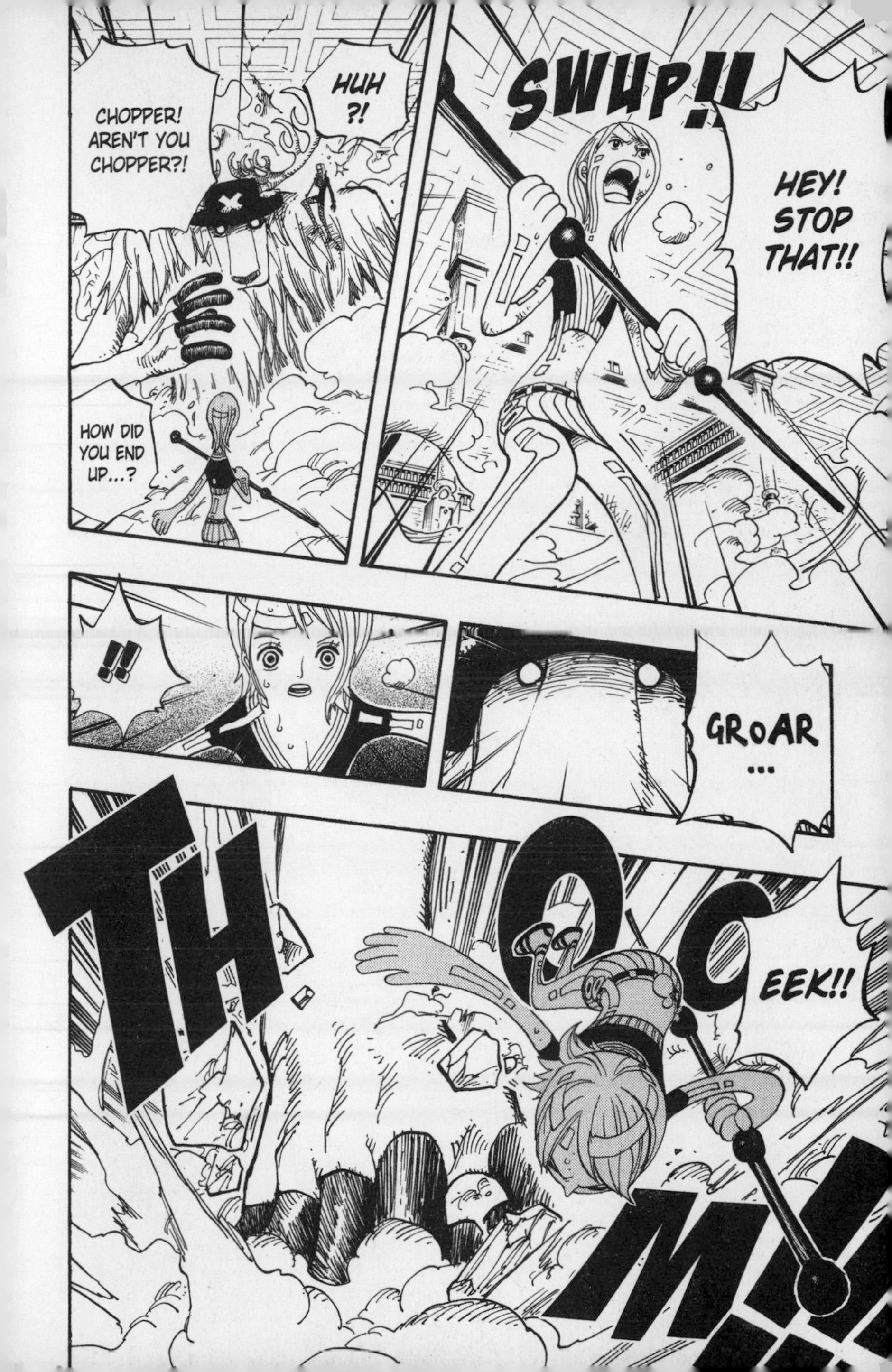
SWUP!!
HEY! STOP THAT!!
HUH ?!
CHOPPER! AREN'T YOU CHOPPER?!
HOW DID YOU END UP...?
GROAR ...
!!
EEK!!
THOOM!!

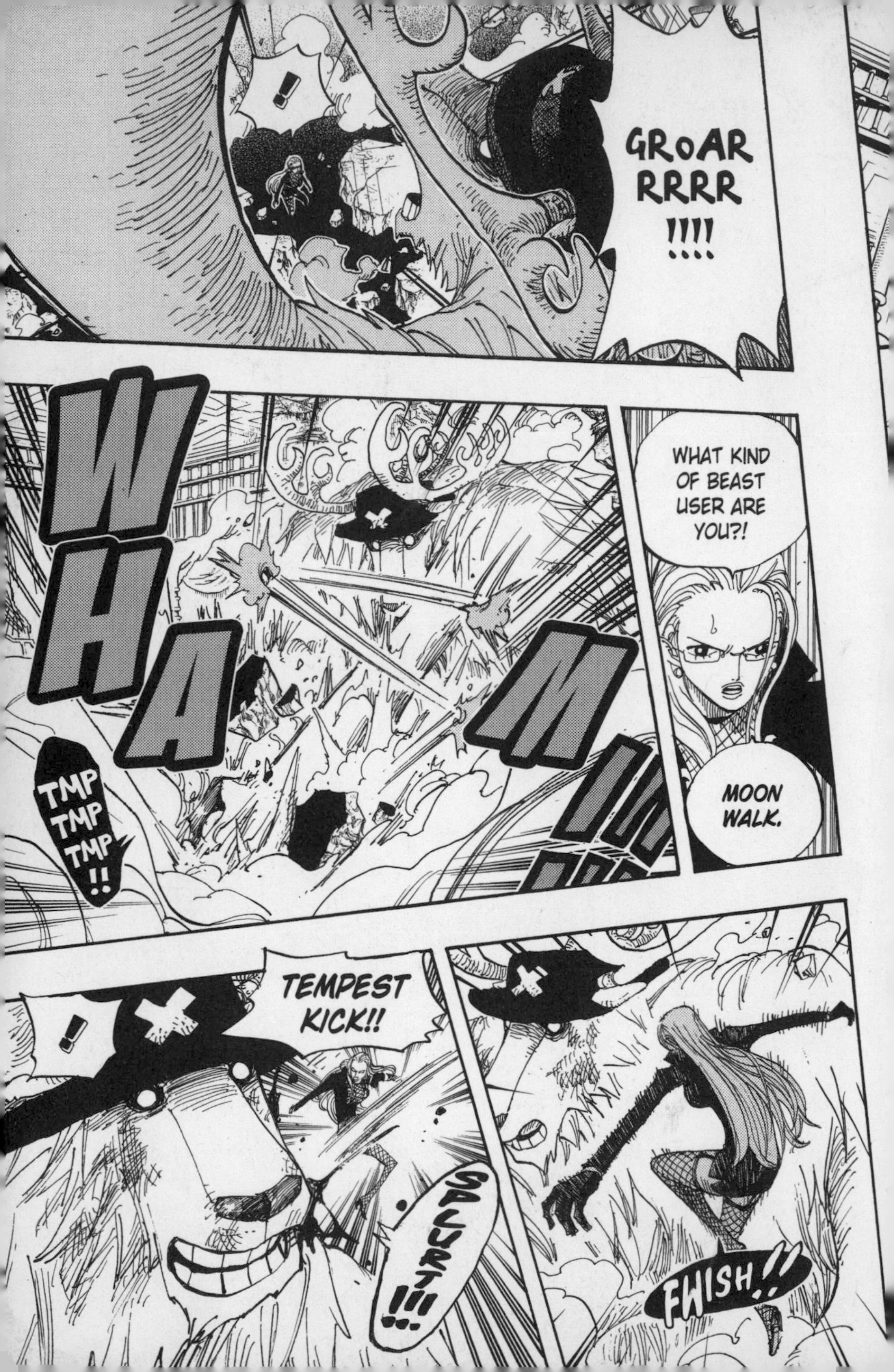
GROAR RRRR !!!!
WHAT KIND OF BEAST USER ARE YOU?!
MOON WALK.
WHAM
TMP TMP TMP!!
FWISH!!
TEMPEST KICK!!
SPLURT!!!

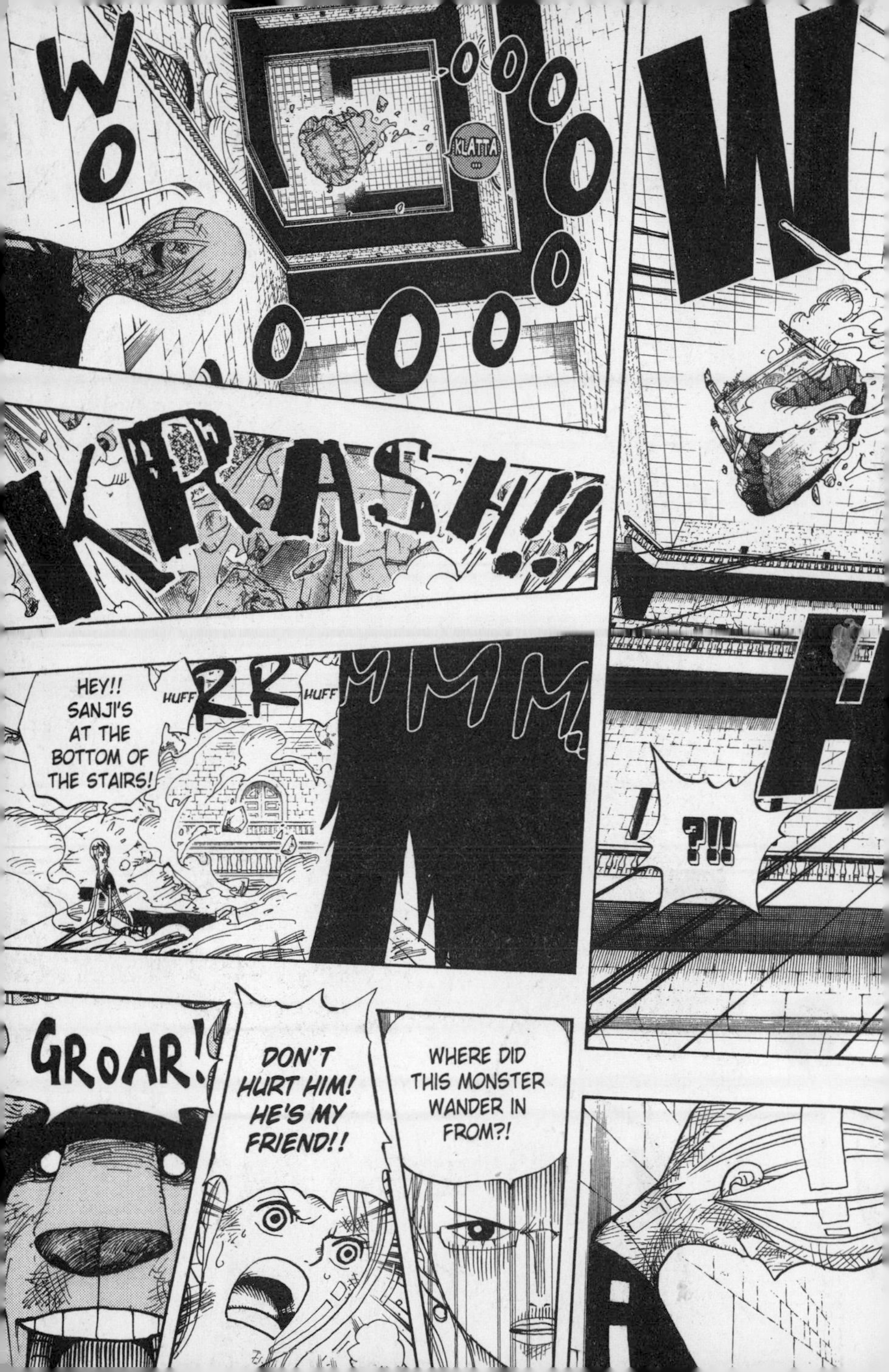
W
?!!
WO
OOOOOOOOO
KLATTA ...
KRASH!!
HUFF
RRMMMM
HUFF
HEY!! SANJI'S AT THE BOTTOM OF THE STAIRS!
WHERE DID THIS MONSTER WANDER IN FROM?!
DON'T HURT HIM! HE'S MY FRIEND!!
GROAR!

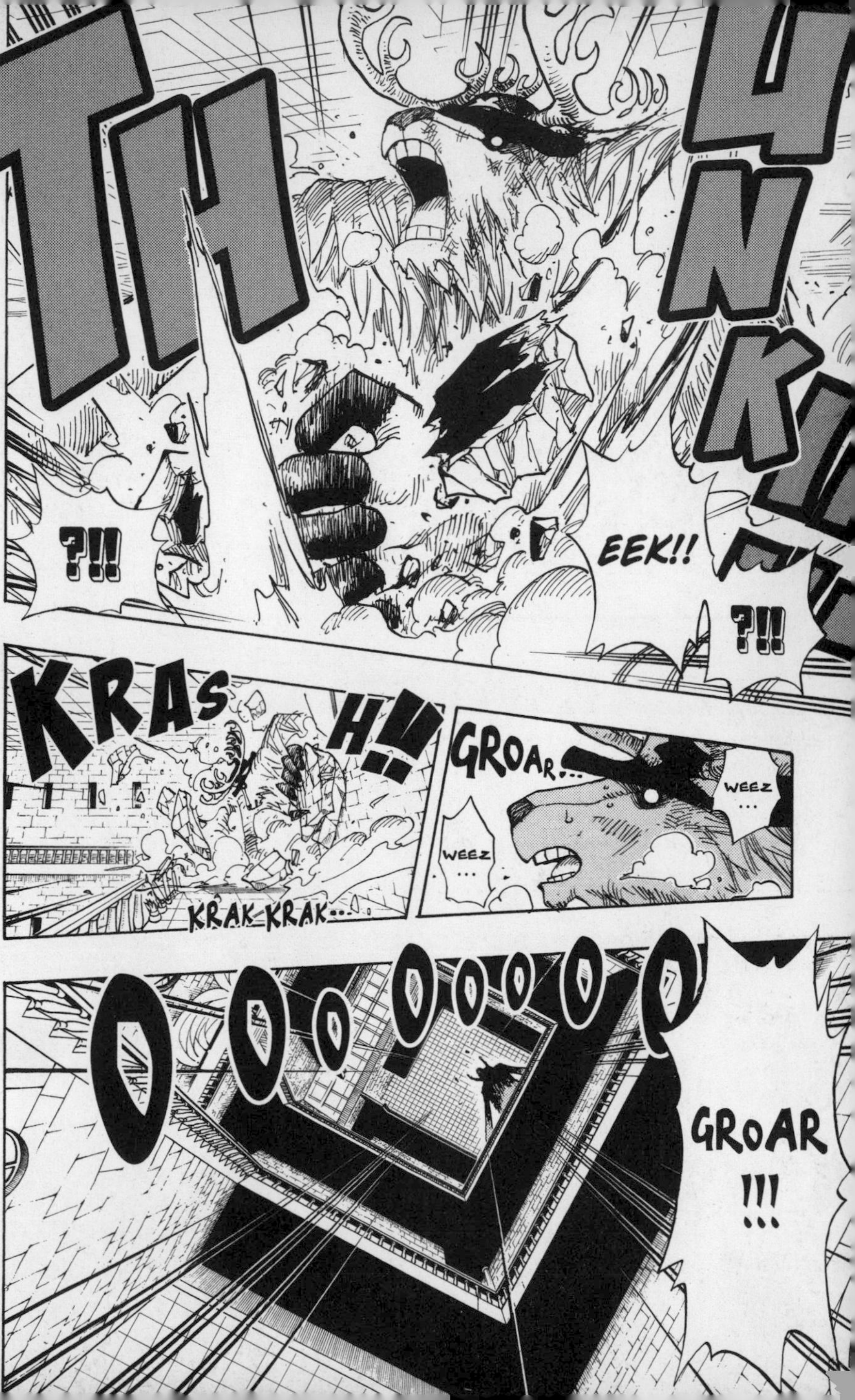

TH
NK
?!!
EEK!!
?!!
GROAR...
WEEZ ...
WEEZ ...
KRASH!!
KRAK KRAK...
OOOOOOOOM
GROAR !!!

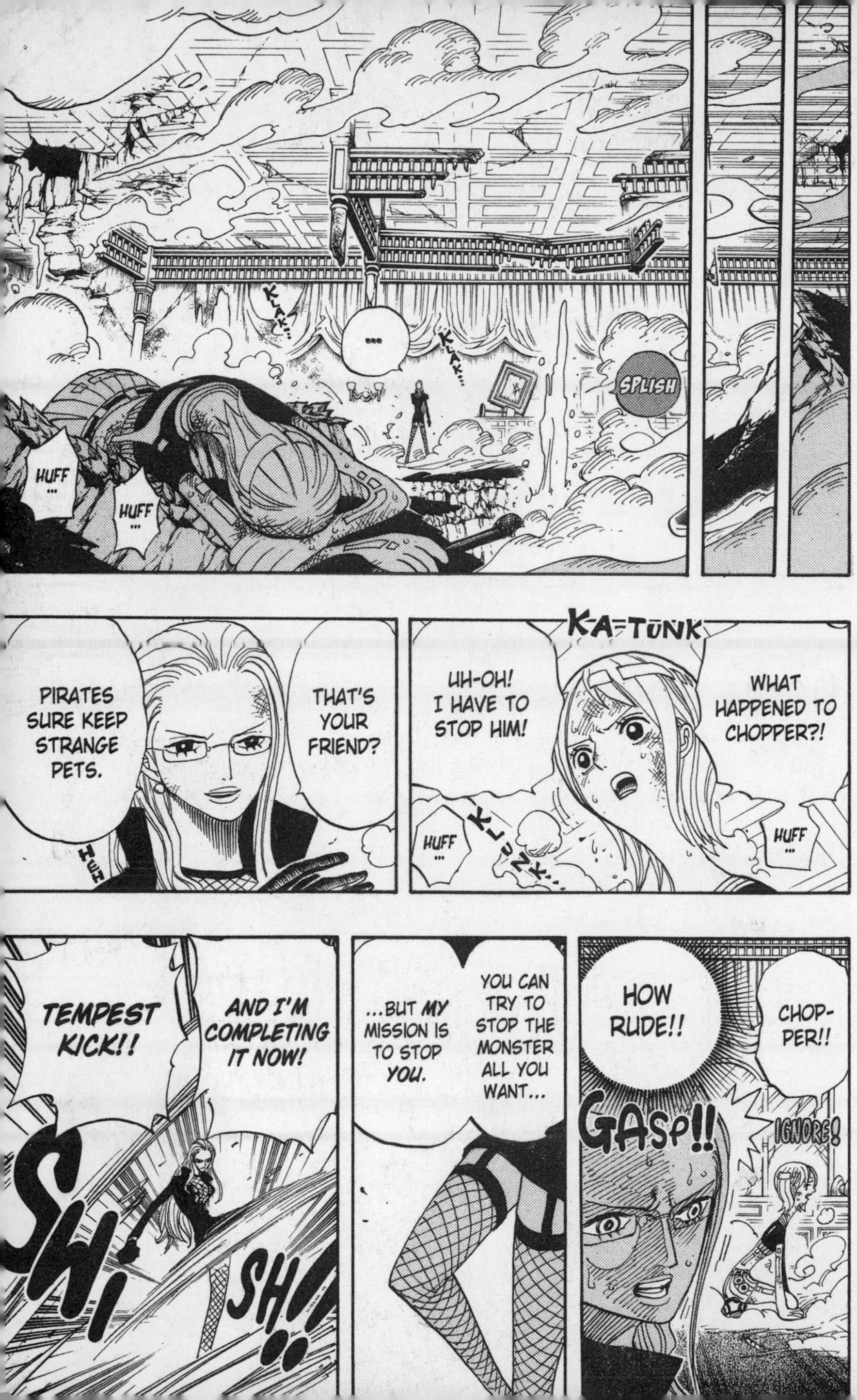
SPLISH
KLAK...
...
KLAK...
HUFF...
HUFF...
KA-TUNK
WHAT HAPPENED TO CHOPPER?!
UH-OH! I HAVE TO STOP HIM!
HUFF...
KLUNK...
HUFF...
THAT'S YOUR FRIEND?
PIRATES SURE KEEP STRANGE PETS.
HEH
CHOP-PER!!
IGNORE!
HOW RUDE!!
GASP!!
YOU CAN TRY TO STOP THE MONSTER ALL YOU WANT...
...BUT MY MISSION IS TO STOP YOU.
AND I'M COMPLETING IT NOW!
TEMPEST KICK!!
SHI
SHI!!

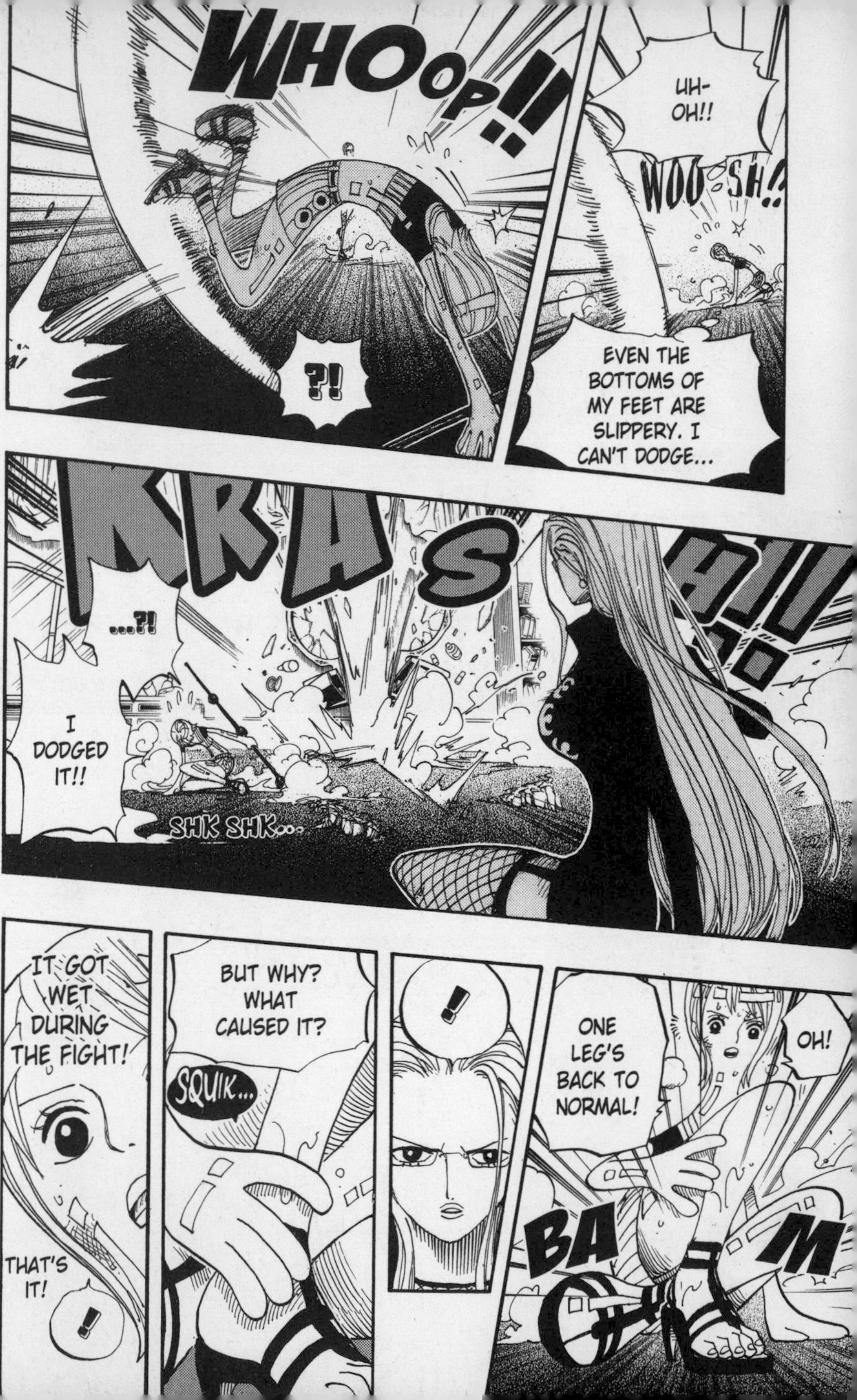
UH-OH!!
WOOSH!!
EVEN THE BOTTOMS OF MY FEET ARE SLIPPERY. I CAN'T DODGE...
WHOOP!!
?!
KRASH!!
...?!
I DODGED IT!!
SHK SHK...
OH!
ONE LEG'S BACK TO NORMAL!
BAM
!
BUT WHY? WHAT CAUSED IT?
SQUIK...
IT GOT WET DURING THE FIGHT!
THAT'S IT!
!

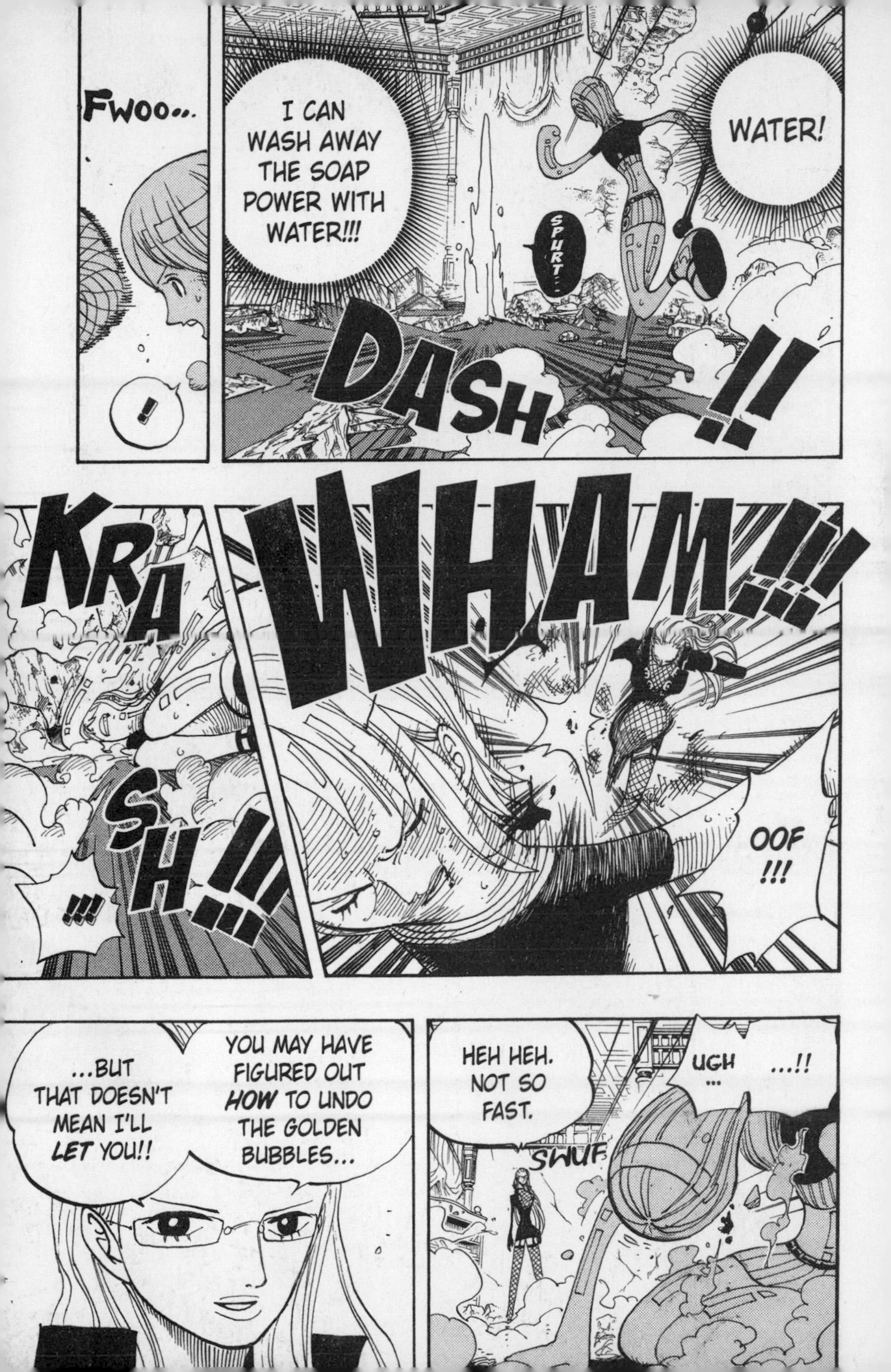
WATER!
I CAN WASH AWAY THE SOAP POWER WITH WATER!!!
SPURT...
DASH!!
FWOO...
!
WHAM!!!
OOF!!!
KRASH!!!
!!!
UGH...
...!!
HEH HEH. NOT SO FAST.
SWUF
YOU MAY HAVE FIGURED OUT HOW TO UNDO THE GOLDEN BUBBLES...
...BUT THAT DOESN'T MEAN I'LL LET YOU!!

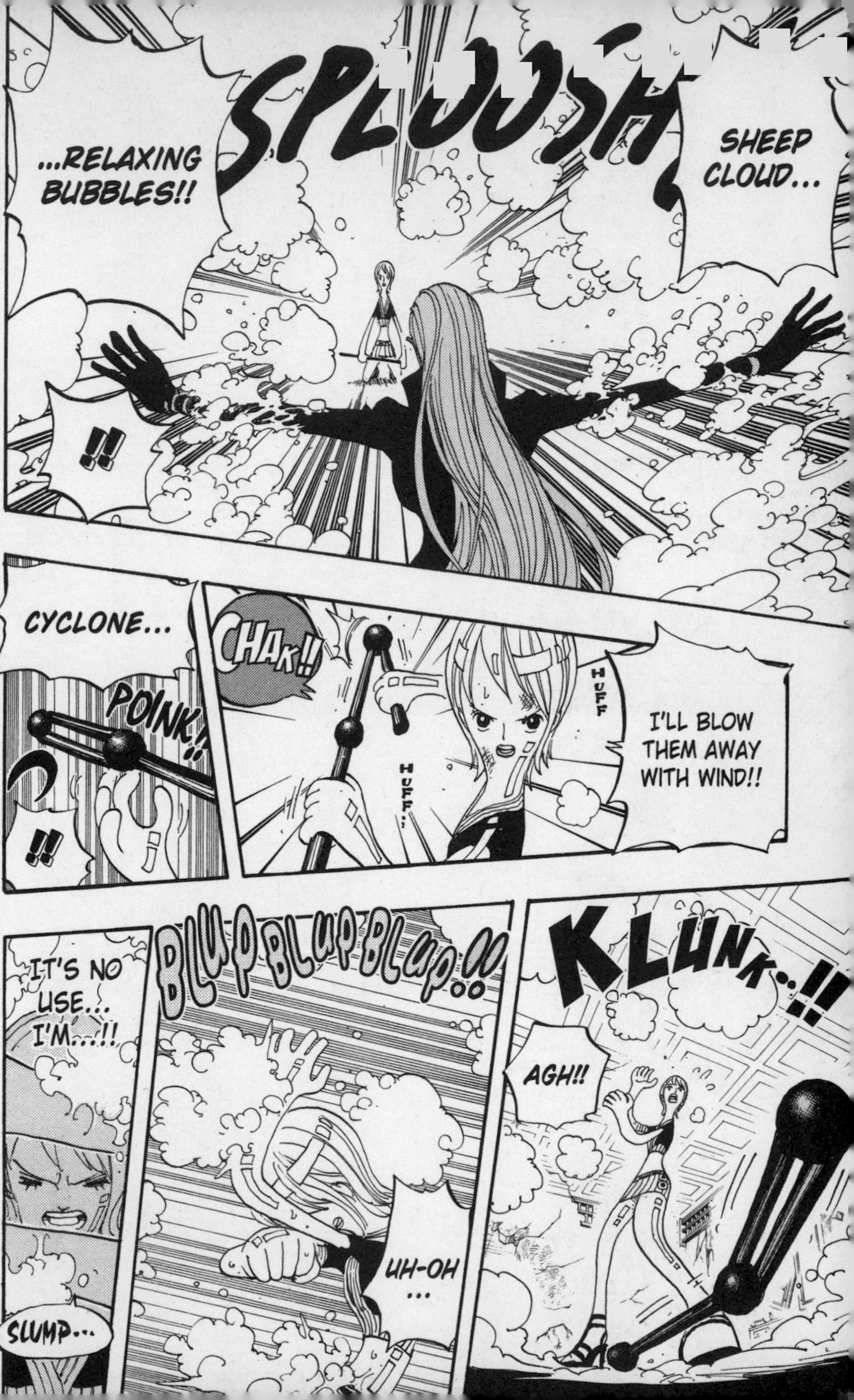
SHEEP CLOUD...
SPLOOSH
...RELAXING BUBBLES!!
!!
I'LL BLOW THEM AWAY WITH WIND!!
HUFF
HUFF..
CHAK!!
CYCLONE...
POINK!!
!!
KLUNK..!!
AGH!!
BLUP BLUP BLUP..!!
UH-OH...
IT'S NO USE... I'M...!!
SLUMP...

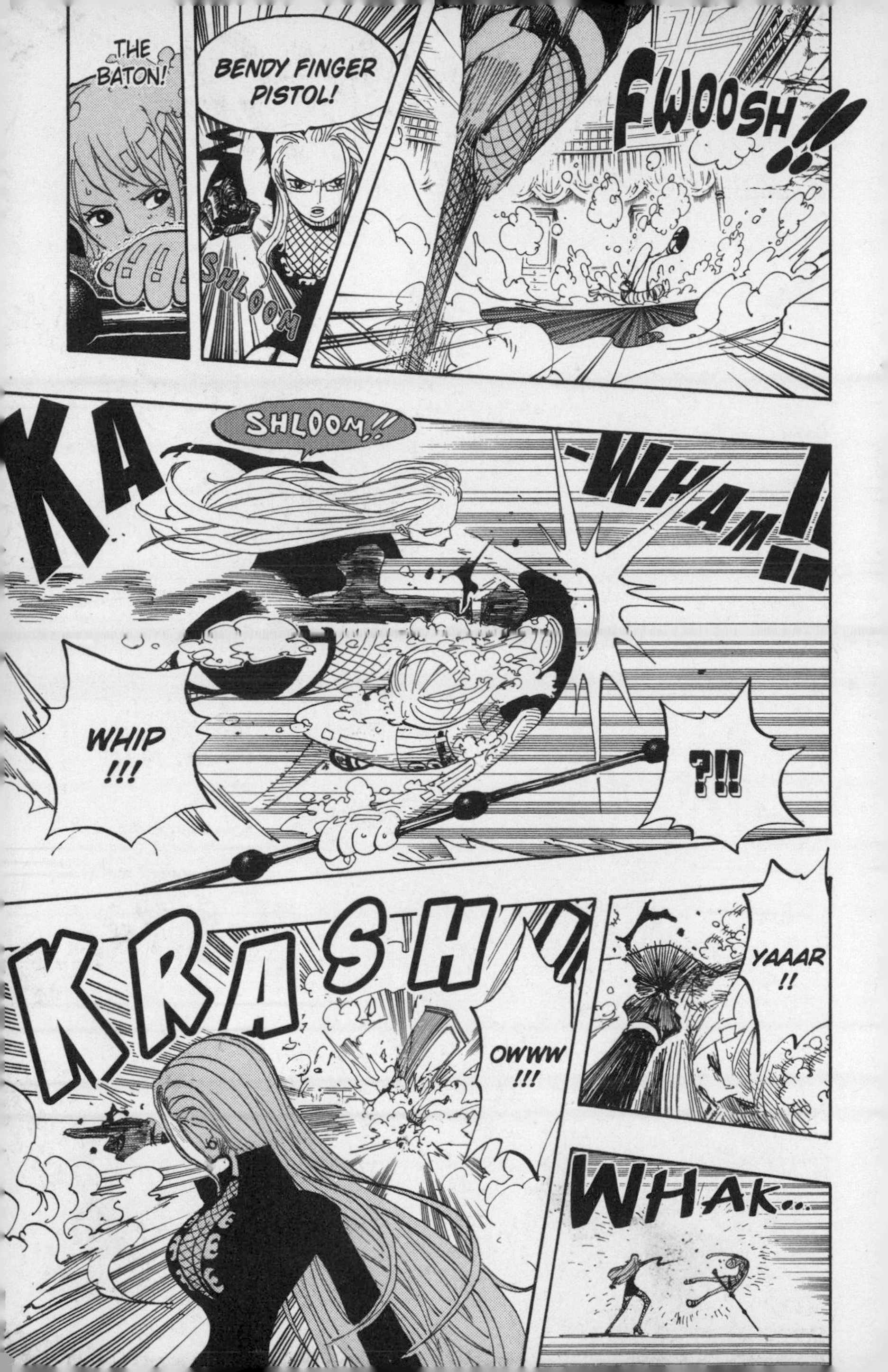
FWOOSH!!
BENDY FINGER PISTOL!
SHLOOM
THE BATON!
KA-WHAM!!
SHLOOM!!
?!!
WHIP!!!
YAAAR!!
WHAK..
KRASH
OWWW!!!

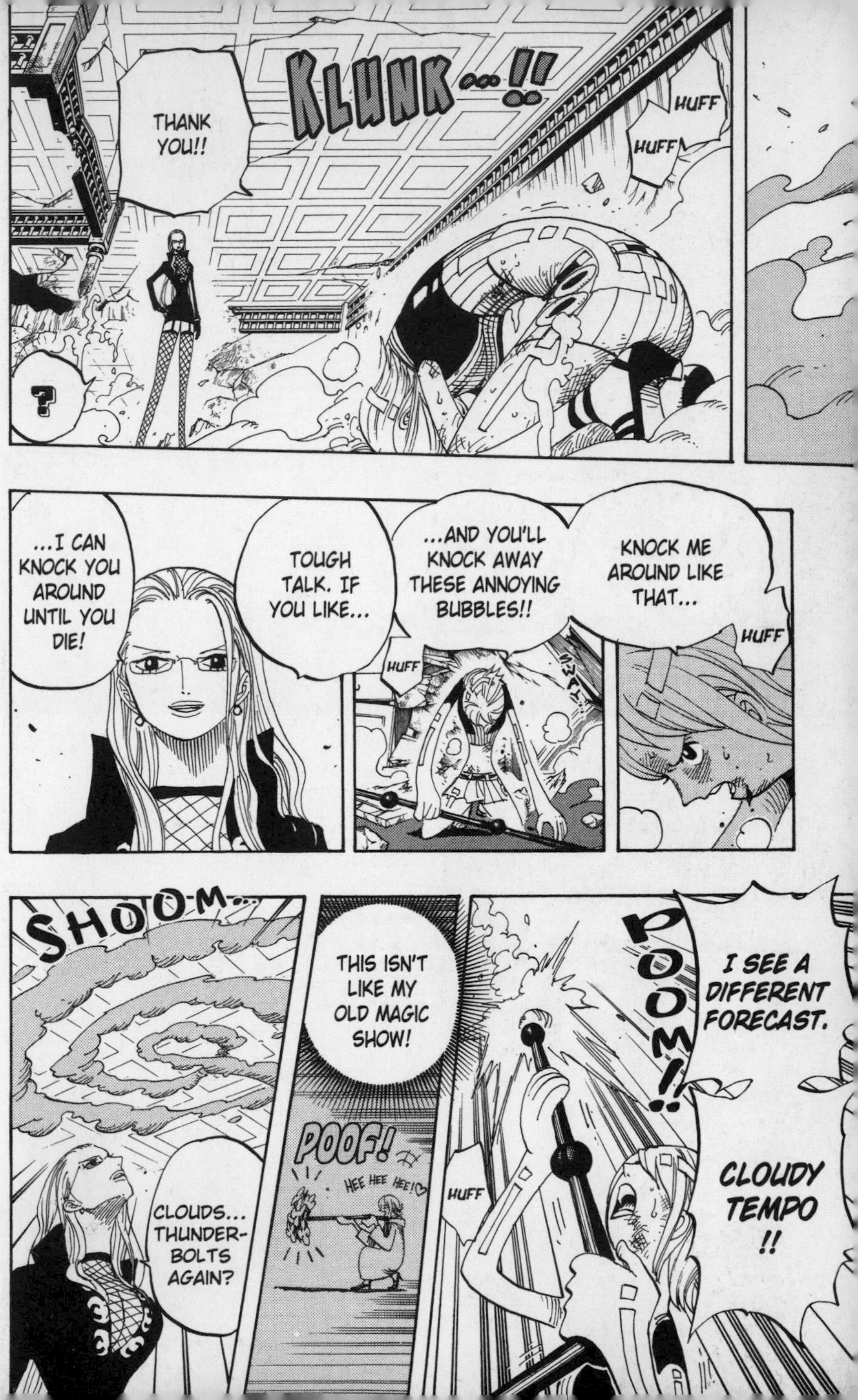
HUFF
HUFF
KLUNK...!!
THANK YOU!!
?
KNOCK ME AROUND LIKE THAT...
HUFF
...AND YOU'LL KNOCK AWAY THESE ANNOYING BUBBLES!!
SWAY
HUFF
TOUGH TALK. IF YOU LIKE...
...I CAN KNOCK YOU AROUND UNTIL YOU DIE!
I SEE A DIFFERENT FORECAST.
POOM!!
CLOUDY TEMPO!!
HUFF
THIS ISN'T LIKE MY OLD MAGIC SHOW!
POOF!
HEE HEE HEE!
SHOOM...
CLOUDS... THUNDER-BOLTS AGAIN?

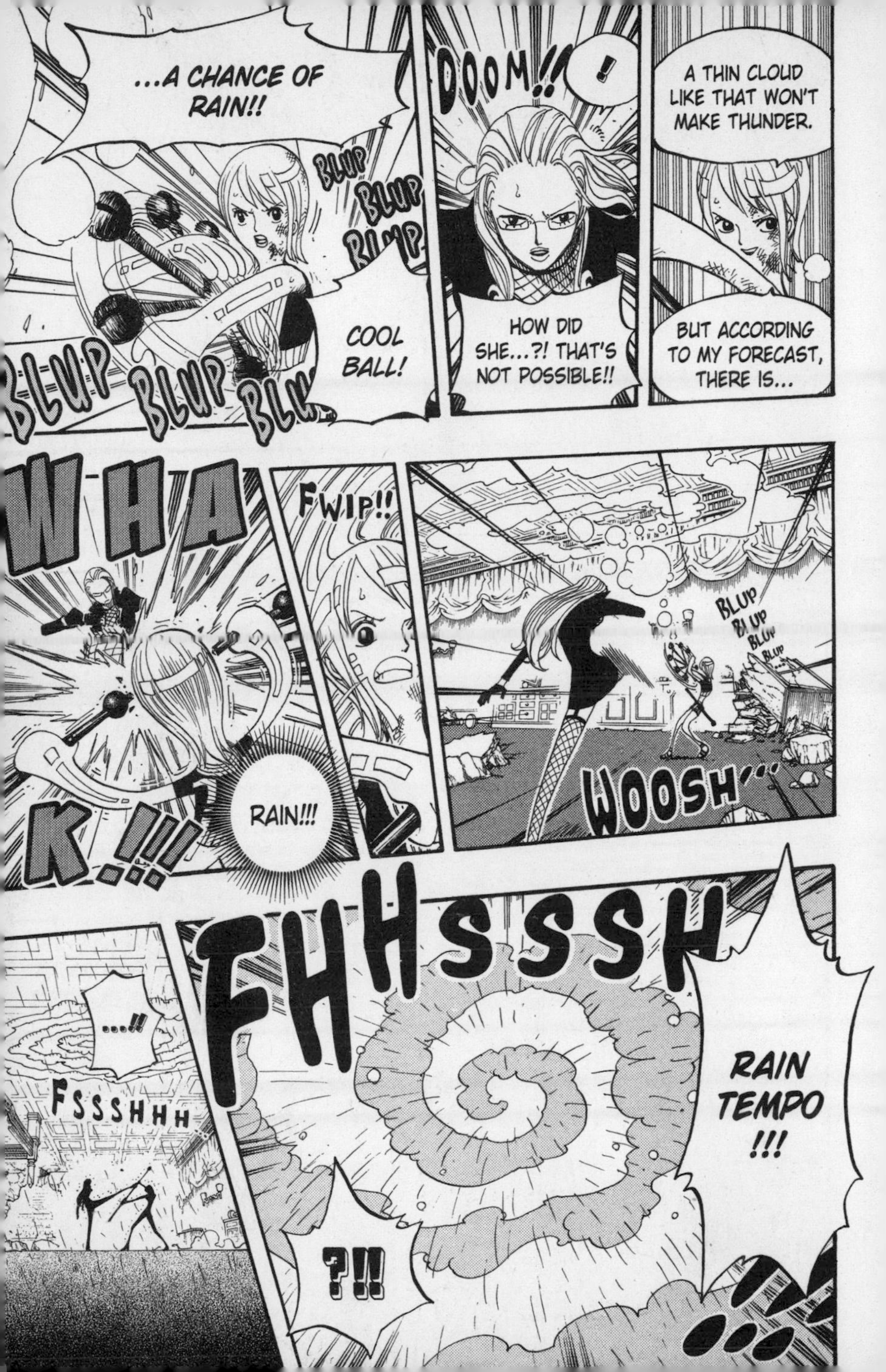
A THIN CLOUD LIKE THAT WON'T MAKE THUNDER.
BUT ACCORDING TO MY FORECAST, THERE IS...
DOOM!!
!
HOW DID SHE...?! THAT'S NOT POSSIBLE!!
...A CHANCE OF RAIN!!
BLUP BLUP BLUP
COOL BALL!
BLUP BLUP
BLUP BLUP BLUP BLUP
WOOSH
FWIP!!
WHAK!!!
RAIN!!!
FHSSSH
RAIN TEMPO!!!
?!!
...!!
FSSSHHH

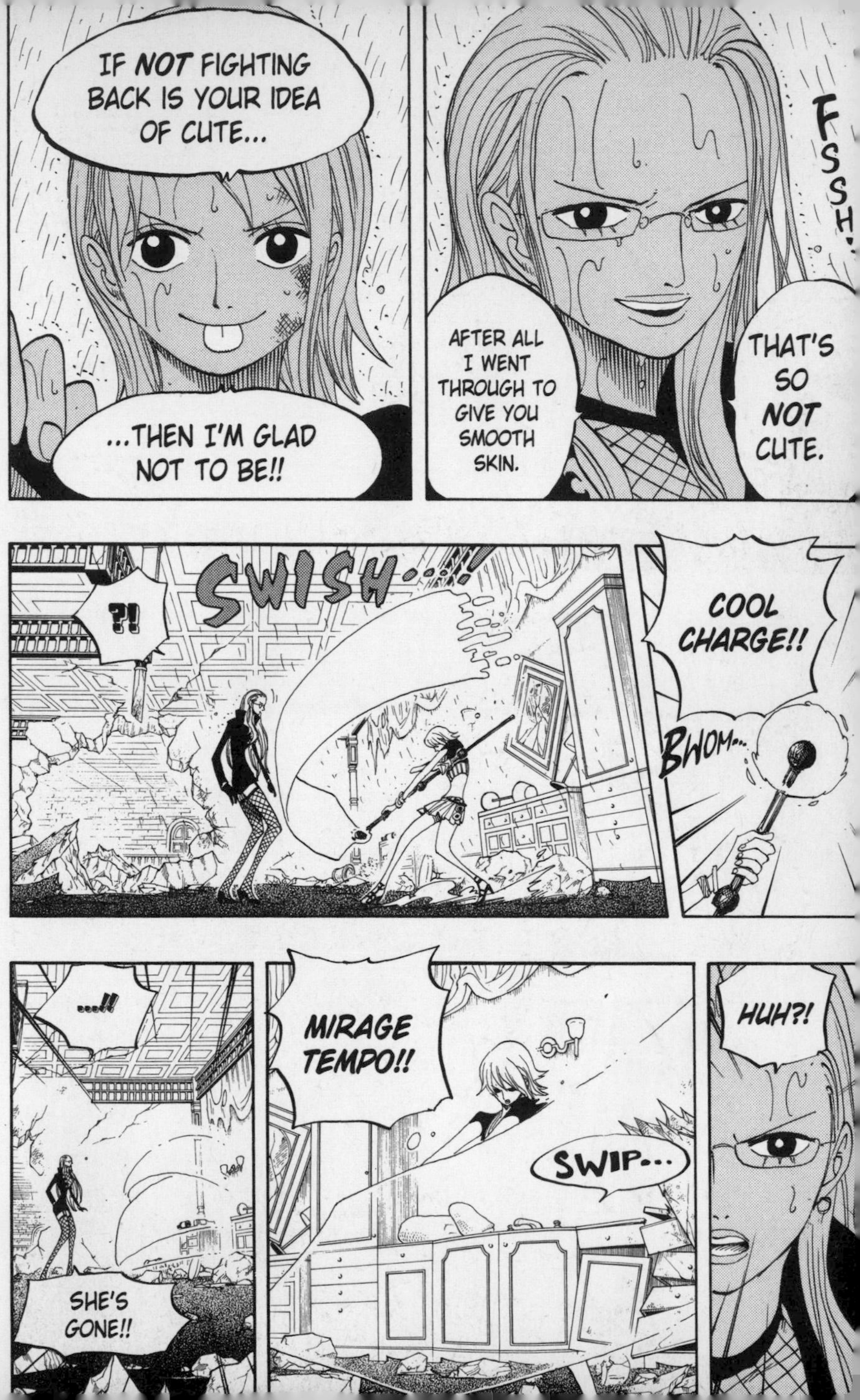
FSSH!
THAT'S SO NOT CUTE.
AFTER ALL I WENT THROUGH TO GIVE YOU SMOOTH SKIN.
IF NOT FIGHTING BACK IS YOUR IDEA OF CUTE...
...THEN I'M GLAD NOT TO BE!!
COOL CHARGE!!
BWOM...
SWISH...!
?!
HUH?!
MIRAGE TEMPO!!
SWIP...
...!!
SHE'S GONE!!

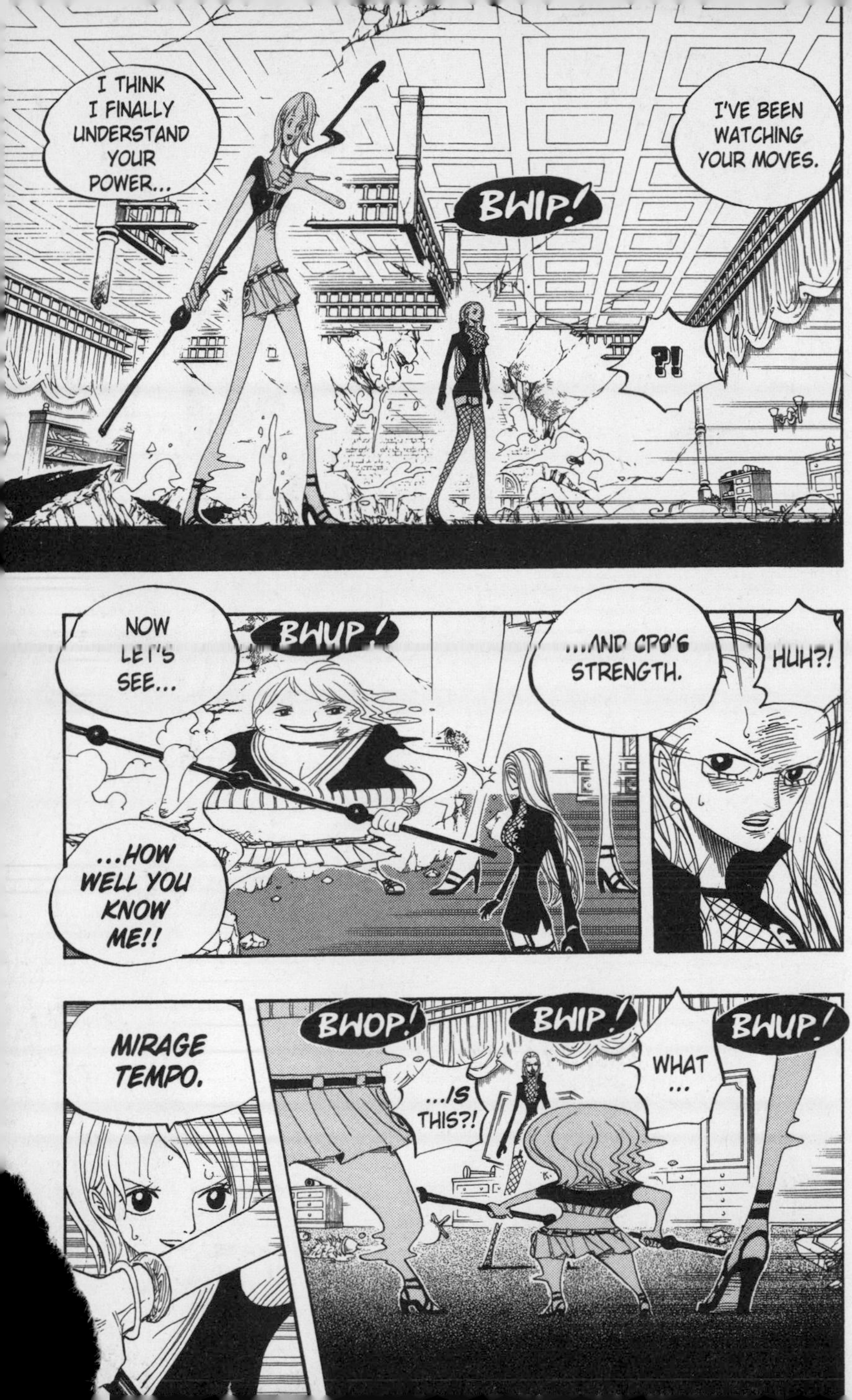
I'VE BEEN WATCHING YOUR MOVES.
BWIP!
?!
I THINK I FINALLY UNDERSTAND YOUR POWER...
HUH?!
...AND CP9'S STRENGTH.
BWUP!
NOW LET'S SEE...
...HOW WELL YOU KNOW ME!!
BWUP!
BWIP!
WHAT ...
BWOP!
...IS THIS?!
MIRAGE TEMPO.

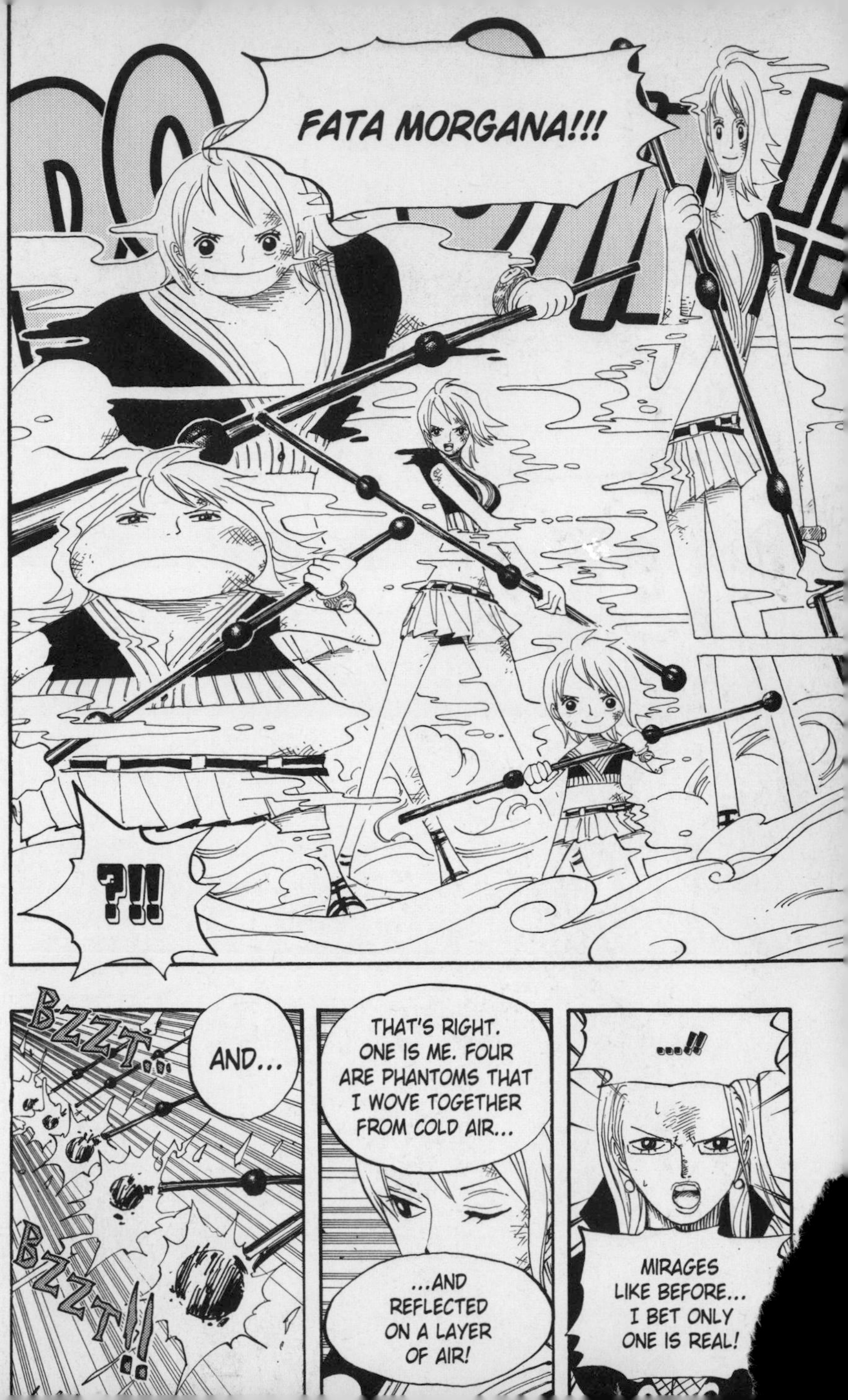
FATA MORGANA!!!
?!!
...!!
MIRAGES LIKE BEFORE... I BET ONLY ONE IS REAL!
THAT'S RIGHT. ONE IS ME. FOUR ARE PHANTOMS THAT I WOVE TOGETHER FROM COLD AIR...
...AND REFLECTED ON A LAYER OF AIR!
BZZZT...
AND...
BZZZT!!

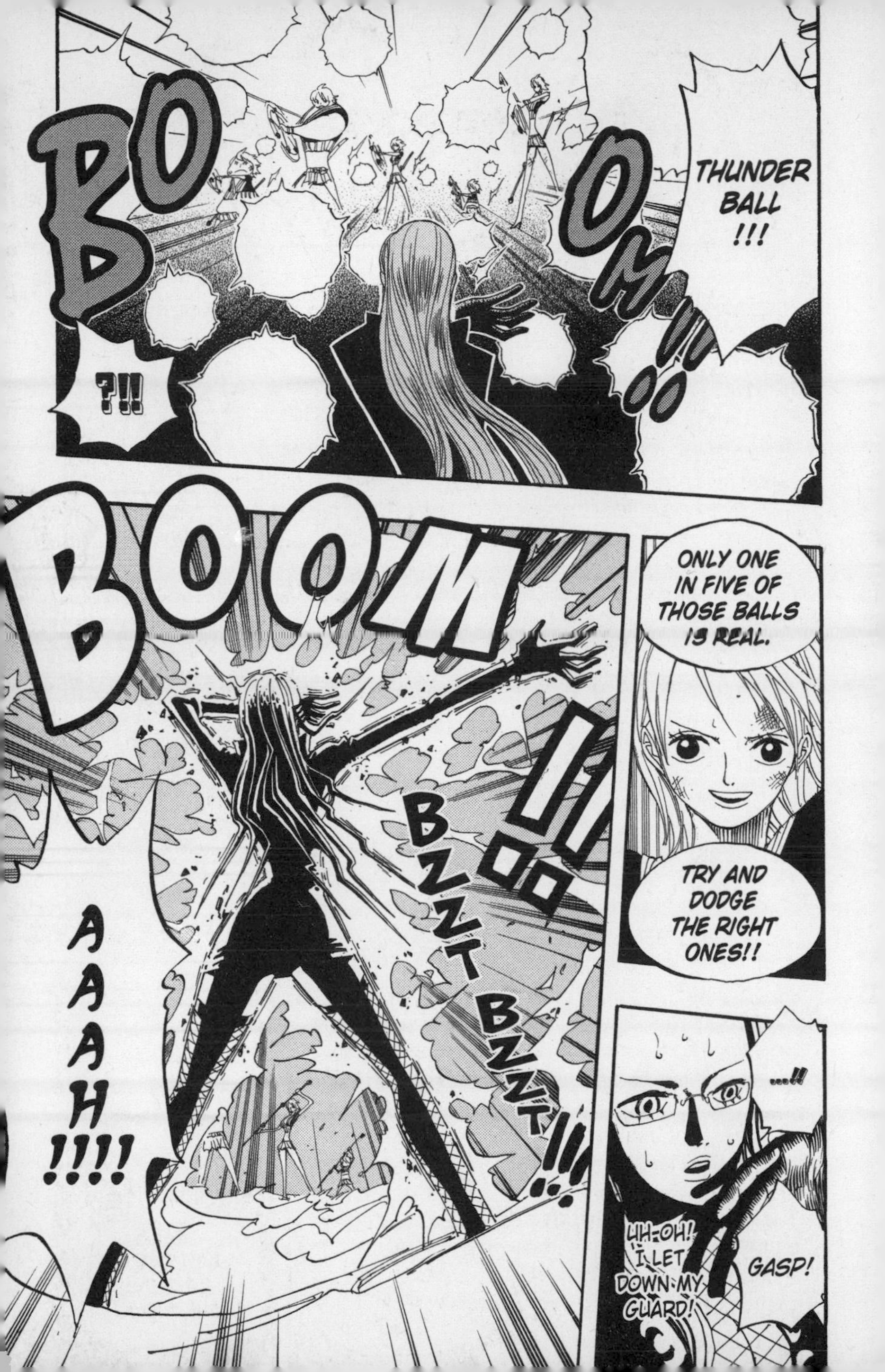
THUNDER BALL !!!
BOOM!!
?!!
ONLY ONE IN FIVE OF THOSE BALLS IS REAL.
TRY AND DODGE THE RIGHT ONES!!
...!!
GASP!
UH-OH! I LET DOWN MY GUARD!
BOOM!!
BZZZT BZZZT!!
AAAAH!!!!

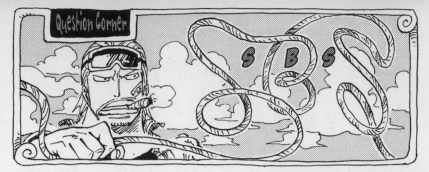

Question Corner
SBS

Q: Is the origin for Sodomu and Gomora the depraved towns of Sodom and Gomorrah in the Old Testament? Sodom and Gomorrah were destroyed by God. Did you decide to have the World Government represent the overwhelming power of God in the story?

--Yoiko

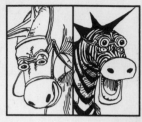

A: One Piece isn't that deep of a story! (Laughs) That's where I got their names, though.

TCH! ALL RIGHT, ALREADY! BUT YOU'LL NEED MORE MONEY TO BUY ALL THAT!

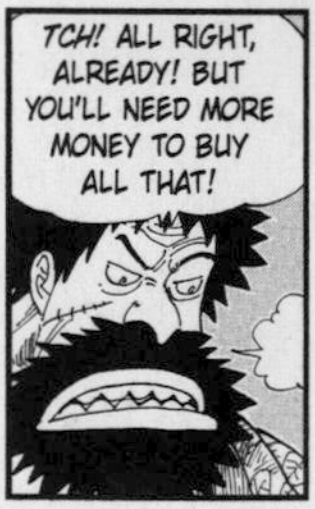

Q: I'd like to know the name of the old man who gave Usopp rice balls in volume 36. He's a good person. (*Cries*)

--Nice Old Man

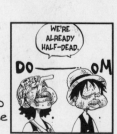

A: Oh, yes. That made me happy. I thanked the old guy even as I drew him. Um...he's a carpenter now, but he used to be Happa--the bandit with a heart. He moved there from the town of good food, Pucci. He's divorced and currently single--meaning he made the rice balls himself. Water Seven's famous dish Water Meat was inside the rice balls, so they tasted good!

WE'RE ALREADY HALF-DEAD.
DO——OM

Q: Punches aren't supposed to work on Luffy, so why does he get goose eggs and bruises when Nami and the others beat him up?! Please, tell me why!!

--Zolo-rin Love

A: When friends beat on each other it's mostly to teach them a lesson. Their punches work because they're full of compassion! They work on one's heart! Nami probably thinks, "My blows hurt my heart!" Okay, so maybe she doesn't...

Chapter 412:
YOU MISSED YOUR CHANCE

**MS. GOLDEN WEEK'S BIG PLAN, A BAROQUE REUNION, VOL. 41:
"MISTERS 0, 1, 2 AND 3"**

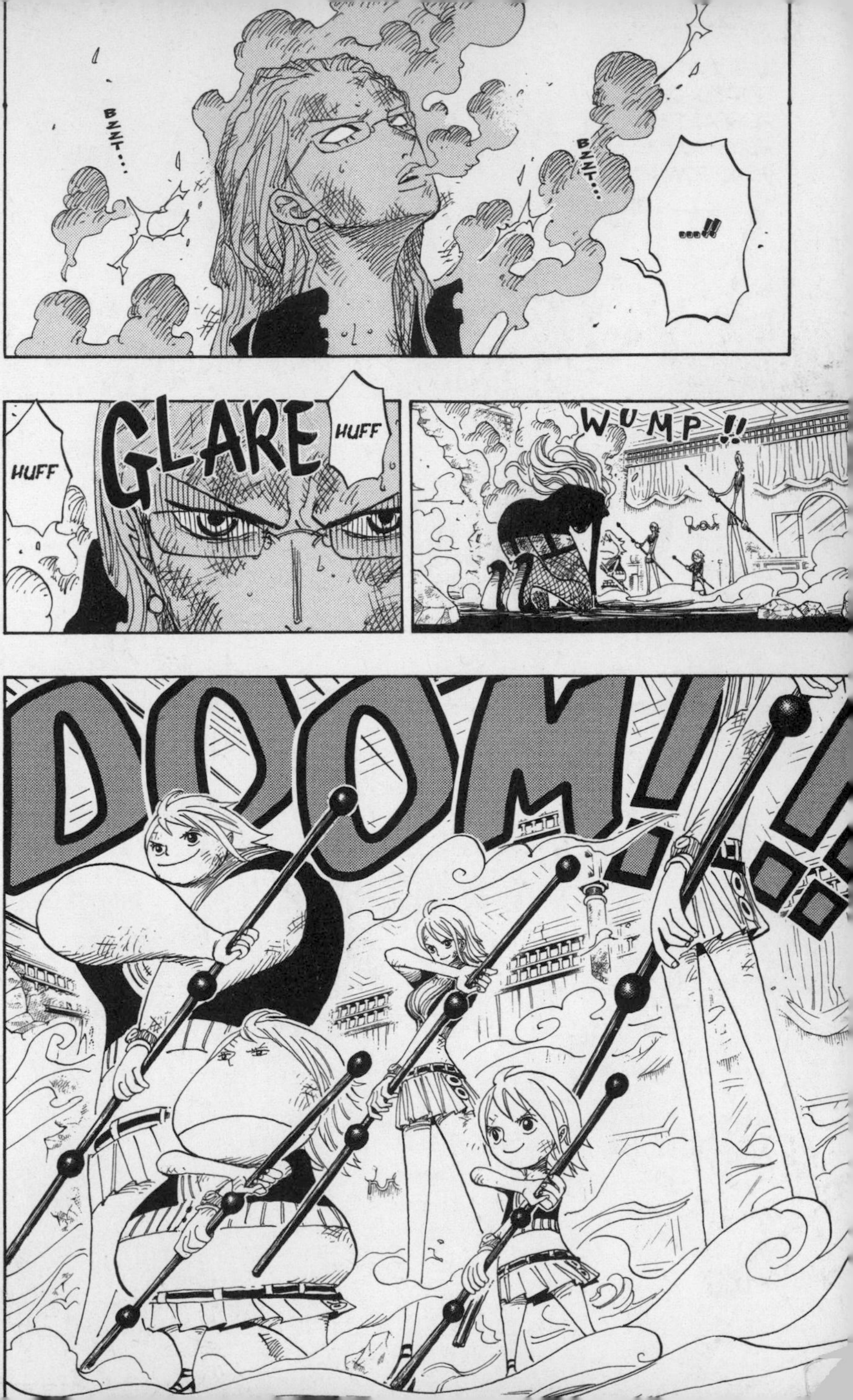
...!!
BZZT...
BZZT...
WUMP!!
HUFF
GLARE
HUFF
DOOM!!

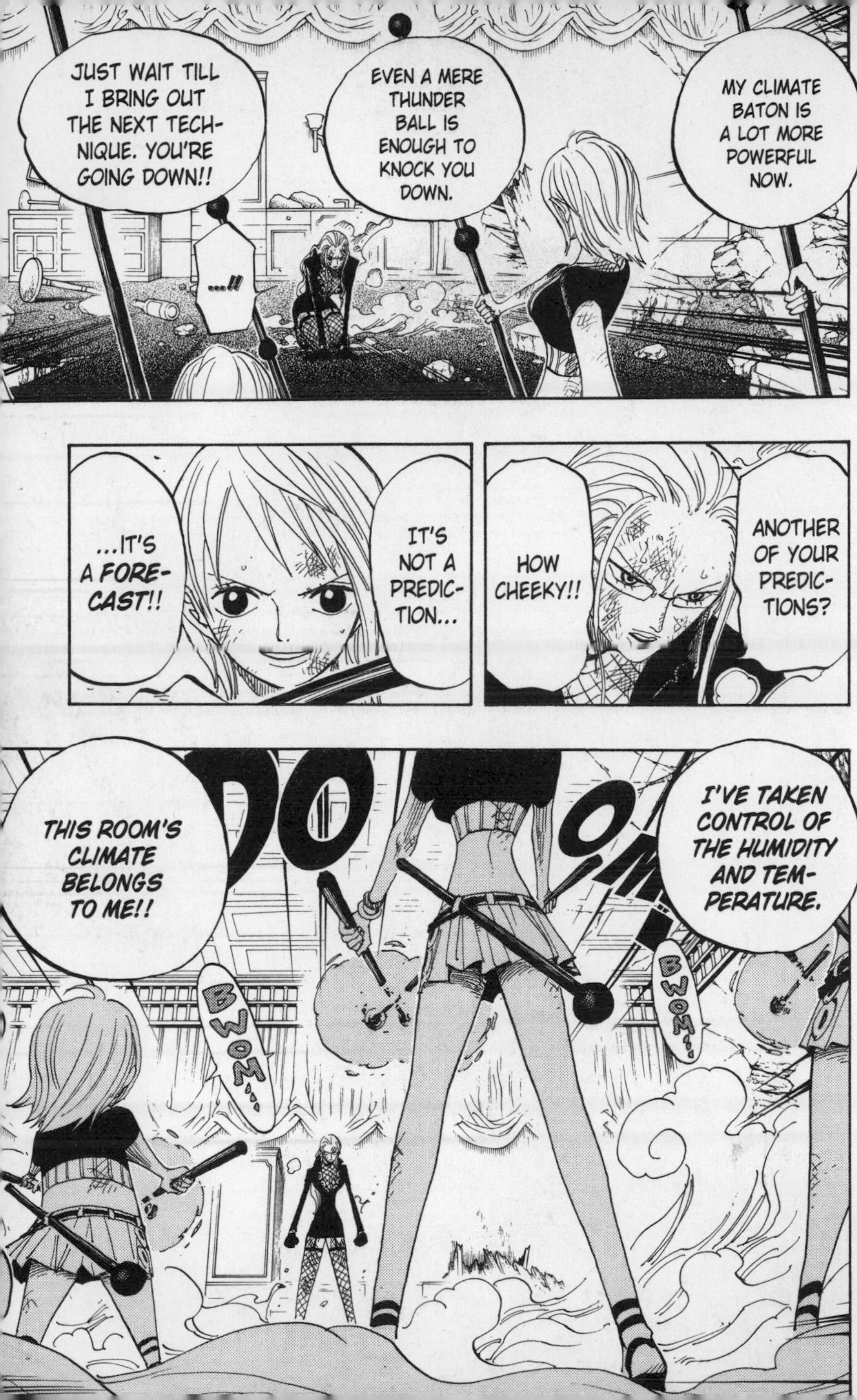
MY CLIMATE BATON IS A LOT MORE POWERFUL NOW.
EVEN A MERE THUNDER BALL IS ENOUGH TO KNOCK YOU DOWN.
JUST WAIT TILL I BRING OUT THE NEXT TECHNIQUE. YOU'RE GOING DOWN!!
...!!
ANOTHER OF YOUR PREDICTIONS?
HOW CHEEKY!!
IT'S NOT A PREDICTION...
...IT'S A *FORECAST!!*
I'VE TAKEN CONTROL OF THE HUMIDITY AND TEMPERATURE.
DOOM
BWOM
BWOM
THIS ROOM'S CLIMATE BELONGS TO ME!!

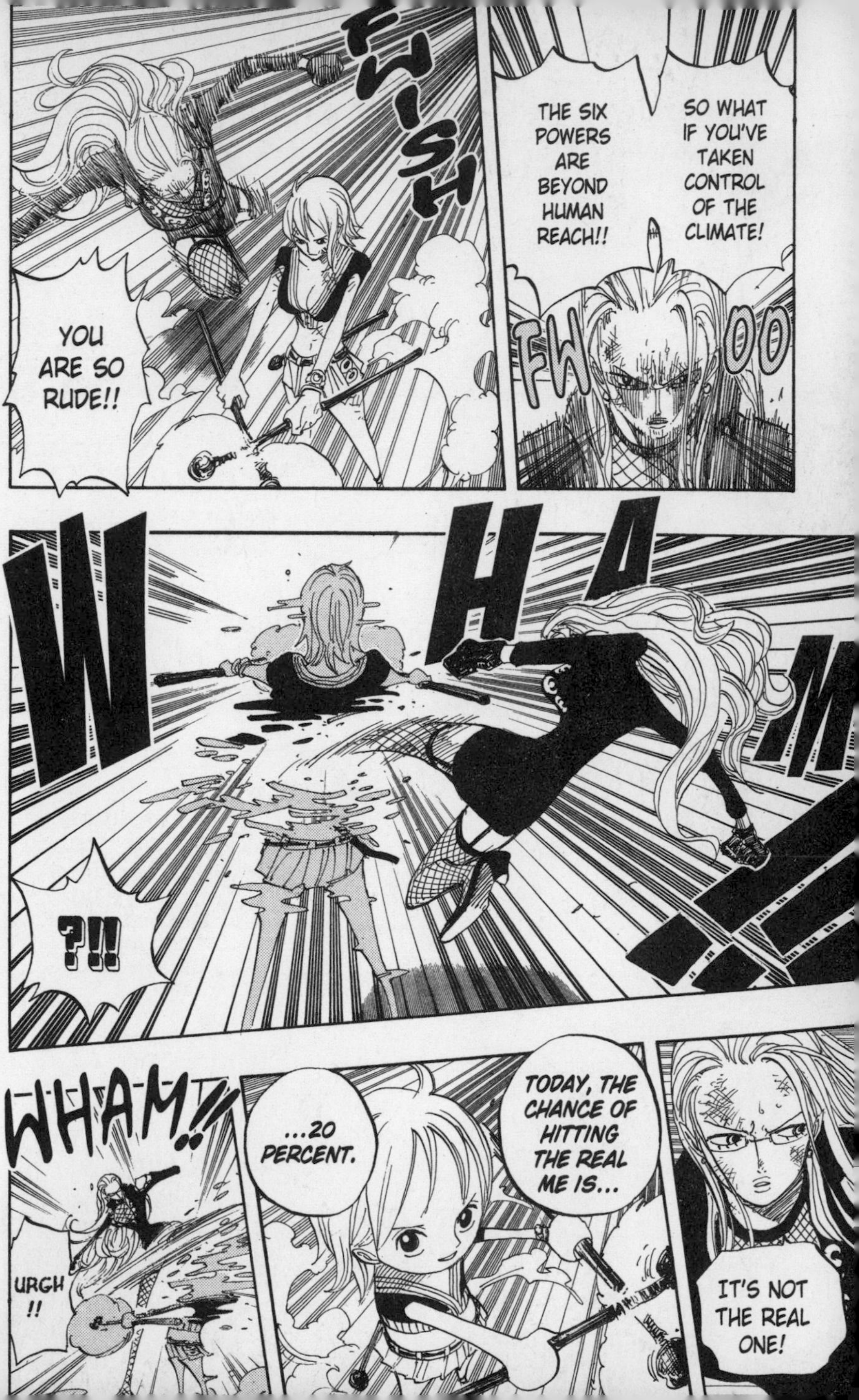

SO WHAT IF YOU'VE TAKEN CONTROL OF THE CLIMATE!
THE SIX POWERS ARE BEYOND HUMAN REACH!!
FWOO
FWISH
YOU ARE SO RUDE!!
WHAM
?!!
IT'S NOT THE REAL ONE!
TODAY, THE CHANCE OF HITTING THE REAL ME IS...
...20 PERCENT.
WHAM!!
URGH!!

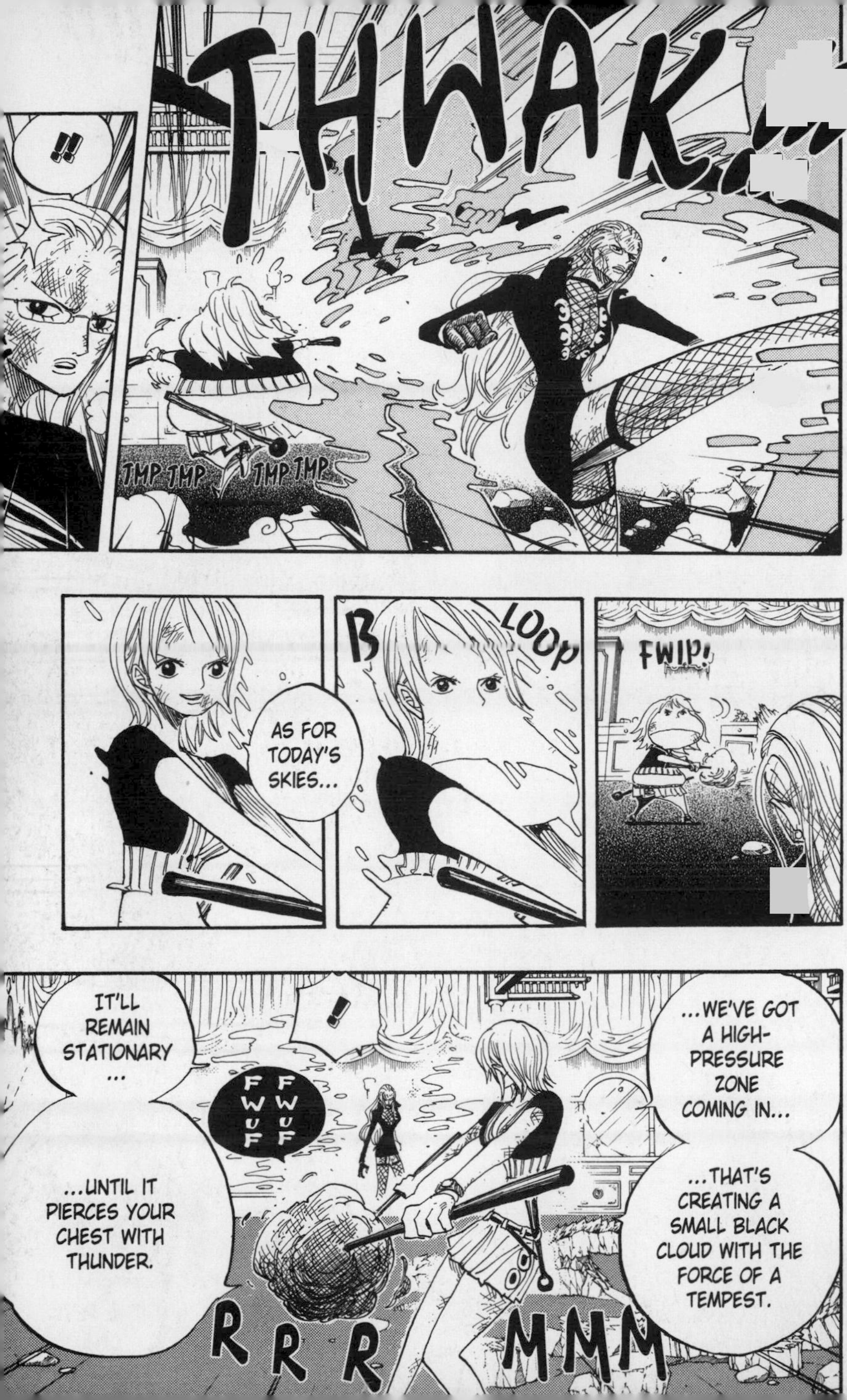
THWAK...
TMP TMP TMP TMP
!!
FWIP!
BLOOP
AS FOR TODAY'S SKIES...
...WE'VE GOT A HIGH-PRESSURE ZONE COMING IN...
...THAT'S CREATING A SMALL BLACK CLOUD WITH THE FORCE OF A TEMPEST.
!
FWUF FWUF
IT'LL REMAIN STATIONARY...
...UNTIL IT PIERCES YOUR CHEST WITH THUNDER.
RRRMMM

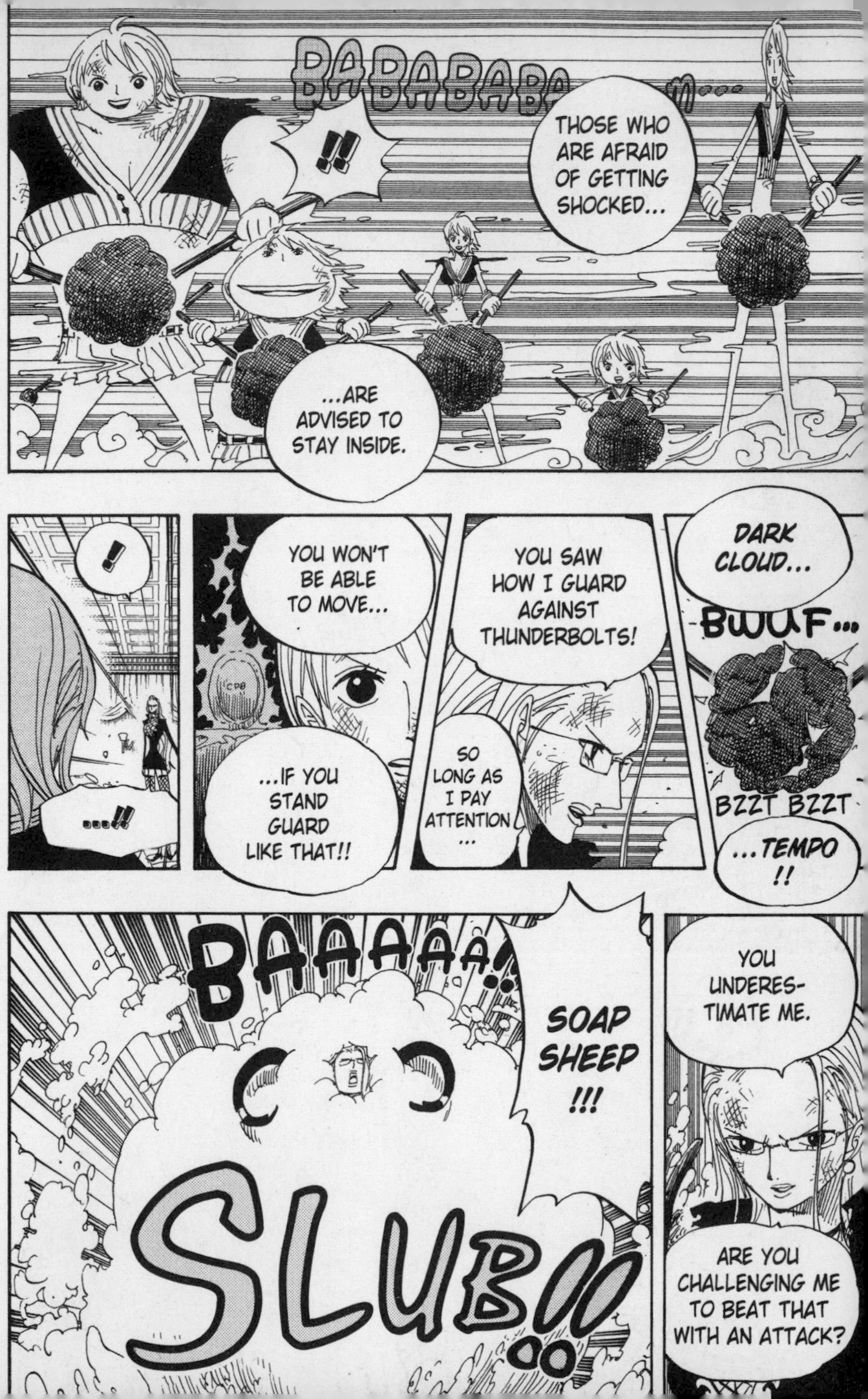
BABABABA
m...
THOSE WHO ARE AFRAID OF GETTING SHOCKED...
!!
...ARE ADVISED TO STAY INSIDE.
DARK CLOUD...
BWUF...
BZZT BZZT
...TEMPO !!
YOU SAW HOW I GUARD AGAINST THUNDERBOLTS!
SO LONG AS I PAY ATTENTION ...
YOU WON'T BE ABLE TO MOVE...
...IF YOU STAND GUARD LIKE THAT!!
!
...!!
YOU UNDERES- TIMATE ME.
ARE YOU CHALLENGING ME TO BEAT THAT WITH AN ATTACK?
BAAAAA!!
SOAP SHEEP !!!
SLUB!!

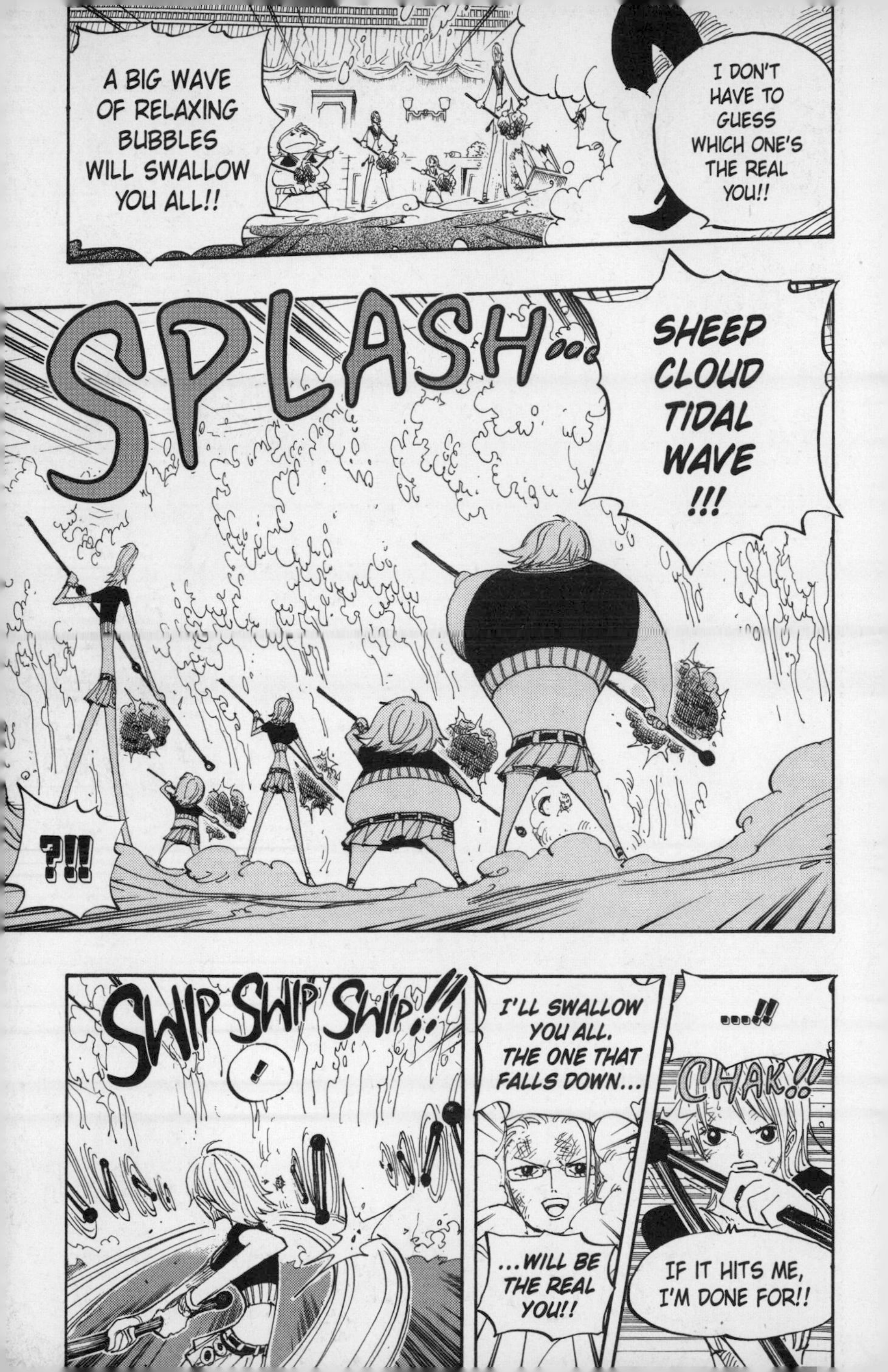
I DON'T HAVE TO GUESS WHICH ONE'S THE REAL YOU!!
A BIG WAVE OF RELAXING BUBBLES WILL SWALLOW YOU ALL!!
SHEEP CLOUD TIDAL WAVE!!!
SPLASH...
?!!
...!!
CHAK!!
IF IT HITS ME, I'M DONE FOR!!
I'LL SWALLOW YOU ALL. THE ONE THAT FALLS DOWN...
...WILL BE THE REAL YOU!!
SWIP SWIP SWIP!!
!

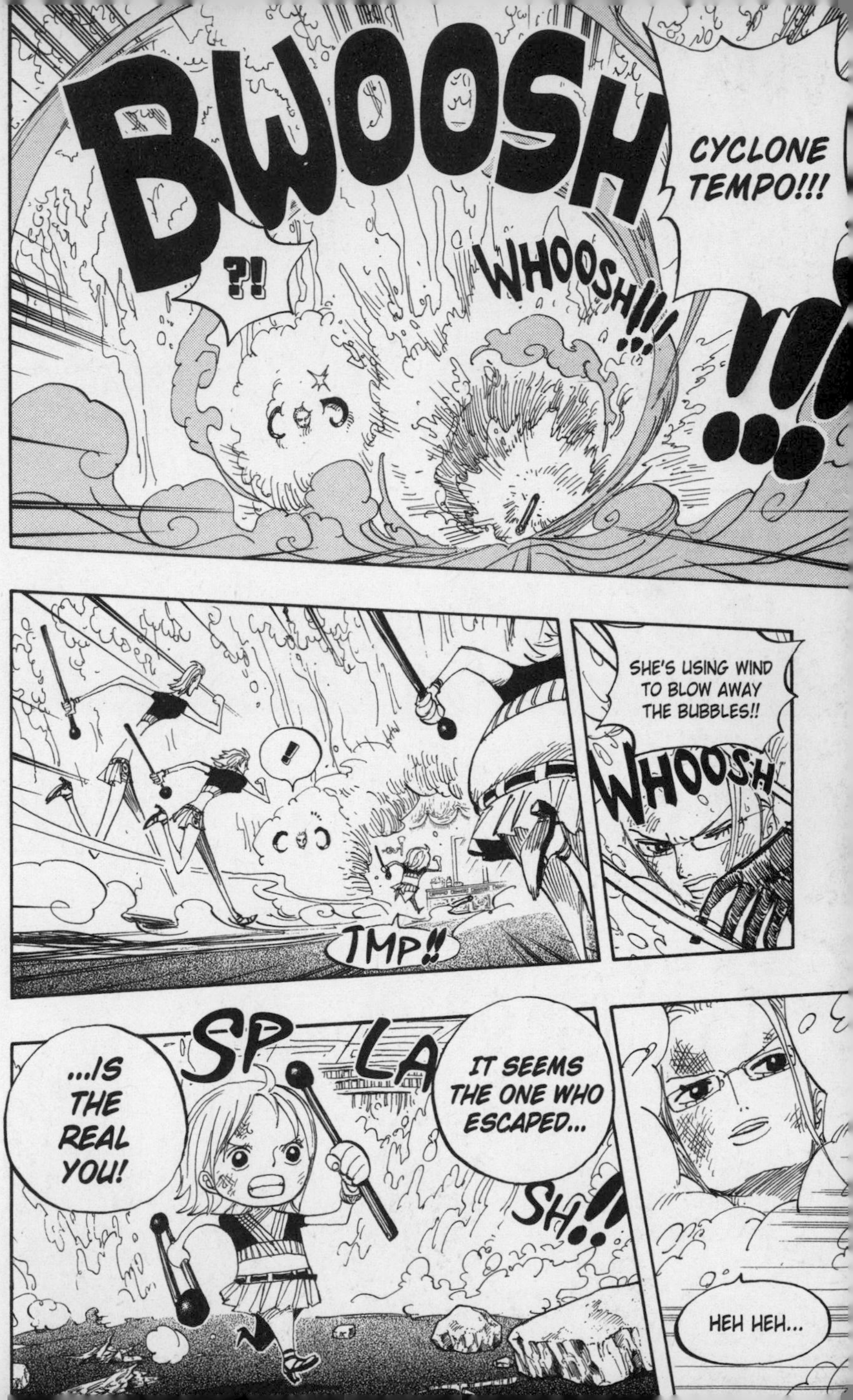
CYCLONE TEMPO!!!
WHOOSH!!!
BWOOSH
?!
SHE'S USING WIND TO BLOW AWAY THE BUBBLES!!
WHOOSH
!
TMP!!
HEH HEH...
IT SEEMS THE ONE WHO ESCAPED...
SPLASH!!
...IS THE REAL YOU!

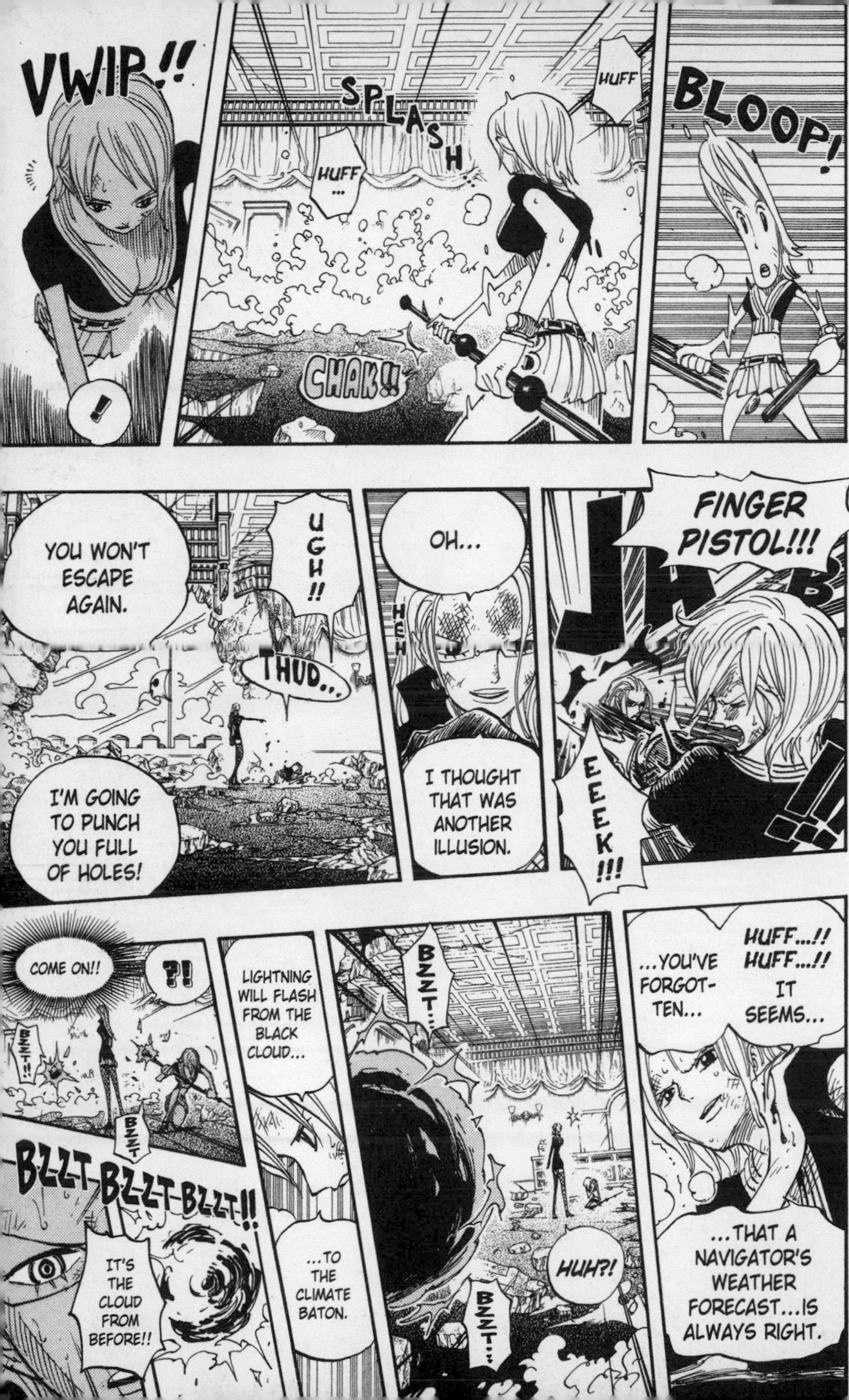
BLOOP!
HUFF
SPLASH
HUFF...
CHAK!!
VWIP!!
!
FINGER PISTOL!!!
EEEK!!!
OH...
HEH
I THOUGHT THAT WAS ANOTHER ILLUSION.
YOU WON'T ESCAPE AGAIN.
UGH!!
THUD...
I'M GOING TO PUNCH YOU FULL OF HOLES!
HUFF...!! HUFF...!!
IT SEEMS...
...YOU'VE FORGOT-TEN...
...THAT A NAVIGATOR'S WEATHER FORECAST...IS ALWAYS RIGHT.
BZZT...
HUH?!
BZZT...
LIGHTNING WILL FLASH FROM THE BLACK CLOUD...
...TO THE CLIMATE BATON.
?!
COME ON!!
BZZT!!
BZZT
B-Z-Z-T-B-Z-Z-T-B-Z-Z-T!!
IT'S THE CLOUD FROM BEFORE!!

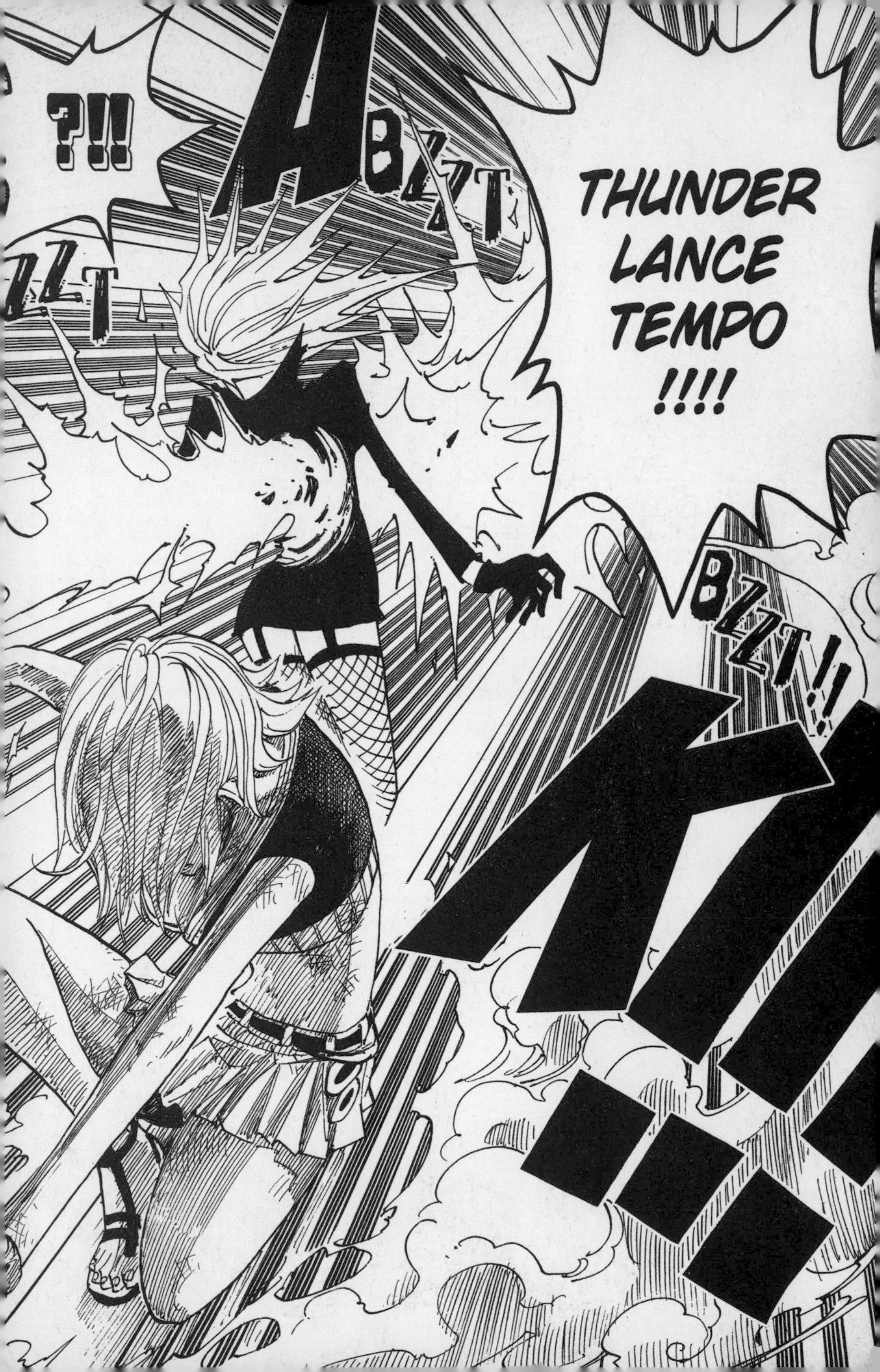
THUNDER LANCE TEMPO !!!!
BZZT
?!!
BZZT
BZZT!!

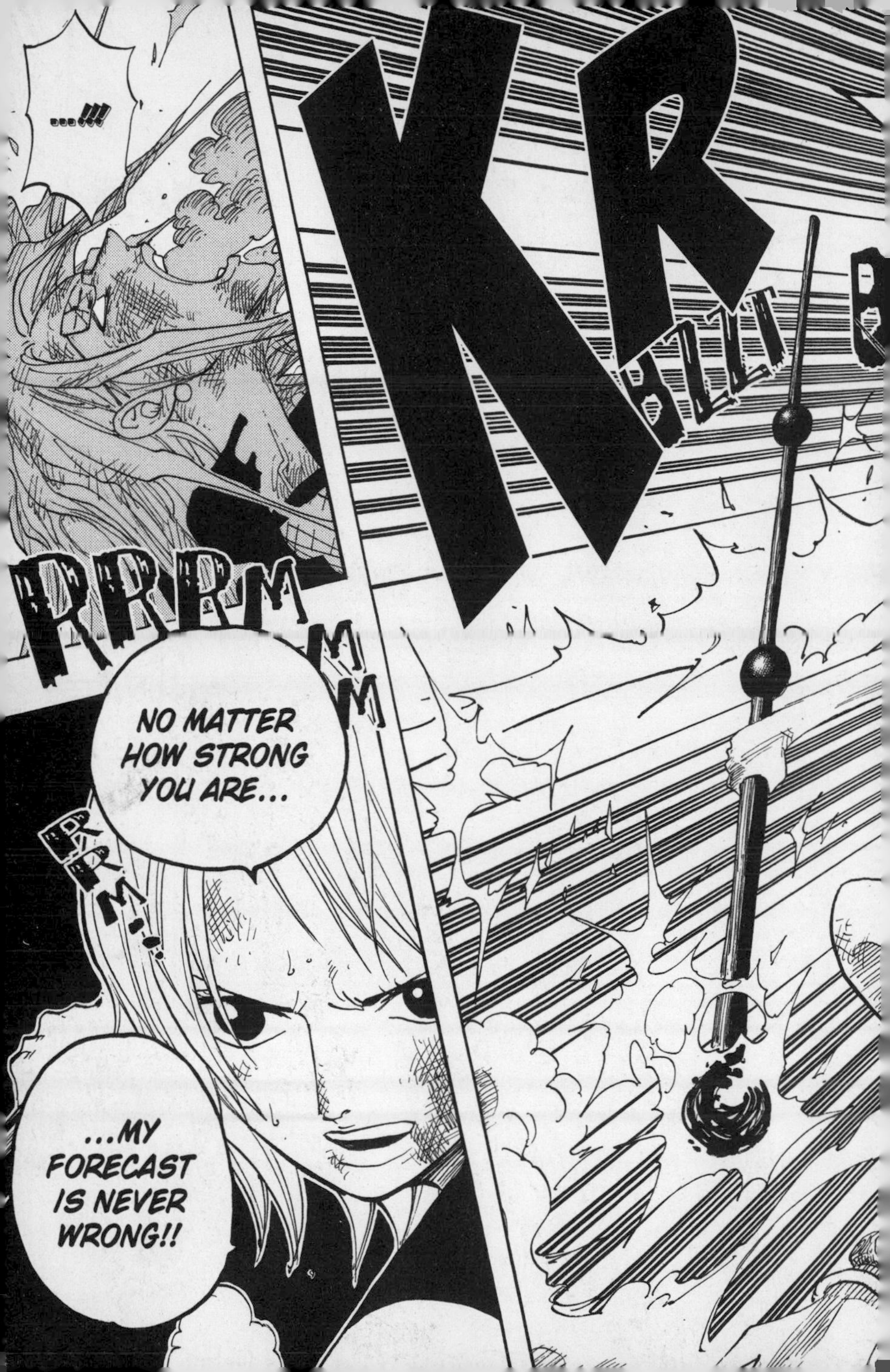
KR
BZZT
B
...!!!
RRRRMMM
NO MATTER HOW STRONG YOU ARE...
RRM
...MY FORECAST IS NEVER WRONG!!

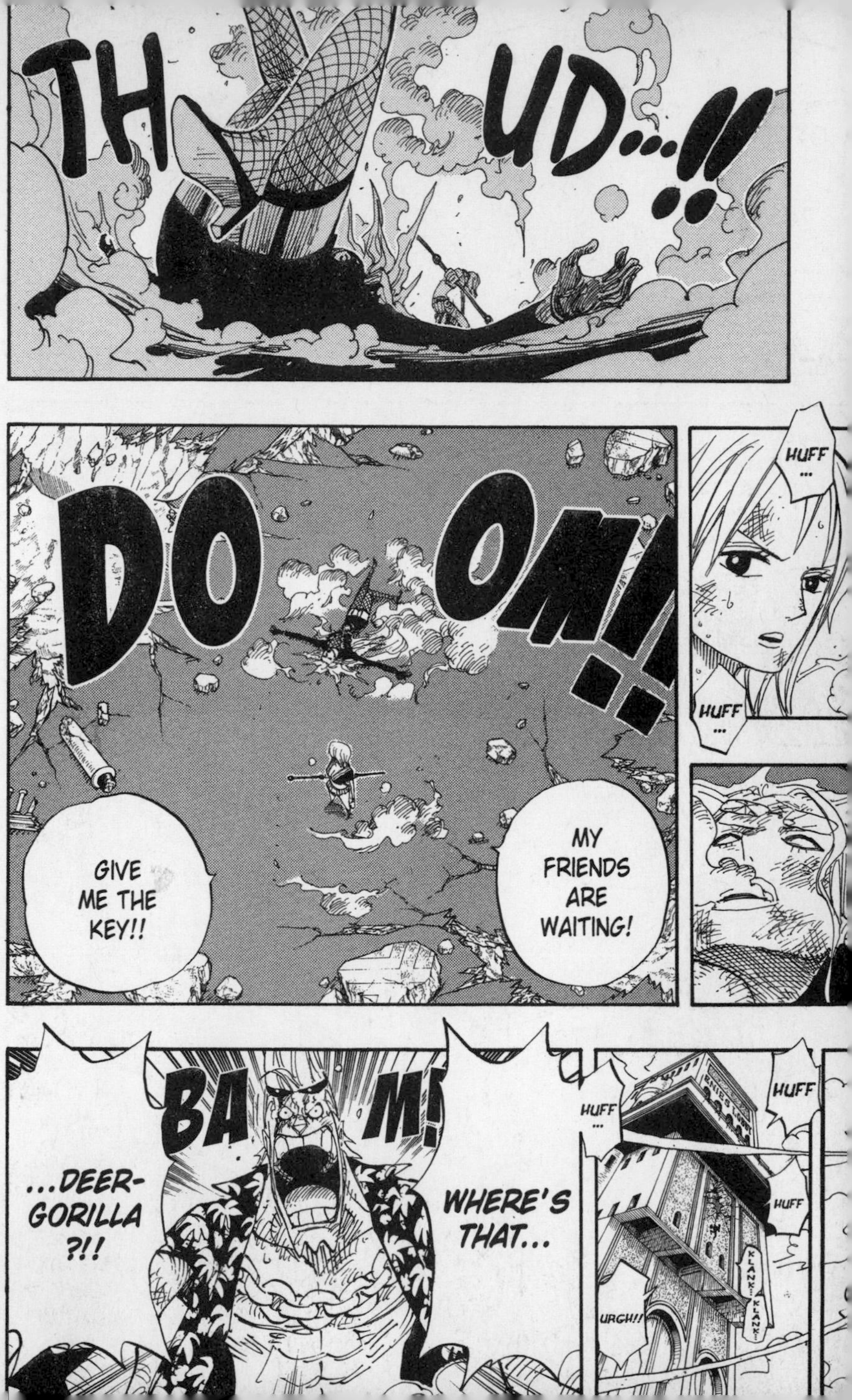
THUD...!!
HUFF...
HUFF...
DOOM!!
MY FRIENDS ARE WAITING!
GIVE ME THE KEY!!
HUFF
HUFF
HUFF...
KLANK! KLANK!
URGH!!
BAM!
WHERE'S THAT...
...DEER-GORILLA?!!

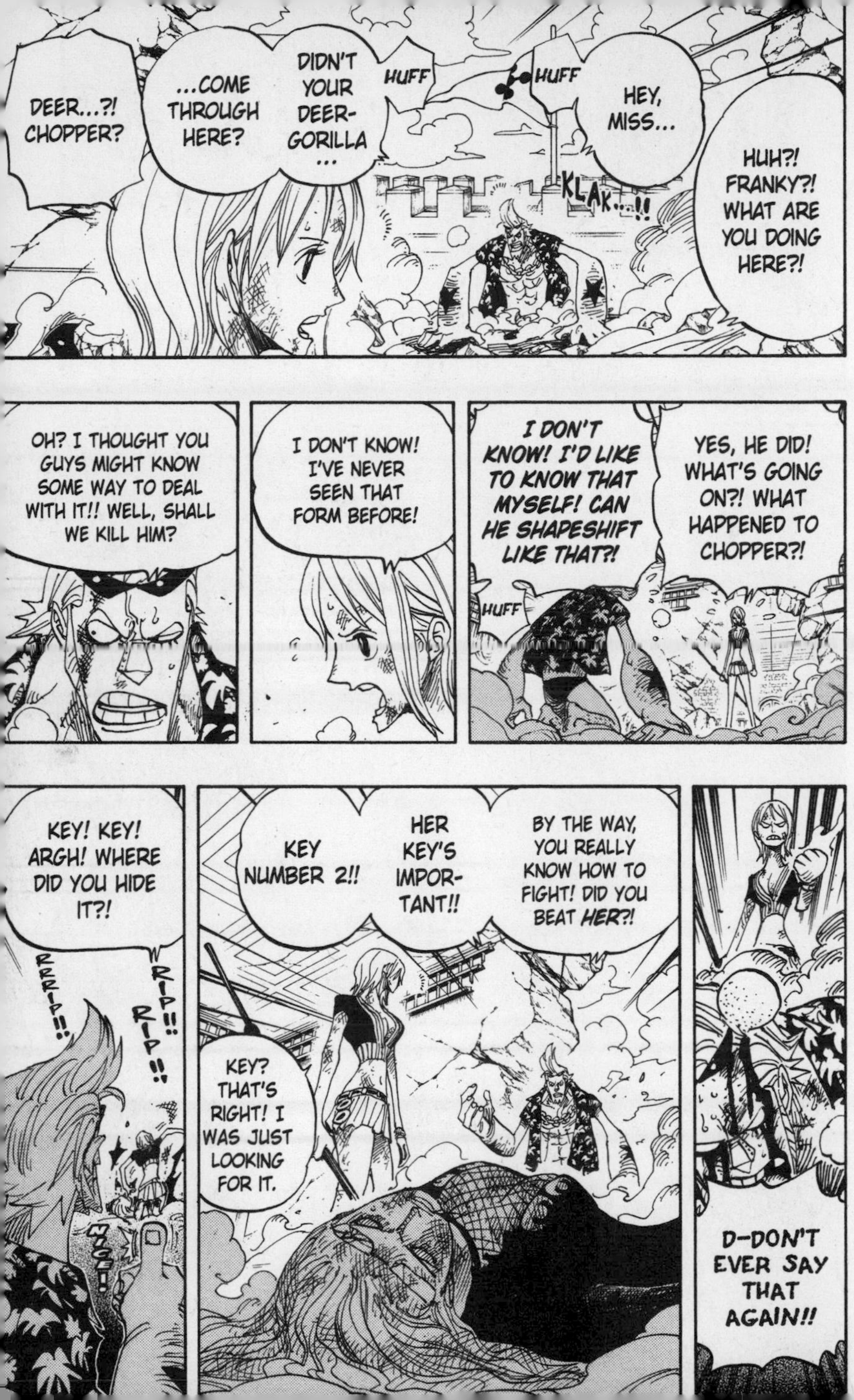
HUH?! FRANKY?! WHAT ARE YOU DOING HERE?!
HEY, MISS...
HUFF
KLAK...!!
HUFF
DIDN'T YOUR DEER-GORILLA ...
...COME THROUGH HERE?
DEER...?! CHOPPER?
YES, HE DID! WHAT'S GOING ON?! WHAT HAPPENED TO CHOPPER?!
I DON'T KNOW! I'D LIKE TO KNOW THAT MYSELF! CAN HE SHAPESHIFT LIKE THAT?!
HUFF
I DON'T KNOW! I'VE NEVER SEEN THAT FORM BEFORE!
OH? I THOUGHT YOU GUYS MIGHT KNOW SOME WAY TO DEAL WITH IT!! WELL, SHALL WE KILL HIM?
D-DON'T EVER SAY THAT AGAIN!!
BY THE WAY, YOU REALLY KNOW HOW TO FIGHT! DID YOU BEAT HER?!
HER KEY'S IMPORTANT!!
KEY NUMBER 2!!
KEY? THAT'S RIGHT! I WAS JUST LOOKING FOR IT.
KEY! KEY! ARGH! WHERE DID YOU HIDE IT?!
RIP!!
RIP!!
RRRIP!!
NICE!

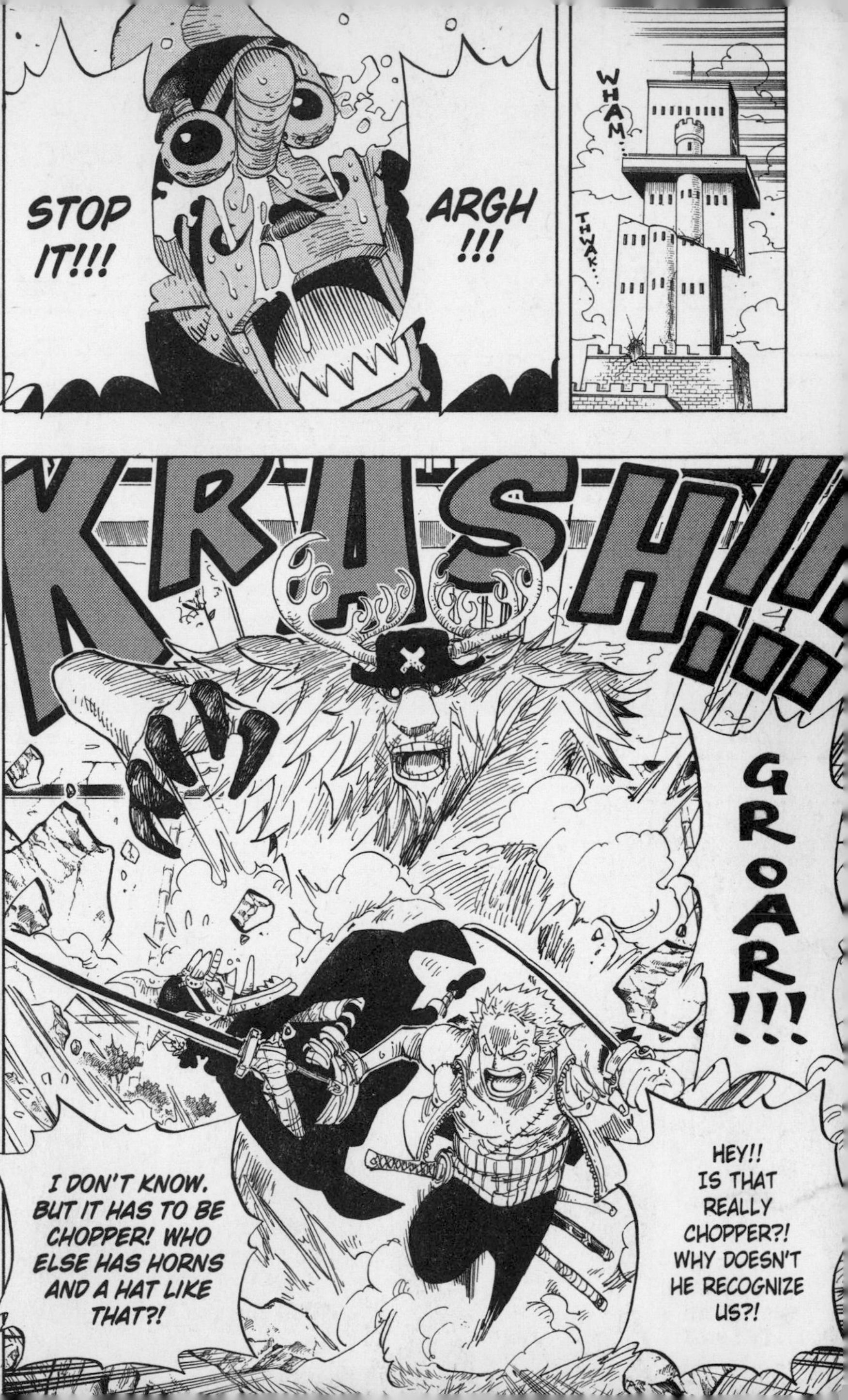
WHAM...
THWAK...
ARGH!!!
STOP IT!!!
KRASH!!
GROAR!!!
HEY!! IS THAT REALLY CHOPPER?! WHY DOESN'T HE RECOGNIZE US?!
I DON'T KNOW. BUT IT HAS TO BE CHOPPER! WHO ELSE HAS HORNS AND A HAT LIKE THAT?!

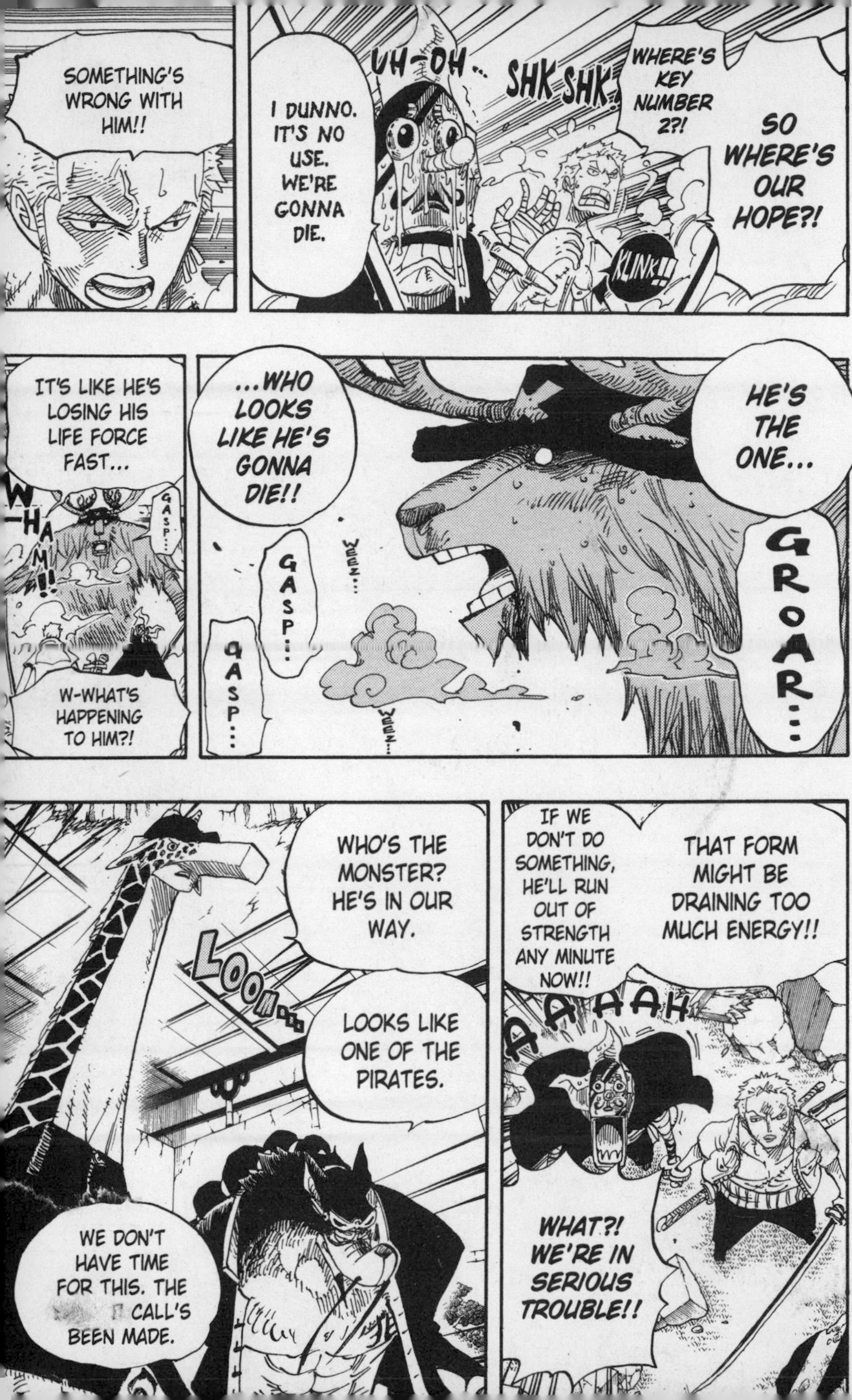
SO WHERE'S OUR HOPE?!
WHERE'S KEY NUMBER 2?!
SHK SHK
UH-OH...
I DUNNO. IT'S NO USE. WE'RE GONNA DIE.
KLINK!!
SOMETHING'S WRONG WITH HIM!!
HE'S THE ONE...
...WHO LOOKS LIKE HE'S GONNA DIE!!
GROAR...
WEEZ...
GASP...
GASP...
WEEZ...
IT'S LIKE HE'S LOSING HIS LIFE FORCE FAST...
WHAM!!
GASP...
W-WHAT'S HAPPENING TO HIM?!
THAT FORM MIGHT BE DRAINING TOO MUCH ENERGY!!
IF WE DON'T DO SOMETHING, HE'LL RUN OUT OF STRENGTH ANY MINUTE NOW!!
AAAAAH
WHAT?! WE'RE IN SERIOUS TROUBLE!!
WHO'S THE MONSTER? HE'S IN OUR WAY.
LOOM...
LOOKS LIKE ONE OF THE PIRATES.
WE DON'T HAVE TIME FOR THIS. THE CALL'S BEEN MADE.

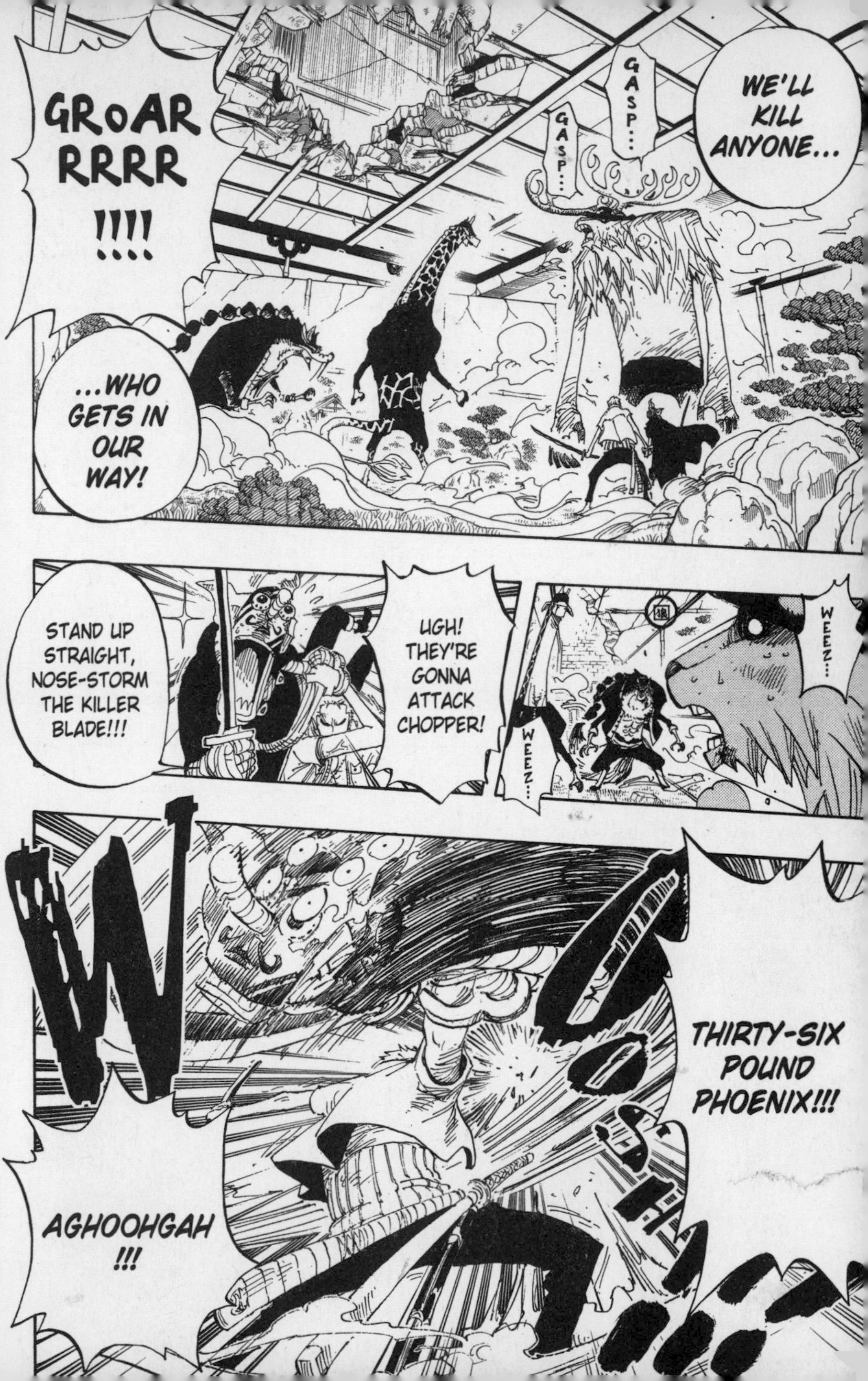
WE'LL KILL ANYONE...
GASP...
GASP...
GROARRRRR!!!!
...WHO GETS IN OUR WAY!
WEEZ...
WEEZ...
UGH! THEY'RE GONNA ATTACK CHOPPER!
STAND UP STRAIGHT, NOSE-STORM THE KILLER BLADE!!!
THIRTY-SIX POUND PHOENIX!!!
AGHOOHGAH!!!

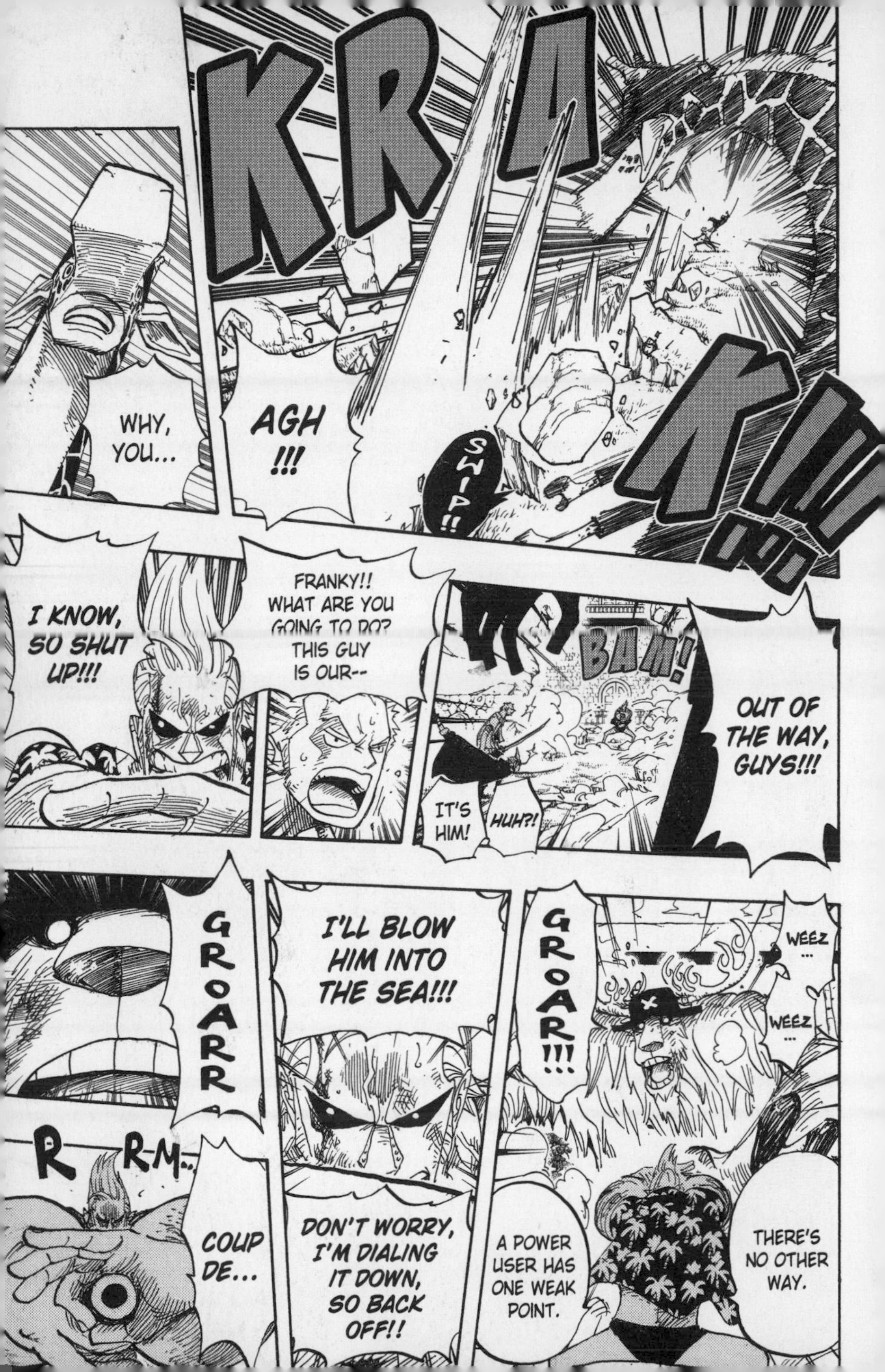
KRA
K!!!
AGH !!!
SWIP!!
WHY, YOU...
OUT OF THE WAY, GUYS!!!
BAM!
HUH?!
IT'S HIM!
FRANKY!! WHAT ARE YOU GOING TO DO? THIS GUY IS OUR--
I KNOW, SO SHUT UP!!!
WEEZ ...
WEEZ ...
GROARR!!!
THERE'S NO OTHER WAY.
A POWER USER HAS ONE WEAK POINT.
I'LL BLOW HIM INTO THE SEA!!!
DON'T WORRY, I'M DIALING IT DOWN, SO BACK OFF!!
GROARR
R R-M..
COUP DE...

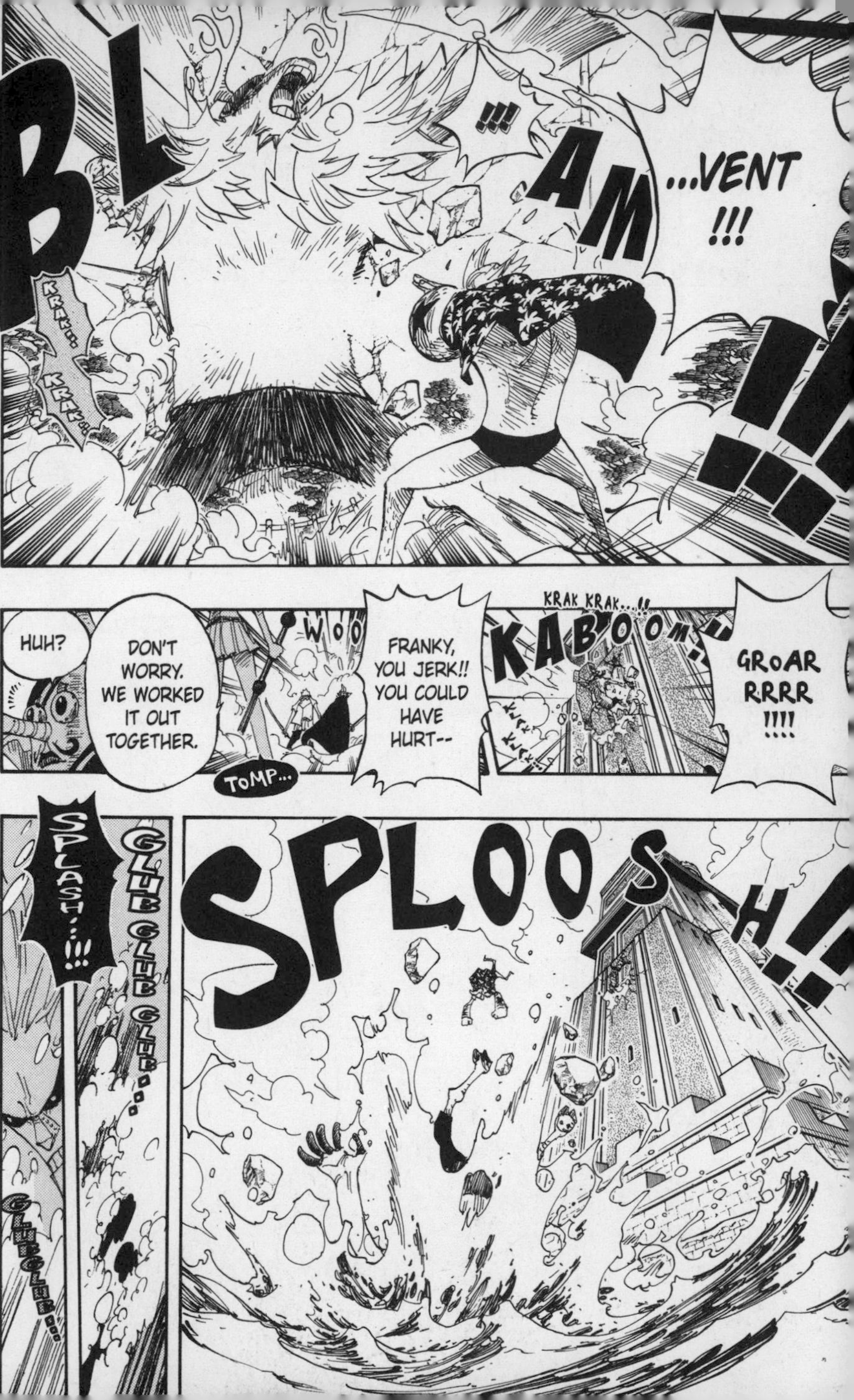
BL
!!!
AM
...VENT
!!!
KRAK..
KRAK..
GRoAR
RRRR
!!!!
KRAK KRAK...!!
KABOOM..!!
FRANKY, YOU JERK!! YOU COULD HAVE HURT--
WOO
TOMP...
DON'T WORRY. WE WORKED IT OUT TOGETHER.
HUH?
SPLOOSH!!
GLUB GLUB GLUB...
SPLASH...!!!
GLUBGLUB...

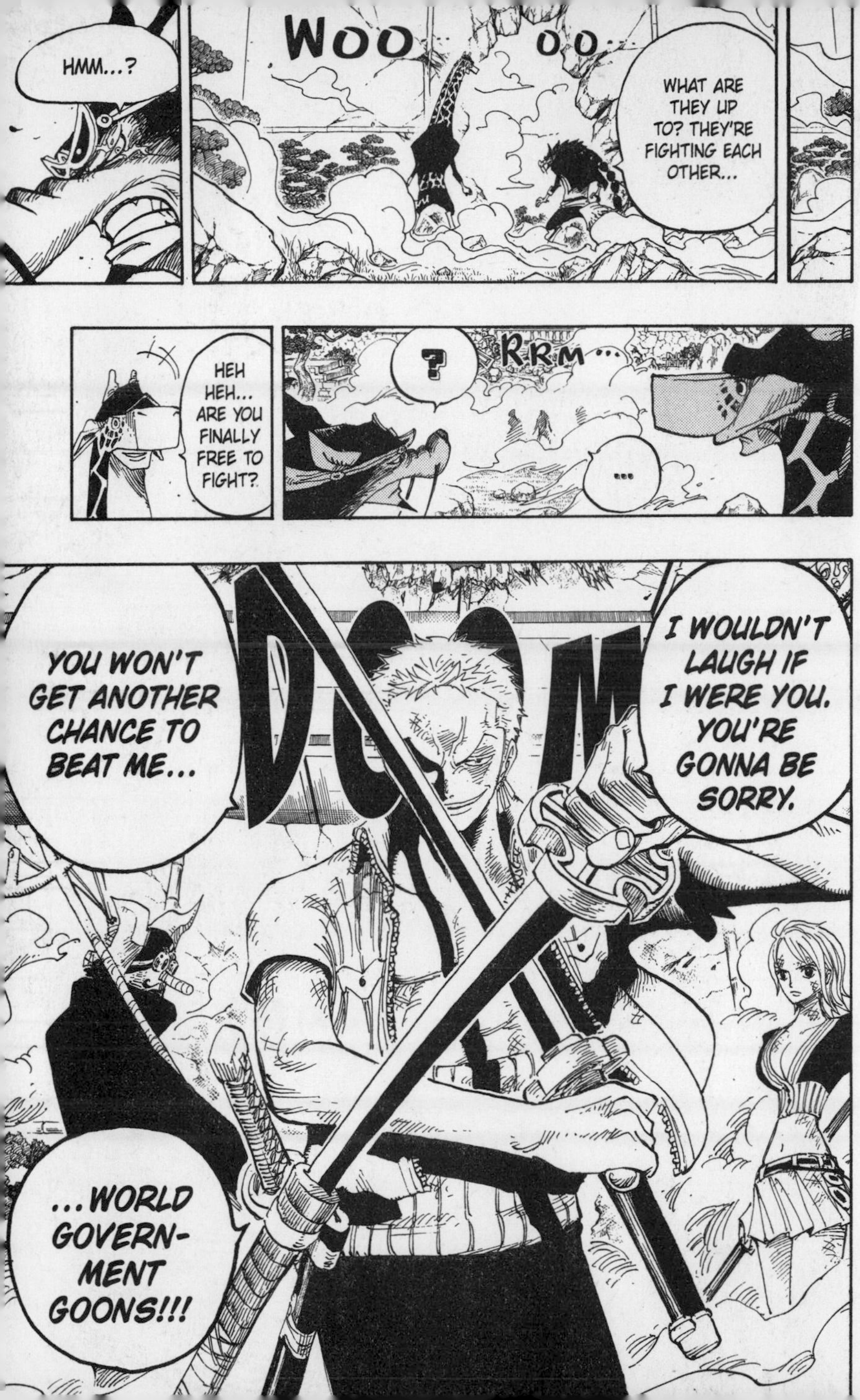
WOO... OO...
WHAT ARE THEY UP TO? THEY'RE FIGHTING EACH OTHER...
HMM...?
?
RRM...
...
HEH HEH... ARE YOU FINALLY FREE TO FIGHT?
I WOULDN'T LAUGH IF I WERE YOU. YOU'RE GONNA BE SORRY.
YOU WON'T GET ANOTHER CHANCE TO BEAT ME...
...WORLD GOVERNMENT GOONS!!!

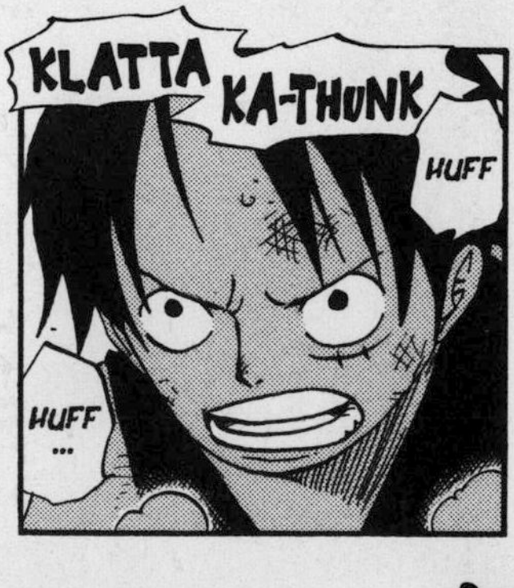

KLATTA
KA-THUNK
HUFF
HUFF ...

Chapter 413:
HUNTER

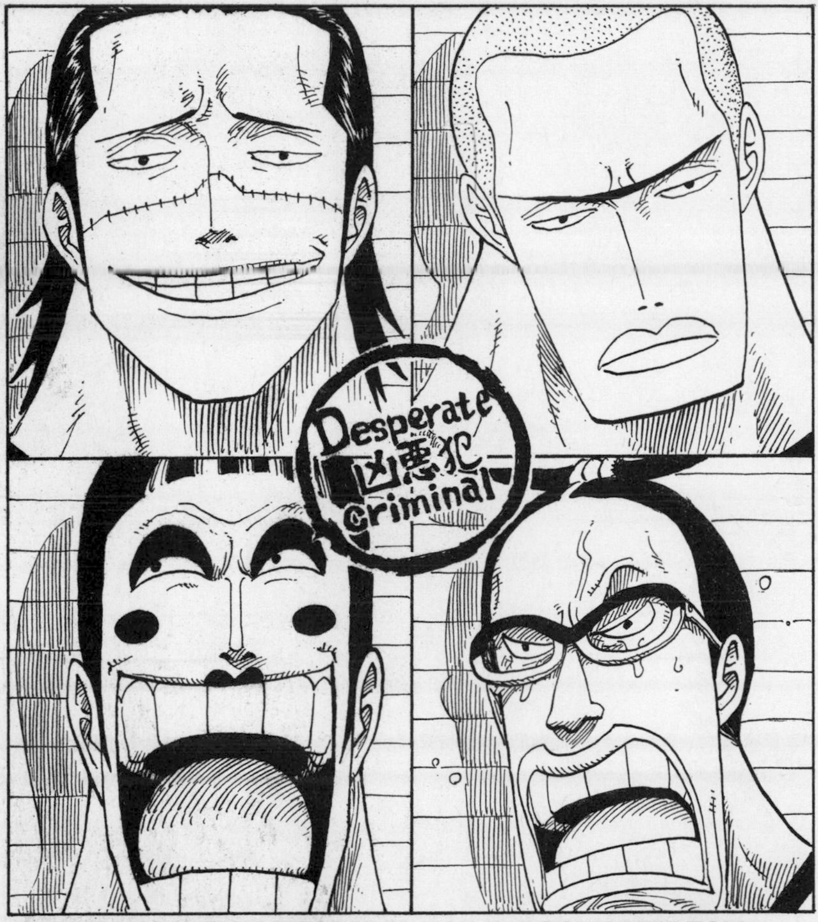
Desperate
凶悪犯
criminal

MS. GOLDEN WEEK'S BIG PLAN, A BAROQUE REUNION, THE FINALE: "SENTENCED TO INCARCERATION IN THE GREAT PRISON IMPEL DOWN"

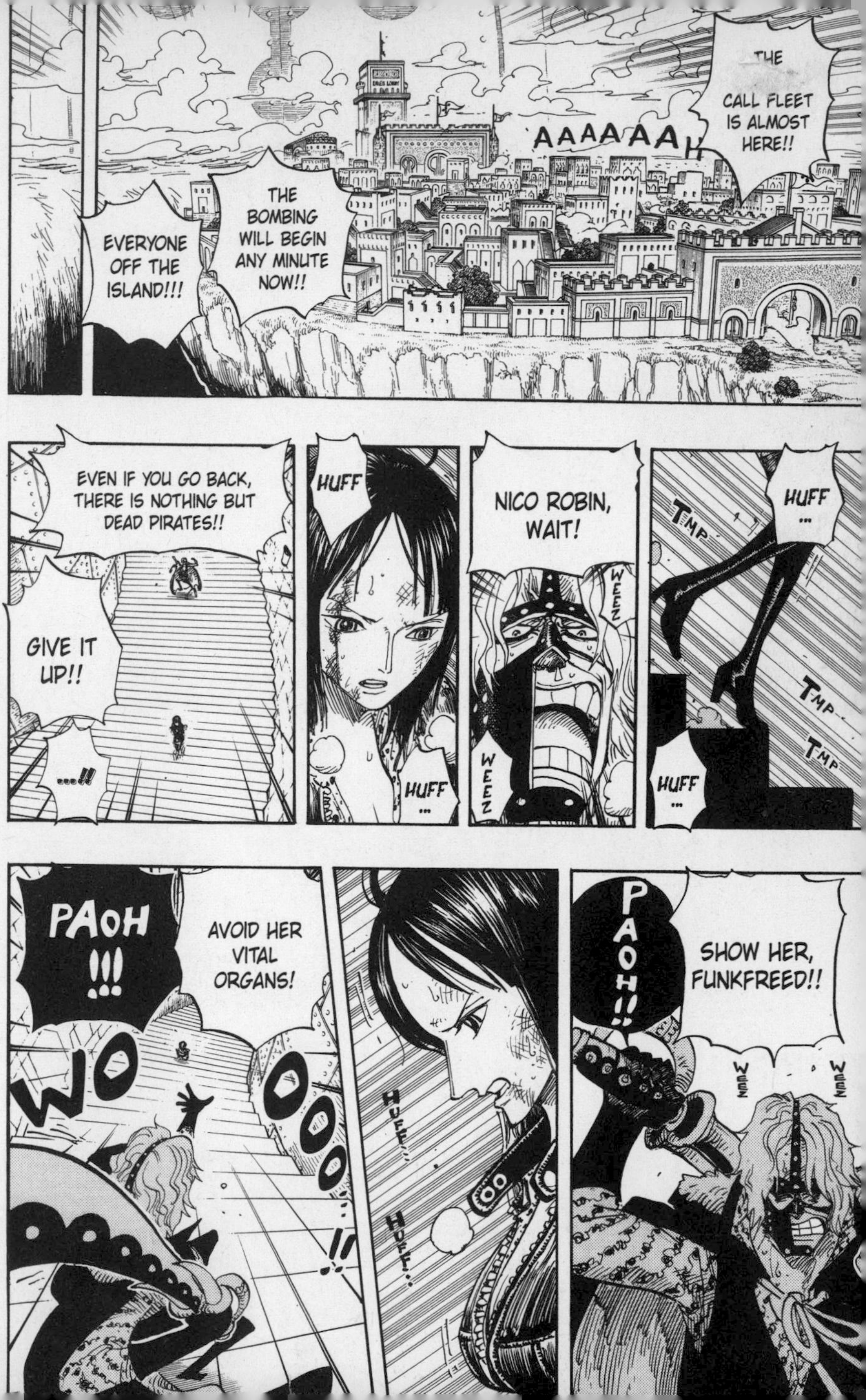
THE CALL FLEET IS ALMOST HERE!!
AAAAAA
THE BOMBING WILL BEGIN ANY MINUTE NOW!!
EVERYONE OFF THE ISLAND!!!
HUFF ...
TMP
TMP
TMP
HUFF ...
NICO ROBIN, WAIT!
WEEZ
WEEZ
HUFF
HUFF ...
EVEN IF YOU GO BACK, THERE IS NOTHING BUT DEAD PIRATES!!
GIVE IT UP!!
...!!
SHOW HER, FUNKFREED!!
PAOH!!
WEEZ
WEEZ
HUFF...
HUFF...
PAOH !!!
AVOID HER VITAL ORGANS!
WOOOOO!!

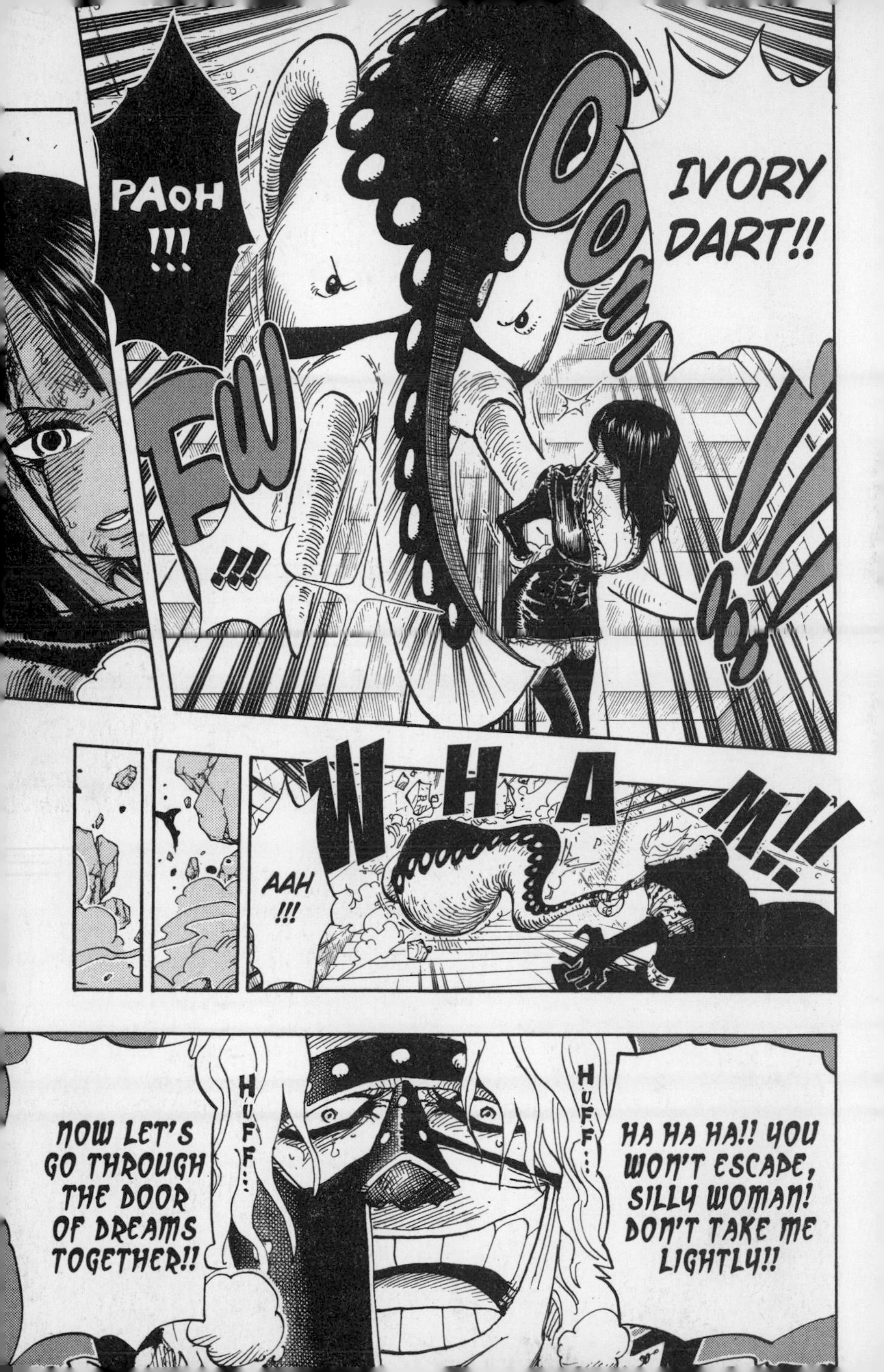
IVORY DART!!
PAOH !!!
WHAM!!
AAH !!!
HA HA HA!! YOU WON'T ESCAPE, SILLY WOMAN! DON'T TAKE ME LIGHTLY!!
HUFF...
HUFF...
NOW LET'S GO THROUGH THE DOOR OF DREAMS TOGETHER!!

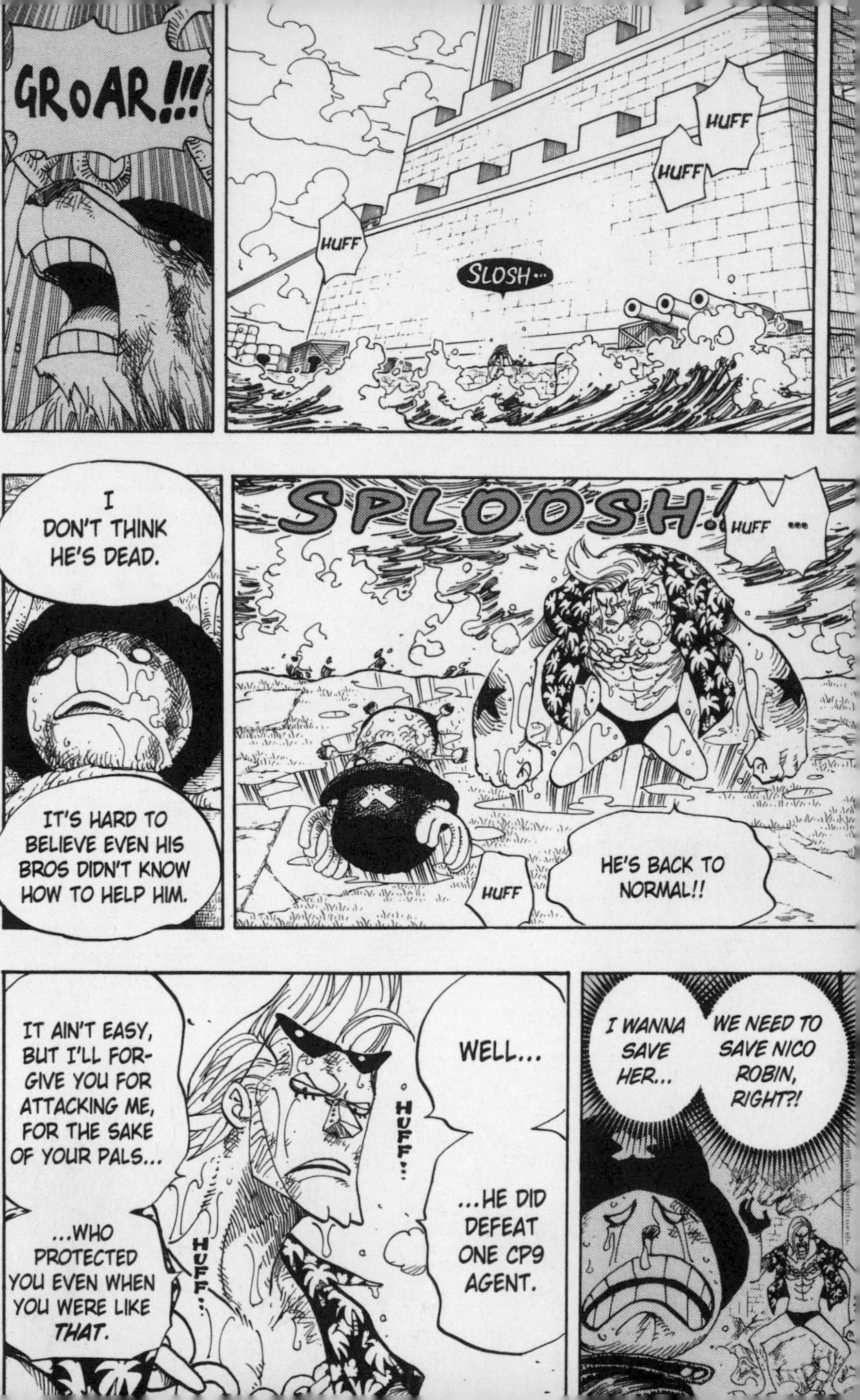
HUFF
HUFF
HUFF
SLOSH...
GROAR!!!
SPLOOSH!
HUFF ...
HE'S BACK TO NORMAL!!
HUFF
I DON'T THINK HE'S DEAD.
IT'S HARD TO BELIEVE EVEN HIS BROS DIDN'T KNOW HOW TO HELP HIM.
WE NEED TO SAVE NICO ROBIN, RIGHT?!
I WANNA SAVE HER...
WELL...
HUFF...
...HE DID DEFEAT ONE CP9 AGENT.
HUFF...
IT AIN'T EASY, BUT I'LL FOR-GIVE YOU FOR ATTACKING ME, FOR THE SAKE OF YOUR PALS...
...WHO PROTECTED YOU EVEN WHEN YOU WERE LIKE *THAT*.

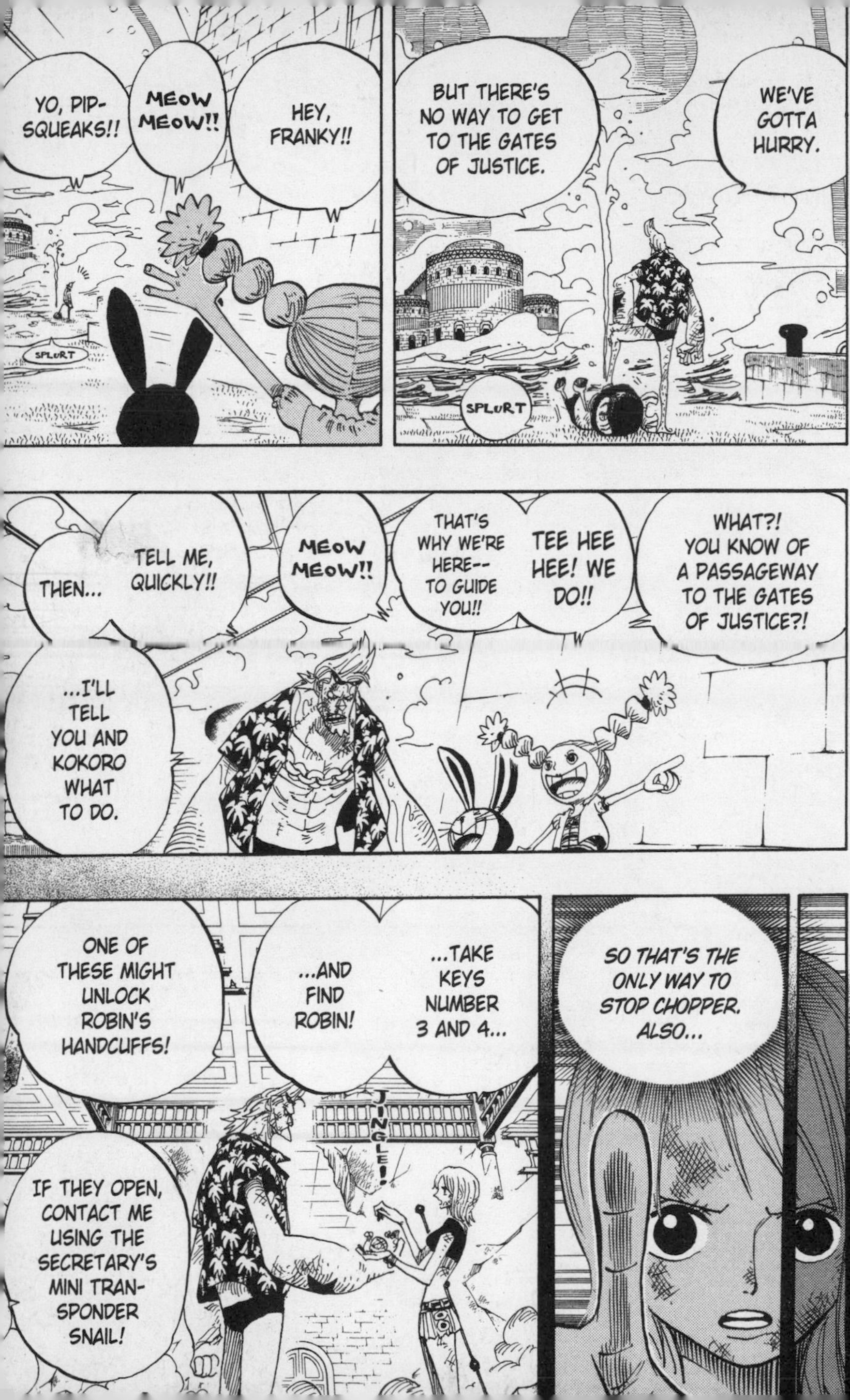
WE'VE GOTTA HURRY.
BUT THERE'S NO WAY TO GET TO THE GATES OF JUSTICE.
SPLURT
HEY, FRANKY!!
MEOW MEOW!!
YO, PIP-SQUEAKS!!
SPLURT
WHAT?! YOU KNOW OF A PASSAGEWAY TO THE GATES OF JUSTICE?!
TEE HEE HEE! WE DO!!
THAT'S WHY WE'RE HERE-- TO GUIDE YOU!!
MEOW MEOW!!
TELL ME, QUICKLY!!
THEN...
...I'LL TELL YOU AND KOKORO WHAT TO DO.
SO THAT'S THE ONLY WAY TO STOP CHOPPER. ALSO...
...TAKE KEYS NUMBER 3 AND 4...
...AND FIND ROBIN!
ONE OF THESE MIGHT UNLOCK ROBIN'S HANDCUFFS!
JINGLE!
IF THEY OPEN, CONTACT ME USING THE SECRETARY'S MINI TRAN-SPONDER SNAIL!

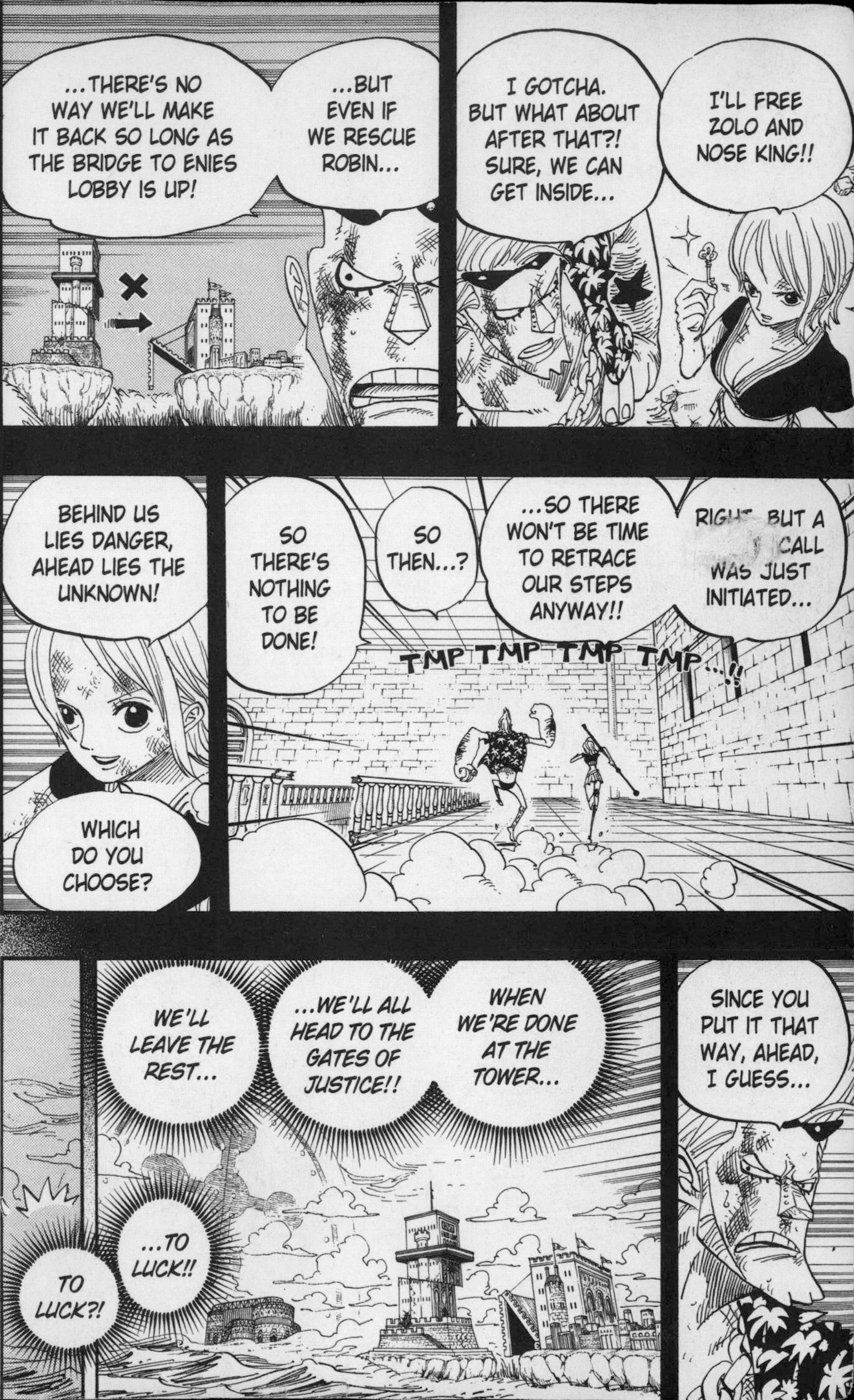
I'LL FREE ZOLO AND NOSE KING!!
I GOTCHA. BUT WHAT ABOUT AFTER THAT?! SURE, WE CAN GET INSIDE...
...BUT EVEN IF WE RESCUE ROBIN...
...THERE'S NO WAY WE'LL MAKE IT BACK SO LONG AS THE BRIDGE TO ENIES LOBBY IS UP!
RIGH BUT A CALL WAS JUST INITIATED...
...SO THERE WON'T BE TIME TO RETRACE OUR STEPS ANYWAY!!
SO THEN...?
SO THERE'S NOTHING TO BE DONE!
TMP TMP TMP TMP...!!
BEHIND US LIES DANGER, AHEAD LIES THE UNKNOWN!
WHICH DO YOU CHOOSE?
SINCE YOU PUT IT THAT WAY, AHEAD, I GUESS...
WHEN WE'RE DONE AT THE TOWER...
...WE'LL ALL HEAD TO THE GATES OF JUSTICE!!
WE'LL LEAVE THE REST...
...TO LUCK!!
TO LUCK?!

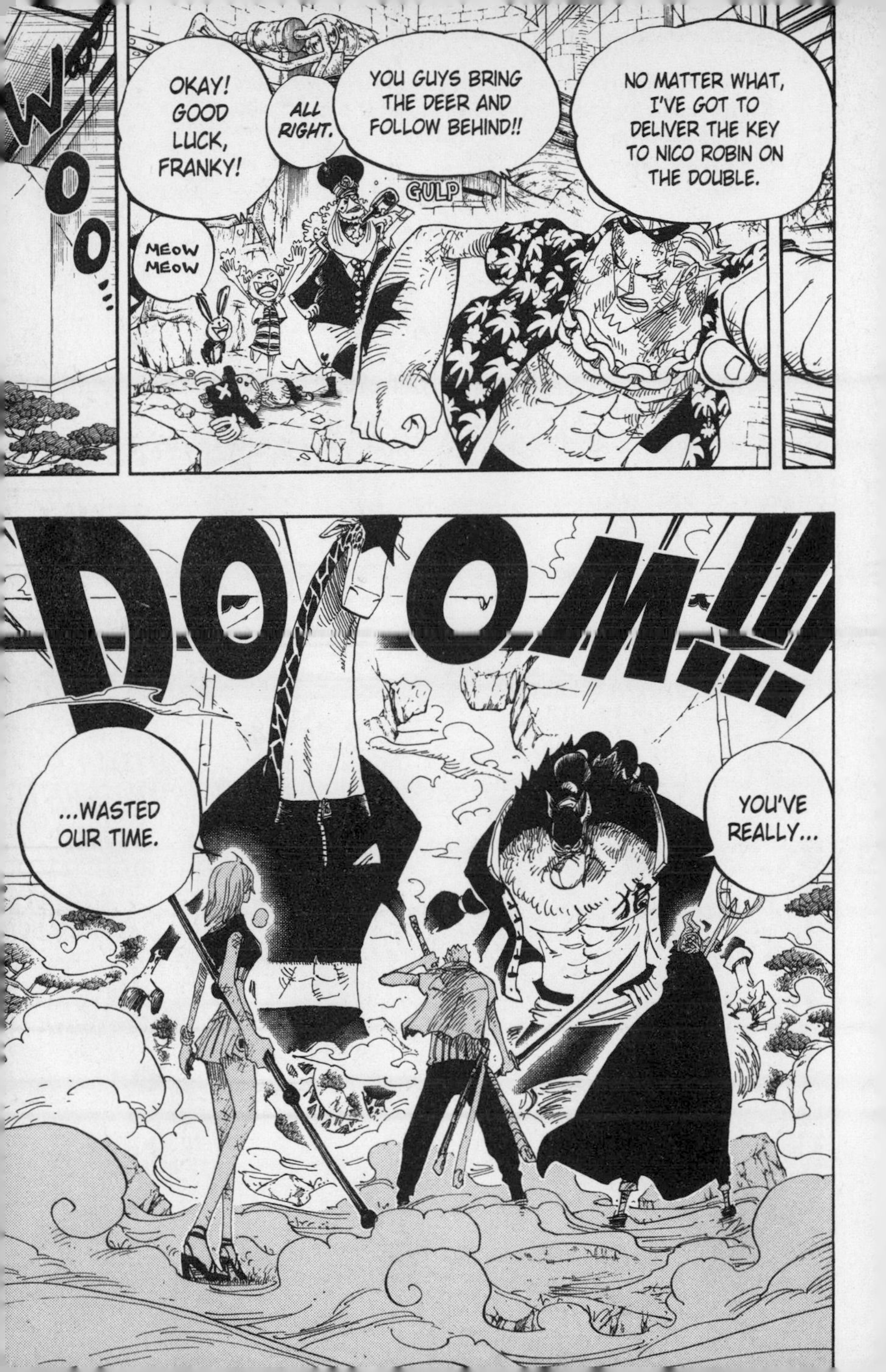
NO MATTER WHAT, I'VE GOT TO DELIVER THE KEY TO NICO ROBIN ON THE DOUBLE.
YOU GUYS BRING THE DEER AND FOLLOW BEHIND!!
ALL RIGHT.
OKAY! GOOD LUCK, FRANKY!
GULP
MEOW MEOW
WOOO...
DOOM!!!
YOU'VE REALLY...
...WASTED OUR TIME.

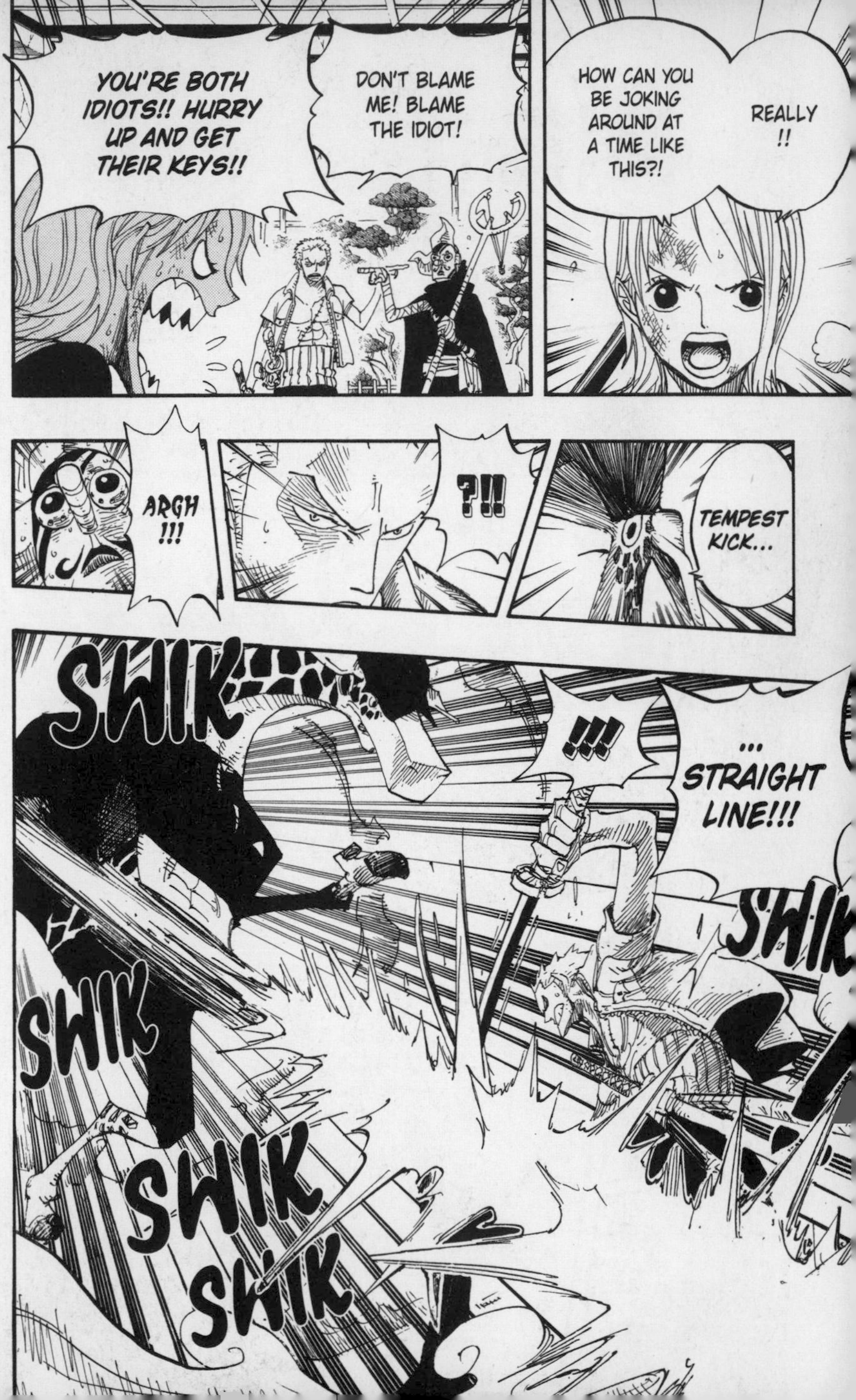
HOW CAN YOU BE JOKING AROUND AT A TIME LIKE THIS?!
REALLY !!
DON'T BLAME ME! BLAME THE IDIOT!
YOU'RE BOTH IDIOTS!! HURRY UP AND GET THEIR KEYS!!
TEMPEST KICK...
?!!
ARGH !!!
... STRAIGHT LINE!!!
SHIK
!!!
SHIK
SHIK
SHIK
SHIK

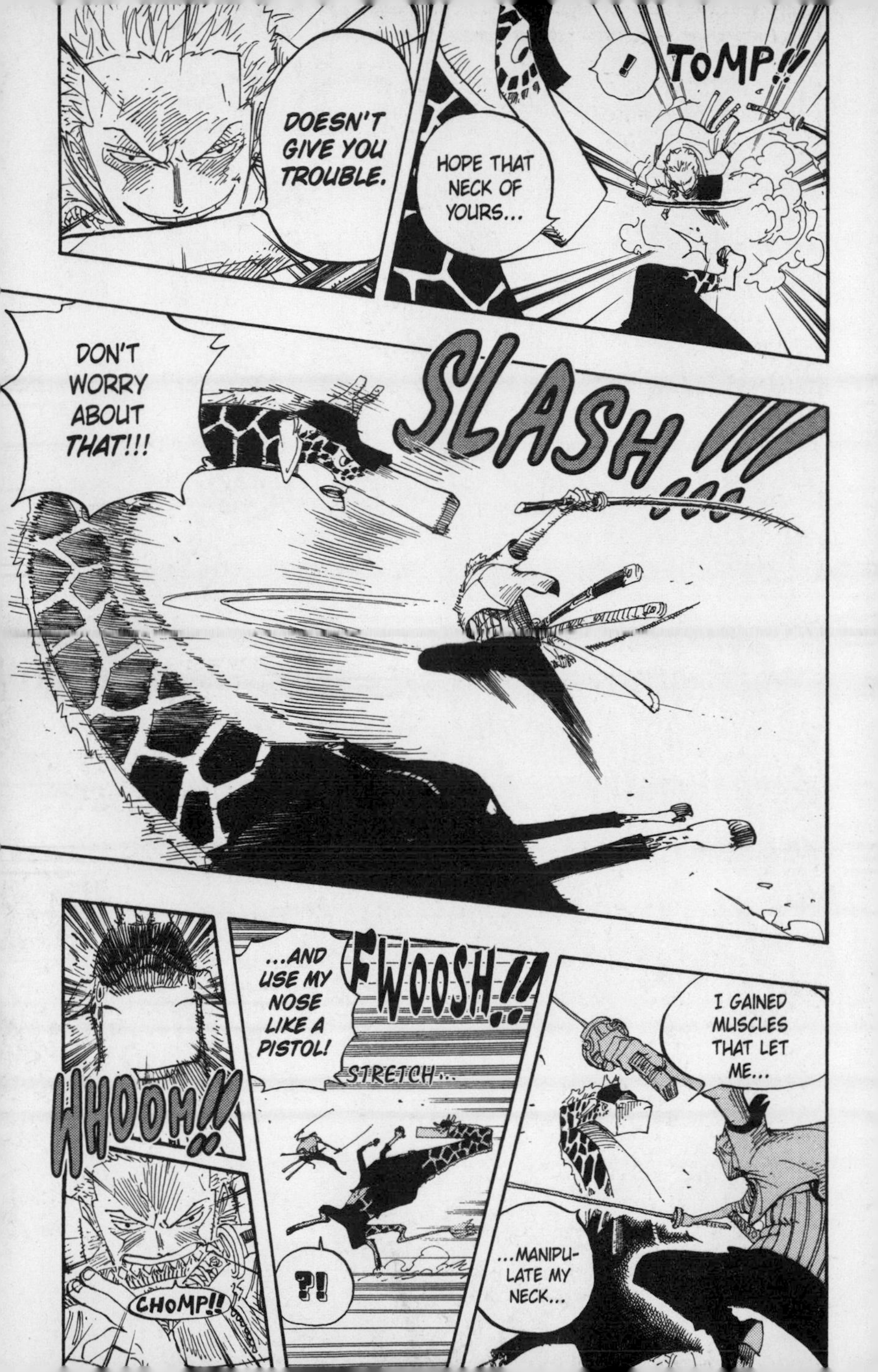
!
TOMP!!
HOPE THAT NECK OF YOURS...
DOESN'T GIVE YOU TROUBLE.
SLASH!!
DON'T WORRY ABOUT THAT!!!
I GAINED MUSCLES THAT LET ME...
...MANIPU-LATE MY NECK...
FWOOSH!!
...AND USE MY NOSE LIKE A PISTOL!
STRETCH...
?!
WHOOM!!
CHOMP!!

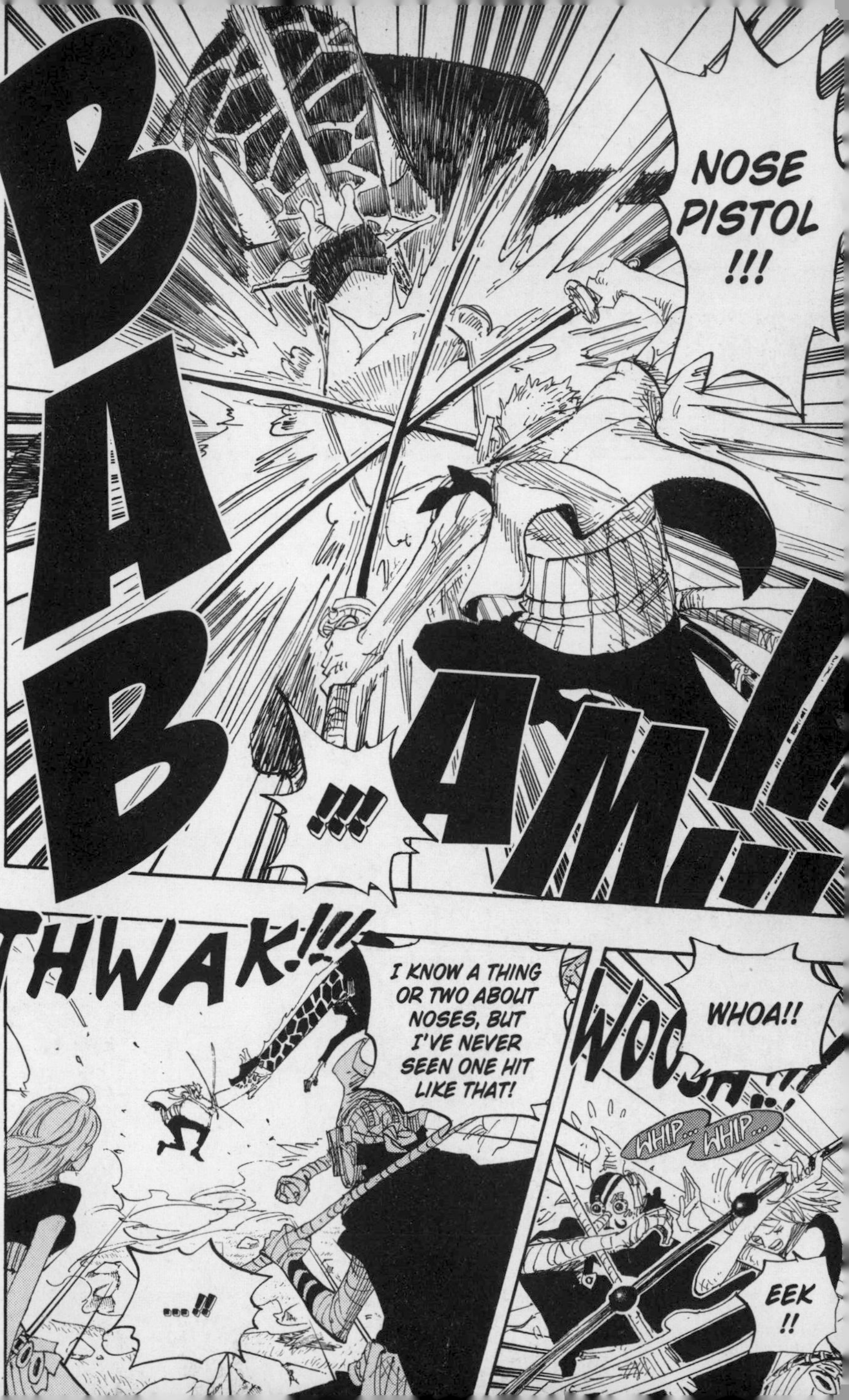

NOSE PISTOL !!!
BABAM!!!
WHOA!!
WOOSH!!
WHIP... WHIP...
EEK !!
I KNOW A THING OR TWO ABOUT NOSES, BUT I'VE NEVER SEEN ONE HIT LIKE THAT!
THWAK!!!
...!!

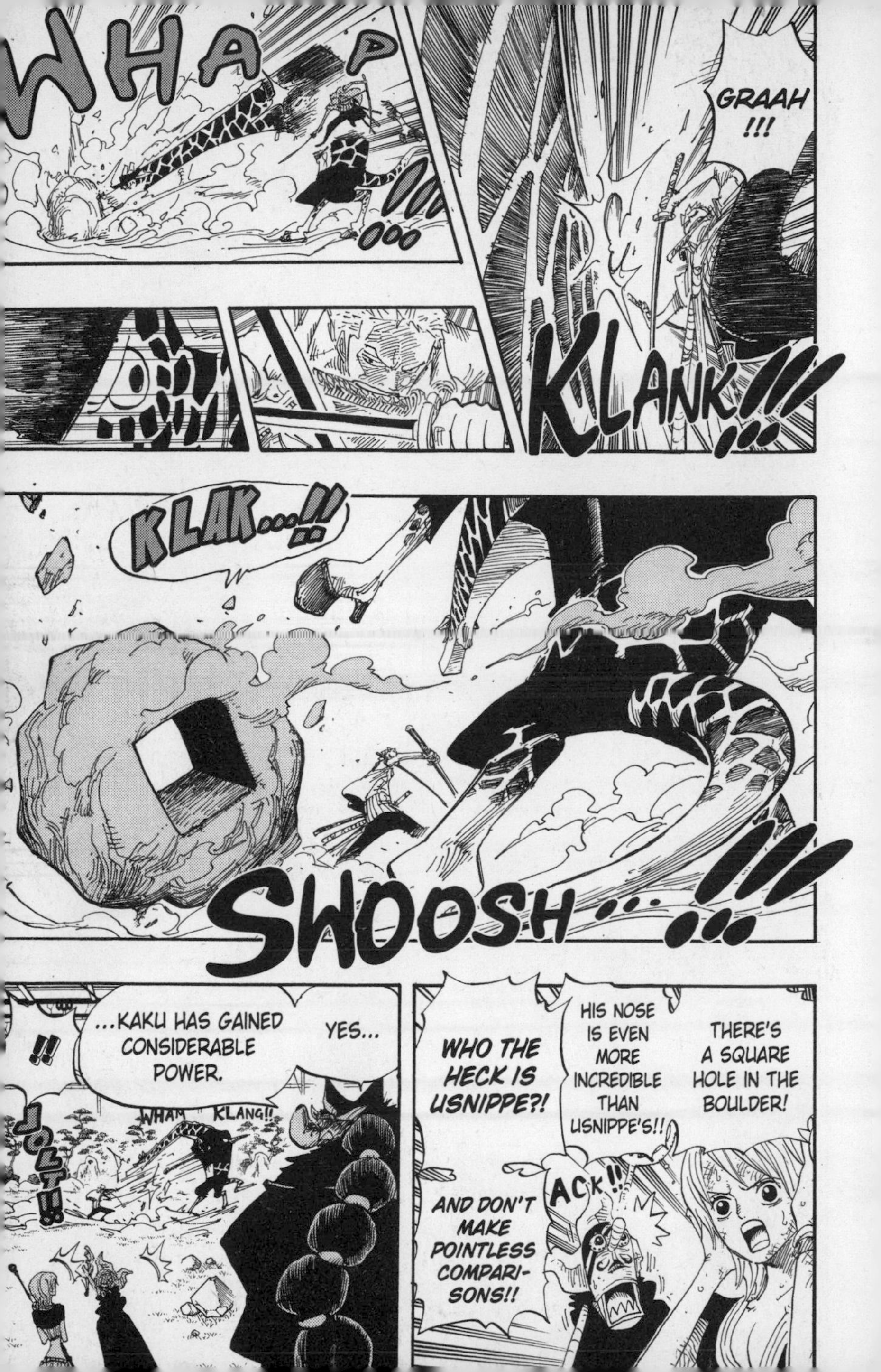
GRAAH!!!
KLANK!!!
WHAP
KLAK...!!
SHOOSH...!!!
THERE'S A SQUARE HOLE IN THE BOULDER!
HIS NOSE IS EVEN MORE INCREDIBLE THAN USNIPPE'S!!
WHO THE HECK IS USNIPPE?!
ACK!!
AND DON'T MAKE POINTLESS COMPARISONS!!
YES...
...KAKU HAS GAINED CONSIDERABLE POWER.
KLANG!!
WHAM
!!
JOLT!!

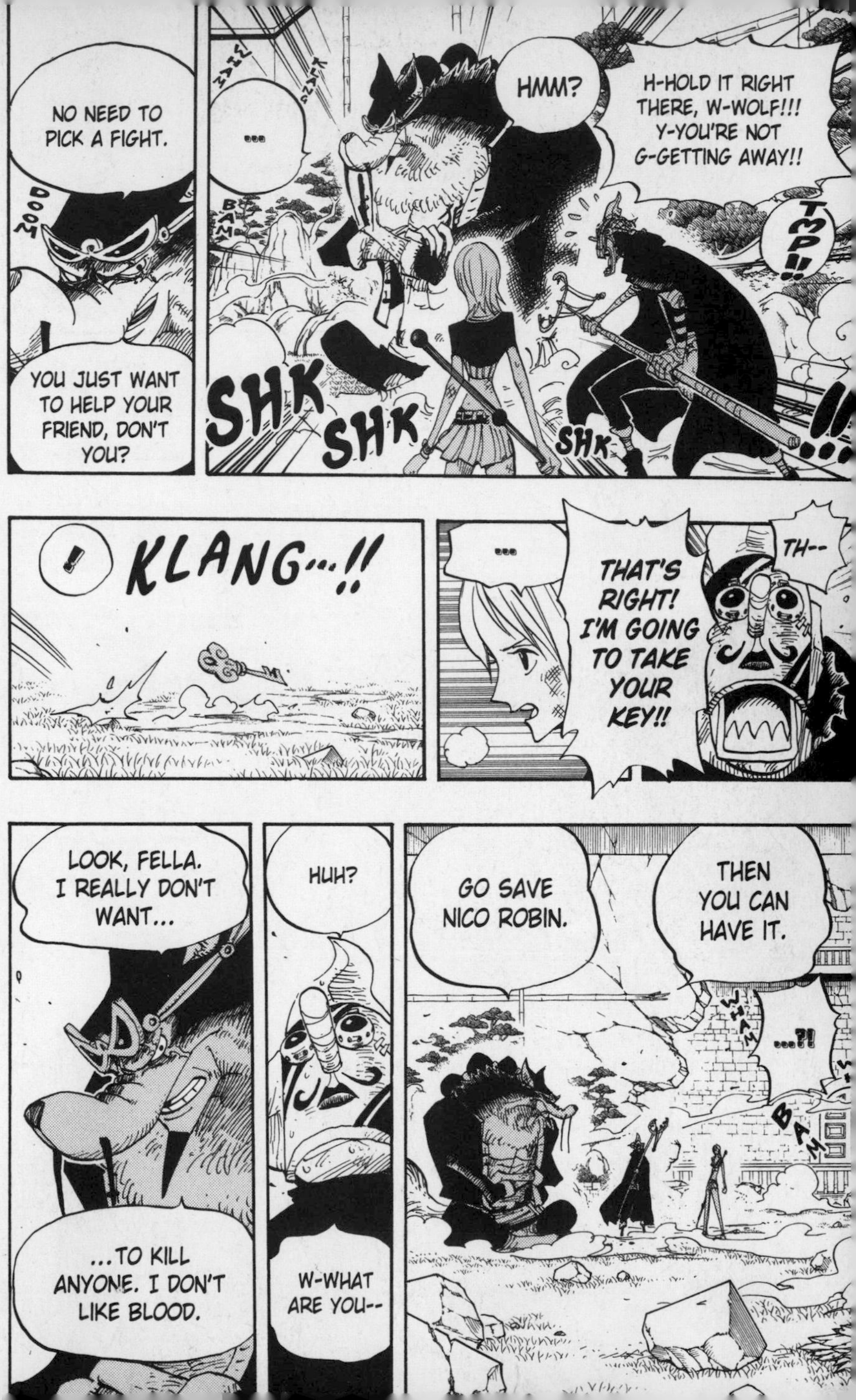
H-HOLD IT RIGHT THERE, W-WOLF!!! Y-YOU'RE NOT G-GETTING AWAY!!
TMP!!
HMM?
...!!
SHK
...
WHAM
KLANG
BAM
SHK
SHK
NO NEED TO PICK A FIGHT.
DOOM
YOU JUST WANT TO HELP YOUR FRIEND, DON'T YOU?
TH--
THAT'S RIGHT! I'M GOING TO TAKE YOUR KEY!!
...
!
KLANG...!!
THEN YOU CAN HAVE IT.
GO SAVE NICO ROBIN.
WHAM
...?!
BAM
HUH?
W-WHAT ARE YOU--
LOOK, FELLA. I REALLY DON'T WANT...
...TO KILL ANYONE. I DON'T LIKE BLOOD.

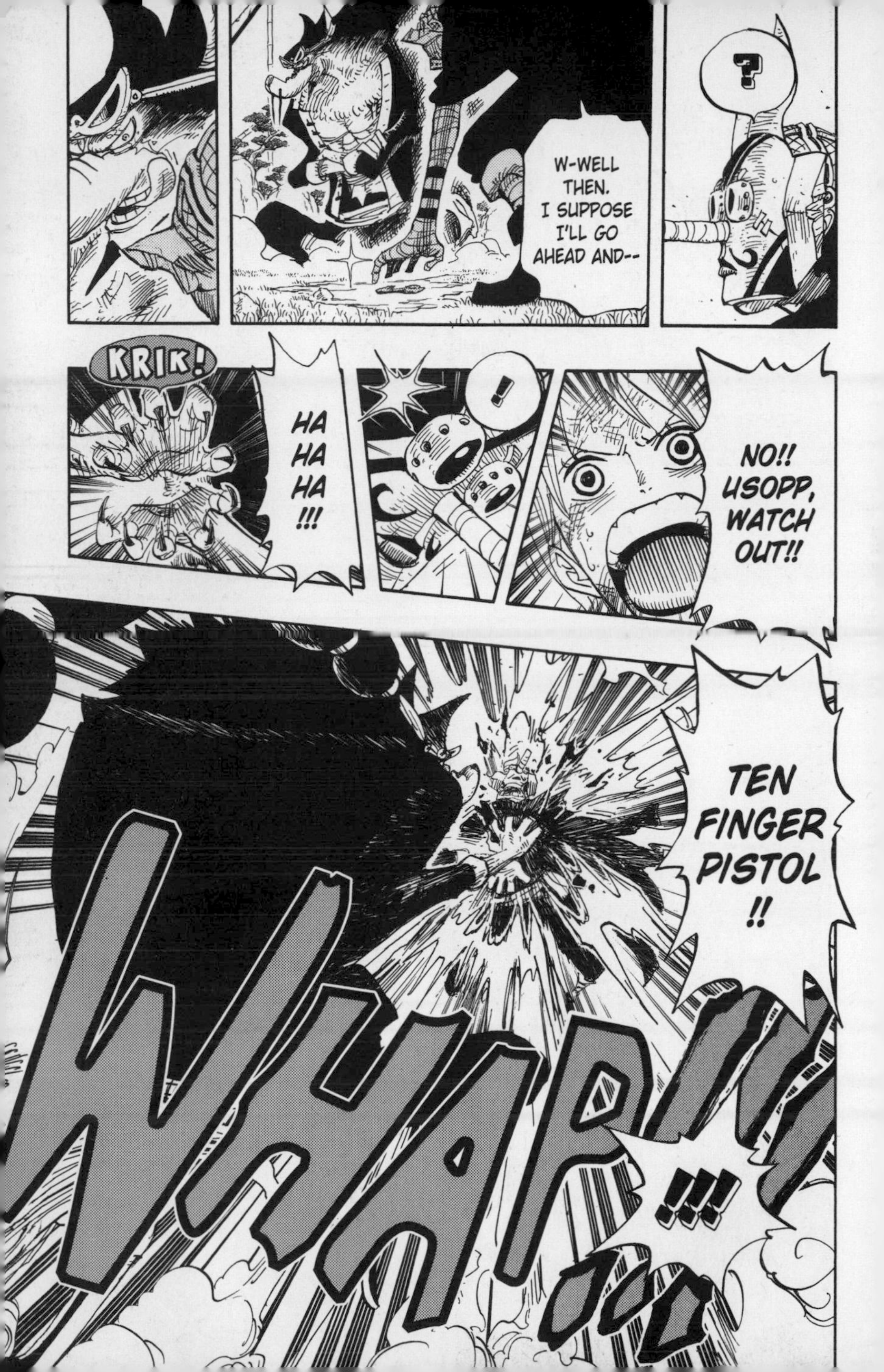
?
W-WELL THEN. I SUPPOSE I'LL GO AHEAD AND--
NO!! USOPP, WATCH OUT!!
!
HA HA HA !!!
KRIK!
TEN FINGER PISTOL !!
WHAP!!!

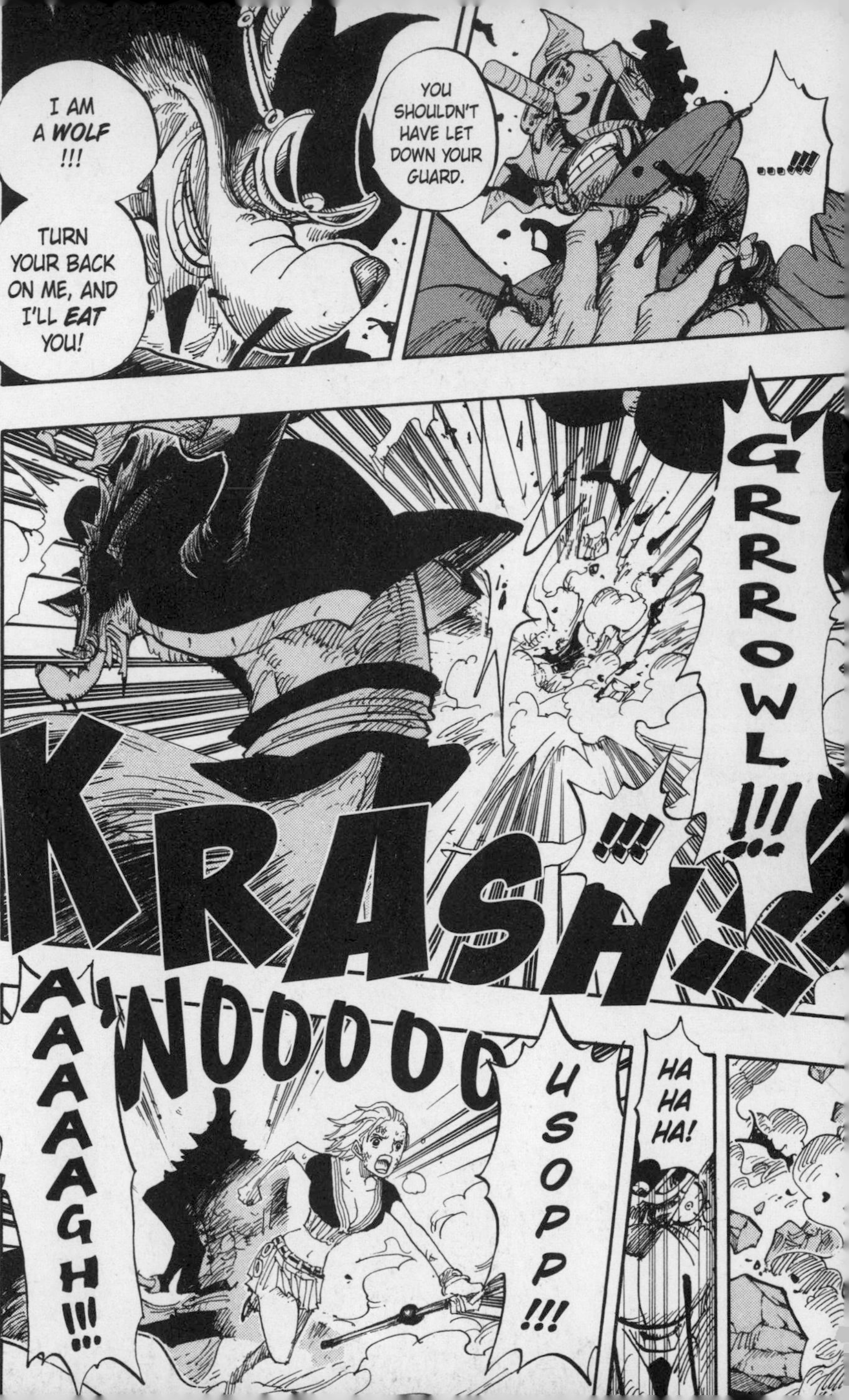
...!!!
YOU SHOULDN'T HAVE LET DOWN YOUR GUARD.
I AM A WOLF!!!
TURN YOUR BACK ON ME, AND I'LL EAT YOU!
GRRROWL!!!
KRASH!!!
HA HA HA!
USOPP!!!
NOOOOO
AAAAAGH!!!

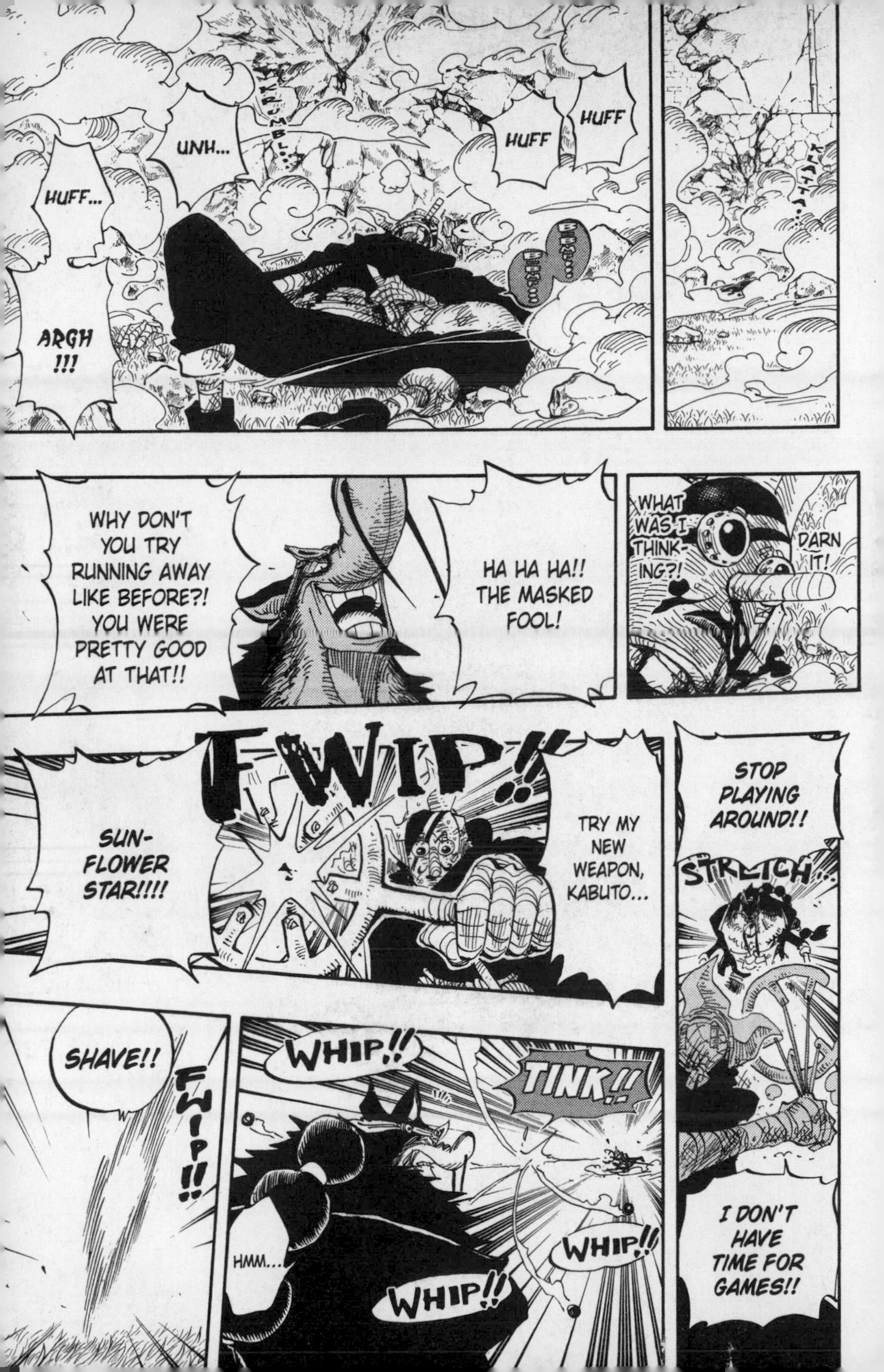
KLATTA...
HUFF
HUFF
KRUMBL...
UNH...
HUFF...
ARGH!!!
DARN IT!
WHAT WAS I THINKING?!
HA HA HA!! THE MASKED FOOL!
WHY DON'T YOU TRY RUNNING AWAY LIKE BEFORE?! YOU WERE PRETTY GOOD AT THAT!!
STOP PLAYING AROUND!!
STRETCH...
I DON'T HAVE TIME FOR GAMES!!
FWIP!!
TRY MY NEW WEAPON, KABUTO...
SUN-FLOWER STAR!!!!
WHIP!!
TINK!!
WHIP!!
WHIP!!
HMM...
SHAVE!!
FWIP!!

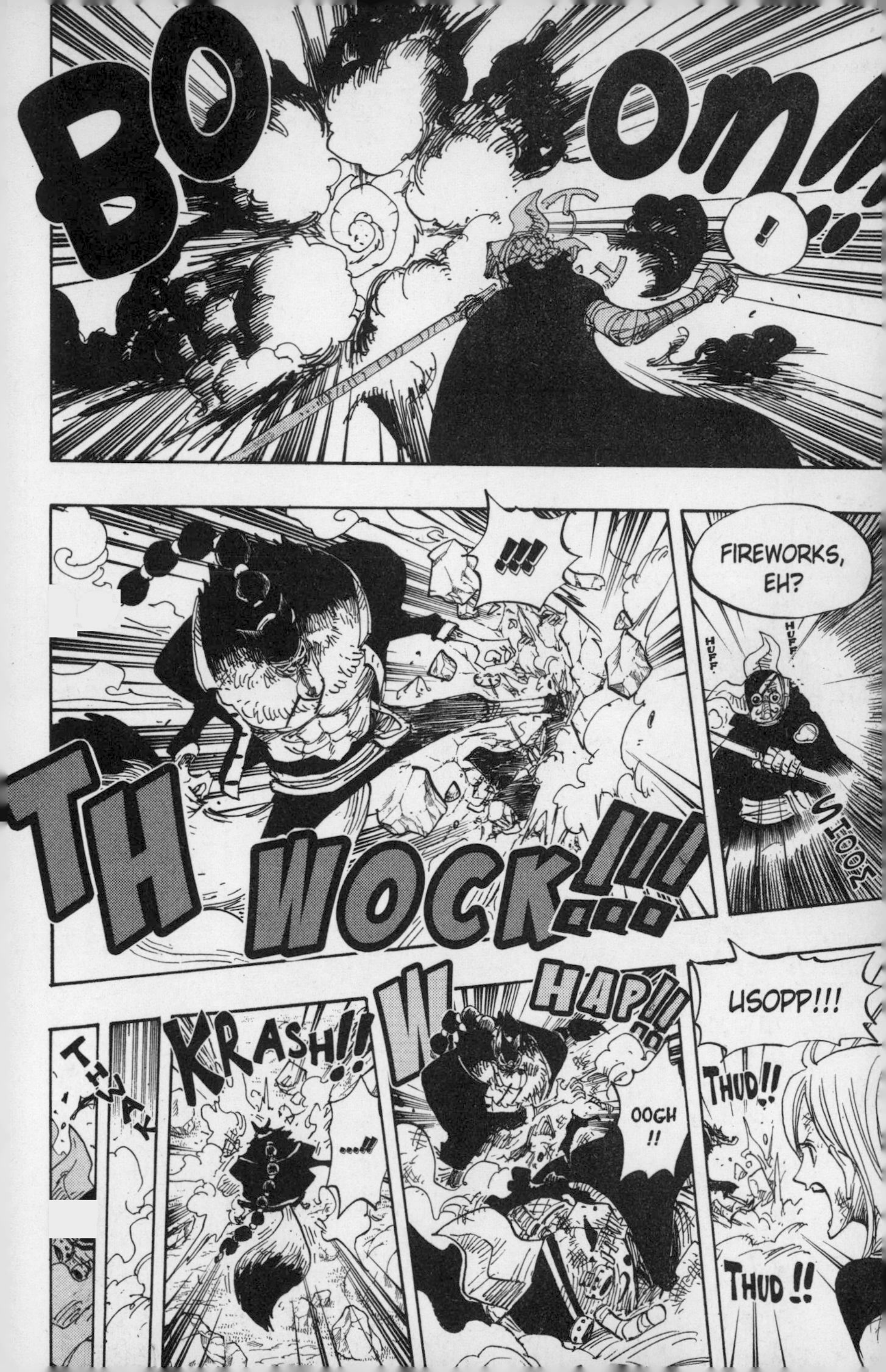
BOOOM!!
!
FIREWORKS, EH?
HUFF
HUFF
!!!
THWOCK!!!
USOPP!!!
THUD!!
THUD!!
WHAP!!
OOGH !!
KRASH!!!
...!!

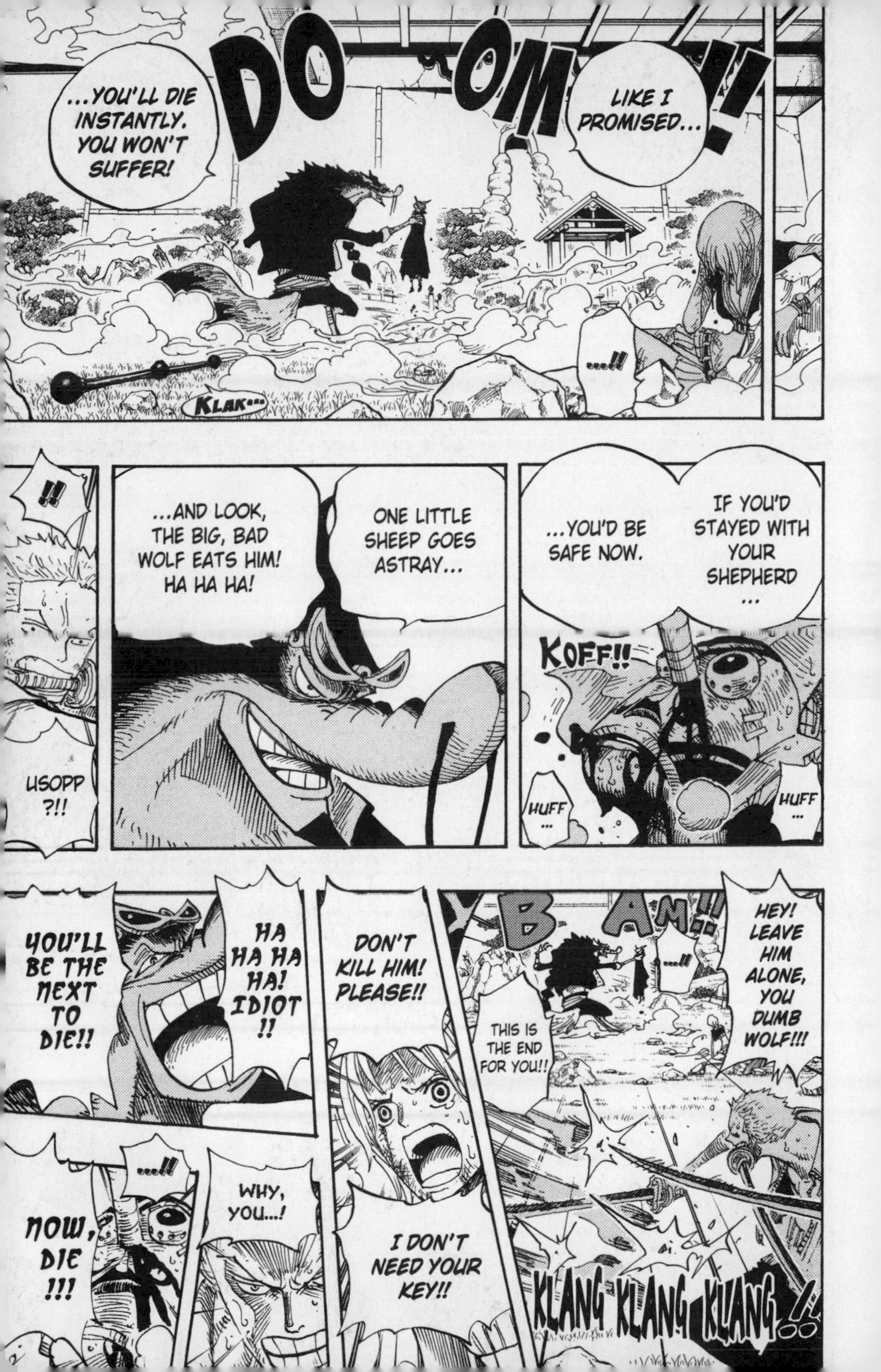
LIKE I PROMISED...
DO-OM!!
...YOU'LL DIE INSTANTLY. YOU WON'T SUFFER!
...!!
KLAK...
IF YOU'D STAYED WITH YOUR SHEPHERD...
...YOU'D BE SAFE NOW.
KOFF!!
HUFF...
HUFF...
ONE LITTLE SHEEP GOES ASTRAY...
...AND LOOK, THE BIG, BAD WOLF EATS HIM! HA HA HA!
!!
USOPP?!!
HEY! LEAVE HIM ALONE, YOU DUMB WOLF!!!
BAM!!
...!!
THIS IS THE END FOR YOU!!
KLANG KLANG KLANG!!
DON'T KILL HIM! PLEASE!!
I DON'T NEED YOUR KEY!!
HA HA HA HA! IDIOT!!
YOU'LL BE THE NEXT TO DIE!!
WHY, YOU...!
...!!
NOW, DIE!!!

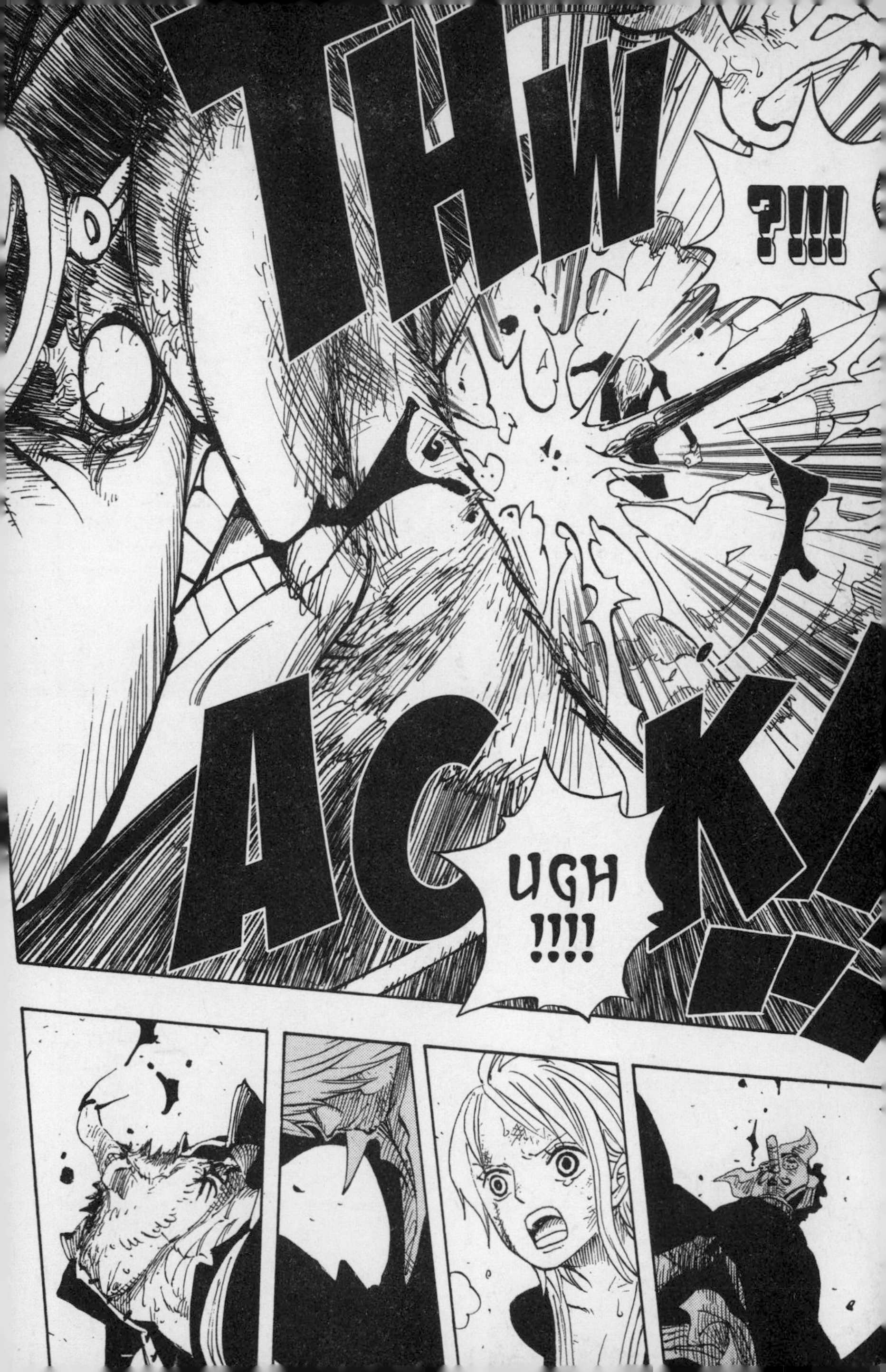
?!!!
THWACK!!
UGH !!!!

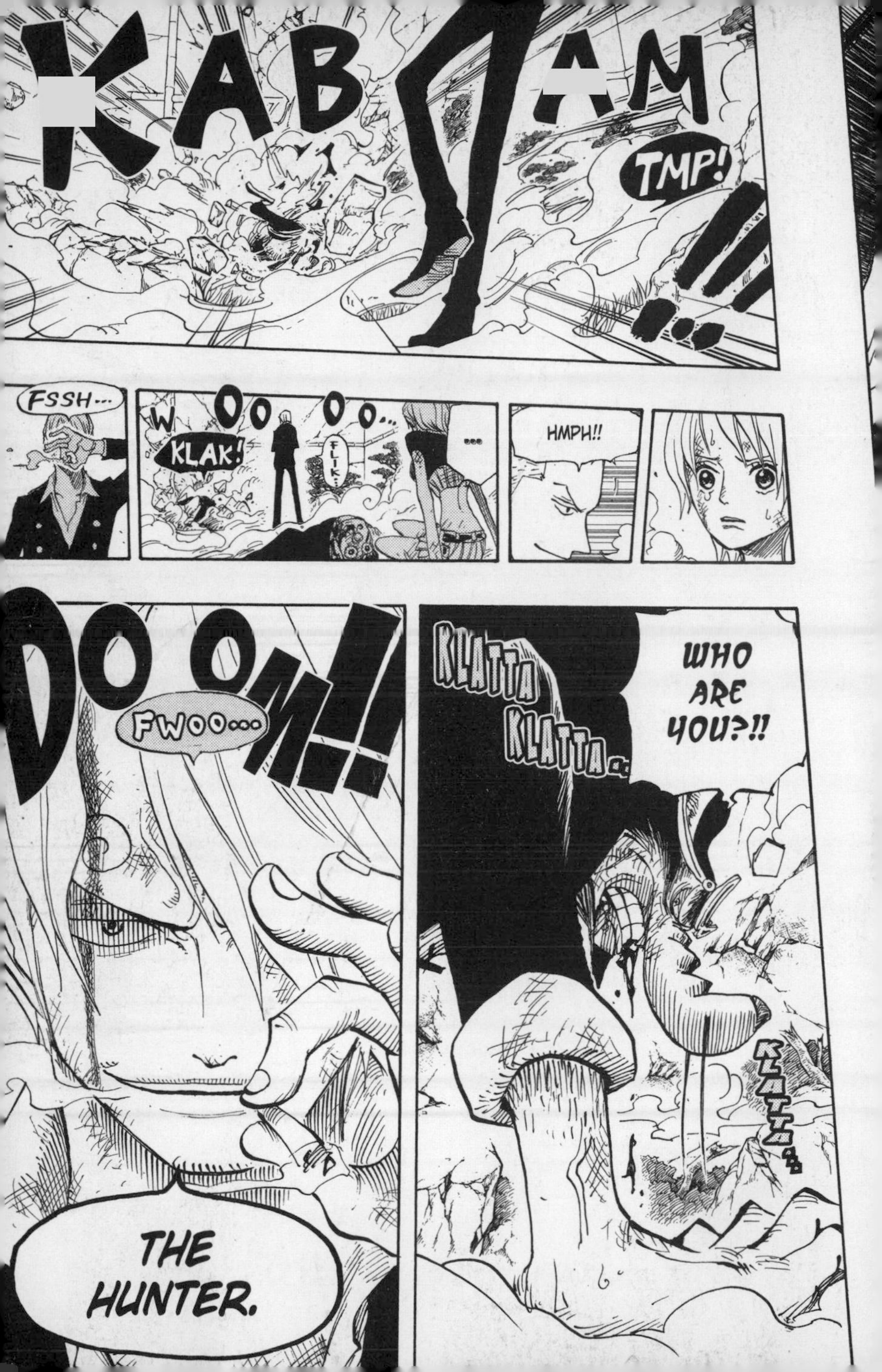
KABLAM
TMP!!
HMPH!!
...
FLIK...
WOO OO...
KLAK!
FSSH...
WHO ARE YOU?!!
KLATTA KLATTA...
KLATTA...
DOOM!!
FWOO...
THE HUNTER.

Question Corner
S B S

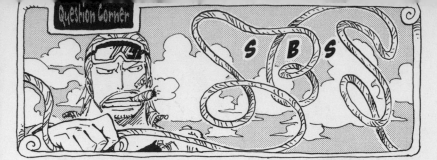

Q: Mr. Oda. I'm sending this letter, and our appreciation, from France! I'm writing this as spokesman for more than one thousand fans of *One Piece* on the Internet. I want everyone to know that *One Piece* has fans overseas! I especially want Japan's fans to know. Question: Oda Sensei, do you have any delicious French bread? When the Question Corner starts, I have to eat delicious French bread because I'm French! One last thing: Que la volonté du D soit avec vous, Mr. Oda! (The will of D is with you!!)

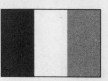

--Signe! La Volonté du D" (The Will of D)

A: Whoa... has the Question Corner finally reached the world stage? Thank you for going to all the trouble of sending your letter to the editorial department in Japan. And after crossing national boundaries, that's your question?! Right now, in my house, there is no French bread! I'd like to have some in France someday, though. I answered your question, but I hear that in France the One Piece graphic novels are about ten volumes behind, so you won't read my answer for another two years. Stay a fan until then! Thank you!!

Q: Odacchi!! These days I'm having trouble sleeping. Kalifa is the only girl in CP9. When she uses the Iron Body technique of the Six Powers, does she bounce? When I go to confirm, I get covered in bubbles... See? Today, too, bubbles smother me... GLUB GLUB... Obajjii! Bind bout bor be!! (Odacchi! Find out for me!!)

--Kyashii Keisuke

PHOO

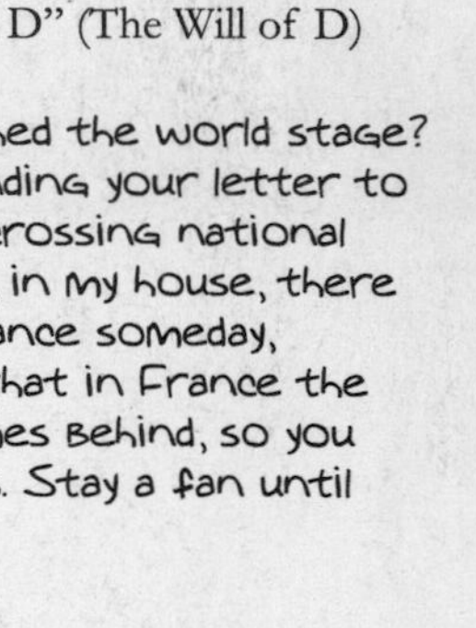

A: Yep, today we've got another girl-crazy question from inside Japan. What the--! Are you telling me to go find out instead of you?! You think I'm some kind of peeper?!

Be bibbin boub. (She didn't bounce.)

Chapter 414:
SANJI VS. JABRA

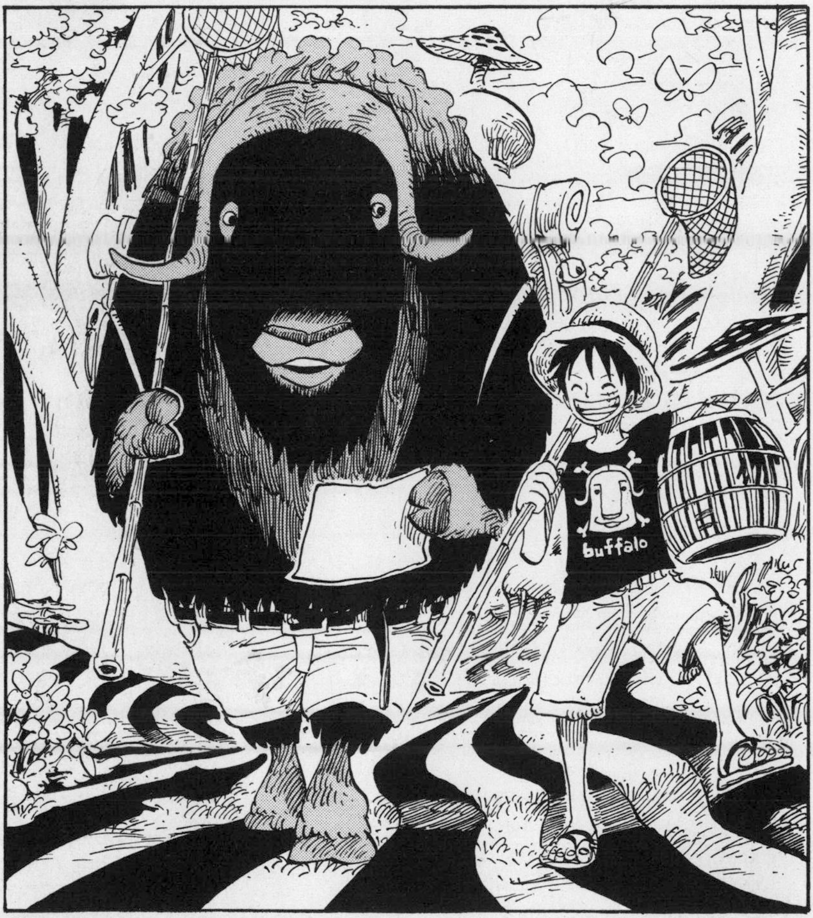
buffalo

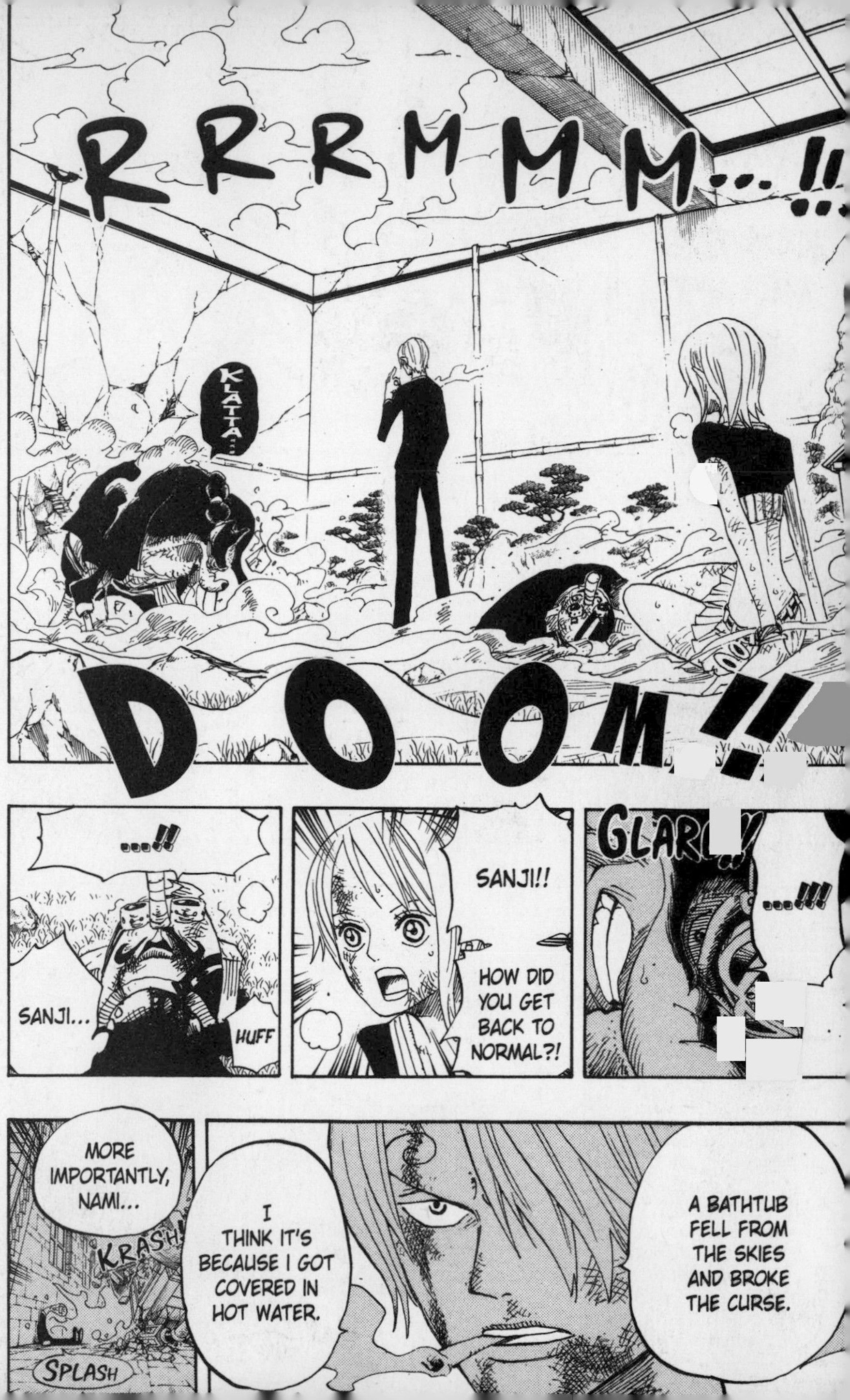
RRRMMM...!!
KLATTA...
DOOM!!
GLAR
...!!!
SANJI!!
HOW DID YOU GET BACK TO NORMAL?!
...!!
SANJI...
HUFF
A BATHTUB FELL FROM THE SKIES AND BROKE THE CURSE.
I THINK IT'S BECAUSE I GOT COVERED IN HOT WATER.
MORE IMPORTANTLY, NAMI...
KRASH!
SPLASH

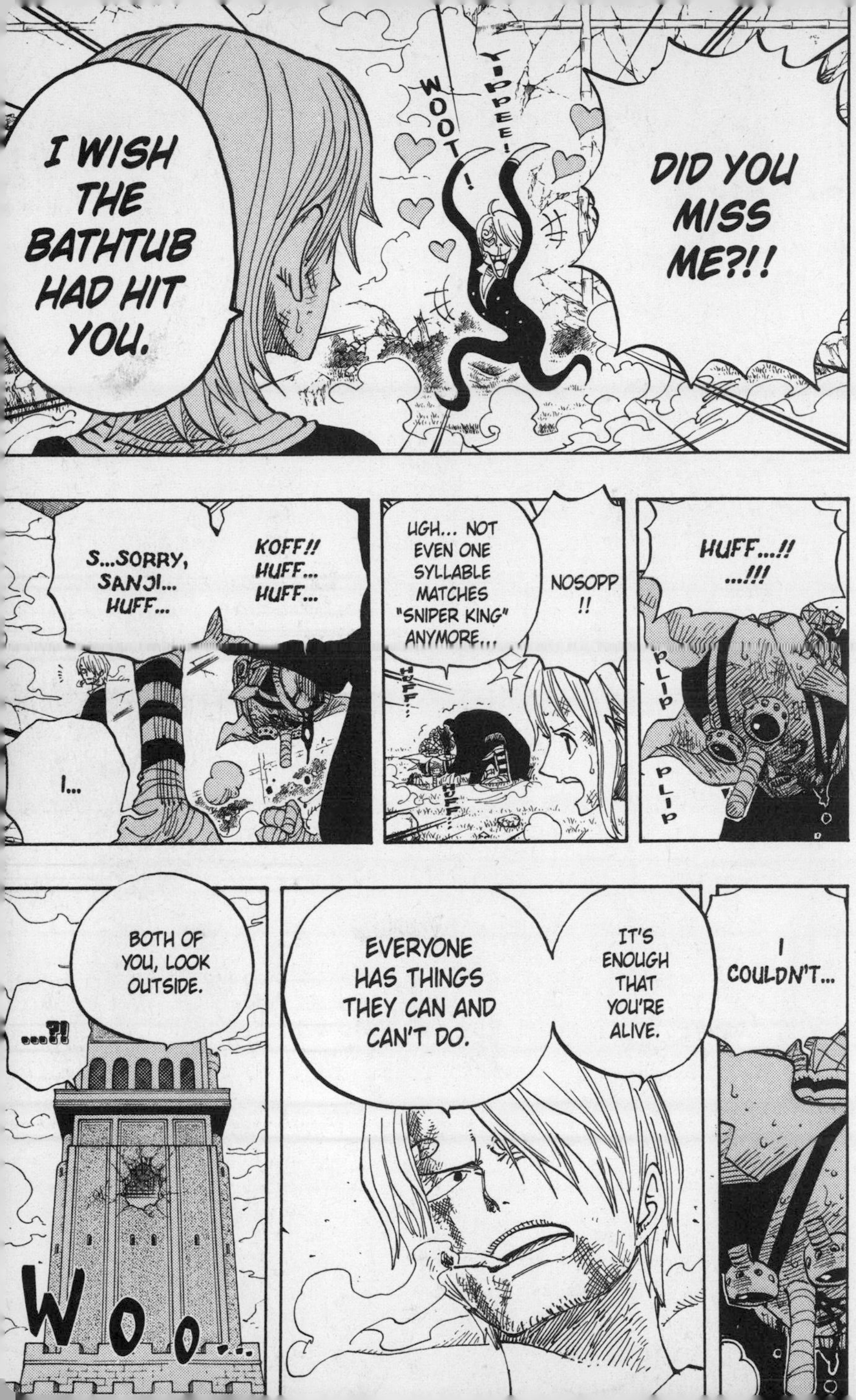
DID YOU MISS ME?!!
YIPPEE!
WOOT!
I WISH THE BATHTUB HAD HIT YOU.
HUFF...!! ...!!!
PLIP
PLIP
NOSOPP !!
UGH... NOT EVEN ONE SYLLABLE MATCHES "SNIPER KING" ANYMORE...
HUFF...
HUFF...
KOFF!! HUFF... HUFF...
S...SORRY, SANJI... HUFF...
I...
I COULDN'T...
IT'S ENOUGH THAT YOU'RE ALIVE.
EVERYONE HAS THINGS THEY CAN AND CAN'T DO.
BOTH OF YOU, LOOK OUTSIDE.
...?!
WOO...

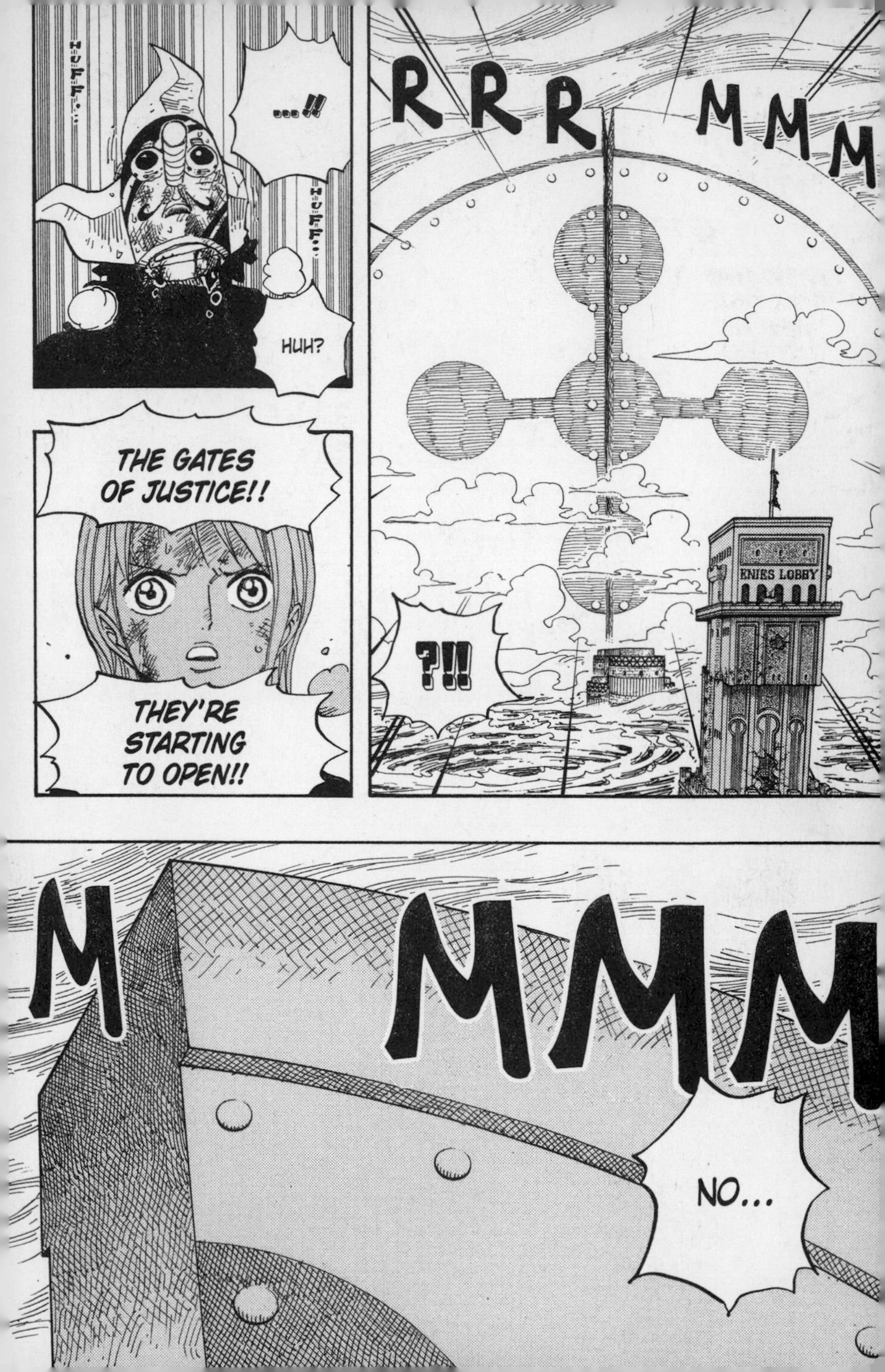
RRRMMM
ENIES LOBBY
?!!
HUFF...
...!!
HUFF...
HUH?
THE GATES OF JUSTICE!!
THEY'RE STARTING TO OPEN!!
MMMM
NO...

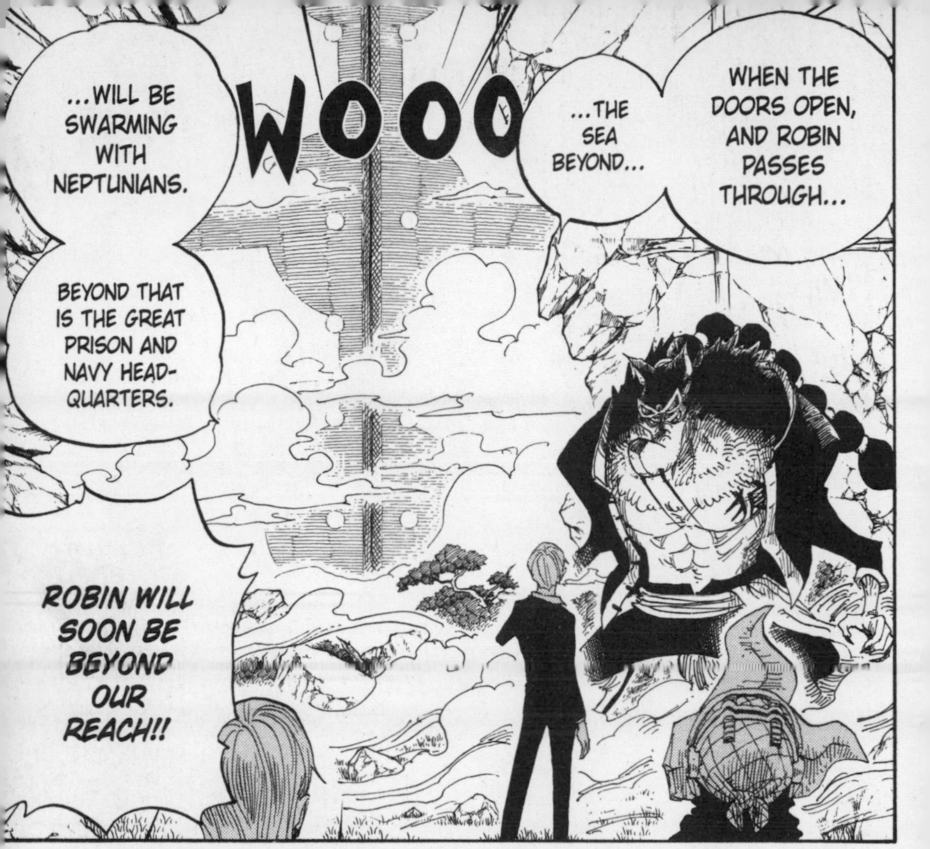
WHEN THE DOORS OPEN, AND ROBIN PASSES THROUGH...
...THE SEA BEYOND...
WOOO
...WILL BE SWARMING WITH NEPTUNIANS.
BEYOND THAT IS THE GREAT PRISON AND NAVY HEAD-QUARTERS.
ROBIN WILL SOON BE BEYOND OUR REACH!!
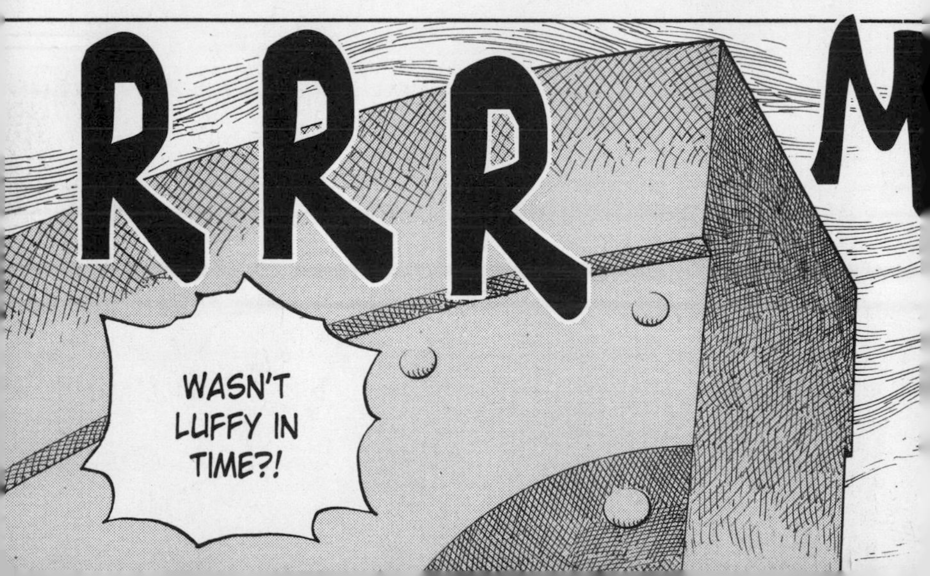
RRRM
WASN'T LUFFY IN TIME?!

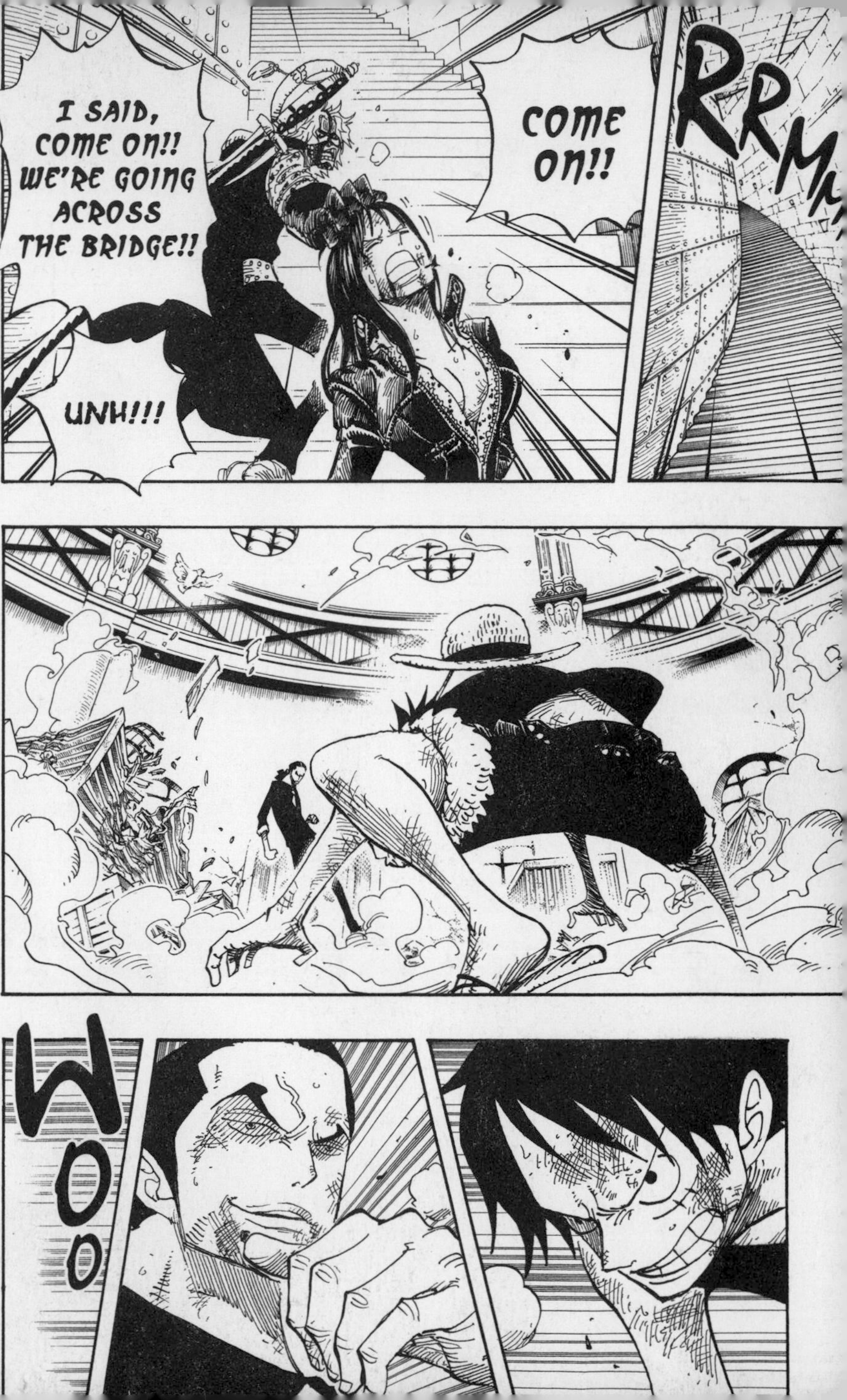
RRM
COME ON!!
I SAID, COME ON!! WE'RE GOING ACROSS THE BRIDGE!!
UNH!!!

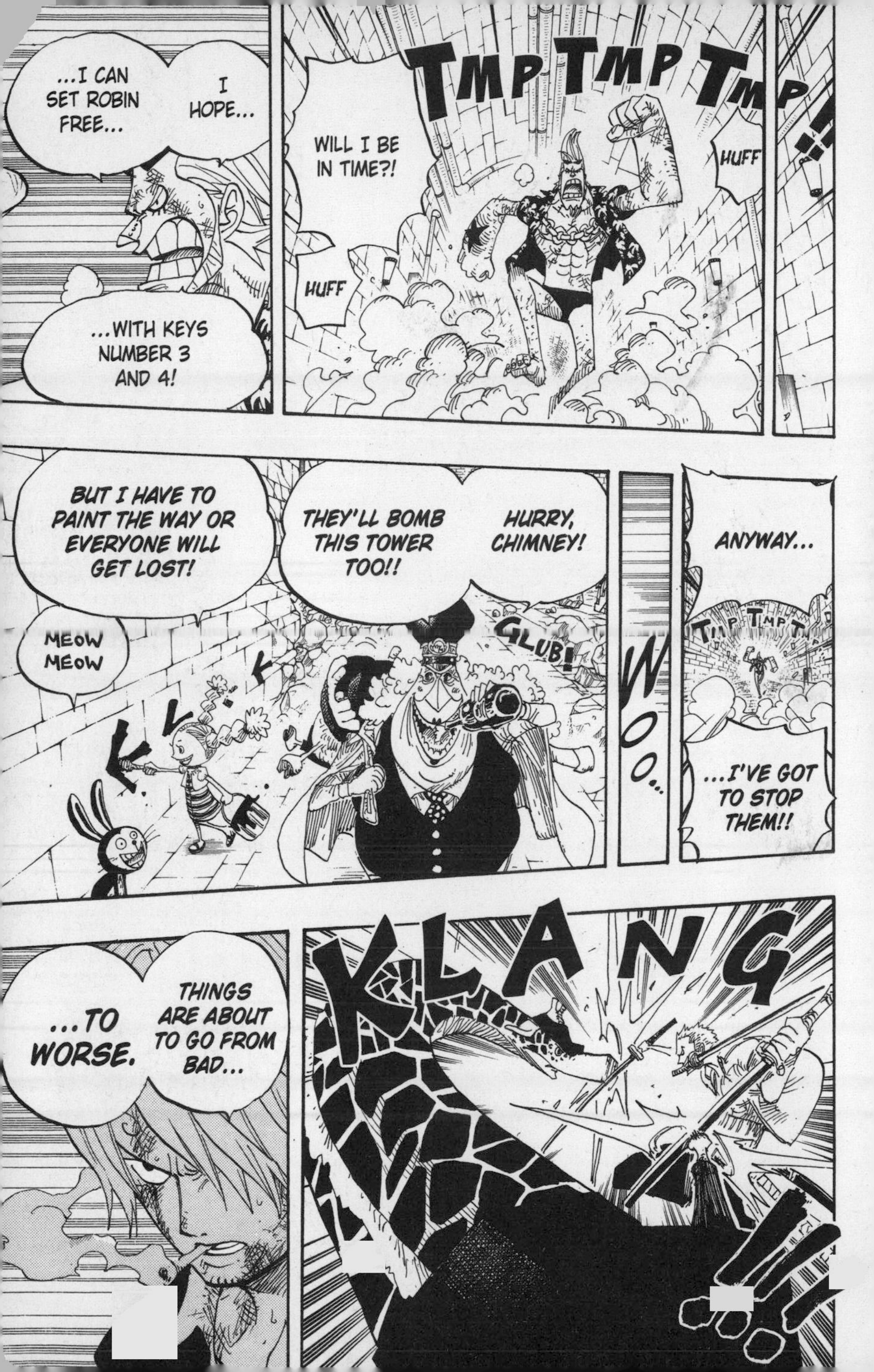

TMP TMP TMP!!
HUFF
WILL I BE IN TIME?!
HUFF
I HOPE...
...I CAN SET ROBIN FREE...
...WITH KEYS NUMBER 3 AND 4!
ANYWAY...
...I'VE GOT TO STOP THEM!!
WOOO...
HURRY, CHIMNEY!
THEY'LL BOMB THIS TOWER TOO!!
GLUB!
BUT I HAVE TO PAINT THE WAY OR EVERYONE WILL GET LOST!
MEOW MEOW
KLANG
THINGS ARE ABOUT TO GO FROM BAD...
...TO WORSE.

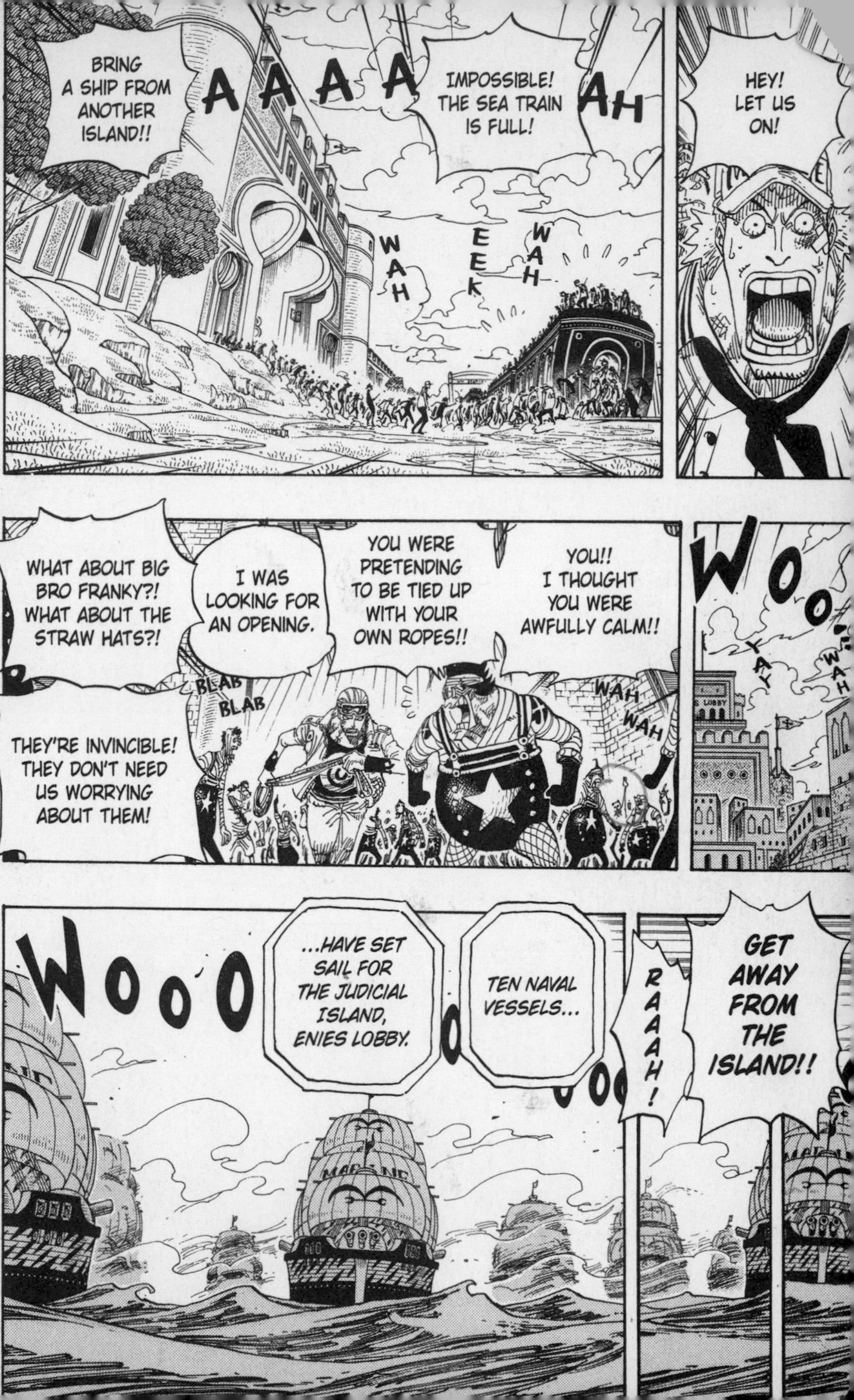
HEY! LET US ON!
AH
IMPOSSIBLE! THE SEA TRAIN IS FULL!
AAAA
BRING A SHIP FROM ANOTHER ISLAND!!
WAH
EEK
WAH
WOOO
YAY
WAH
YOU!! I THOUGHT YOU WERE AWFULLY CALM!!
YOU WERE PRETENDING TO BE TIED UP WITH YOUR OWN ROPES!!
I WAS LOOKING FOR AN OPENING.
WHAT ABOUT BIG BRO FRANKY?! WHAT ABOUT THE STRAW HATS?!
WAH WAH
BLAB BLAB
THEY'RE INVINCIBLE! THEY DON'T NEED US WORRYING ABOUT THEM!
GET AWAY FROM THE ISLAND!!
RAAAAH!
TEN NAVAL VESSELS...
...HAVE SET SAIL FOR THE JUDICIAL ISLAND, ENIES LOBBY.
WOOOO

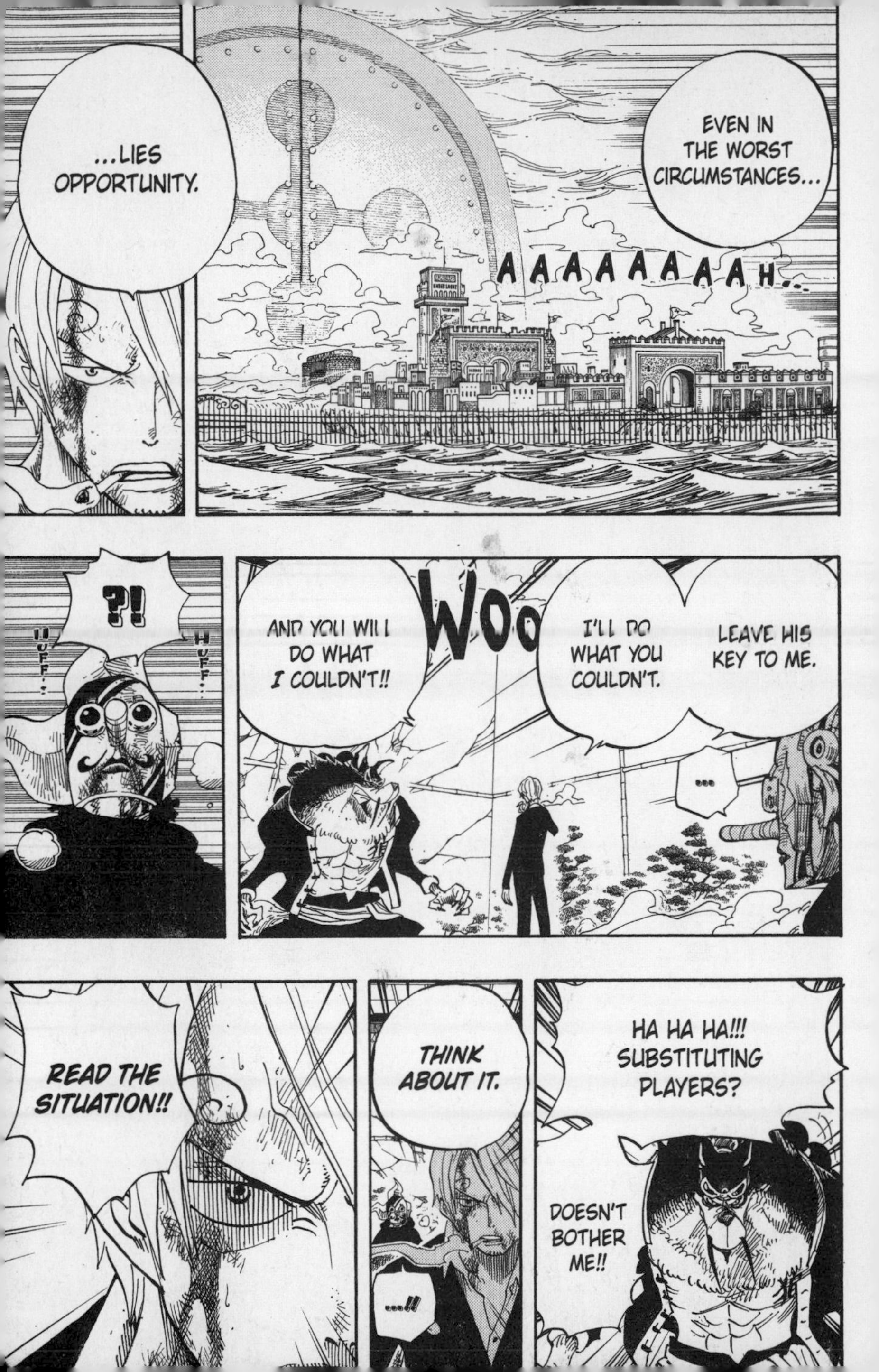

EVEN IN THE WORST CIRCUMSTANCES...
AAAAAAAAH...
...LIES OPPORTUNITY.
LEAVE HIS KEY TO ME.
I'LL DO WHAT YOU COULDN'T.
WOO
AND YOU WILL DO WHAT I COULDN'T!!
...
?!
HUFF...
HUFF...
HA HA HA!!! SUBSTITUTING PLAYERS?
DOESN'T BOTHER ME!!
THINK ABOUT IT.
...!!
READ THE SITUATION!!

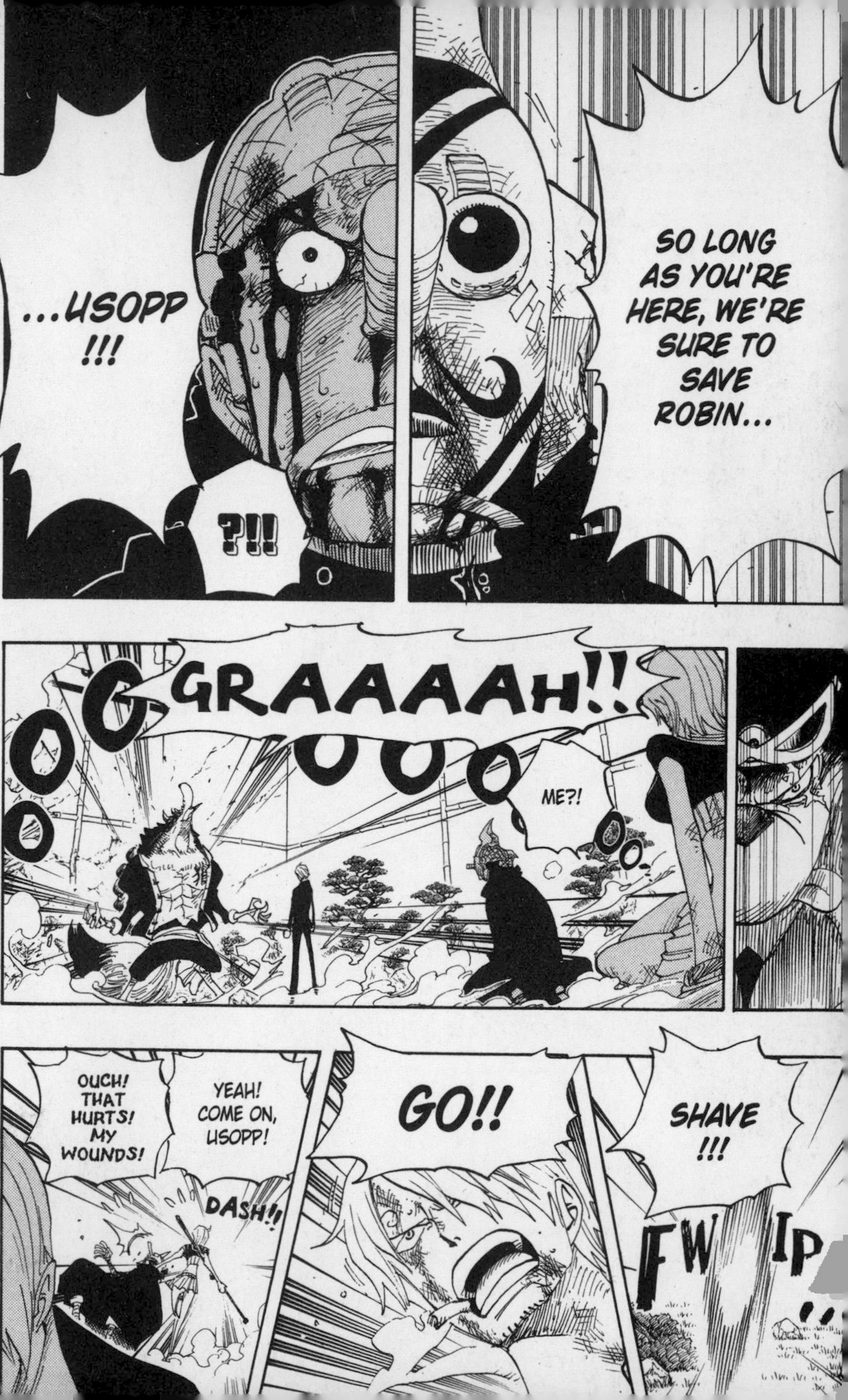
SO LONG AS YOU'RE HERE, WE'RE SURE TO SAVE ROBIN...
...USOPP !!!
?!!
GRAAAAH!!
OOOOOOOOOOO
ME?!
SHAVE !!!
FW IP..
GO!!
YEAH! COME ON, USOPP!
OUCH! THAT HURTS! MY WOUNDS!
DASH!!

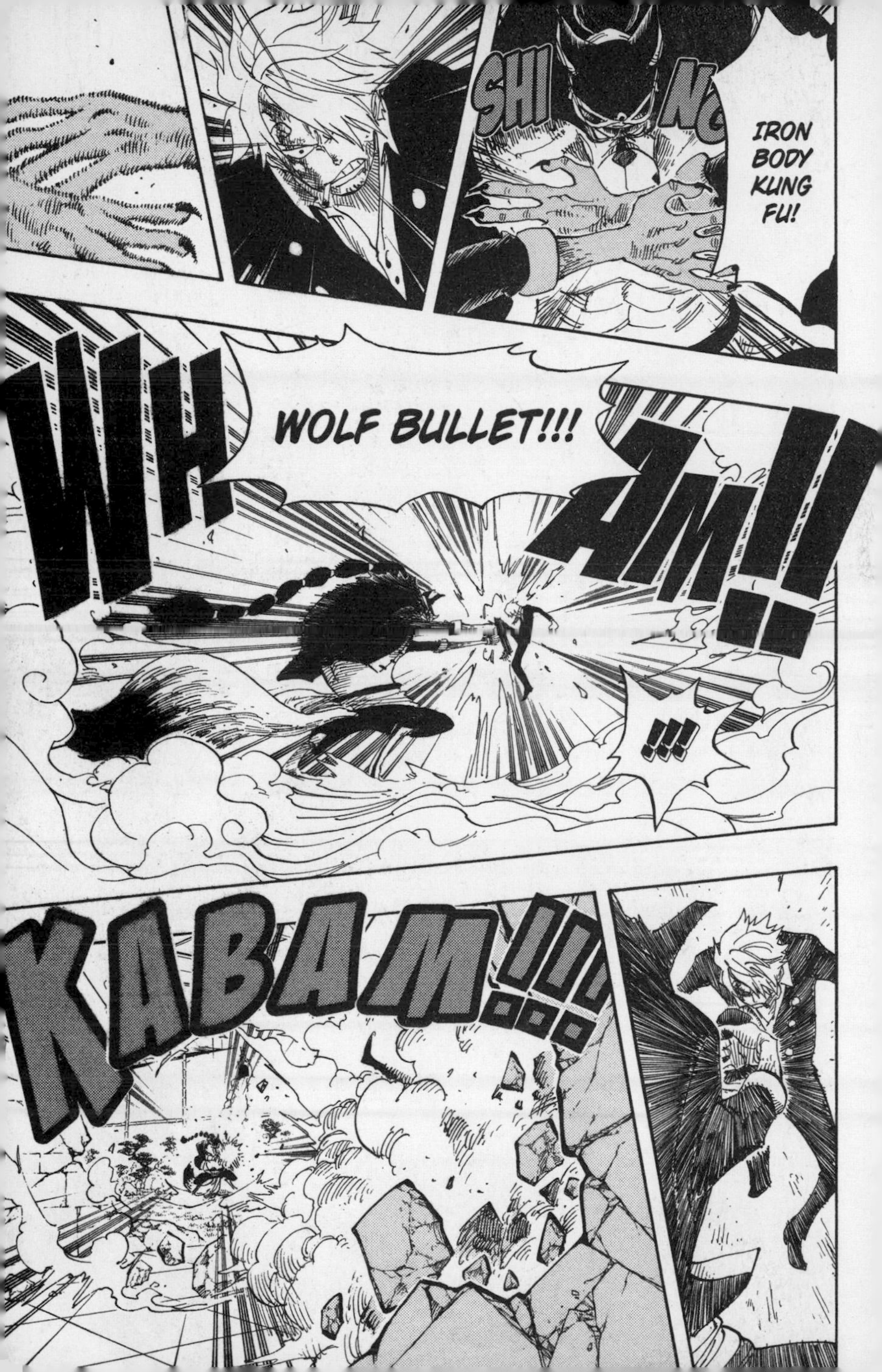
IRON BODY KUNG FU!
SHI NG
WOLF BULLET!!!
WH AM!!
!!!
KABAM!!!

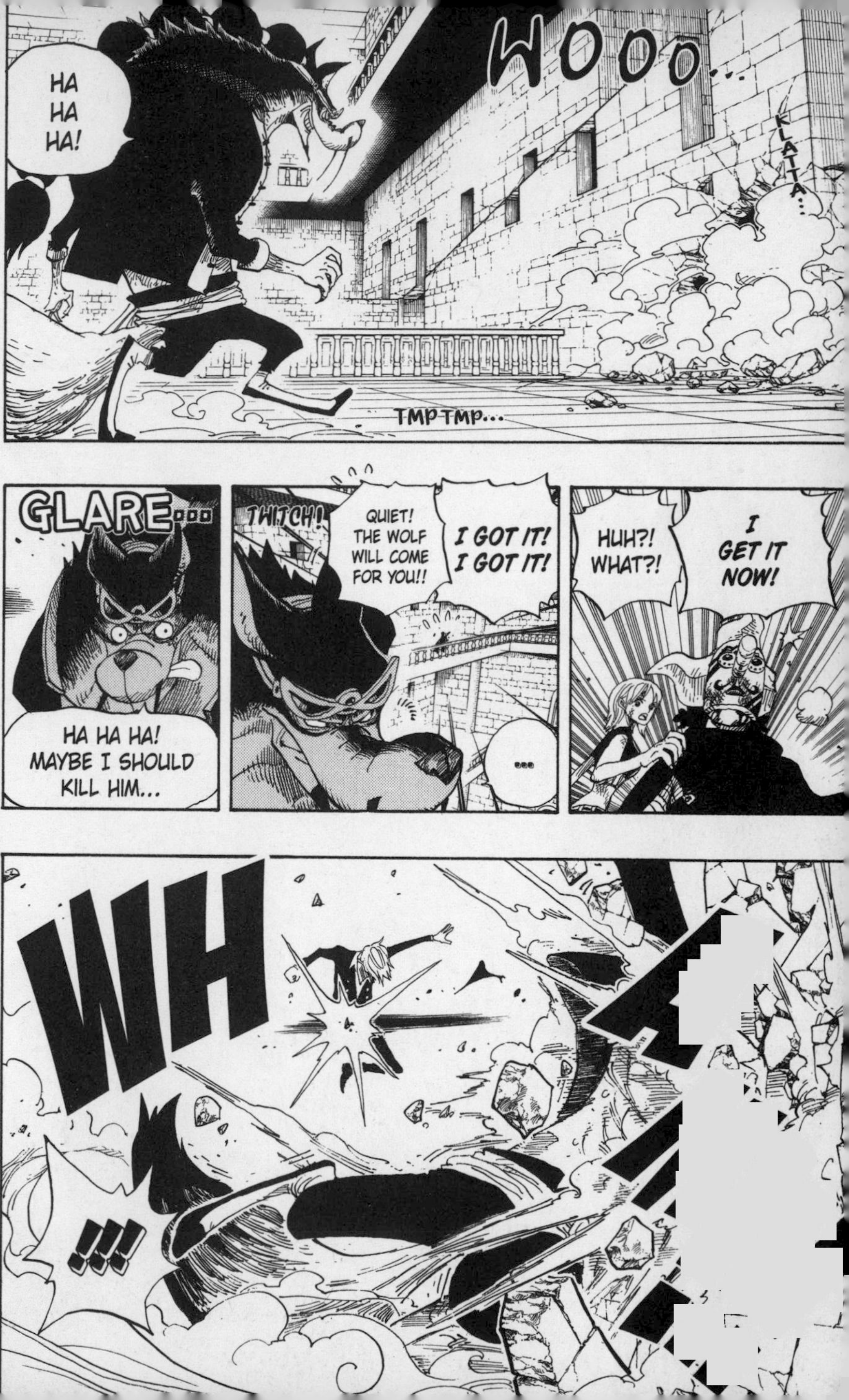
WOOO...
KLATTA...
HA HA HA!
TMP TMP...
I GET IT NOW!
HUH?! WHAT?!
I GOT IT! I GOT IT!
QUIET! THE WOLF WILL COME FOR YOU!!
TWITCH!
...
GLARE...
HA HA HA! MAYBE I SHOULD KILL HIM...
WH
!!!

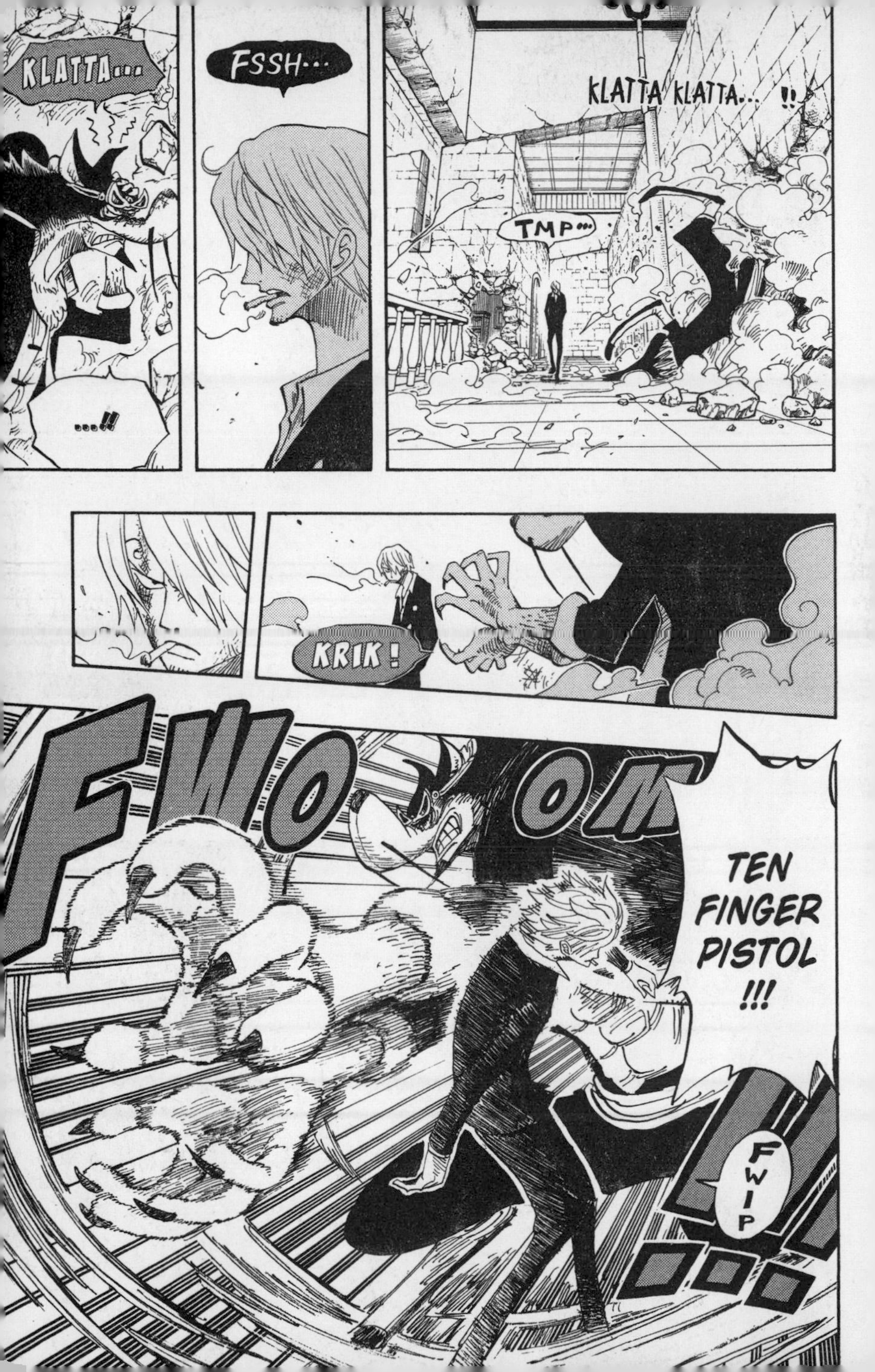
KLATTA KLATTA... !!
TMP...
FSSH...
KLATTA...
...!!
KRIK!
FWOOM
TEN FINGER PISTOL !!!
FWIP

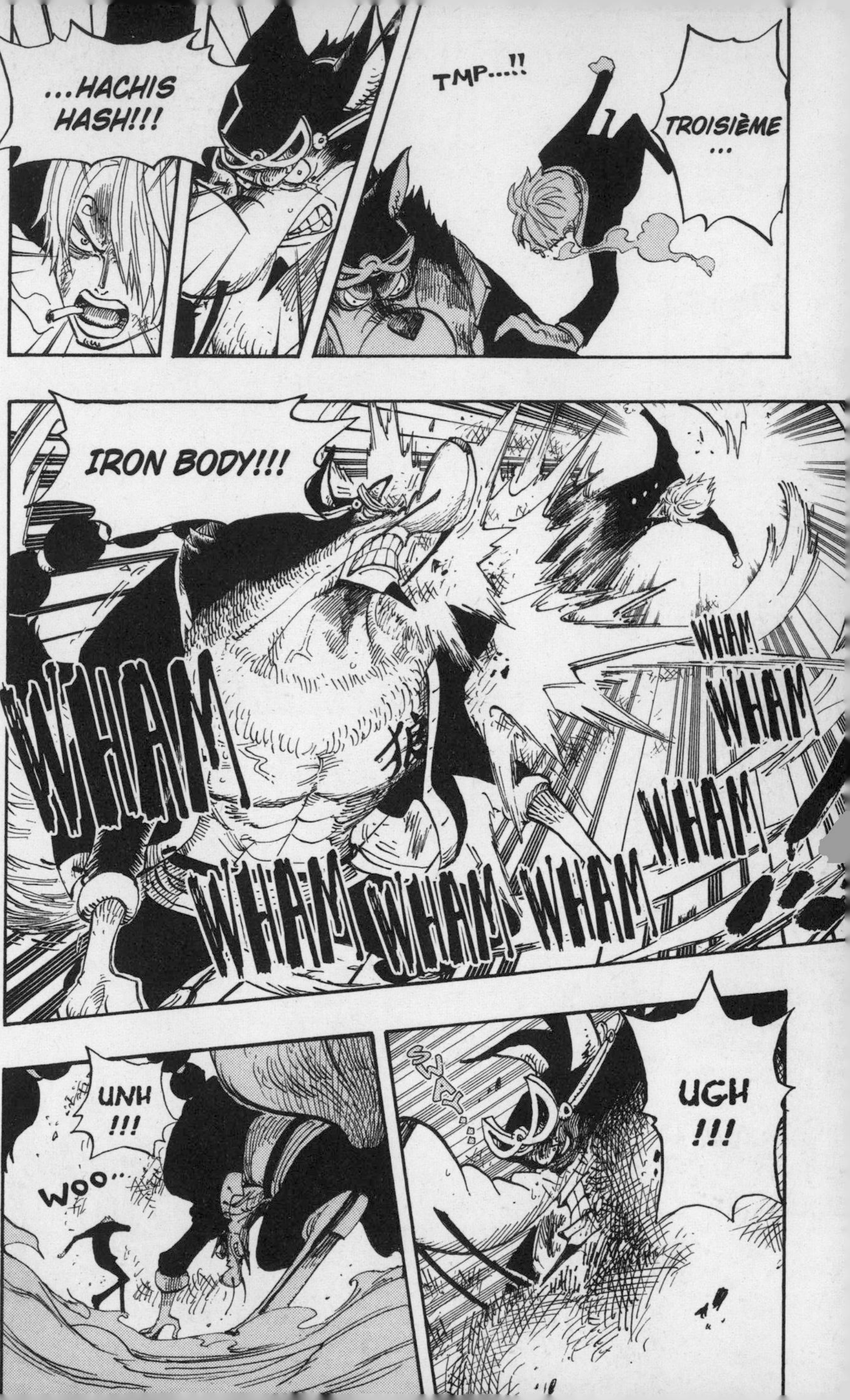
TMP...!!
TROISIÈME ...
...HACHIS HASH!!!
IRON BODY!!!
WHAM WHAM WHAM
WHAM WHAM WHAM WHAM WHAM
UGH !!!
SWAY
UNH !!!
WOO...

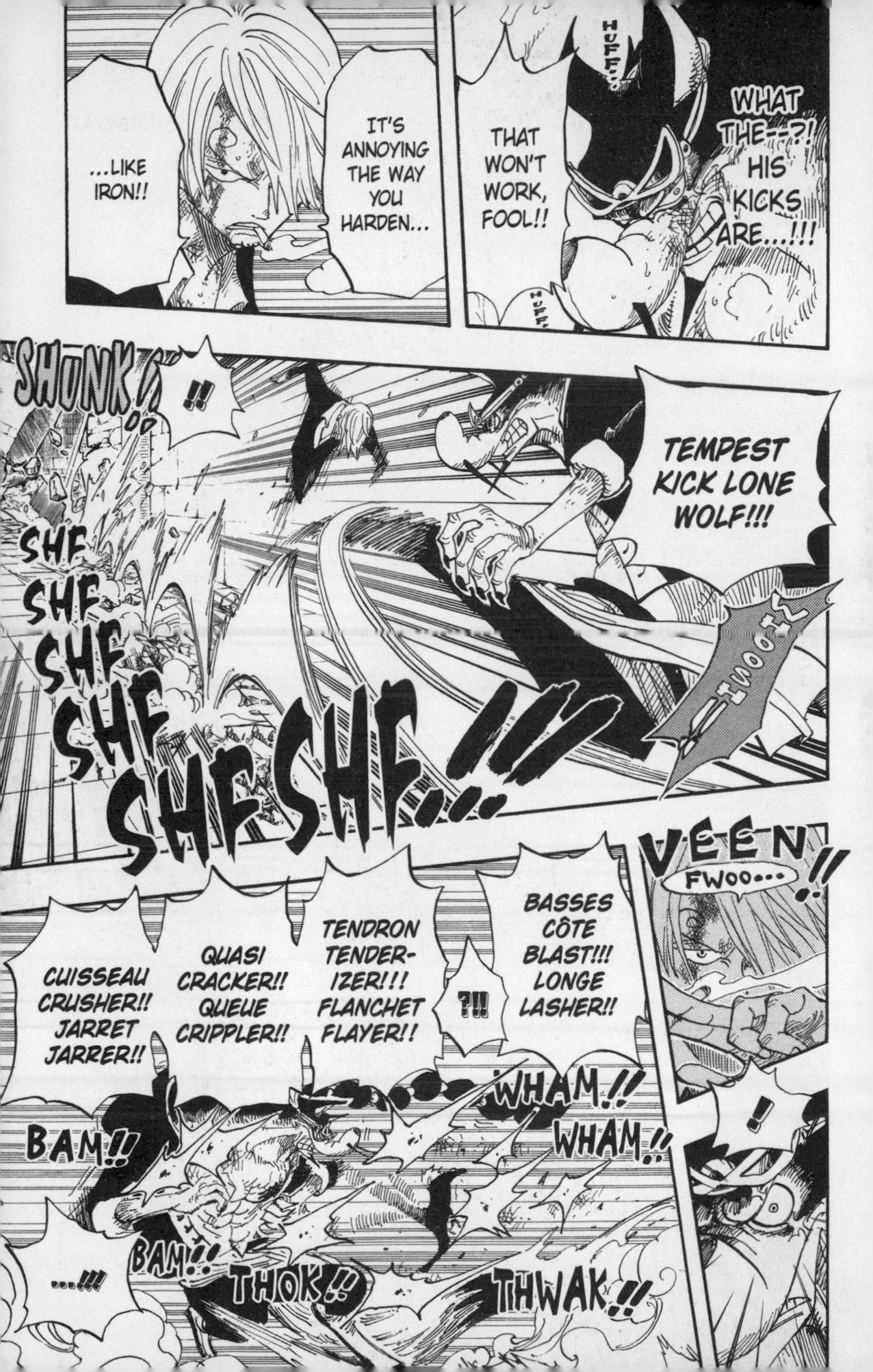

WHAT THE--?! HIS KICKS ARE...!!!
HUFF
THAT WON'T WORK, FOOL!!
HUFF
IT'S ANNOYING THE WAY YOU HARDEN...
...LIKE IRON!!
TEMPEST KICK LONE WOLF!!!
!!
SHUNK
SHF
SHF
SHF
SHF
SHFSHF...!!
VEEN!!
FWOO...
!
BASSES CÔTE BLAST!!! LONGE LASHER!!
?!!
TENDRON TENDER-IZER!!! FLANCHET FLAYER!!
QUASI CRACKER!! QUEUE CRIPPLER!!
CUISSEAU CRUSHER!! JARRET JARRER!!
WHAM!!
WHAM!!
BAM!!
THWAK!!
THOK!!
BAM!!
...!!!

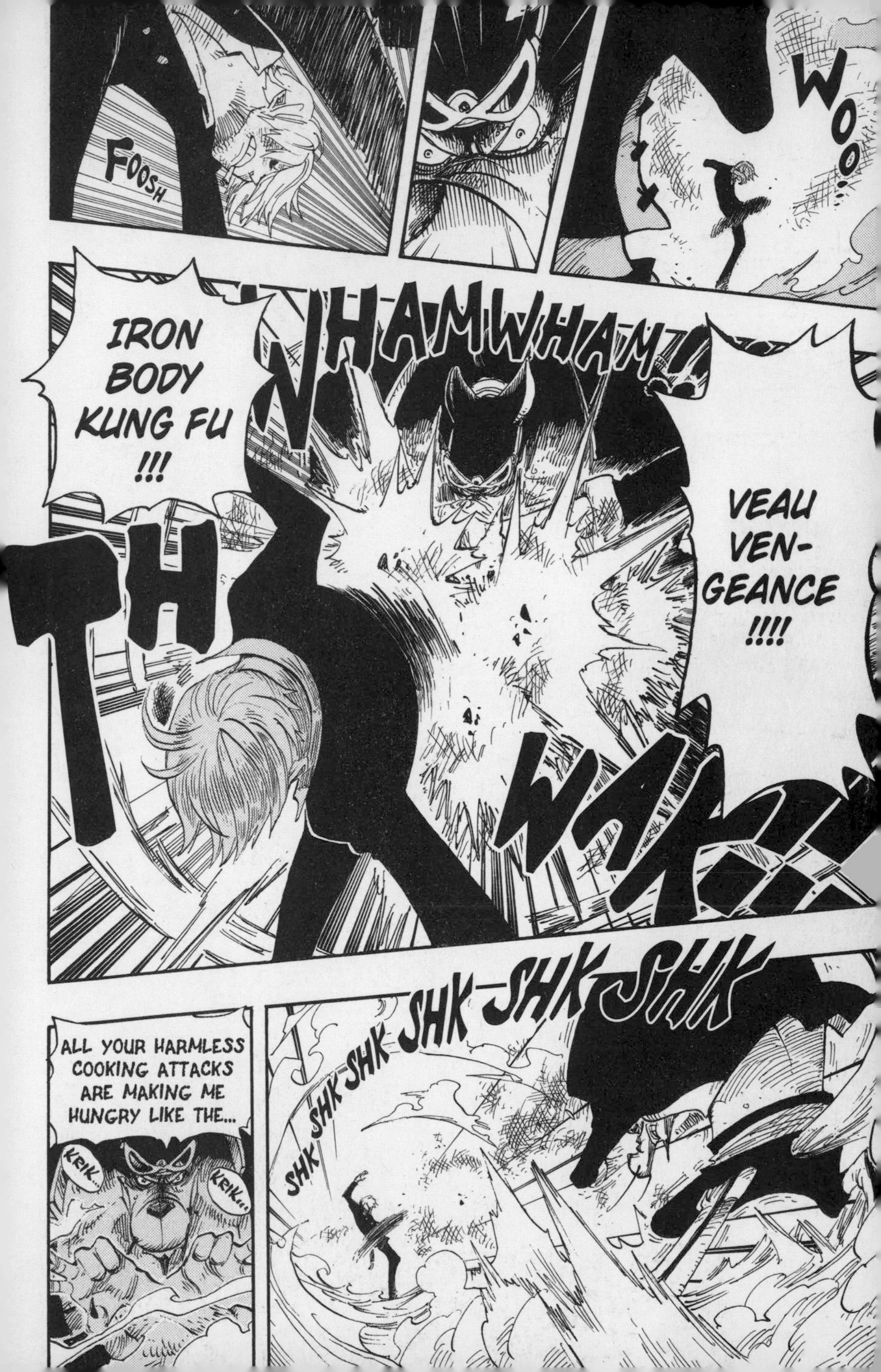
WOO!
FOOSH
WHAMWHAM!!
VEAU VEN-GEANCE !!!!
IRON BODY KUNG FU !!!
TH
WACK
SHK-SHK-SHK-SHK-SHK-SHK-SHK
ALL YOUR HARMLESS COOKING ATTACKS ARE MAKING ME HUNGRY LIKE THE...
KRIK...
KRIK...

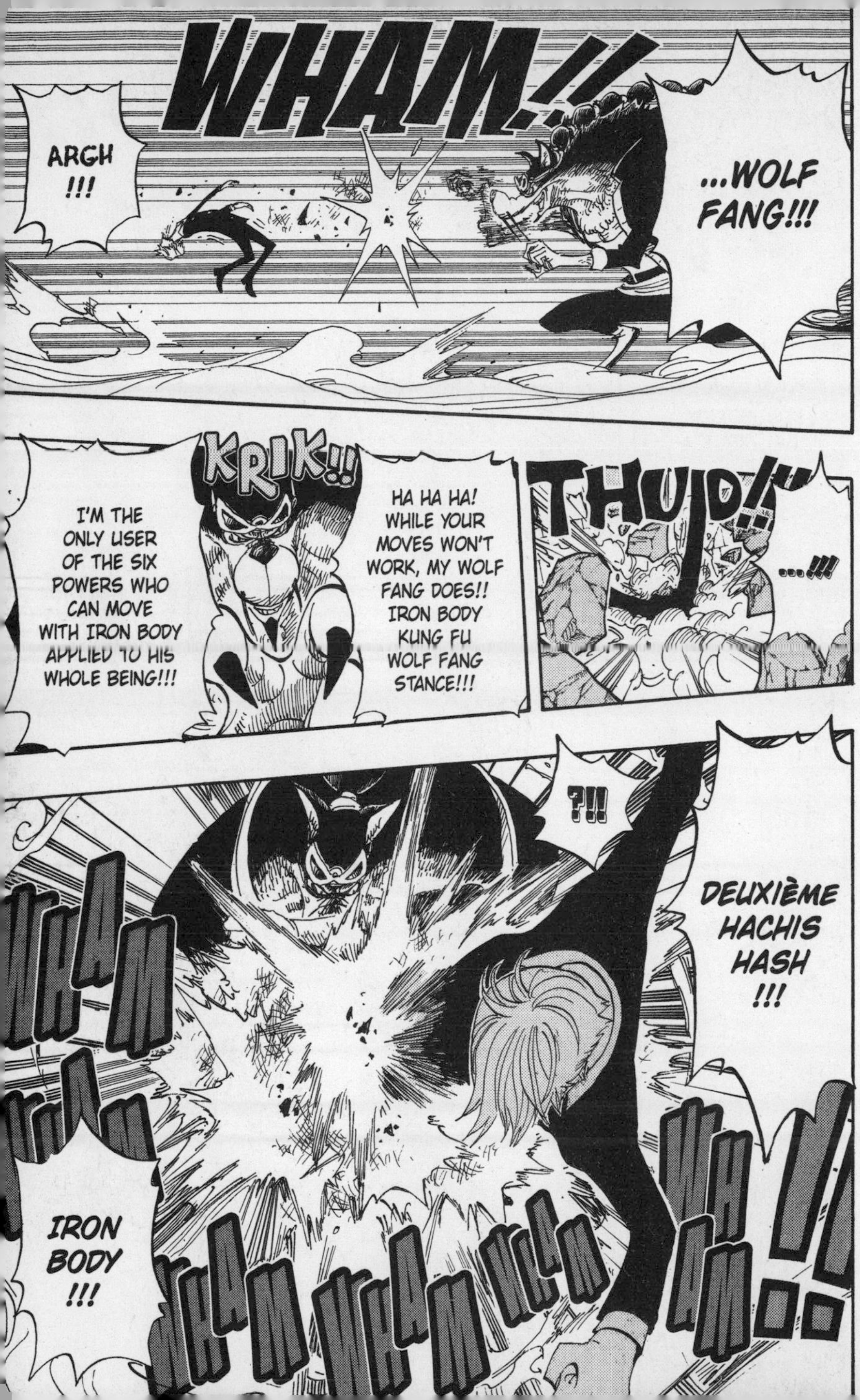
...WOLF FANG!!!
WHAM!!
ARGH !!!
THUD!!
...!!!
KRIK!!
HA HA HA! WHILE YOUR MOVES WON'T WORK, MY WOLF FANG DOES!! IRON BODY KUNG FU WOLF FANG STANCE!!!
I'M THE ONLY USER OF THE SIX POWERS WHO CAN MOVE WITH IRON BODY APPLIED TO HIS WHOLE BEING!!!
?!!
DEUXIÈME HACHIS HASH !!!
IRON BODY !!!

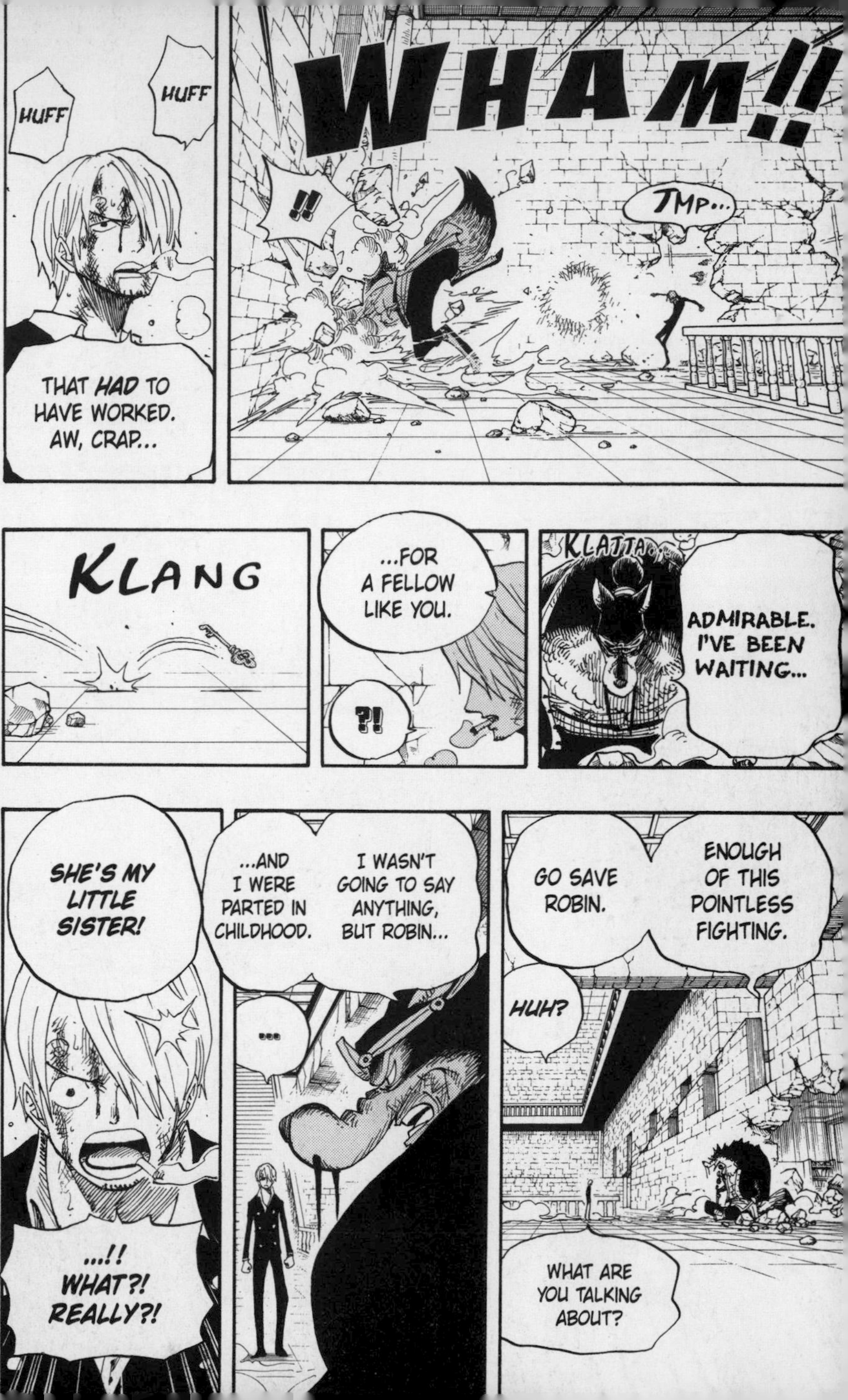
WHAM!!
!!
TMP...
HUFF
HUFF
THAT HAD TO HAVE WORKED. AW, CRAP...
KLATTA
ADMIRABLE. I'VE BEEN WAITING...
...FOR A FELLOW LIKE YOU.
?!
KLANG
ENOUGH OF THIS POINTLESS FIGHTING.
GO SAVE ROBIN.
HUH?
WHAT ARE YOU TALKING ABOUT?
I WASN'T GOING TO SAY ANYTHING, BUT ROBIN...
...AND I WERE PARTED IN CHILDHOOD.
...
SHE'S MY LITTLE SISTER!
...!! WHAT?! REALLY?!

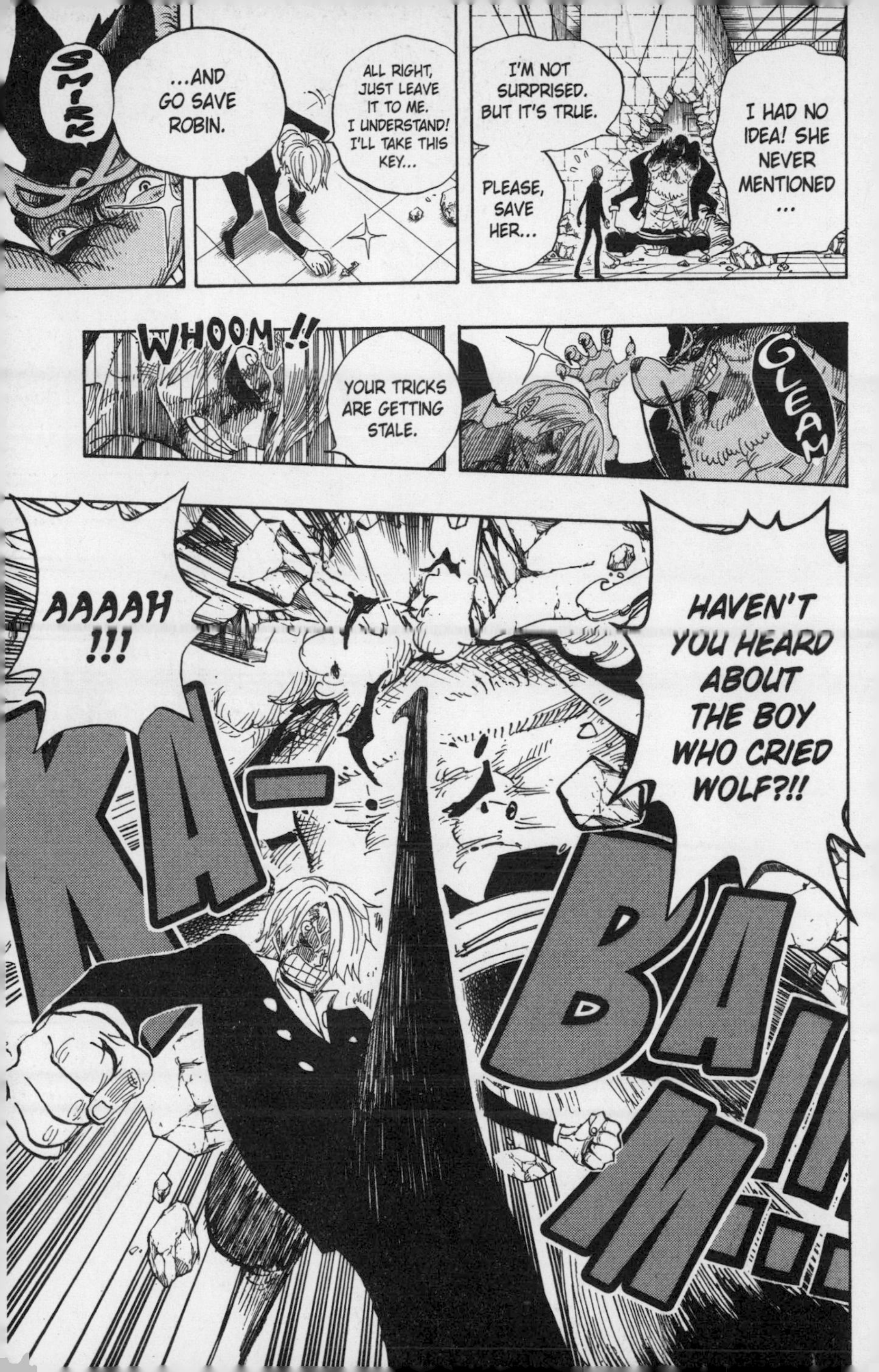
I HAD NO IDEA! SHE NEVER MENTIONED ...
I'M NOT SURPRISED. BUT IT'S TRUE.
PLEASE, SAVE HER...
ALL RIGHT, JUST LEAVE IT TO ME. I UNDERSTAND! I'LL TAKE THIS KEY...
...AND GO SAVE ROBIN.
SMIRK
GLEAM
YOUR TRICKS ARE GETTING STALE.
WHOOM!!
HAVEN'T YOU HEARD ABOUT THE BOY WHO CRIED WOLF?!!
AAAAH !!!
KA-BAM...

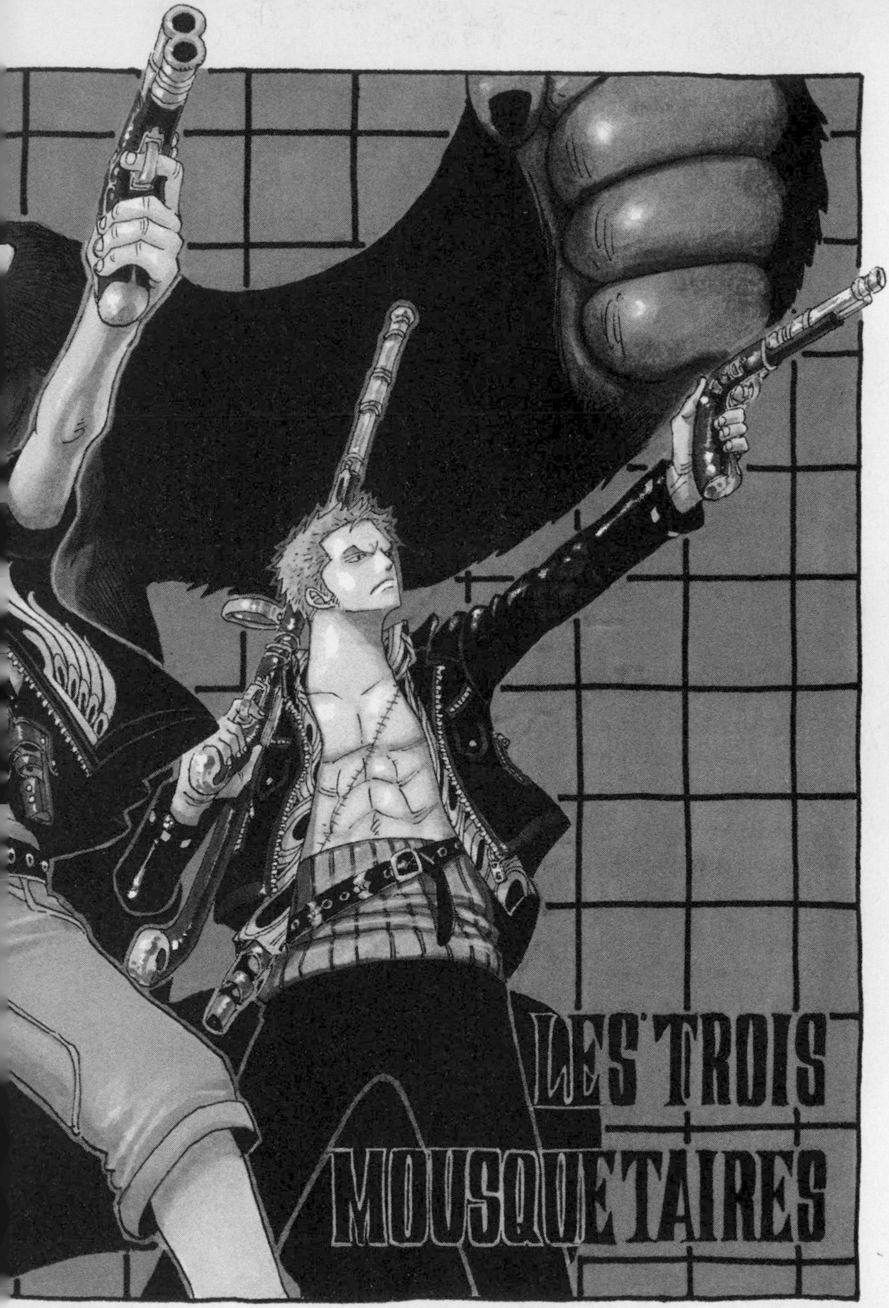
LES TROIS
MOUSQUETAIRES

Chapter 415: HEAT UP

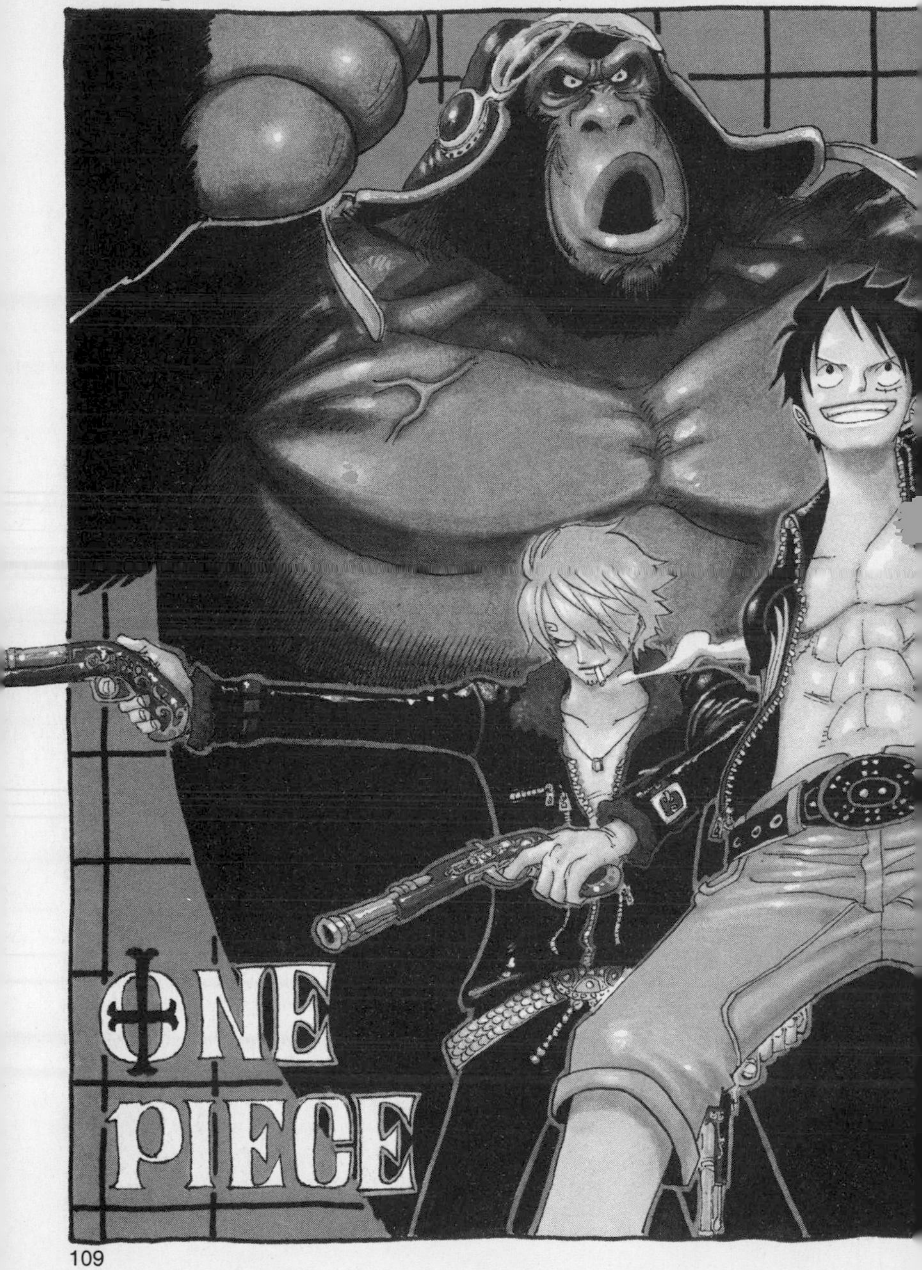
ONE PIECE

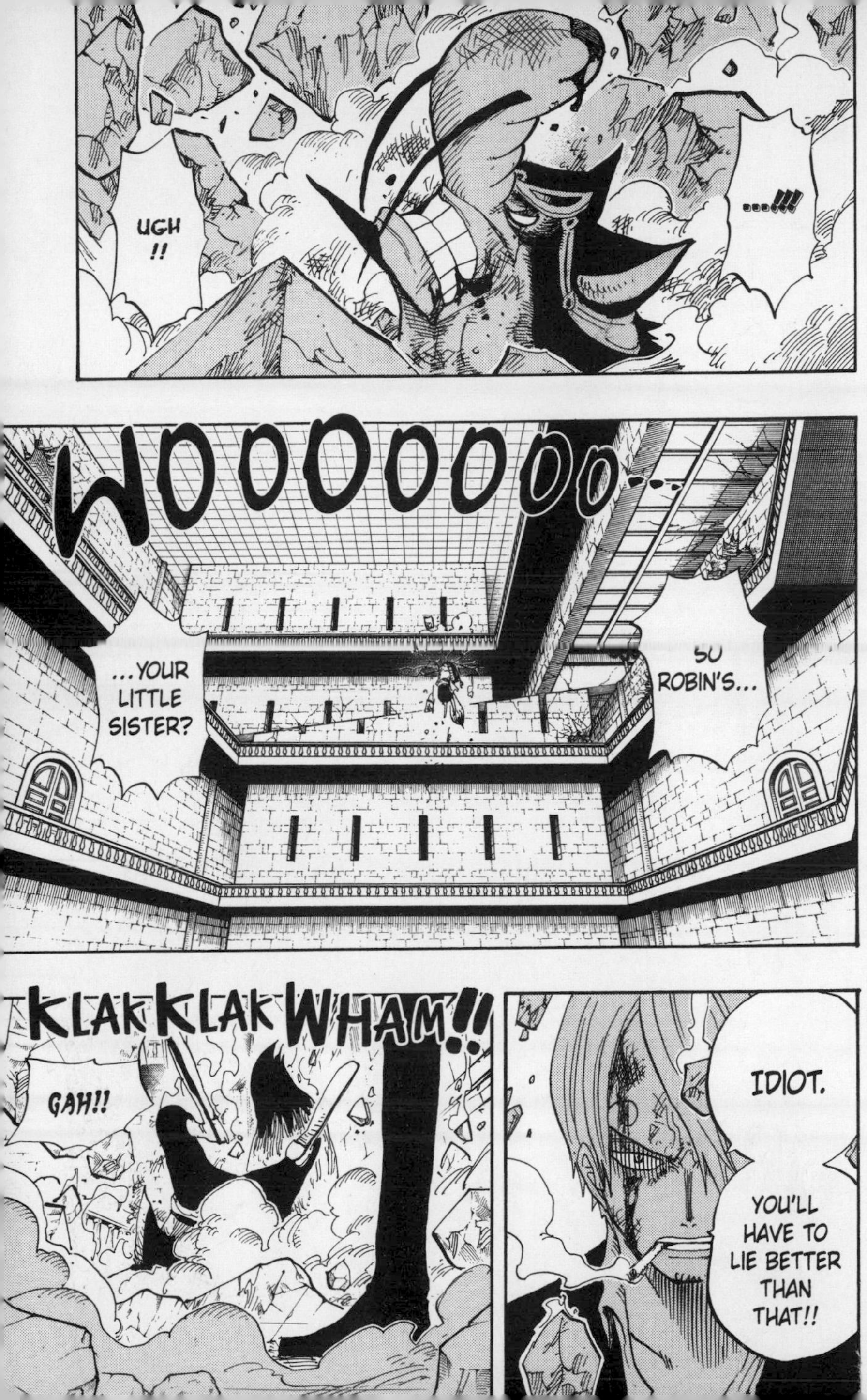
...!!!
UGH !!
WOOOOOOO...
SO ROBIN'S...
...YOUR LITTLE SISTER?
IDIOT.
YOU'LL HAVE TO LIE BETTER THAN THAT!!
KLAK KLAK WHAM!!
GAH!!

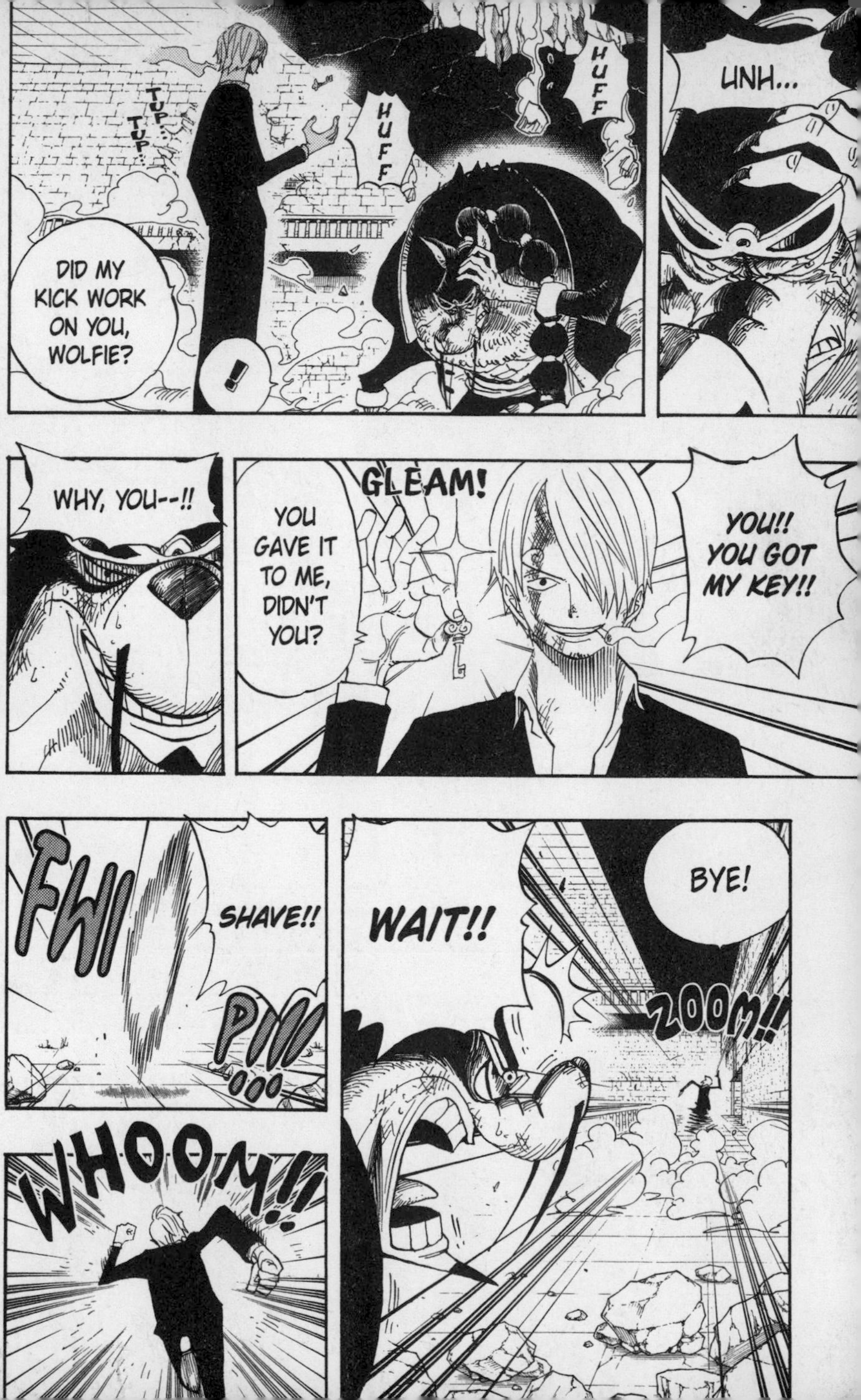
UNH...
HUFF
HUFF
TUP...
TUP...
DID MY KICK WORK ON YOU, WOLFIE?
!
YOU!! YOU GOT MY KEY!!
GLEAM!
YOU GAVE IT TO ME, DIDN'T YOU?
WHY, YOU--!!
BYE!
WAIT!!
ZOOM!!
SHAVE!!
FWI
PIOOO
WHOOM!!

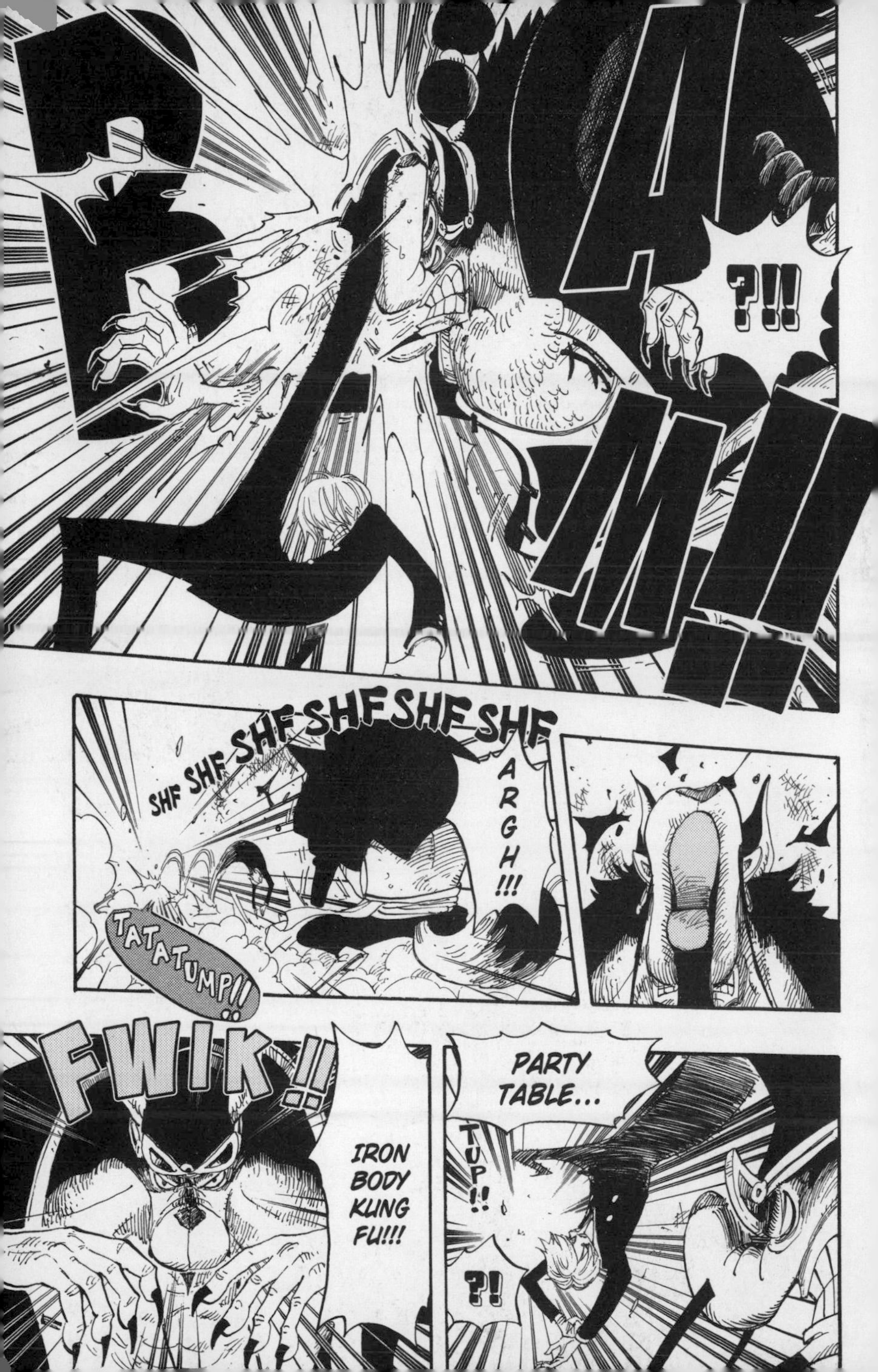
?!!
BAM!!
SHF SHF SHF SHF SHF SHF
ARGH!!!
TATATUMP!!
PARTY TABLE...
TUP!!
?!
FWIK!!
IRON BODY KUNG FU!!!

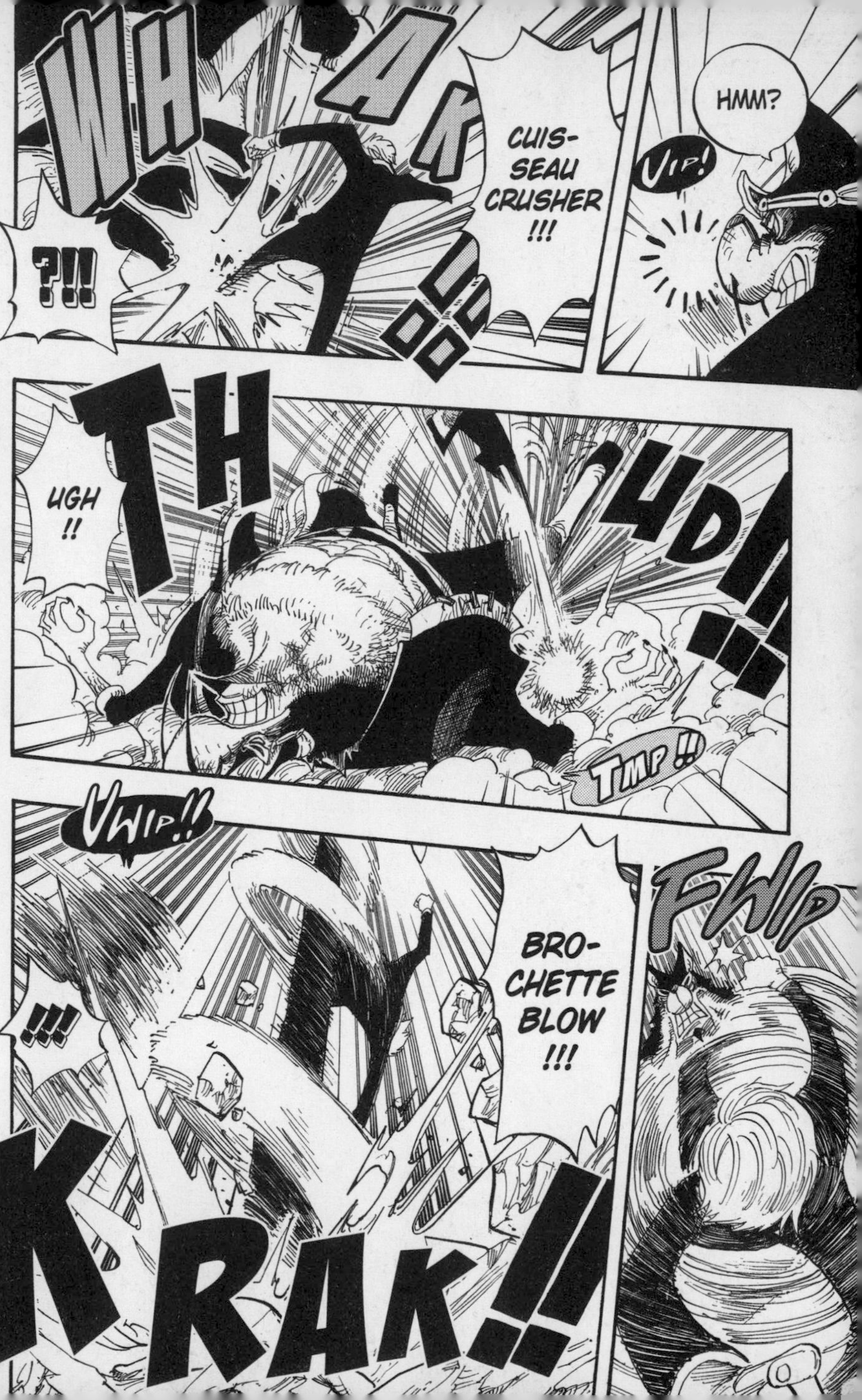
HMM?
VIP!
CUIS-
SEAU
CRUSHER
!!!
WHAK
?!!
THUD!!
UGH
!!
TMP!!
FWIP
VWIP!!
BRO-
CHETTE
BLOW
!!!
!!!
KRAK!!

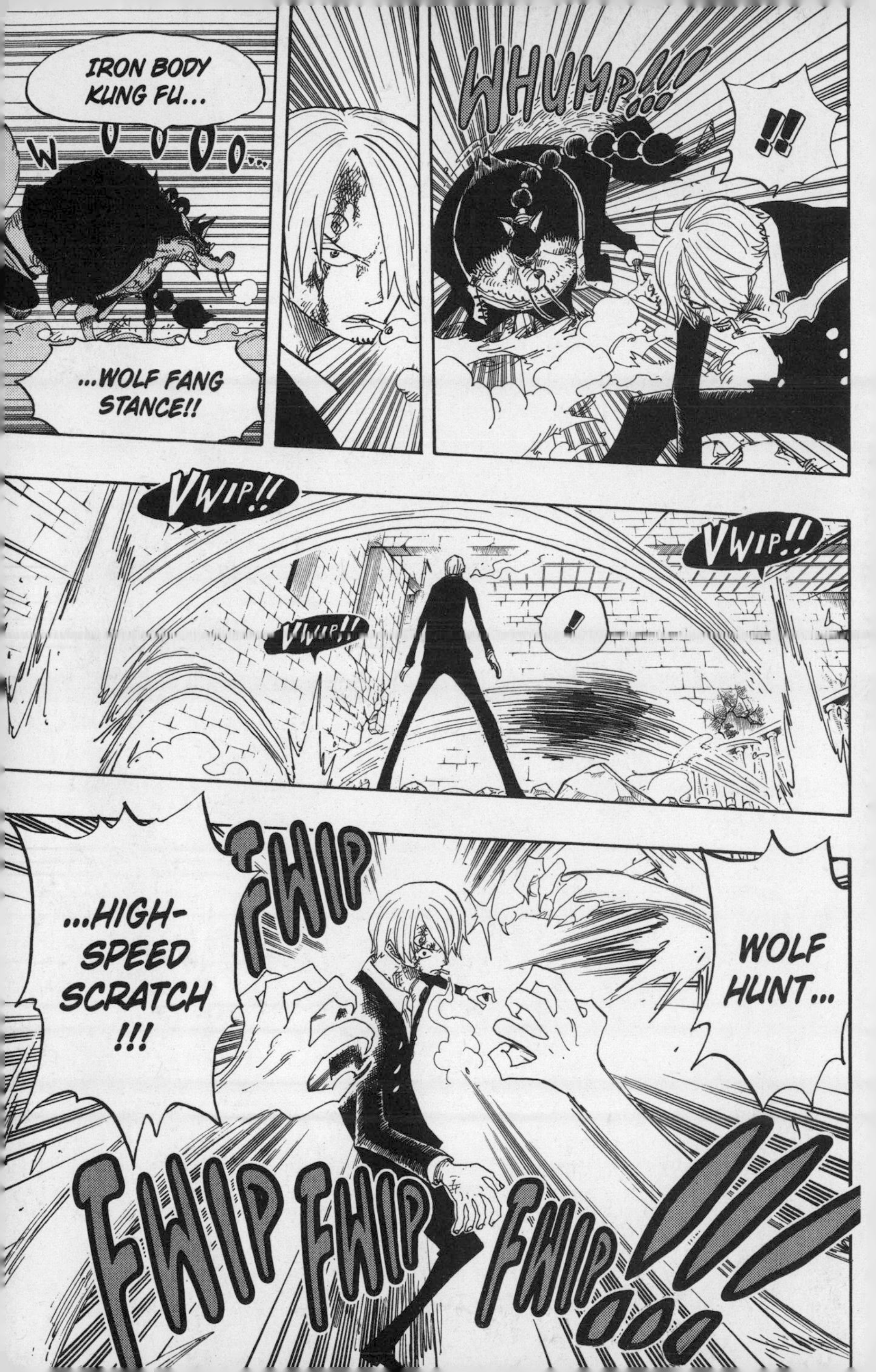
WHUMP!!!
!!
IRON BODY KUNG FU...
WOOOO...
...WOLF FANG STANCE!!
VWIP!!
!
VWIP!!
VWIP!!
WOLF HUNT...
FWIP
...HIGH-SPEED SCRATCH!!!
FWIP FWIP FWIP...!!!

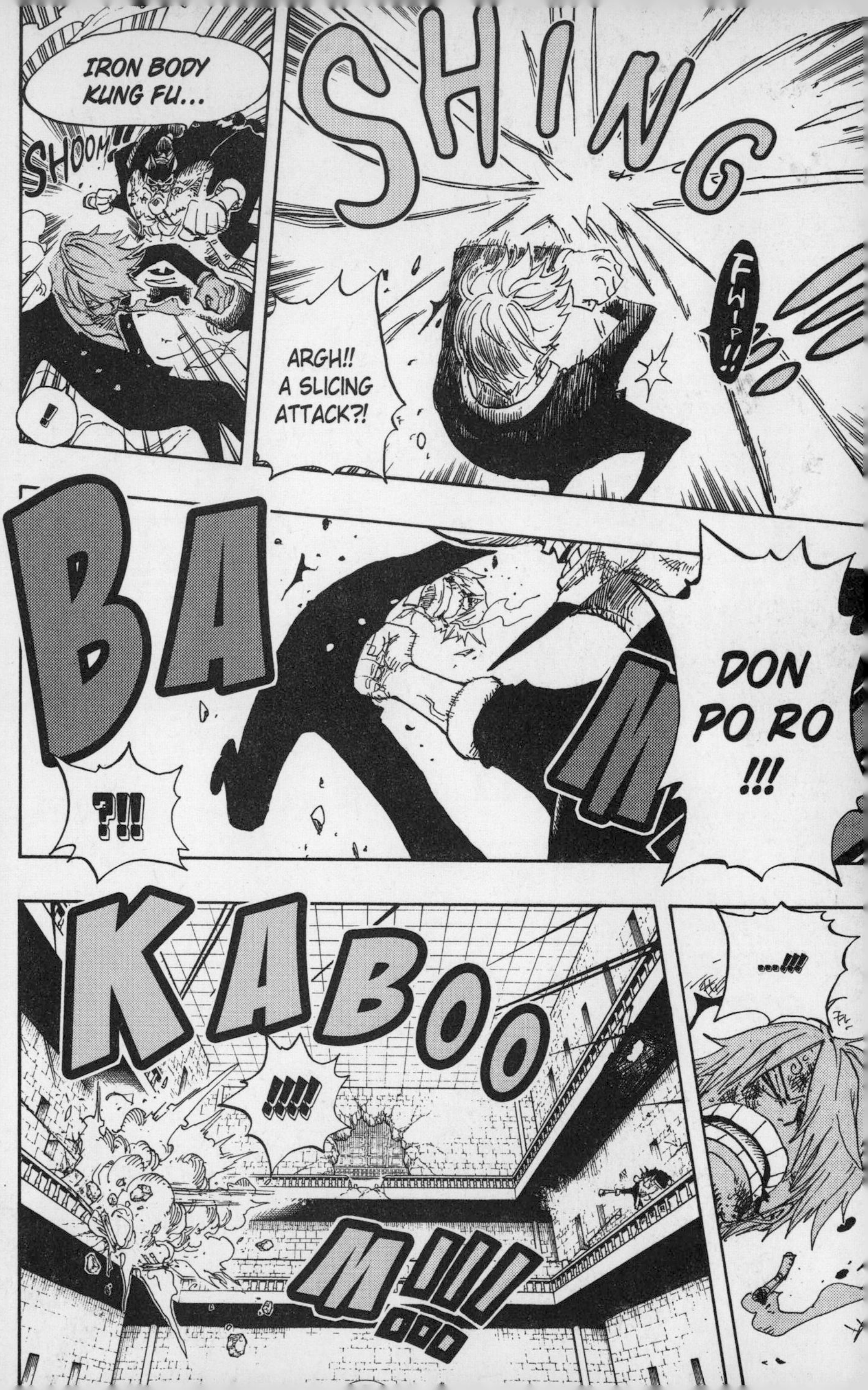
SHING
FWIP!!
ARGH!! A SLICING ATTACK?!
IRON BODY KUNG FU...
SHOOM!!
!
DON PO RO !!!
BAM
?!!
...!!!
KABOOOM!!!
!!!!

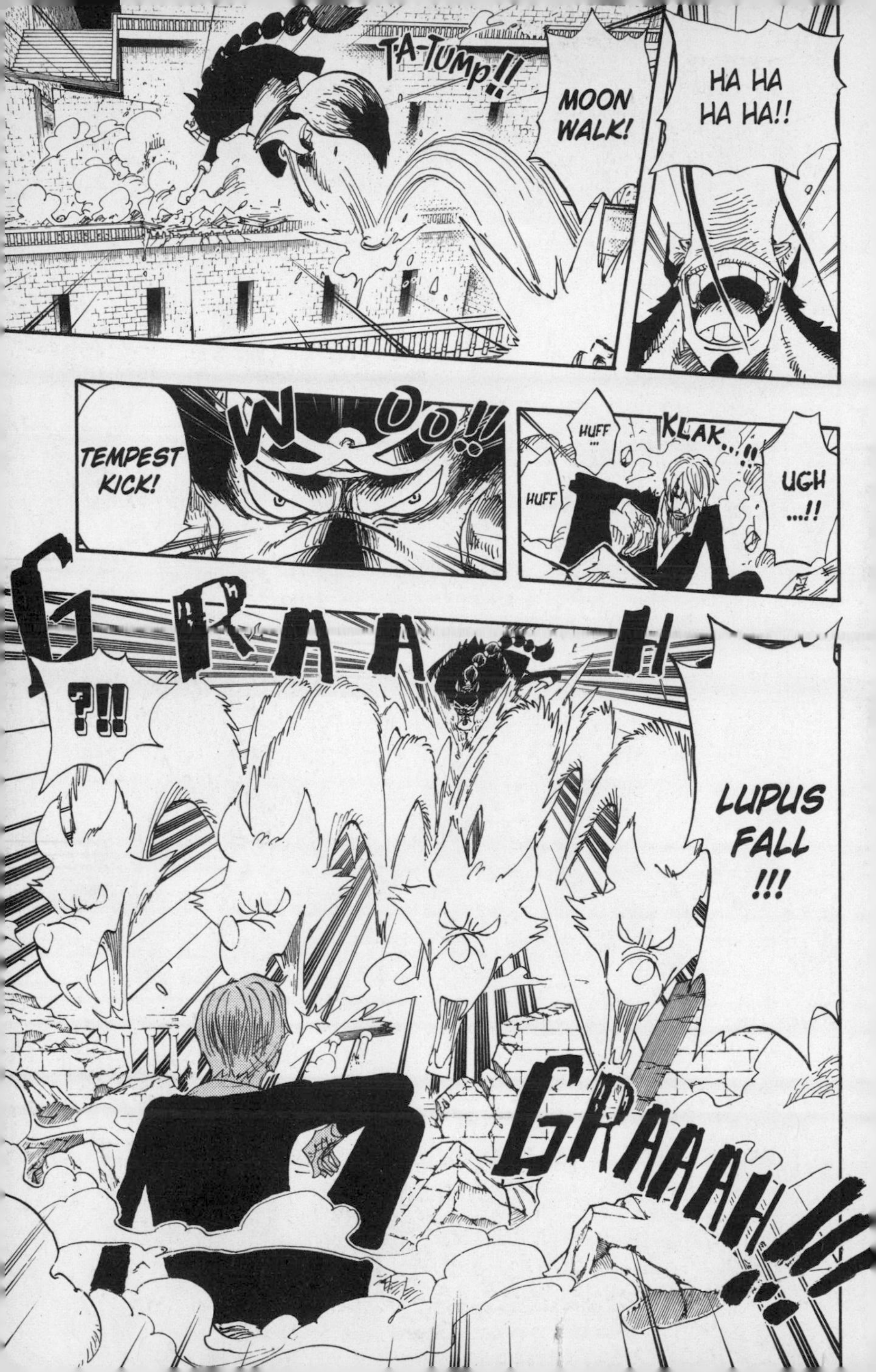
HA HA
HA HA!!
MOON
WALK!
TA-TUMP!!
UGH
...!!
KLAK...!!
HUFF
...
HUFF
WOOO!!
TEMPEST
KICK!
GRAAH
LUPUS
FALL
!!!
?!!
GRAAAH!!!

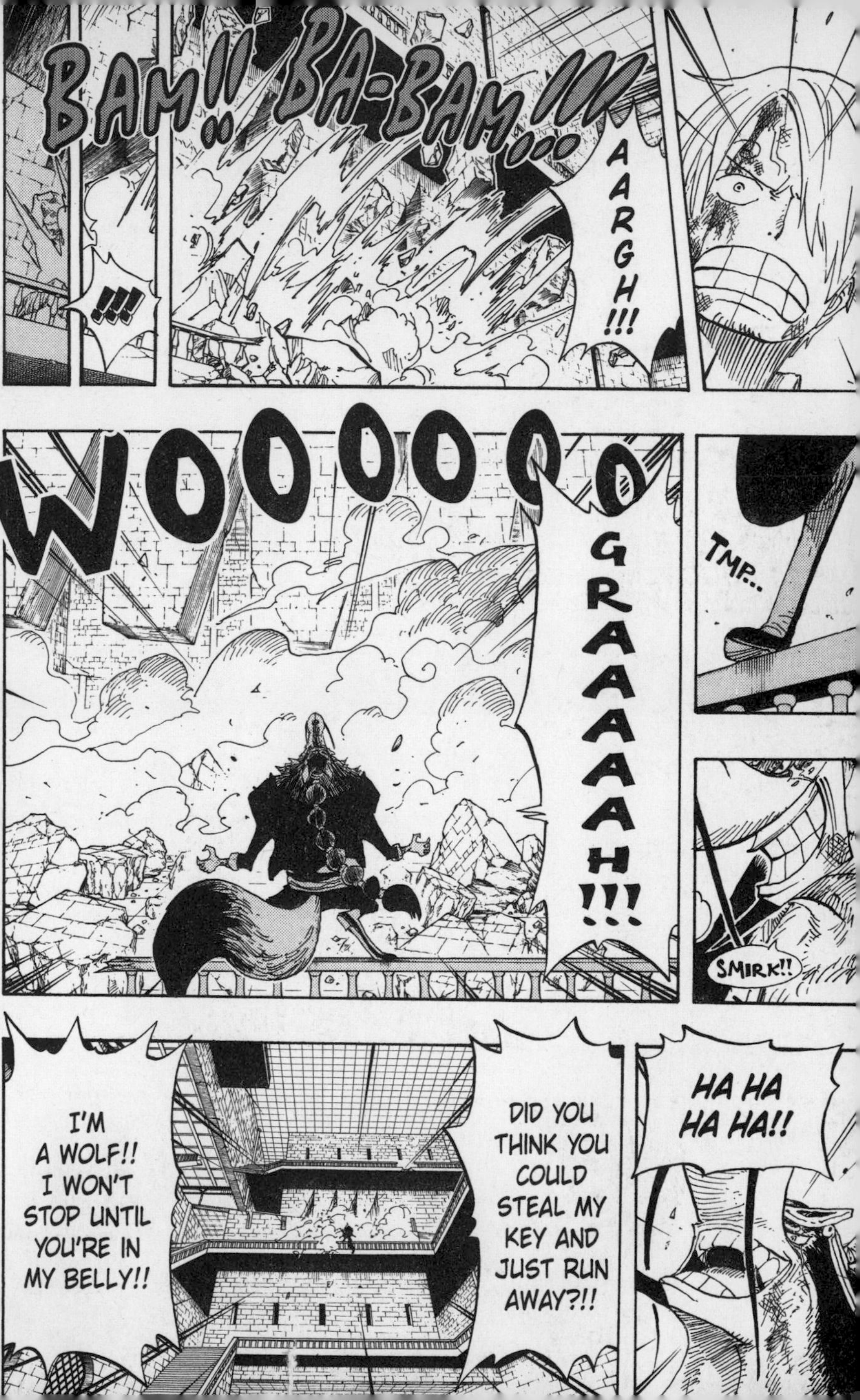
BAM!! BA-BAM!!!
AARGH!!!
!!!
TMP...
SMIRK!!
WOOOOOO
GRAAAAAAH!!!
HA HA HA HA!!
DID YOU THINK YOU COULD STEAL MY KEY AND JUST RUN AWAY?!!
I'M A WOLF!! I WON'T STOP UNTIL YOU'RE IN MY BELLY!!

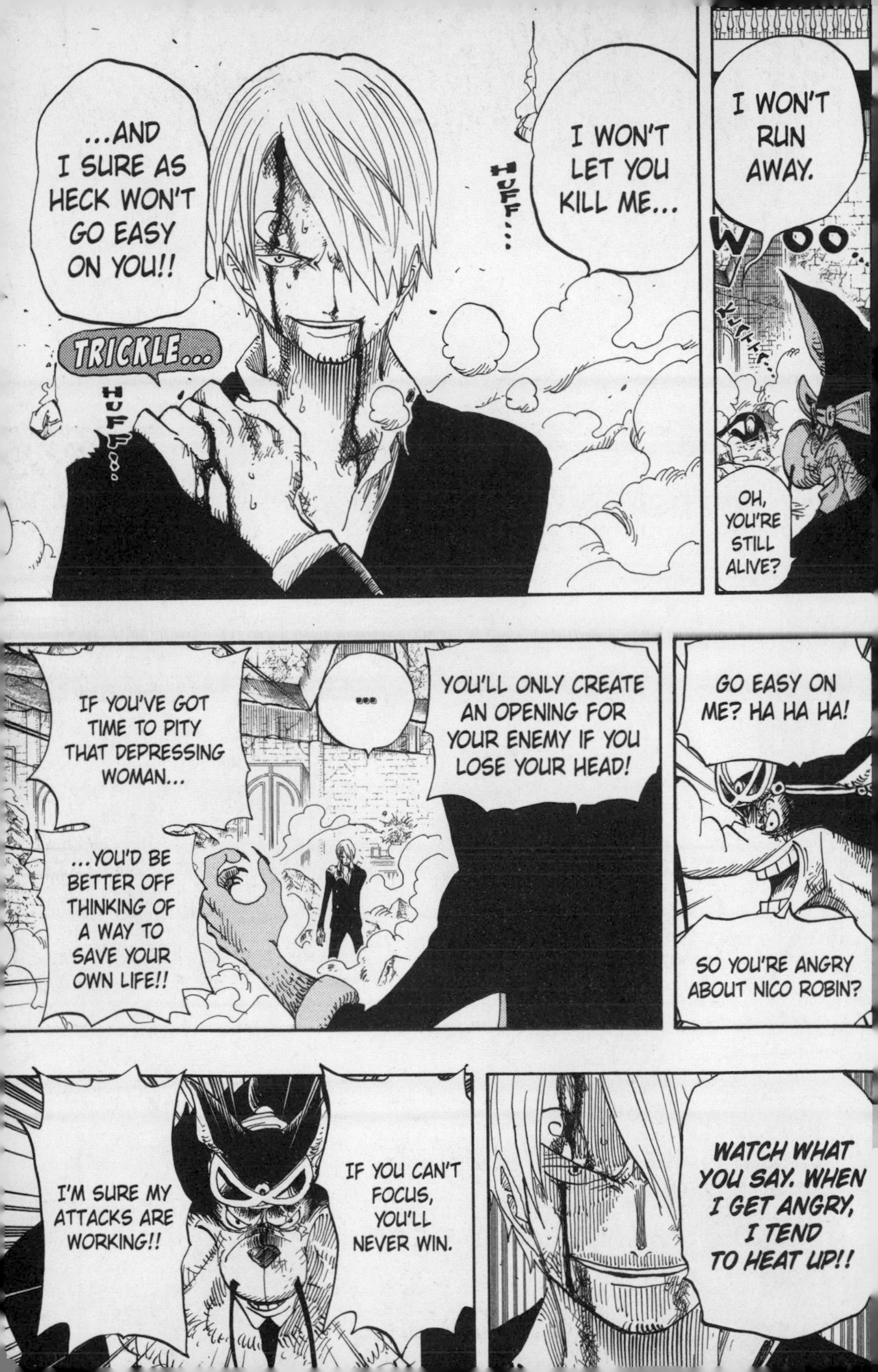
I WON'T RUN AWAY.
WOO...
OH, YOU'RE STILL ALIVE?
I WON'T LET YOU KILL ME...
HUFF...
...AND I SURE AS HECK WON'T GO EASY ON YOU!!
TRICKLE...
HUFF...
GO EASY ON ME? HA HA HA!
SO YOU'RE ANGRY ABOUT NICO ROBIN?
YOU'LL ONLY CREATE AN OPENING FOR YOUR ENEMY IF YOU LOSE YOUR HEAD!
...
IF YOU'VE GOT TIME TO PITY THAT DEPRESSING WOMAN...
...YOU'D BE BETTER OFF THINKING OF A WAY TO SAVE YOUR OWN LIFE!!
WATCH WHAT YOU SAY. WHEN I GET ANGRY, I TEND TO HEAT UP!!
IF YOU CAN'T FOCUS, YOU'LL NEVER WIN.
I'M SURE MY ATTACKS ARE WORKING!!

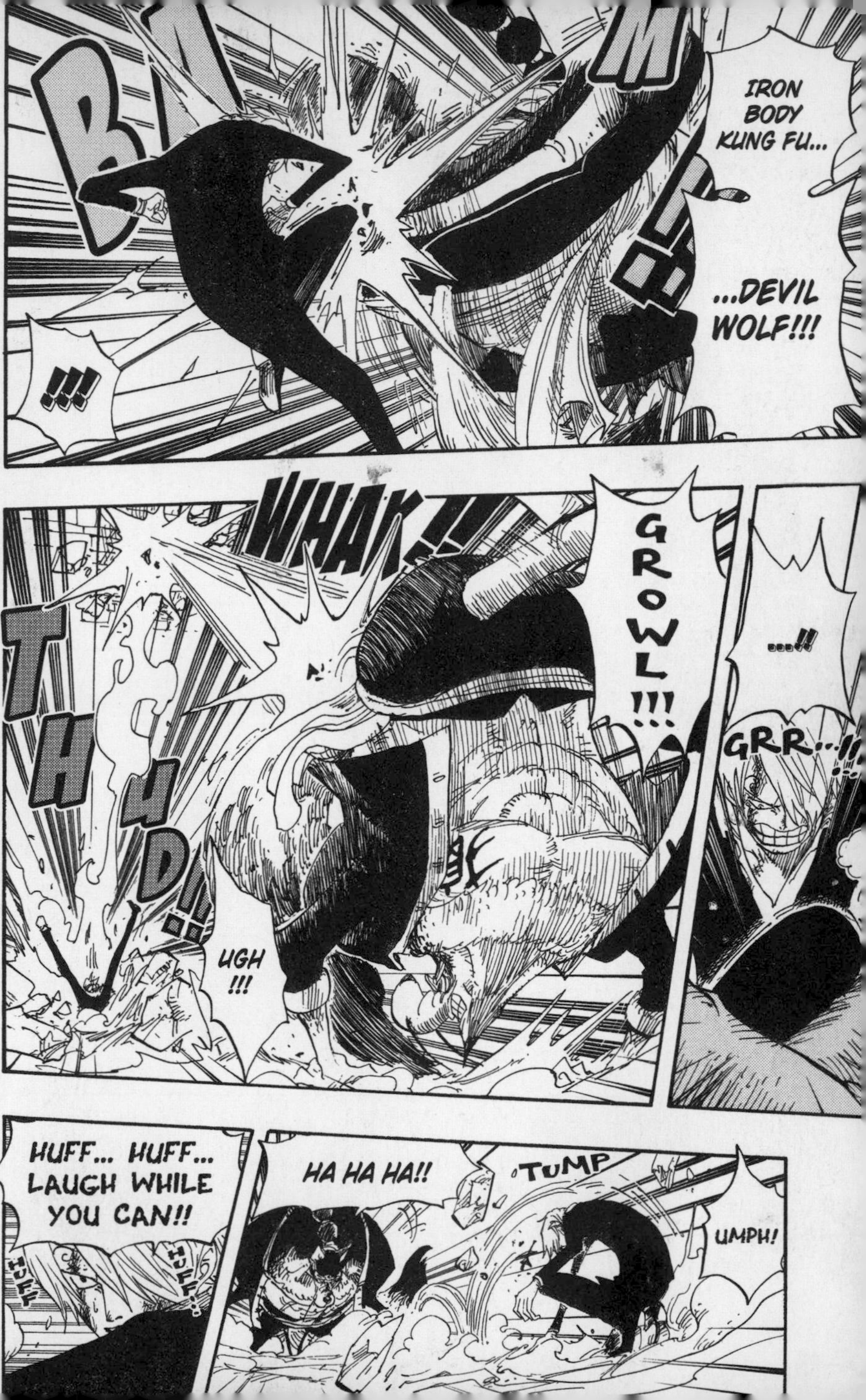
IRON BODY KUNG FU...
...DEVIL WOLF!!!
!!!
...!!
GRR...!!
GROWL!!!
WHAK!!
THUD!!
UGH !!!
TUMP
UMPH!
HA HA HA!!
HUFF... HUFF... LAUGH WHILE YOU CAN!!
HUFF
HUFF...

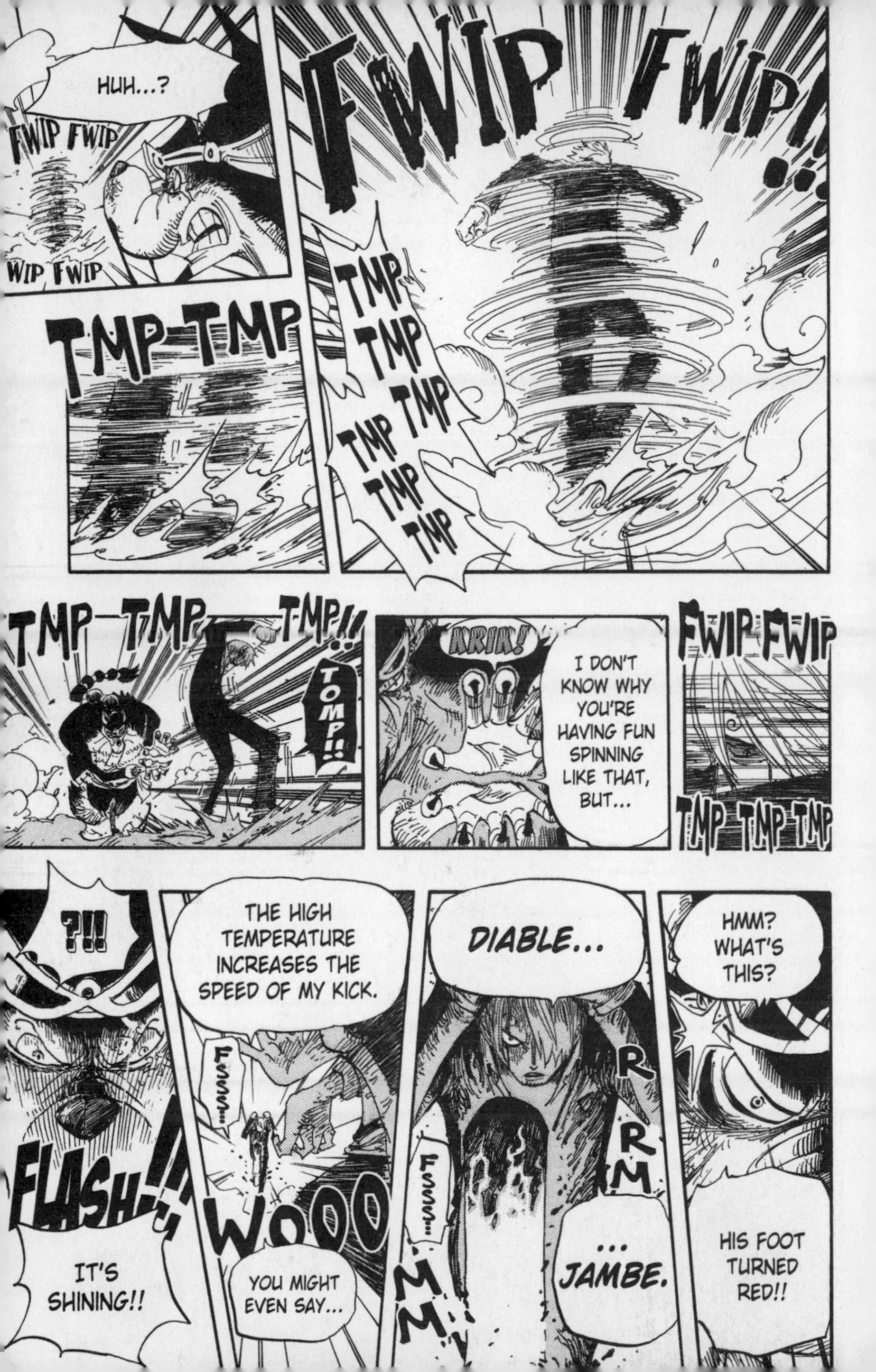
FWIP FWIP!!
TMP TMP TMP TMP TMP TMP TMP
HUH...?
FWIP FWIP
WIP FWIP
TMP TMP
FWIP FWIP
TMP TMP TMP
KRIK!
I DON'T KNOW WHY YOU'RE HAVING FUN SPINNING LIKE THAT, BUT...
TMP TMP TMP!!
TOMP!!
HMM? WHAT'S THIS?
HIS FOOT TURNED RED!!
DIABLE...
RRRM
Fssss...
...JAMBE.
THE HIGH TEMPERATURE INCREASES THE SPEED OF MY KICK.
Fssss...
WOOOMM
YOU MIGHT EVEN SAY...
?!!
FLASH!!!
IT'S SHINING!!

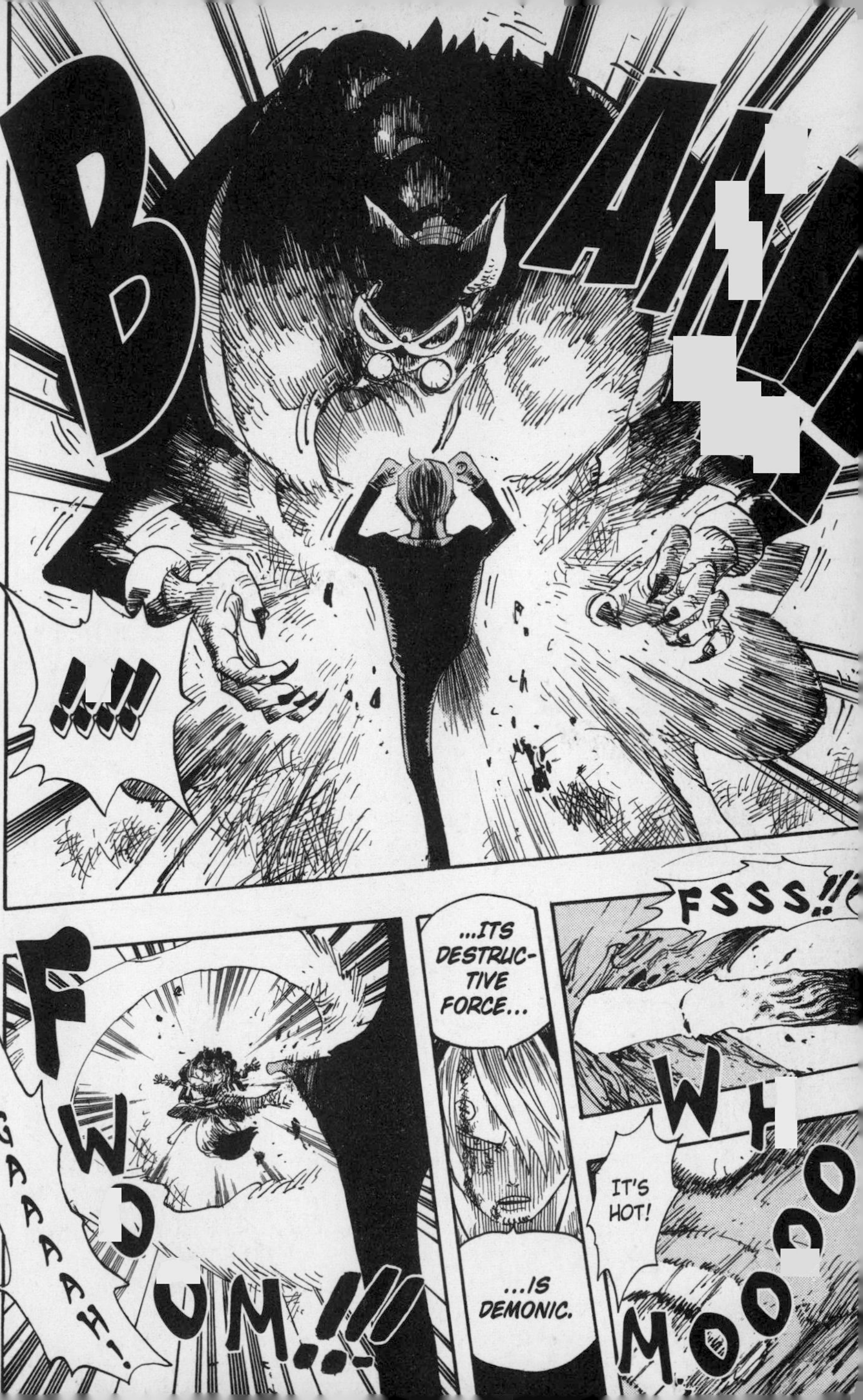
!!!!
FSSS!!
IT'S HOT!
...ITS DESTRUCTIVE FORCE...
...IS DEMONIC.
GAAAAAH!!

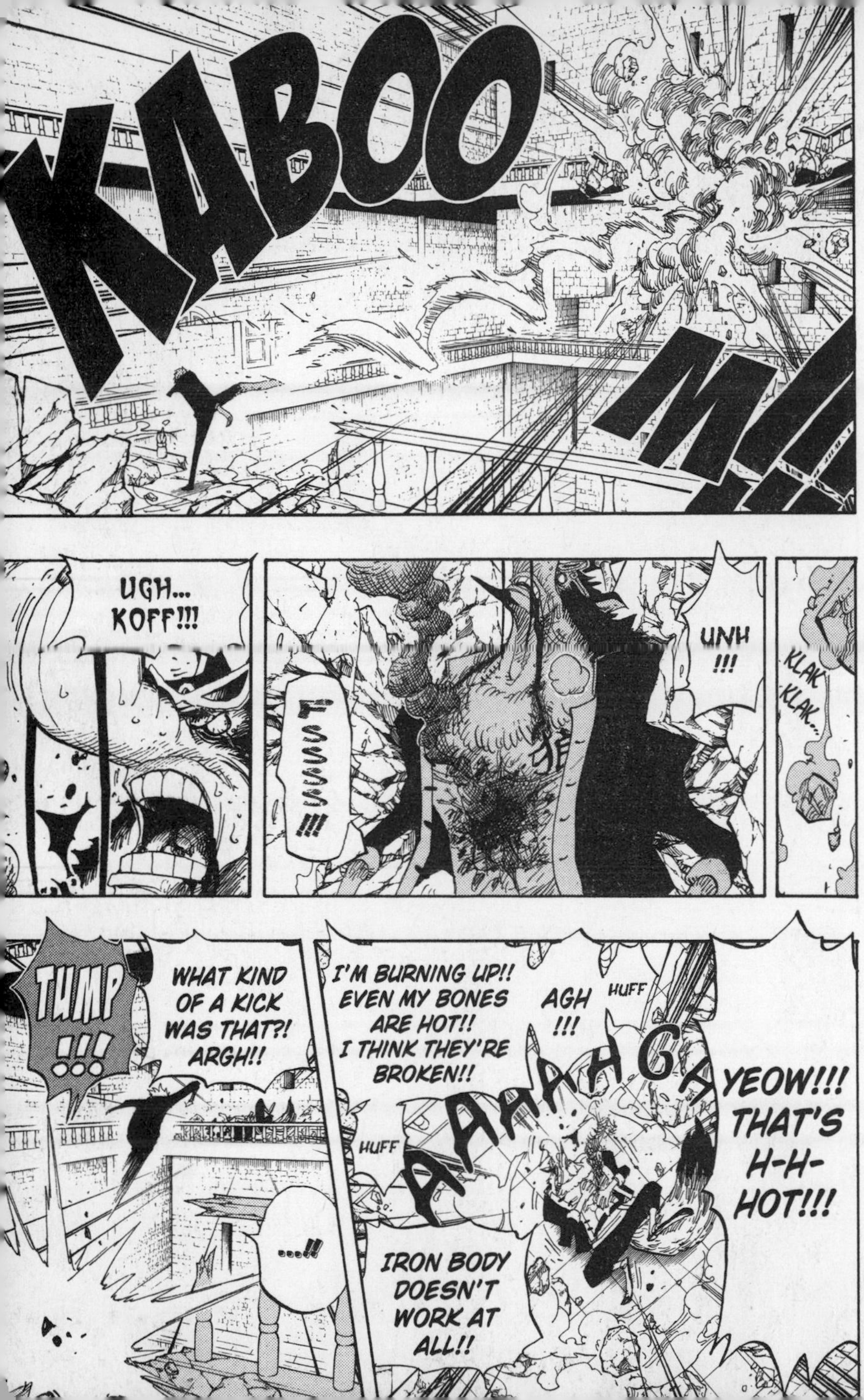

KABOOOM!!
KLAK KLAK...
UNH!!!
FSSSSS!!!
UGH... KOFF!!!
YEOW!!! THAT'S H-H-HOT!!!
HUFF
AGH!!!
I'M BURNING UP!! EVEN MY BONES ARE HOT!! I THINK THEY'RE BROKEN!!
AAAAHGA
HUFF
IRON BODY DOESN'T WORK AT ALL!!
WHAT KIND OF A KICK WAS THAT?! ARGH!!
TUMP!!!
...!!

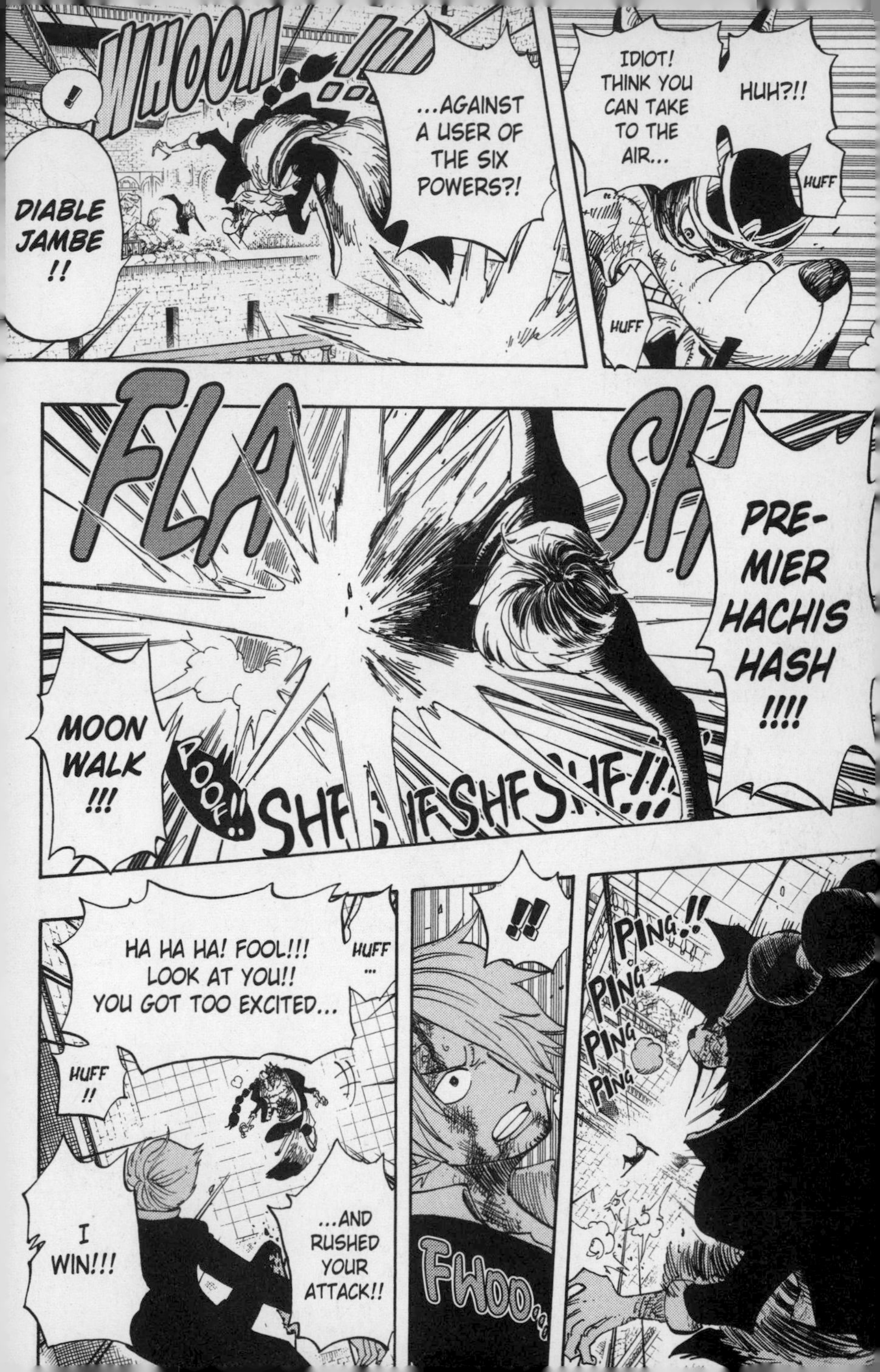
HUH?!!
IDIOT! THINK YOU CAN TAKE TO THE AIR...
HUFF
HUFF
...AGAINST A USER OF THE SIX POWERS?!
WHOOM...!!
!
DIABLE JAMBE !!
FLA SH
PRE-MIER HACHIS HASH !!!!
SHF SHF!!
POOF!!
MOON WALK !!!
PING!!
PING
PING
PING
!!
FHOO...
HUFF ...
HA HA HA! FOOL!!! LOOK AT YOU!! YOU GOT TOO EXCITED...
HUFF !!
...AND RUSHED YOUR ATTACK!!
I WIN!!!

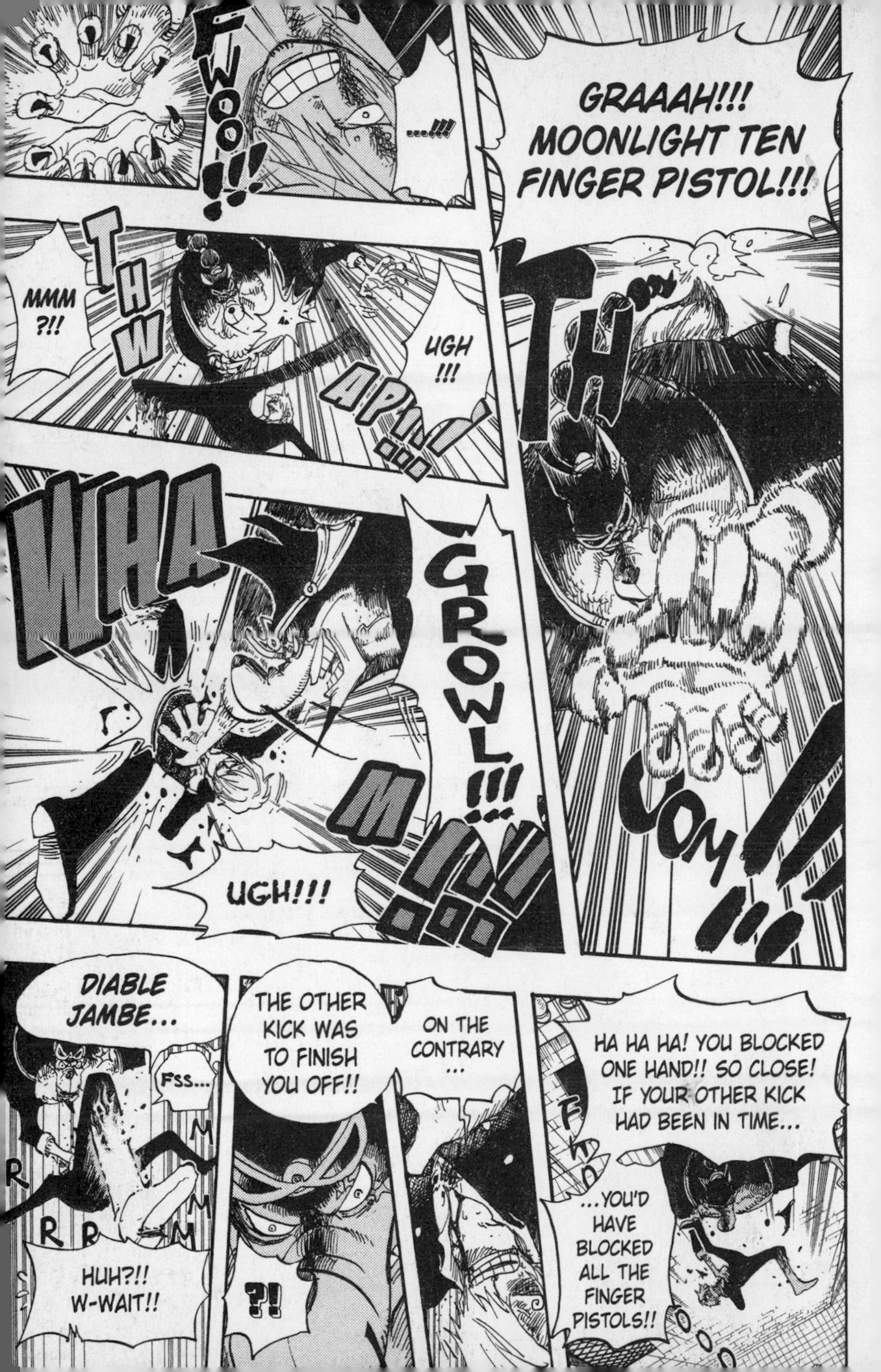
GRAAAH!!! MOONLIGHT TEN FINGER PISTOL!!!
THOOM!!
...!!!
FWOO!!!
MMM ?!!
THWAP!!!
UGH !!!
GROWL!!!
WHAM!!!
UGH!!!
HA HA HA! YOU BLOCKED ONE HAND!! SO CLOSE! IF YOUR OTHER KICK HAD BEEN IN TIME...
...YOU'D HAVE BLOCKED ALL THE FINGER PISTOLS!!
ON THE CONTRARY ...
THE OTHER KICK WAS TO FINISH YOU OFF!!
?!
DIABLE JAMBE...
FSS...
MMM
RRR
HUH?!! W-WAIT!!

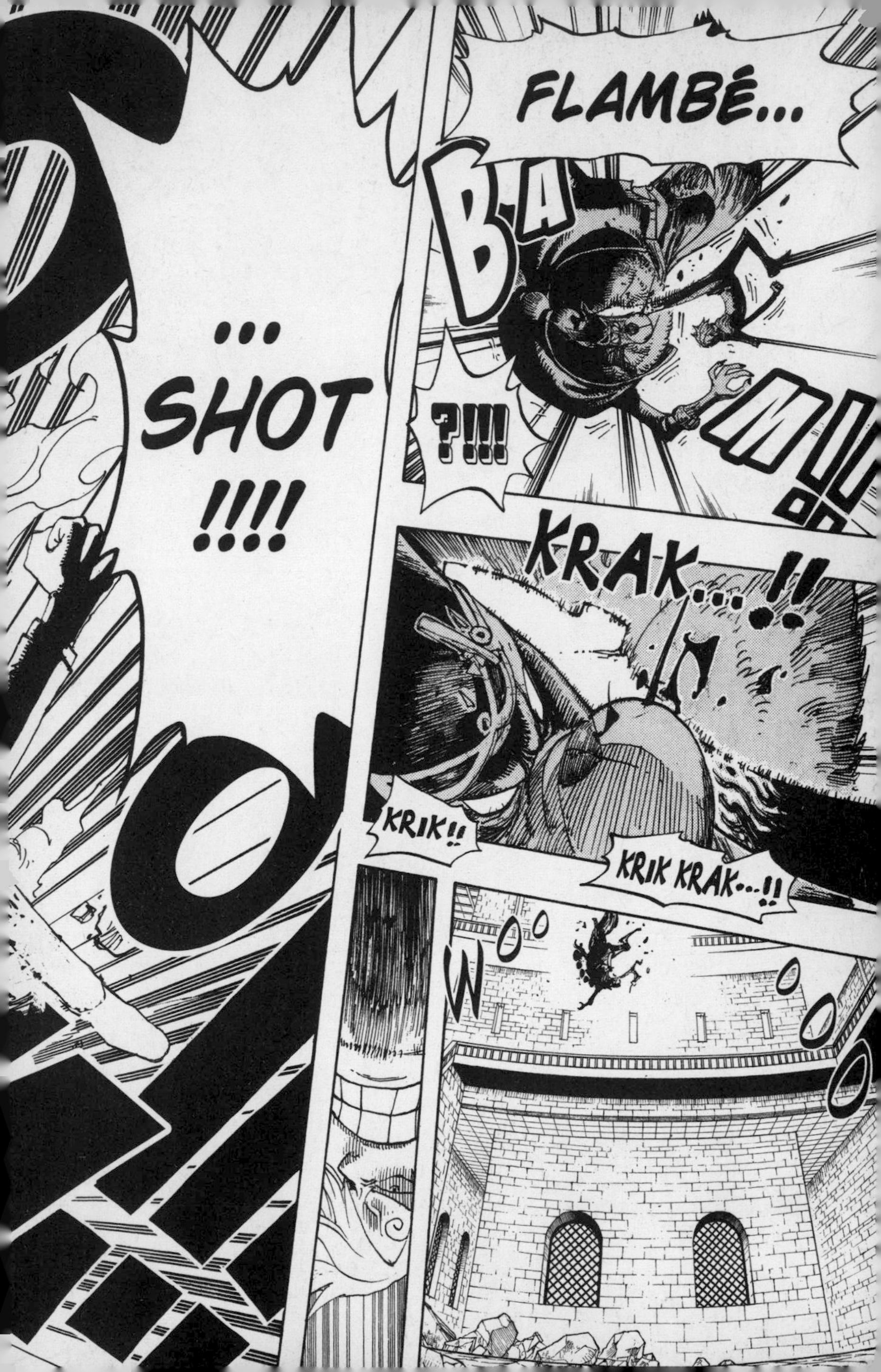

FLAMBÉ...
BAM
?!!!
KRAK...!!
KRIK!!
KRIK KRAK...!!
WOOOOO
...SHOT !!!!

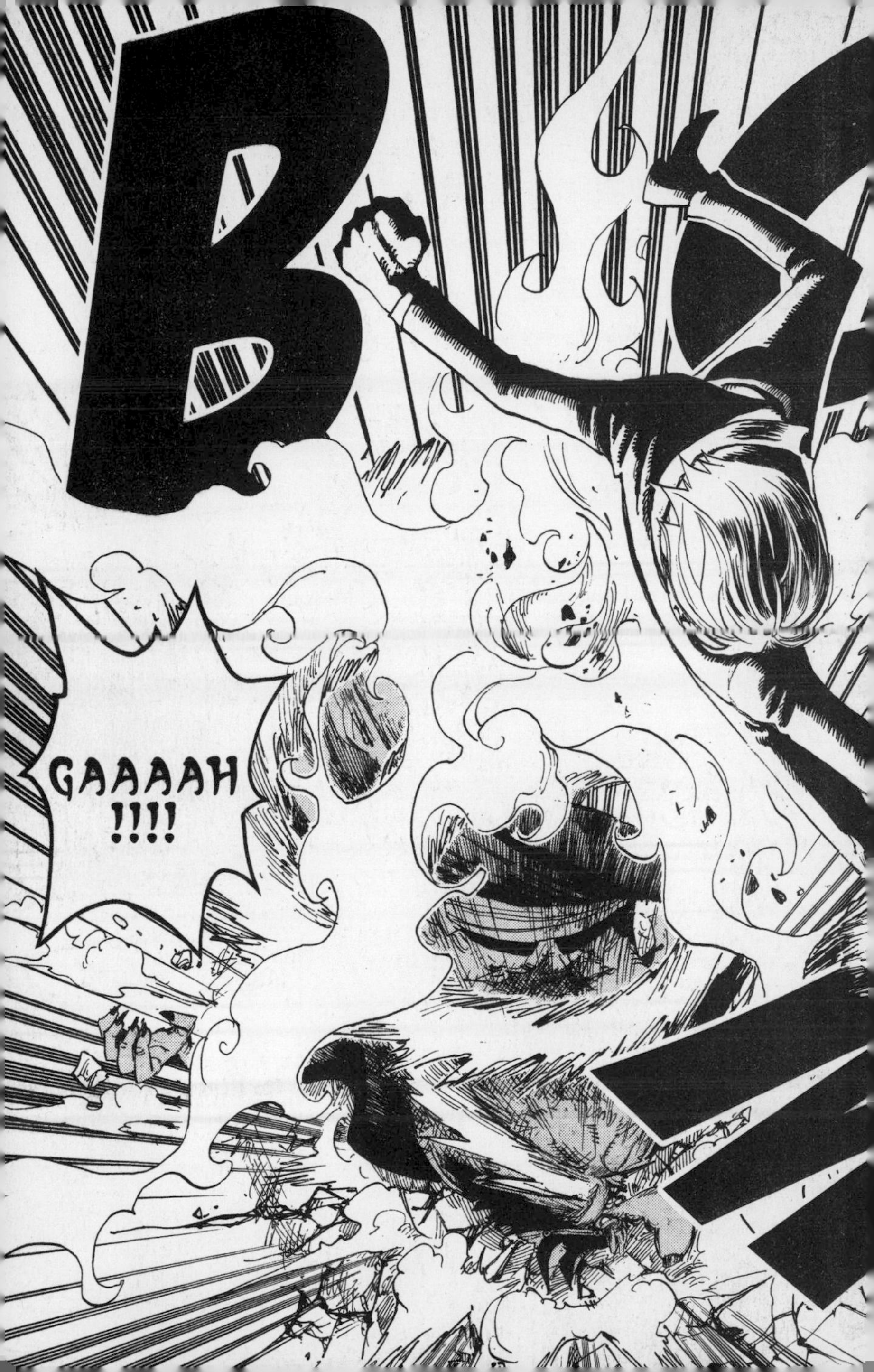
GAAAAH !!!!

Q: I'll get right to it. The reader's corner, S (Set) B (Birthdays) S (Simply) is almost becoming a regular feature, so I'd like to lay down some birthdays for the Water Seven and CP9 story arcs.

• Iceberg	アイスバーグ 1/3	Ice	(アイス)…イ＝1, ス＝3
• Franky	フランキ 3/9	Cyborg	(サイボーグ)…サ＝3, グ＝9
• Paulie	パウリ 7/8	Rope	(縄, なわ)…な＝7, わ＝8
• Rob Lucci	ルブ•ルッチ 6/2	Rob	(ロブ)…ロ＝6, ぶ＝2
• Kaku	カク 8/7	Nose	(はな)…は＝8, な＝7
• Kalifa	カリファ 4/23	Secretary's Day	

That should be all right, shouldn't it? ★ Good luck with your work, Sensei!!

--Exam Student

Parts of each character's name can suggest numbers in Japanese. The reader made up the birthdays by combining the associated numbers.--Ed.

A: Oh... I see... So that's how it is... Hmm... Is there such a thing as Secretary's Day? Hmm... Yeah... Um... Okay, let's go with those dates.

Q: I've got a question! If the Kami Eneru came down to the Blue Sea, how much would the reward for him be? Also, what would happen to the Blue Sea?

--Gorozolo

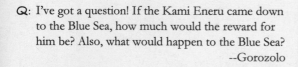

A: I see. Interesting question. The reward would probably go over 500 million, considering how troublesome Eneru is. Luffy lucked out because he's rubber. But like Luffy said, there are other guys out there on the Blue Sea who surpass him in strength. Eneru can't be No. 1!

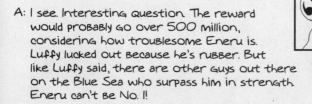

Chapter 416:
ZOLO VS. KAKU

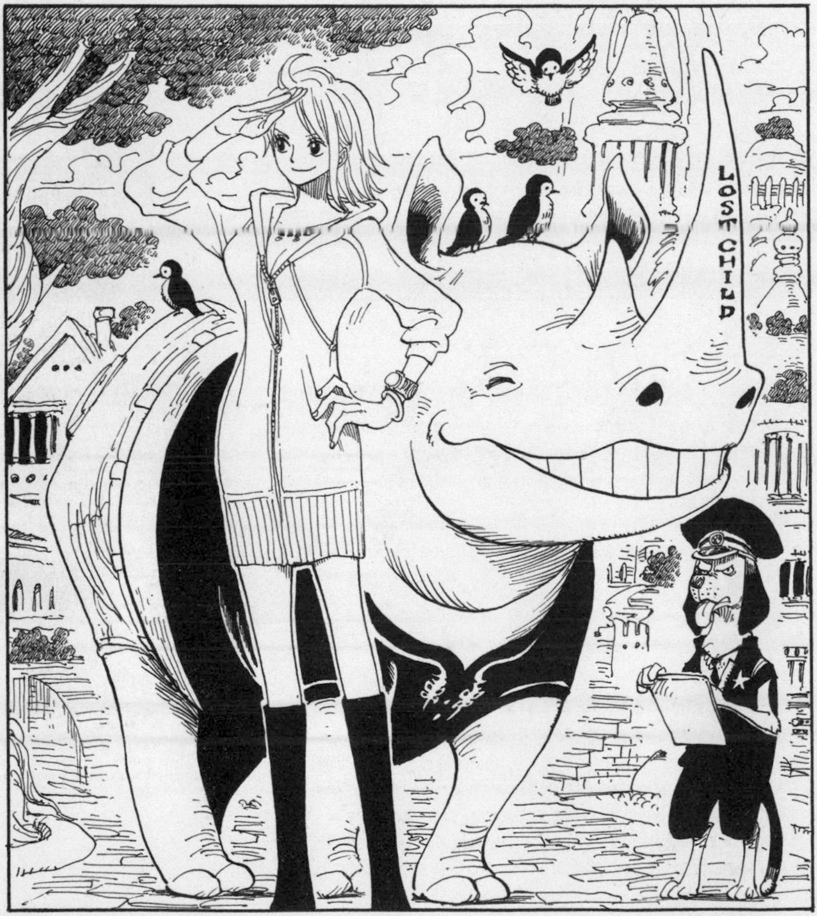
LOST CHILD

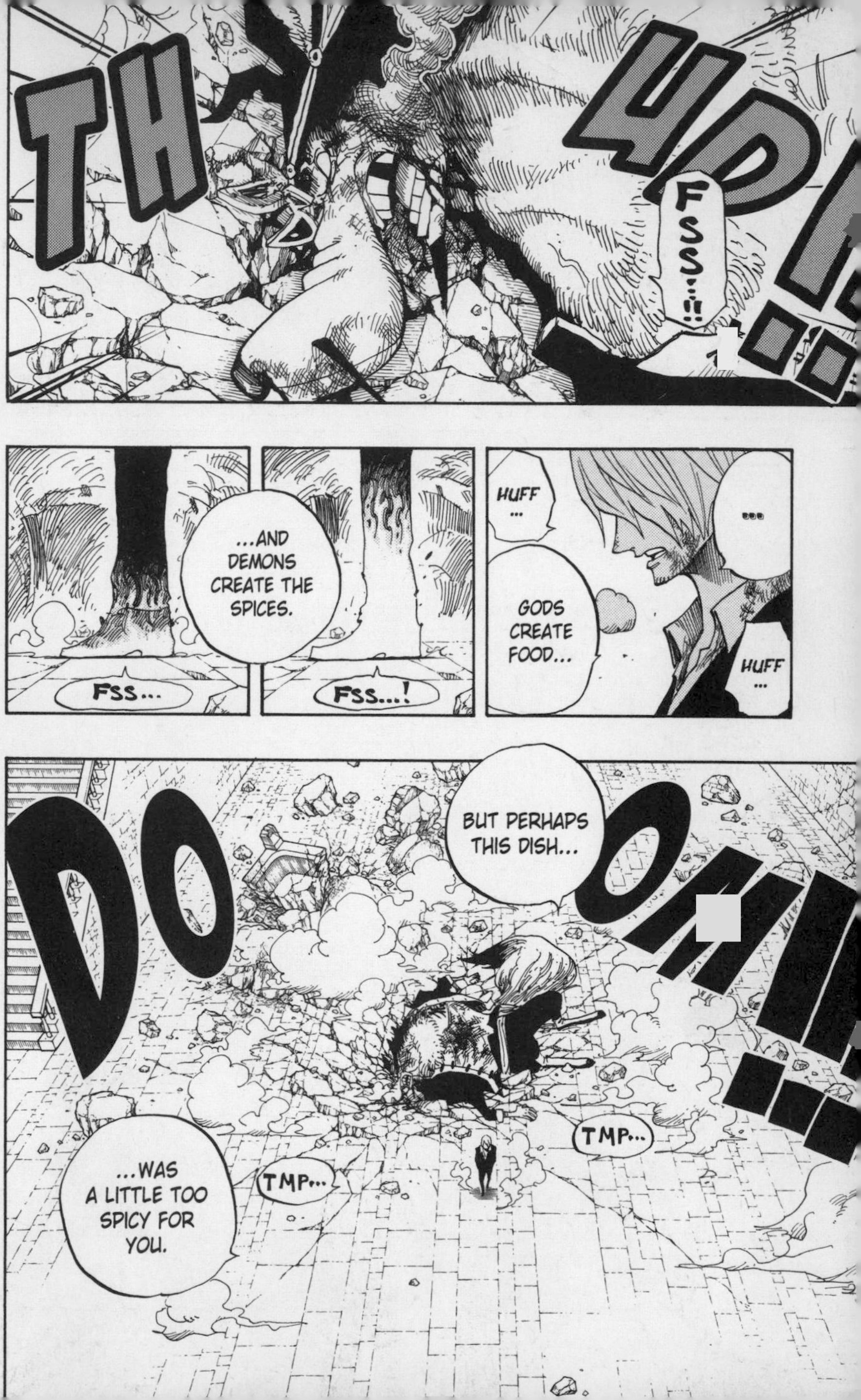
THUD!!
FSS...!!
...
HUFF...
GODS CREATE FOOD...
HUFF...
...AND DEMONS CREATE THE SPICES.
FSS...!
FSS...
DOOM!!!!
BUT PERHAPS THIS DISH...
TMP...
TMP...
...WAS A LITTLE TOO SPICY FOR YOU.

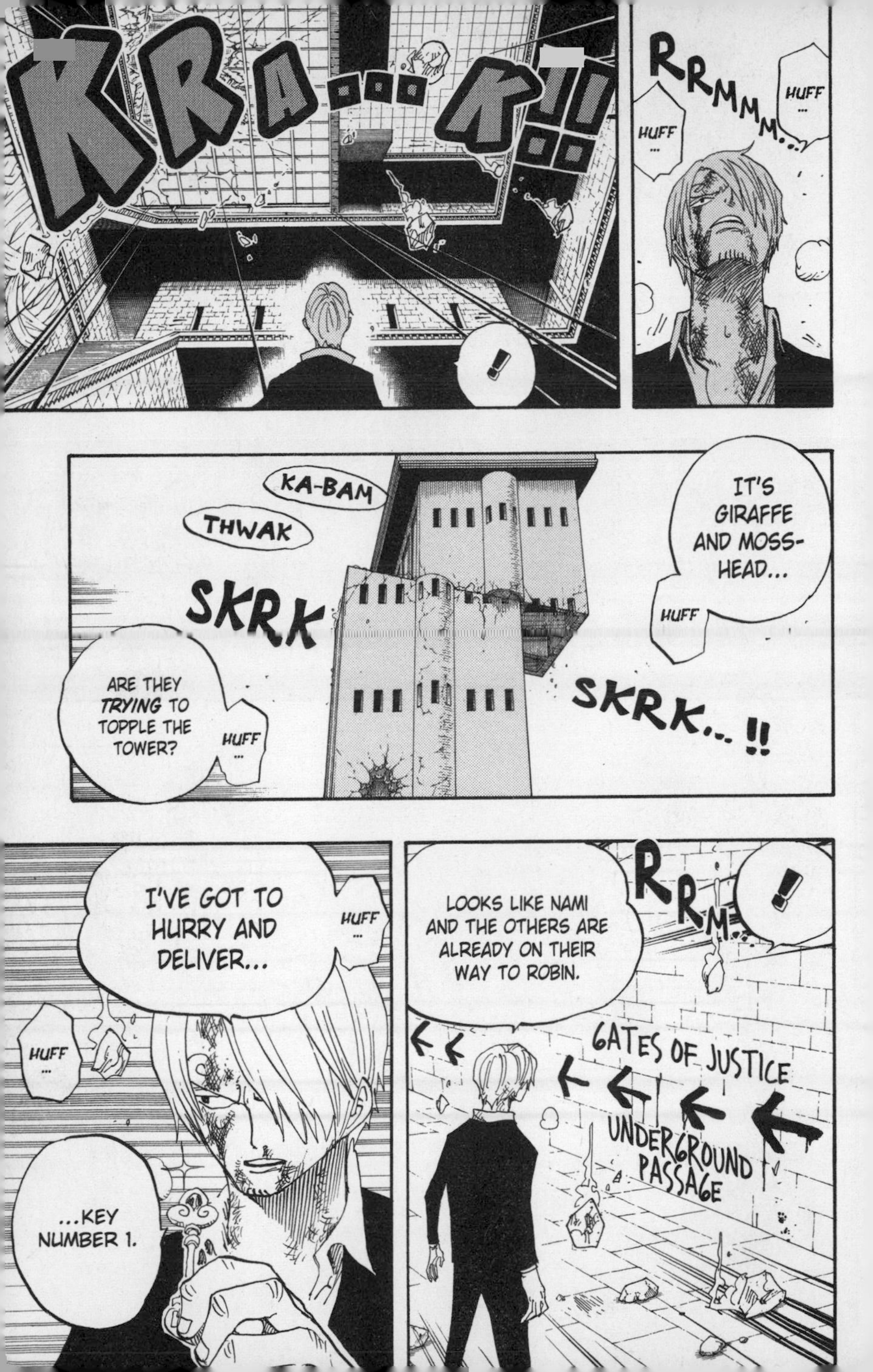
RRMMM...
HUFF...
HUFF...
KRA...K!!
!
IT'S GIRAFFE AND MOSS-HEAD...
HUFF
SKRK...!!
KA-BAM
THWAK
SKRK
ARE THEY *TRYING* TO TOPPLE THE TOWER?
HUFF...
RRM...
!
LOOKS LIKE NAMI AND THE OTHERS ARE ALREADY ON THEIR WAY TO ROBIN.
GATES OF JUSTICE
UNDERGROUND PASSAGE
HUFF...
I'VE GOT TO HURRY AND DELIVER...
HUFF...
...KEY NUMBER 1.

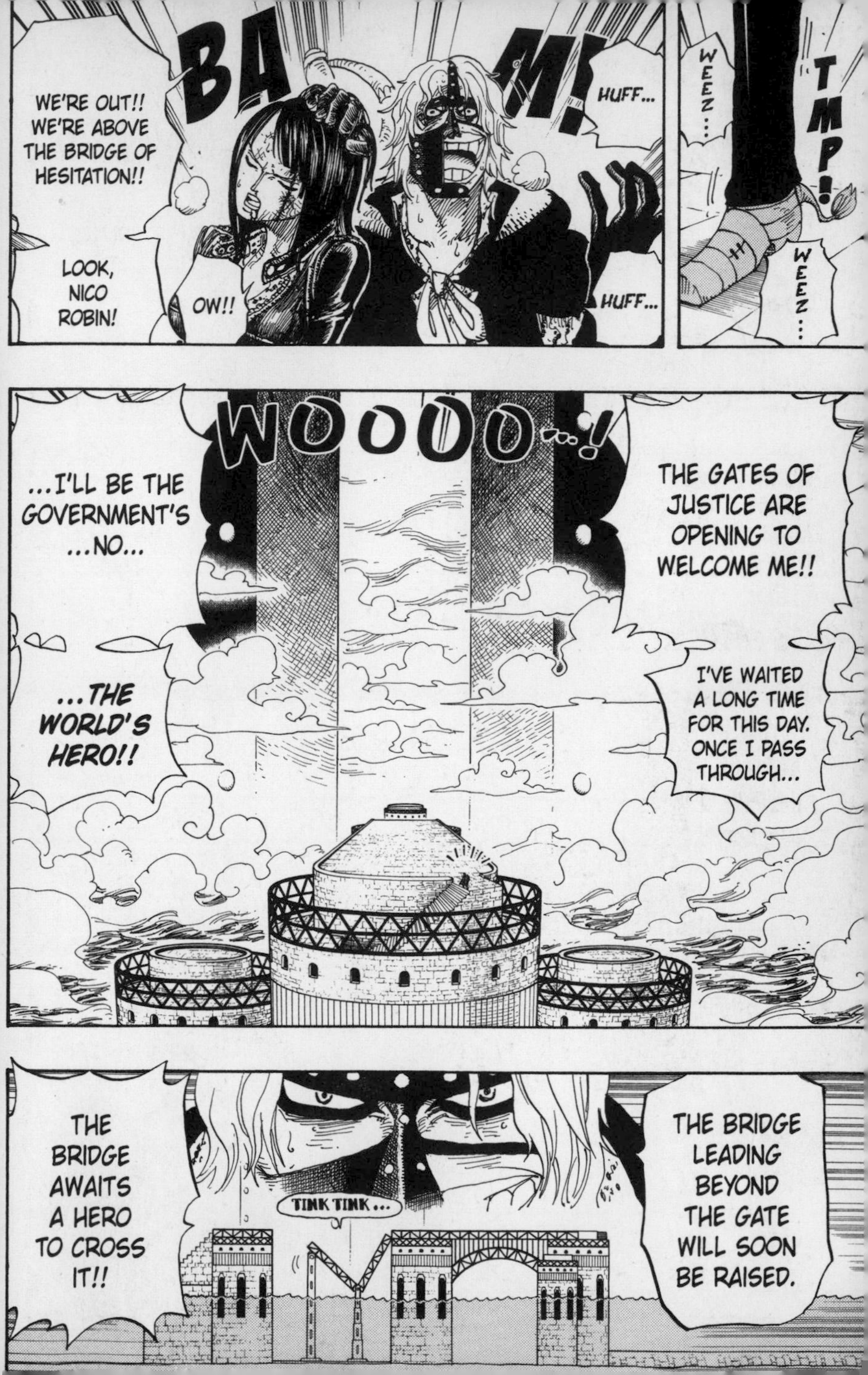
WEEZ...
TMP!
WEEZ...
HUFF...
BAM!
WE'RE OUT!! WE'RE ABOVE THE BRIDGE OF HESITATION!!
HUFF...
OW!!
LOOK, NICO ROBIN!
WOOOO...!
THE GATES OF JUSTICE ARE OPENING TO WELCOME ME!!
I'VE WAITED A LONG TIME FOR THIS DAY. ONCE I PASS THROUGH...
...I'LL BE THE GOVERNMENT'S ...NO...
...THE WORLD'S HERO!!
THE BRIDGE LEADING BEYOND THE GATE WILL SOON BE RAISED.
TINK TINK...
THE BRIDGE AWAITS A HERO TO CROSS IT!!

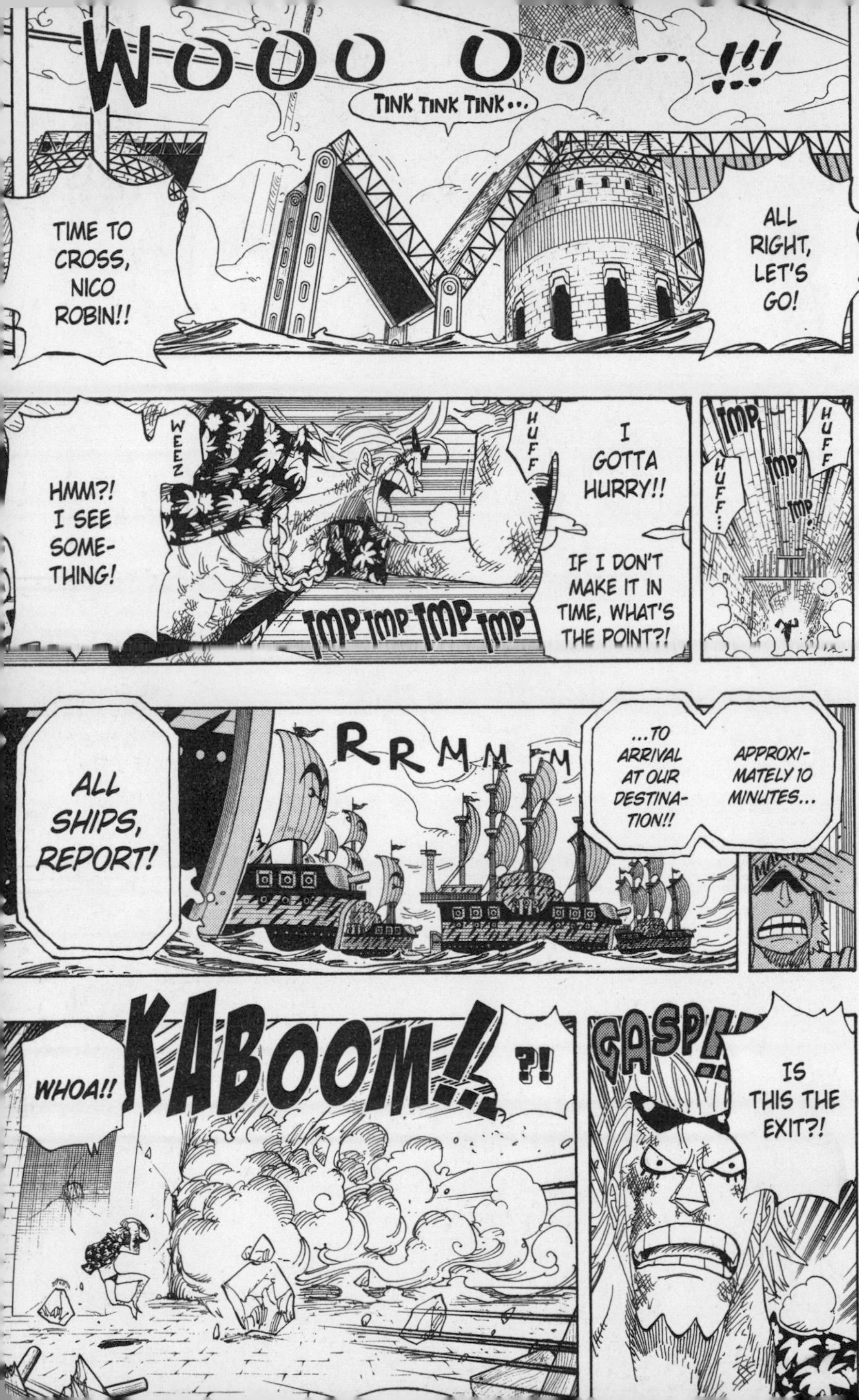
WOOOO OO...!!!
TINK TINK TINK...
ALL RIGHT, LET'S GO!
TIME TO CROSS, NICO ROBIN!!
TMP
HUFF
HUFF...
TMP
TMP
HUFF
I GOTTA HURRY!!
IF I DON'T MAKE IT IN TIME, WHAT'S THE POINT?!
WEEZ
HMM?! I SEE SOME-THING!
TMP TMP TMP TMP
APPROXI-MATELY 10 MINUTES...
...TO ARRIVAL AT OUR DESTINA-TION!!
RRMMMM
ALL SHIPS, REPORT!
GASP!!
IS THIS THE EXIT?!
?!
KABOOM!!
WHOA!!

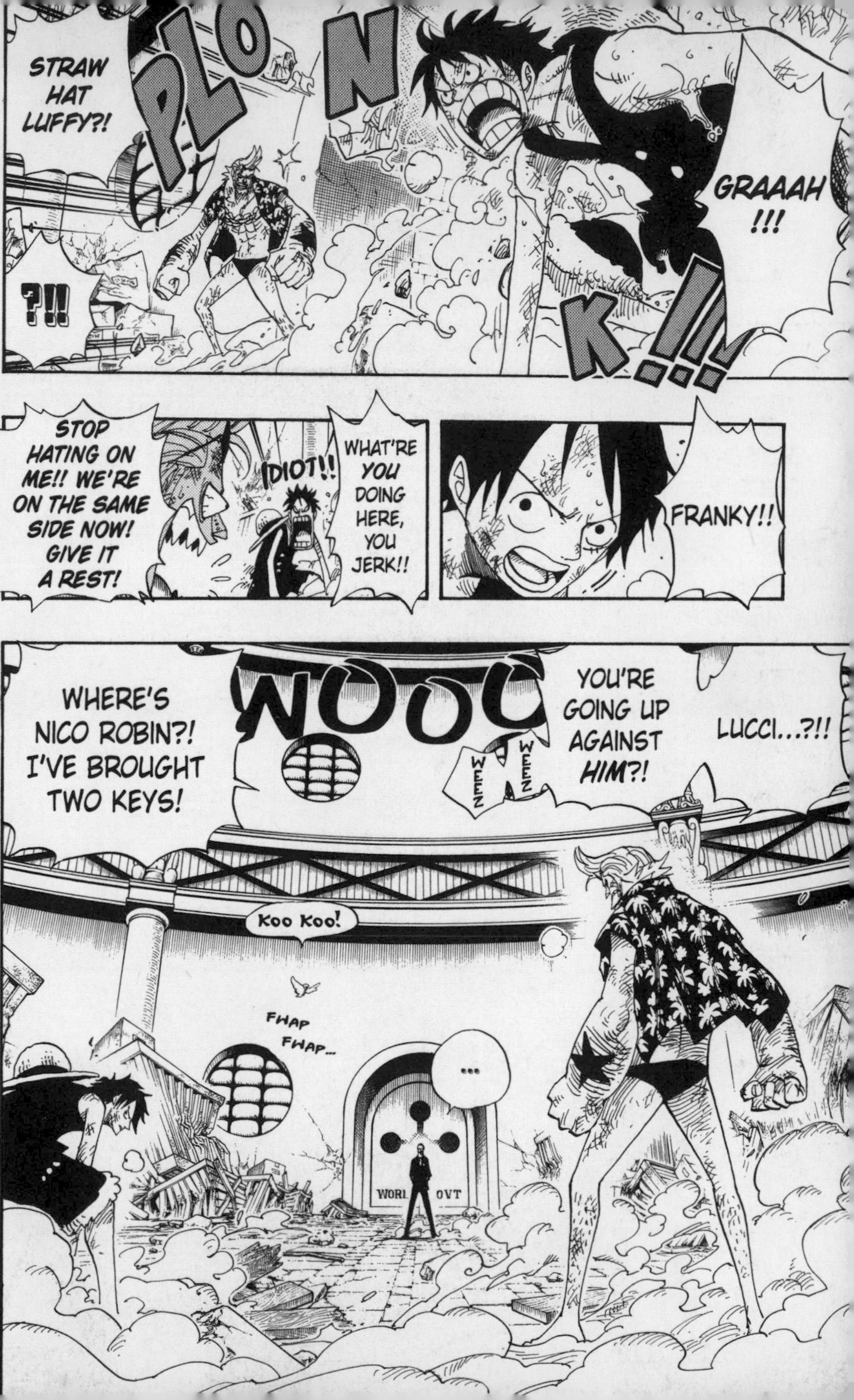
GRAAAH!!!
PLONK!!!
STRAW HAT LUFFY?!
?!!
FRANKY!!
WHAT'RE YOU DOING HERE, YOU JERK!!
IDIOT!!
STOP HATING ON ME!! WE'RE ON THE SAME SIDE NOW! GIVE IT A REST!
LUCCI...?!!
YOU'RE GOING UP AGAINST HIM?!
WEEZ
WEEZ
WOOO
WHERE'S NICO ROBIN?! I'VE BROUGHT TWO KEYS!
Koo Koo!
FWAP FWAP...
...

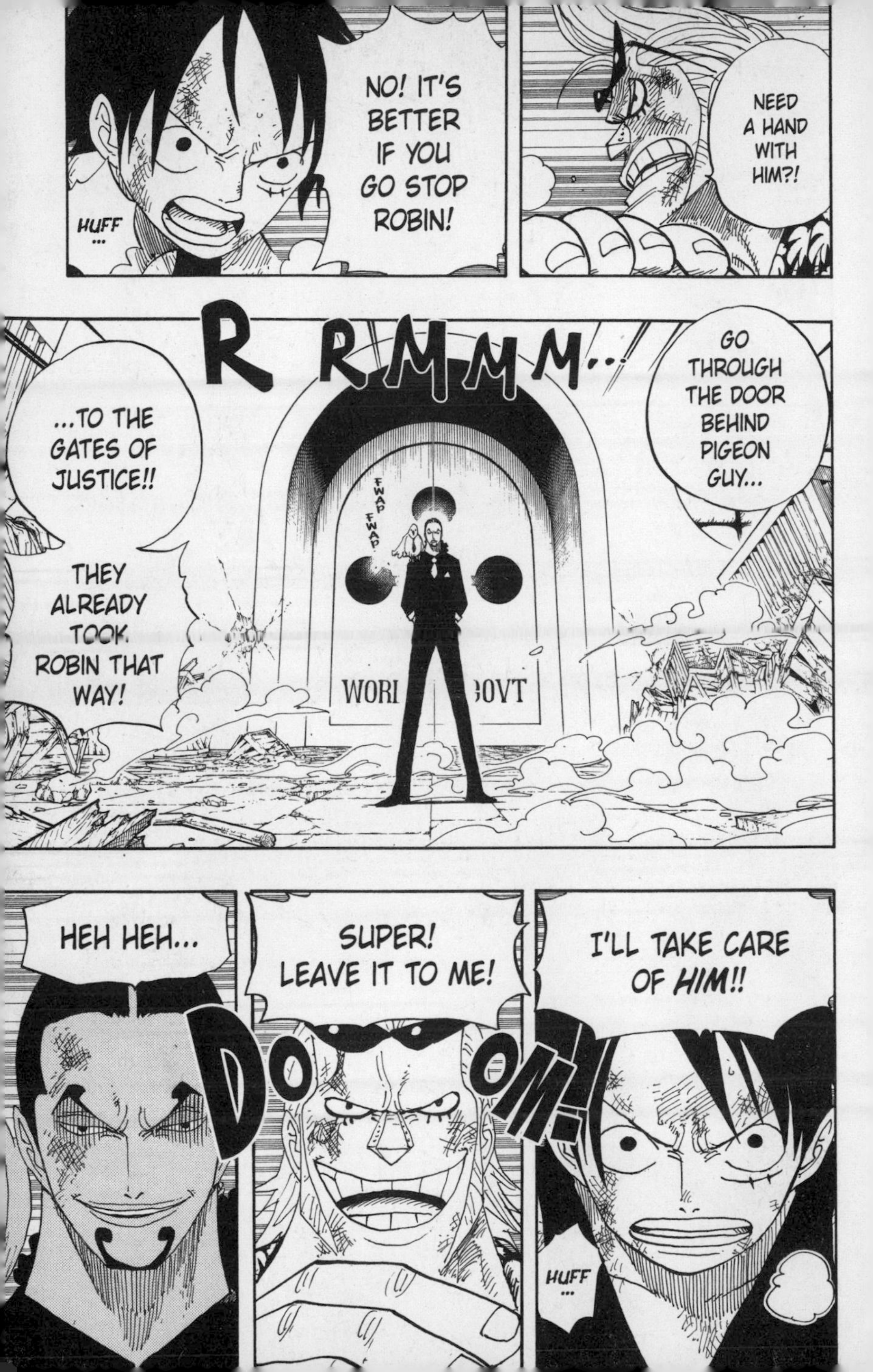
NEED A HAND WITH HIM?!
NO! IT'S BETTER IF YOU GO STOP ROBIN!
HUFF ...
RRMMM...
GO THROUGH THE DOOR BEHIND PIGEON GUY...
...TO THE GATES OF JUSTICE!!
THEY ALREADY TOOK ROBIN THAT WAY!
FWAP FWAP
I'LL TAKE CARE OF *HIM*!!
HUFF ...
DOOM!
SUPER! LEAVE IT TO ME!
HEH HEH...

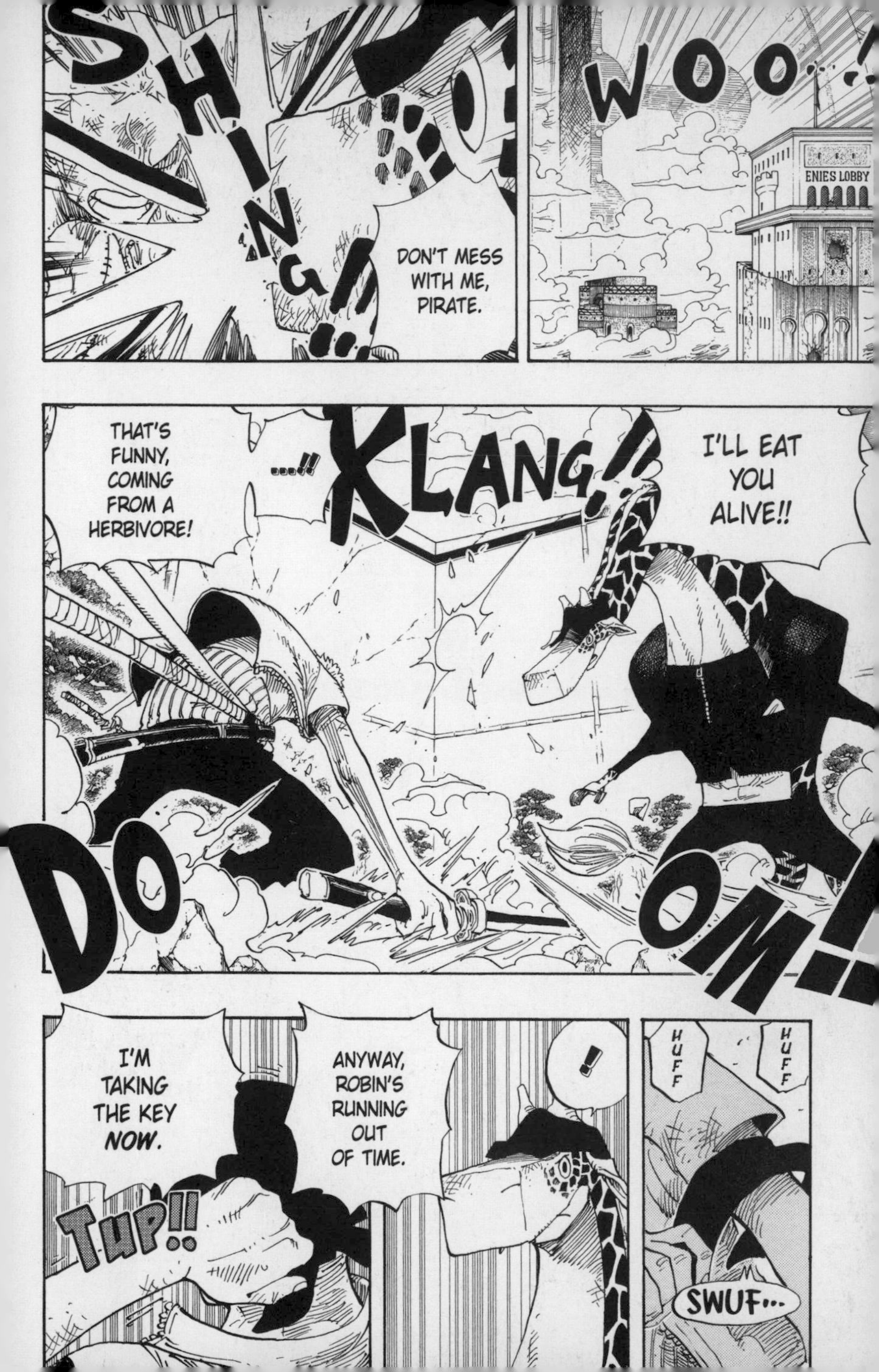
WOO
ENIES LOBBY
SHING
DON'T MESS WITH ME, PIRATE.
I'LL EAT YOU ALIVE!!
KLANG!!
...!!
THAT'S FUNNY, COMING FROM A HERBIVORE!
DOOM!!
HUFF
HUFF
SWUF...
!
ANYWAY, ROBIN'S RUNNING OUT OF TIME.
I'M TAKING THE KEY *NOW*.
TUP!!

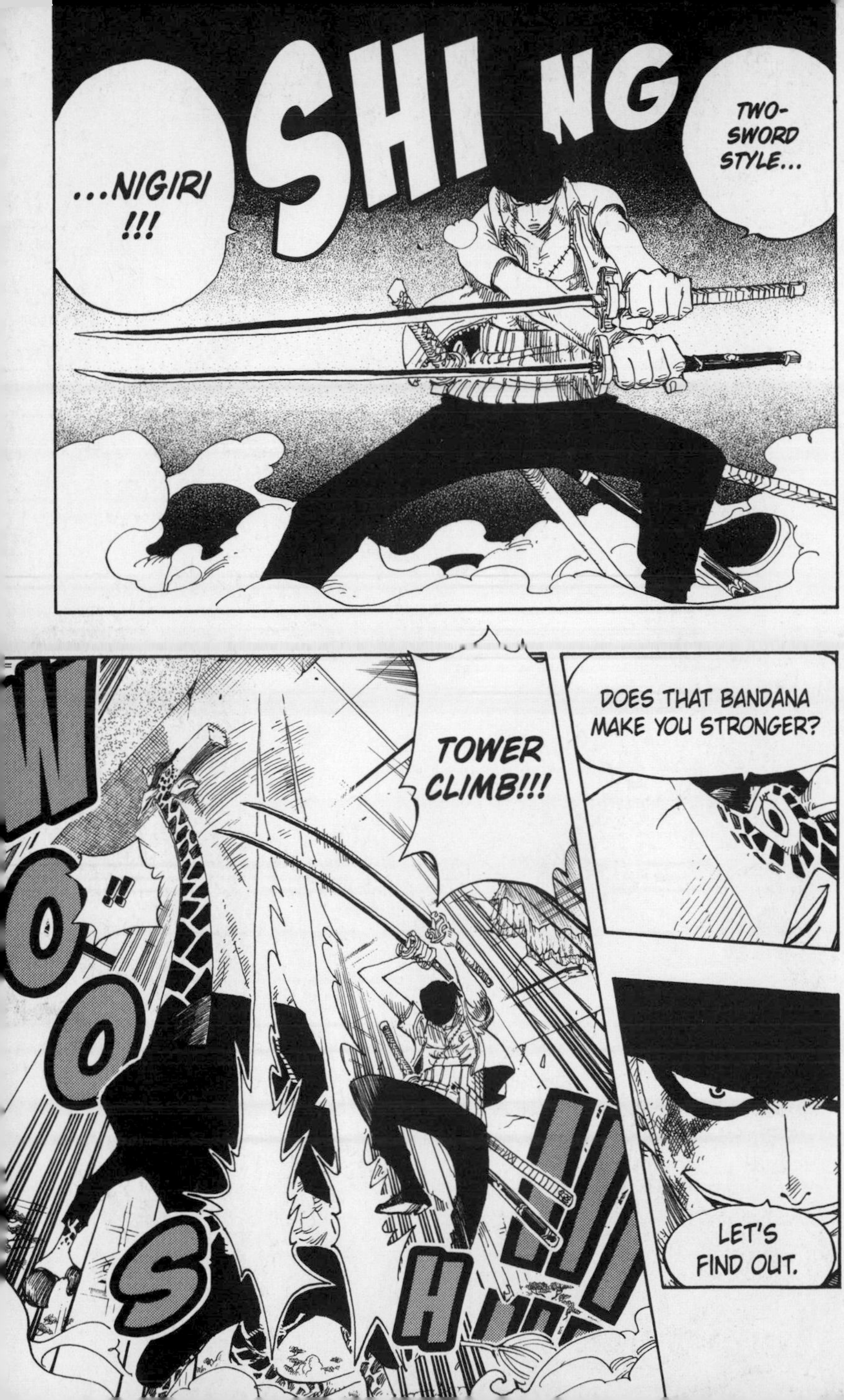
TWO-SWORD STYLE...
SHING
...NIGIRI !!!
DOES THAT BANDANA MAKE YOU STRONGER?
LET'S FIND OUT.
TOWER CLIMB!!!
!!
WOOSH

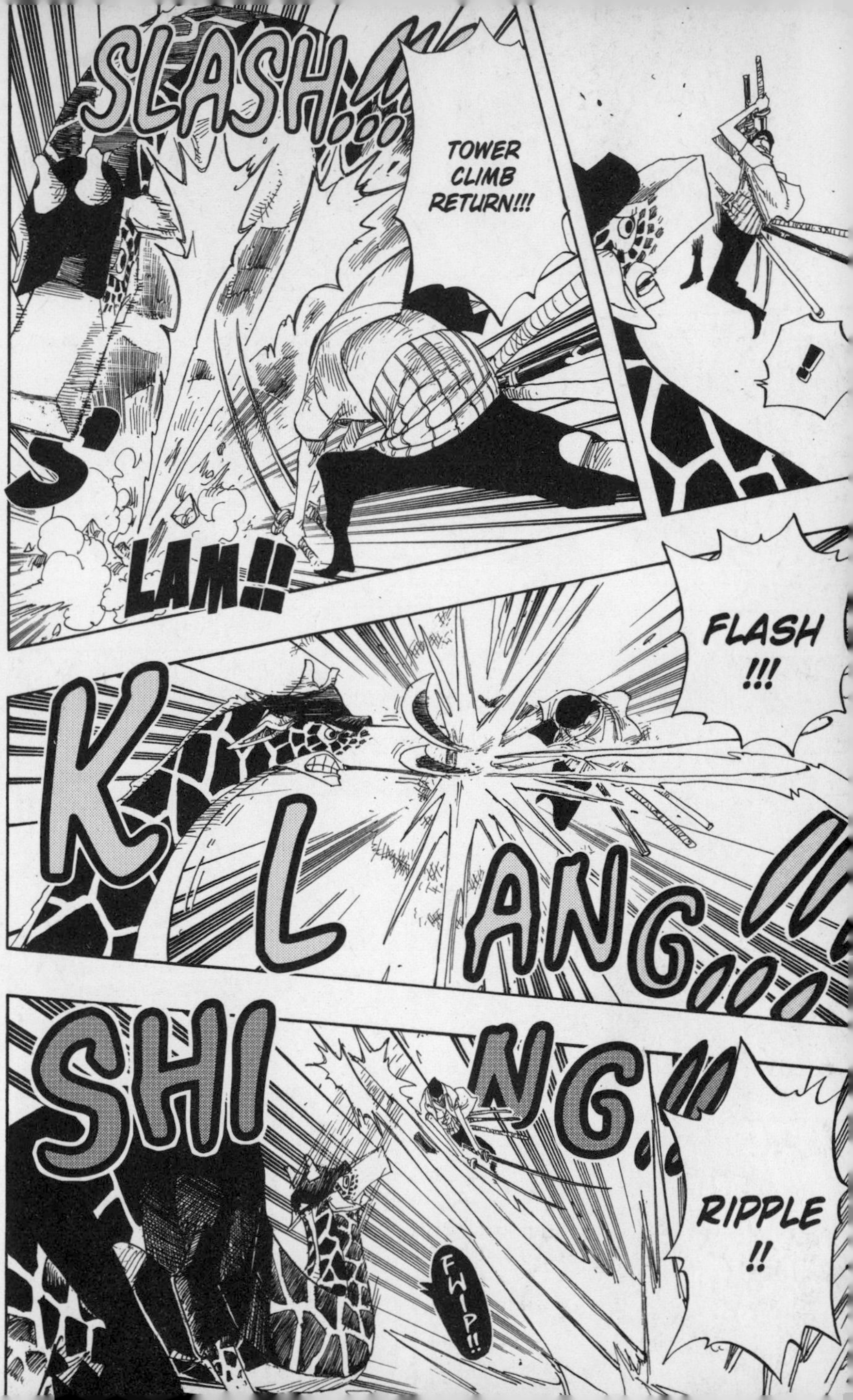
!
TOWER CLIMB RETURN!!!
SLASH...!!
LAM!!
FLASH !!!
KLANG...!!
RIPPLE !!
SHING...!!
FWIP!!

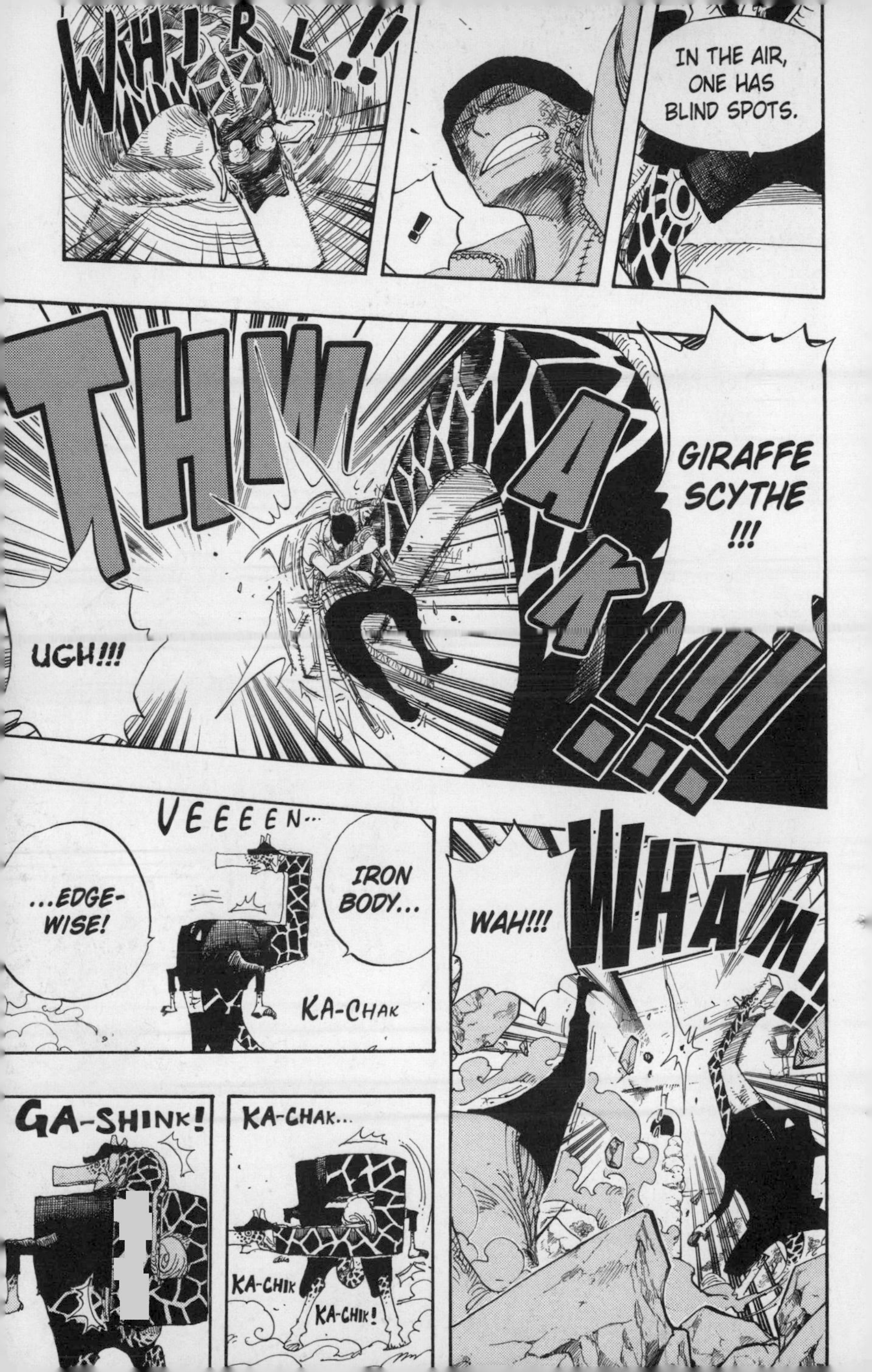
IN THE AIR, ONE HAS BLIND SPOTS.
!
WHIRL!!
GIRAFFE SCYTHE !!!
THWAK!!!!
UGH!!!
WHAM!!
WAH!!!
VEEEEN...
IRON BODY...
...EDGE-WISE!
KA-CHAK
KA-CHAK...
KA-CHIK
KA-CHIK!
GA-SHINK!

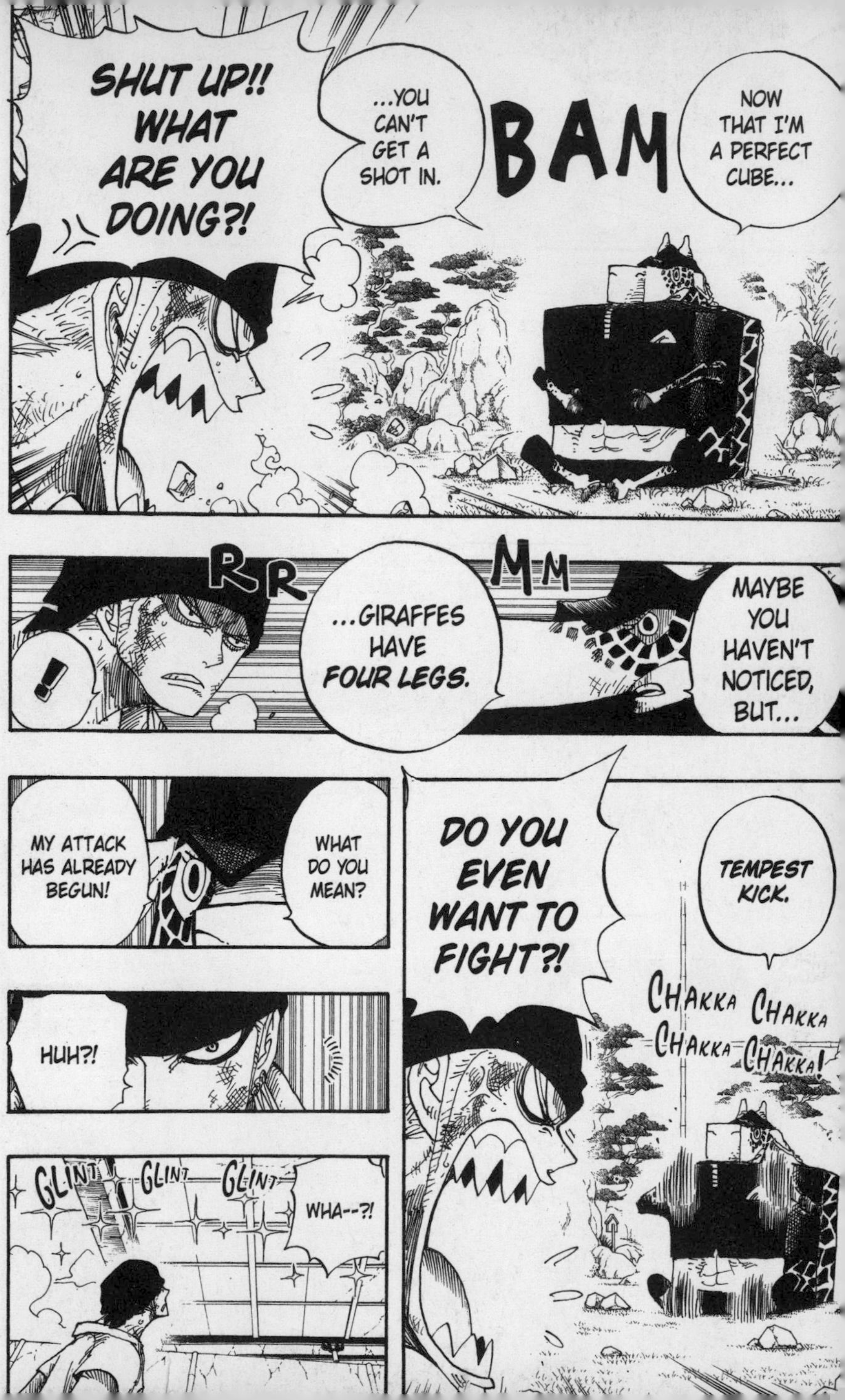
NOW THAT I'M A PERFECT CUBE...
BAM
...YOU CAN'T GET A SHOT IN.
SHUT UP!! WHAT ARE YOU DOING?!
MAYBE YOU HAVEN'T NOTICED, BUT...
MM
...GIRAFFES HAVE FOUR LEGS.
RR
!
TEMPEST KICK.
DO YOU EVEN WANT TO FIGHT?!
CHAKKA CHAKKA
CHAKKA CHAKKA!
WHAT DO YOU MEAN?
MY ATTACK HAS ALREADY BEGUN!
HUH?!
WHA--?!
GLINT GLINT GLINT

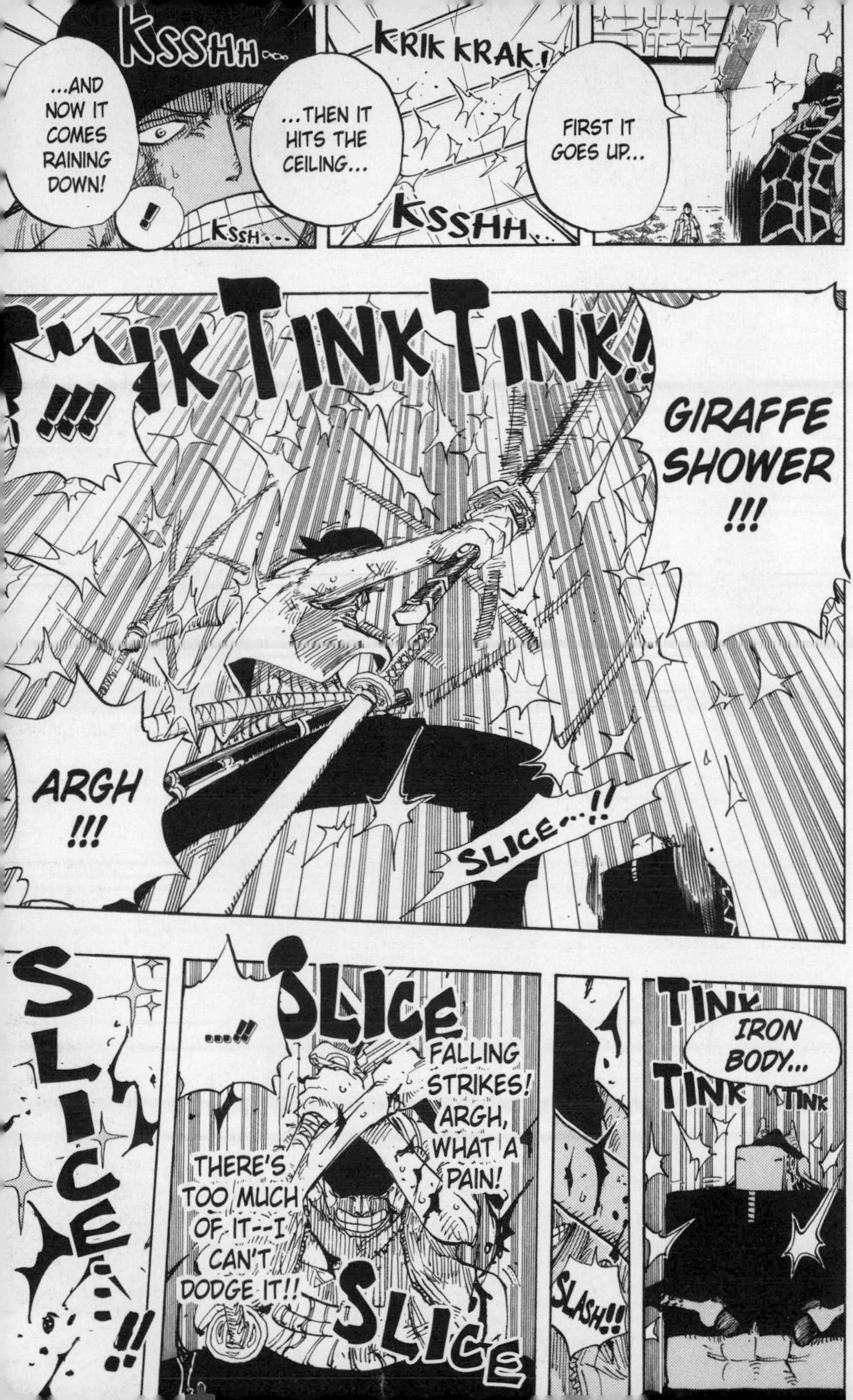
FIRST IT GOES UP...
KRIK KRAK!
...THEN IT HITS THE CEILING...
KSSHH...
KSSHH...
...AND NOW IT COMES RAINING DOWN!
!
KSSH...
KTINKTINK!!
!!!
GIRAFFE SHOWER !!!
ARGH !!!
SLICE...!!
TINK TINK
IRON BODY...
TINK
SLASH!!
SLICE
FALLING STRIKES! ARGH, WHAT A PAIN!
...!!
THERE'S TOO MUCH OF IT--I CAN'T DODGE IT!!
SLICE
SLICE
SLICE...!!

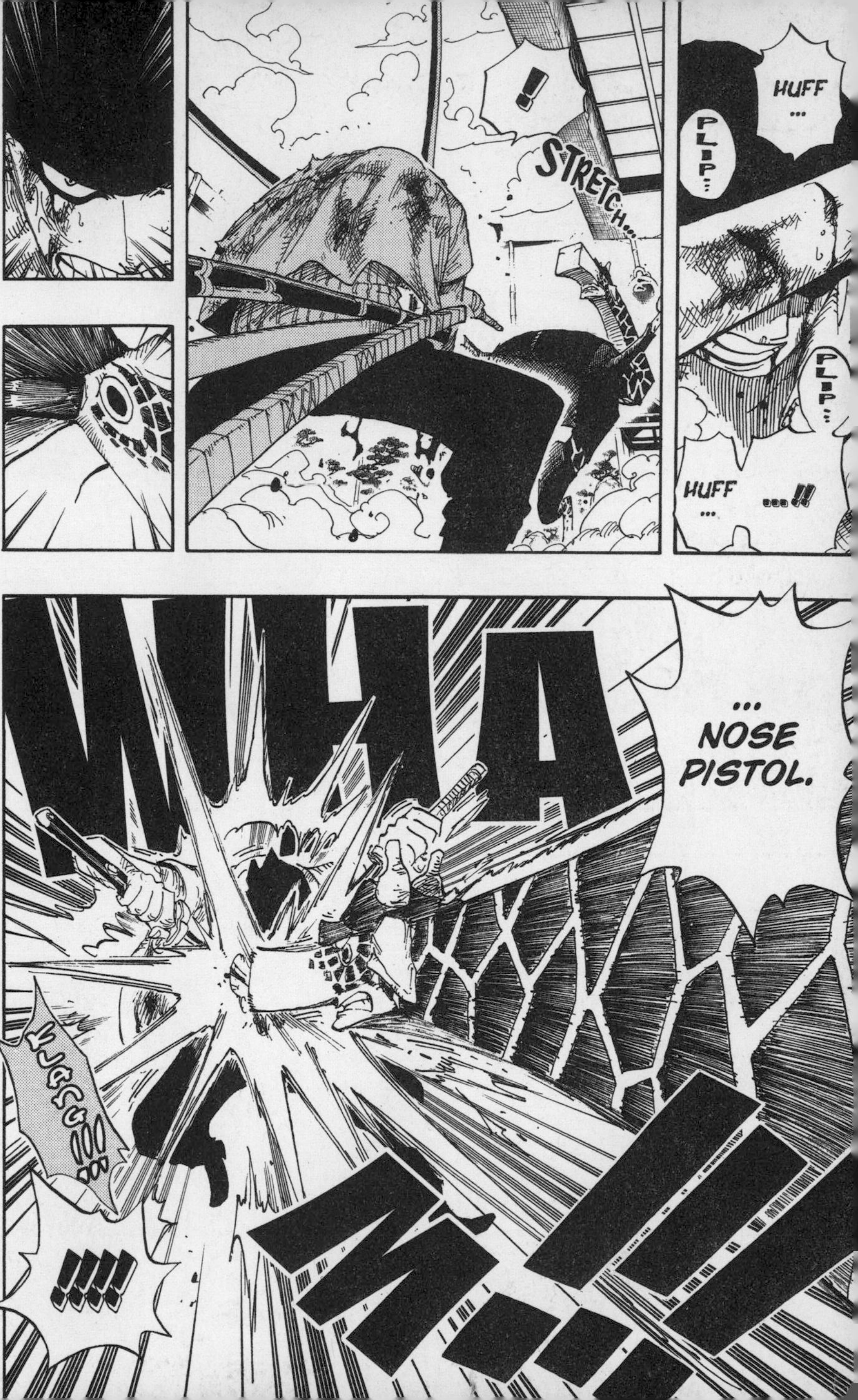
HUFF ...
PLIP...
PLIP...
HUFF ...
...!!
!
STRETCH...
... NOSE PISTOL.
WHAM...!!!
!!!!

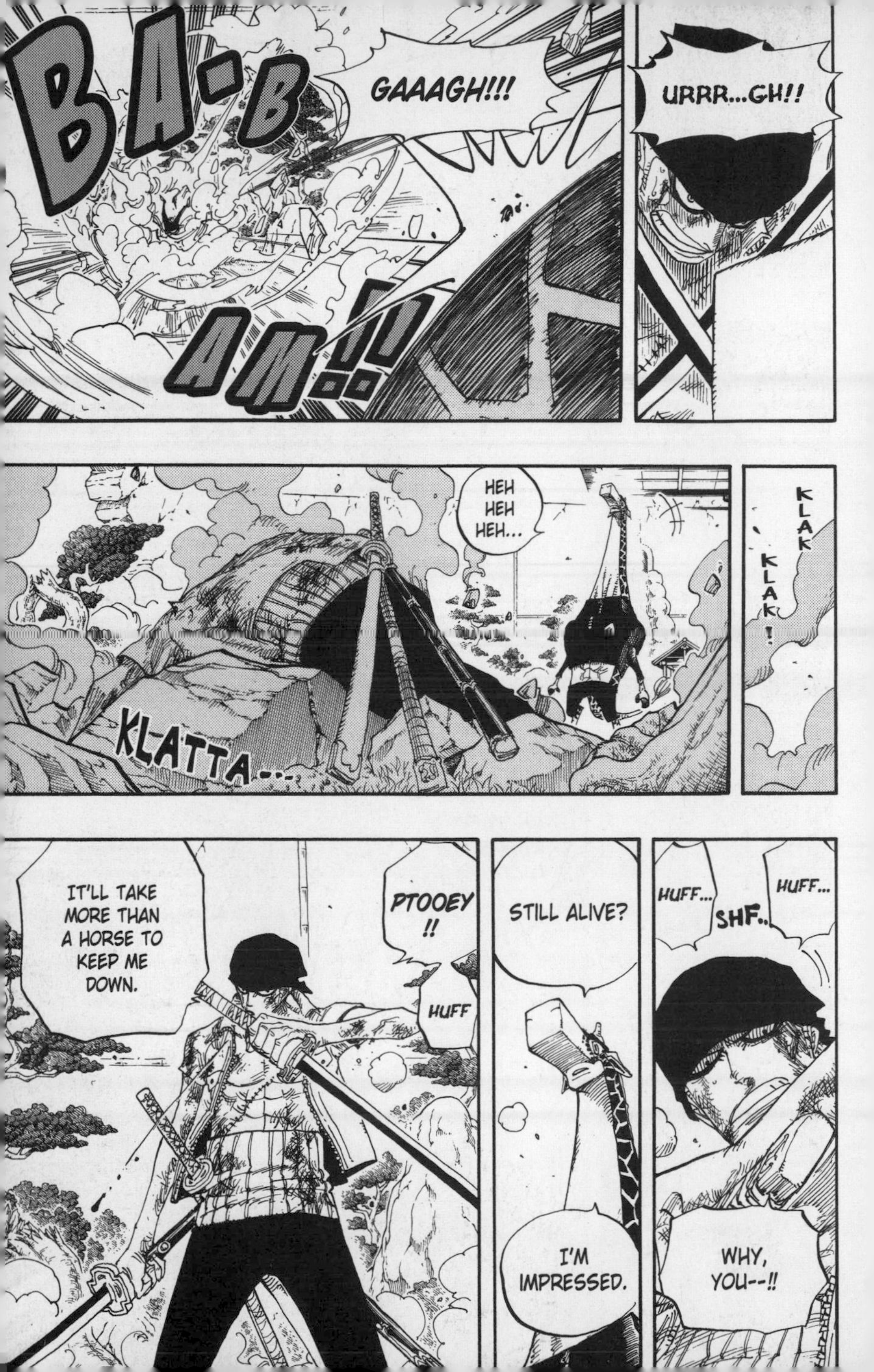
URRR...GH!!
GAAAGH!!!
BA-B
AM!!
KLAK KLAK!
HEH HEH HEH...
KLATTA...
HUFF...
HUFF...
SHF..
WHY, YOU--!!
STILL ALIVE?
I'M IMPRESSED.
PTOOEY!!
HUFF
IT'LL TAKE MORE THAN A HORSE TO KEEP ME DOWN.

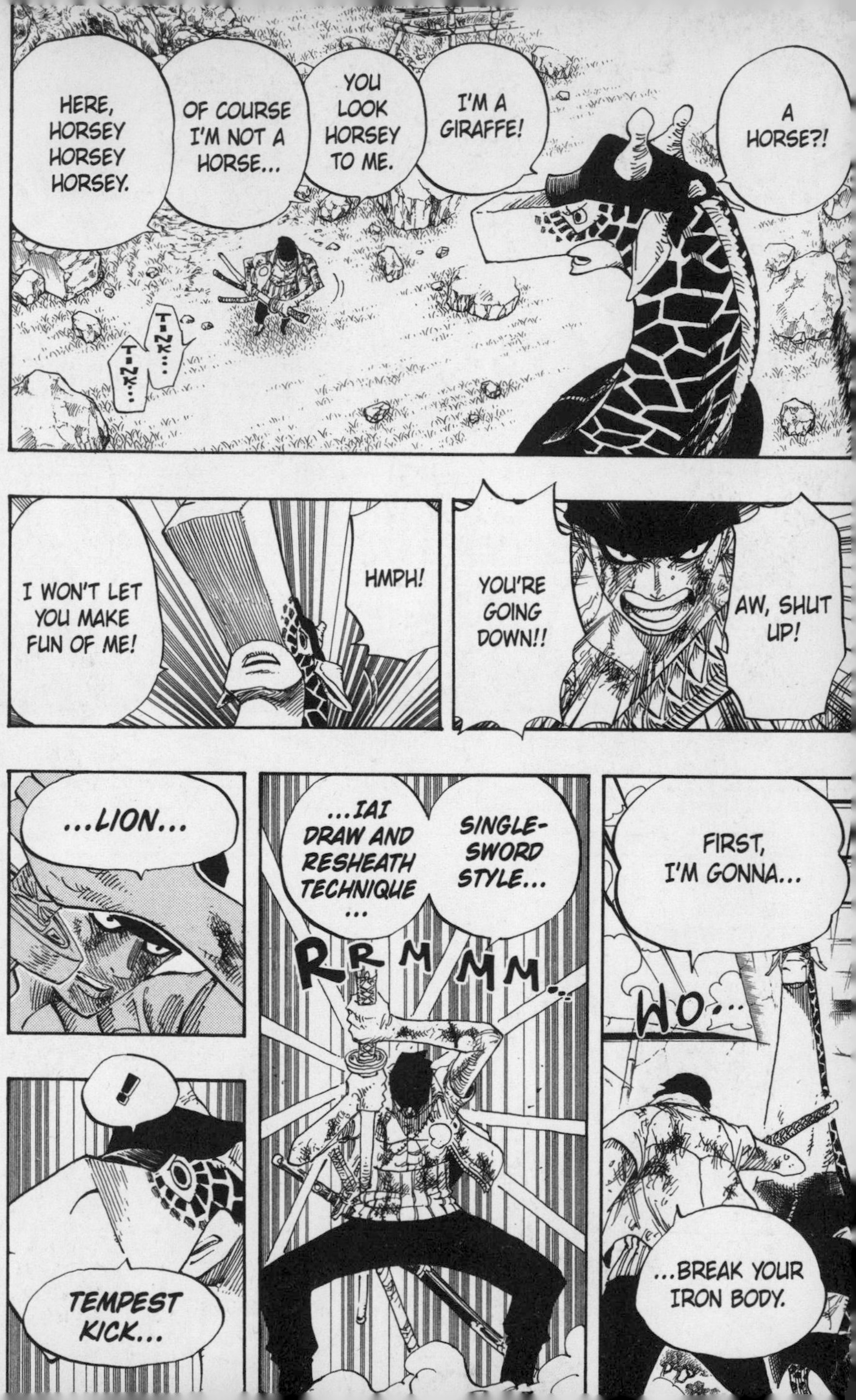
A HORSE?!
I'M A GIRAFFE!
YOU LOOK HORSEY TO ME.
OF COURSE I'M NOT A HORSE...
HERE, HORSEY HORSEY HORSEY.
TINK...
TINK...
AW, SHUT UP!
YOU'RE GOING DOWN!!
HMPH!
I WON'T LET YOU MAKE FUN OF ME!
FIRST, I'M GONNA...
WO...
...BREAK YOUR IRON BODY.
SINGLE-SWORD STYLE...
...IAI DRAW AND RESHEATH TECHNIQUE...
RRMMMM..
...LION...
!
TEMPEST KICK...

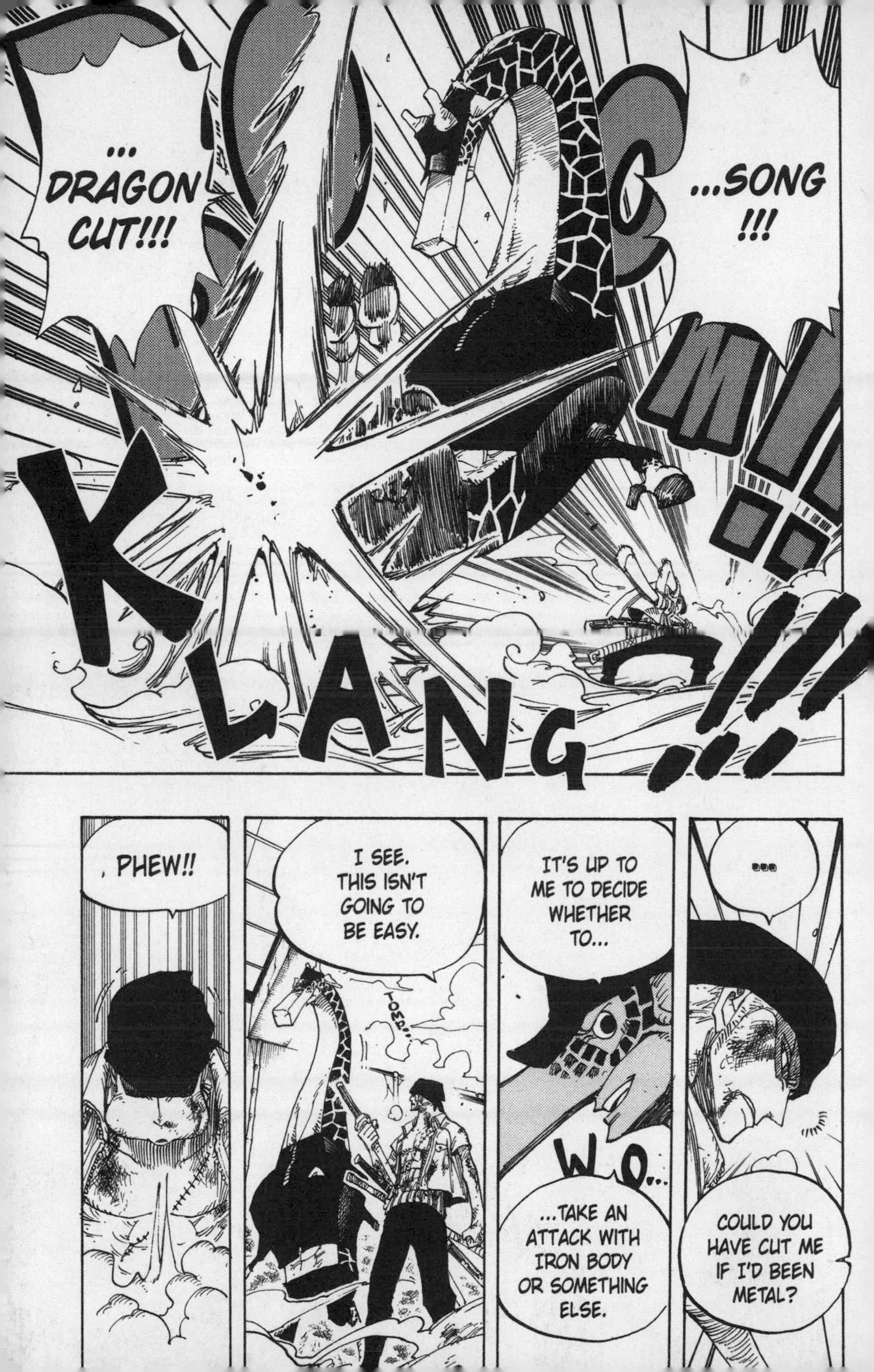
...SONG !!!
... DRAGON CUT!!!
KLANG!!!
...
COULD YOU HAVE CUT ME IF I'D BEEN METAL?
IT'S UP TO ME TO DECIDE WHETHER TO...
WO...
...TAKE AN ATTACK WITH IRON BODY OR SOMETHING ELSE.
I SEE. THIS ISN'T GOING TO BE EASY.
TOMP...
PHEW!!

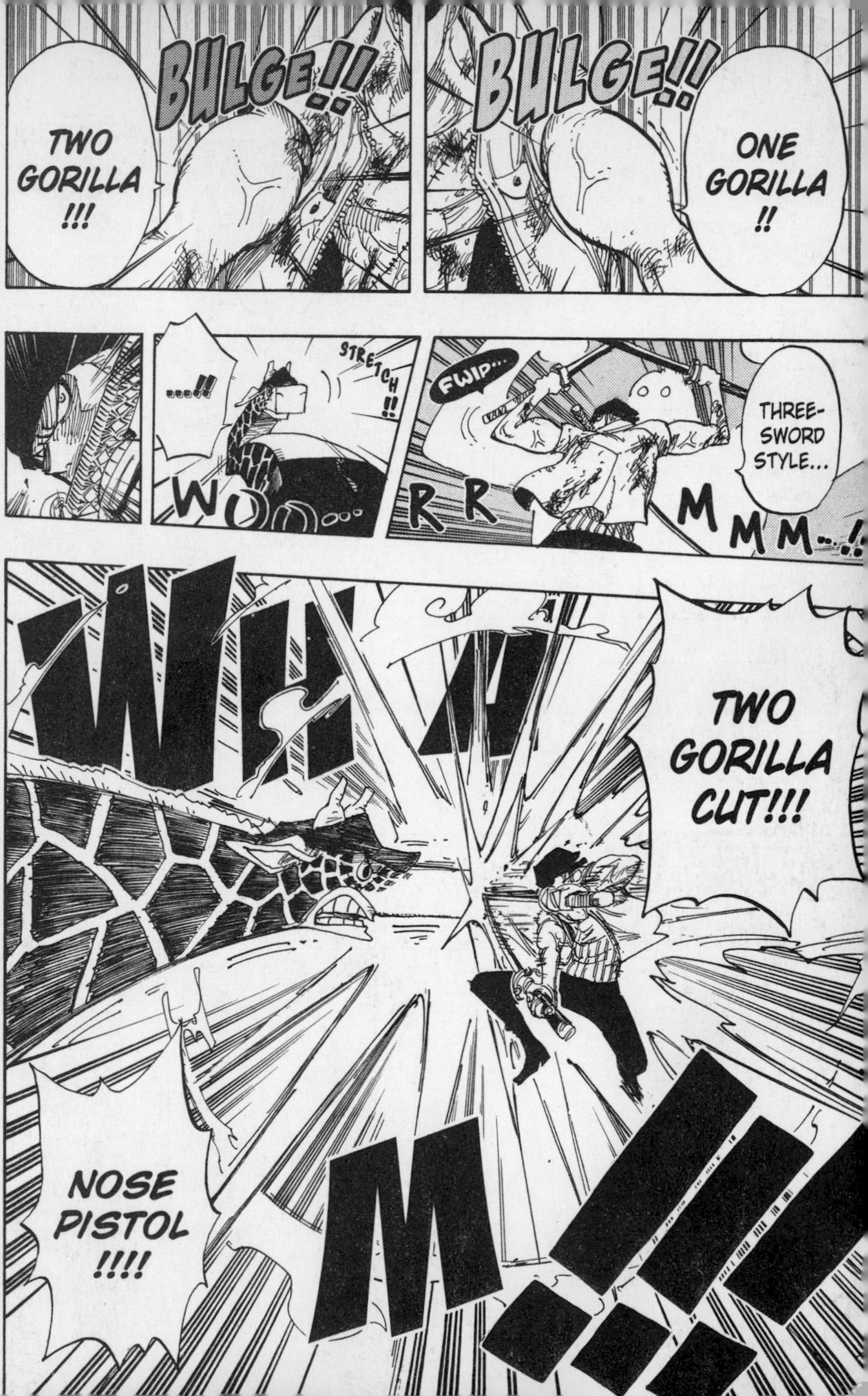
BULGE!!
ONE GORILLA !!
BULGE!!
TWO GORILLA !!!
FWIP...
THREE-SWORD STYLE...
STRETCH!!
...!!
WOOO R R MMM..!!
TWO GORILLA CUT!!!
WHAM!!
NOSE PISTOL !!!!

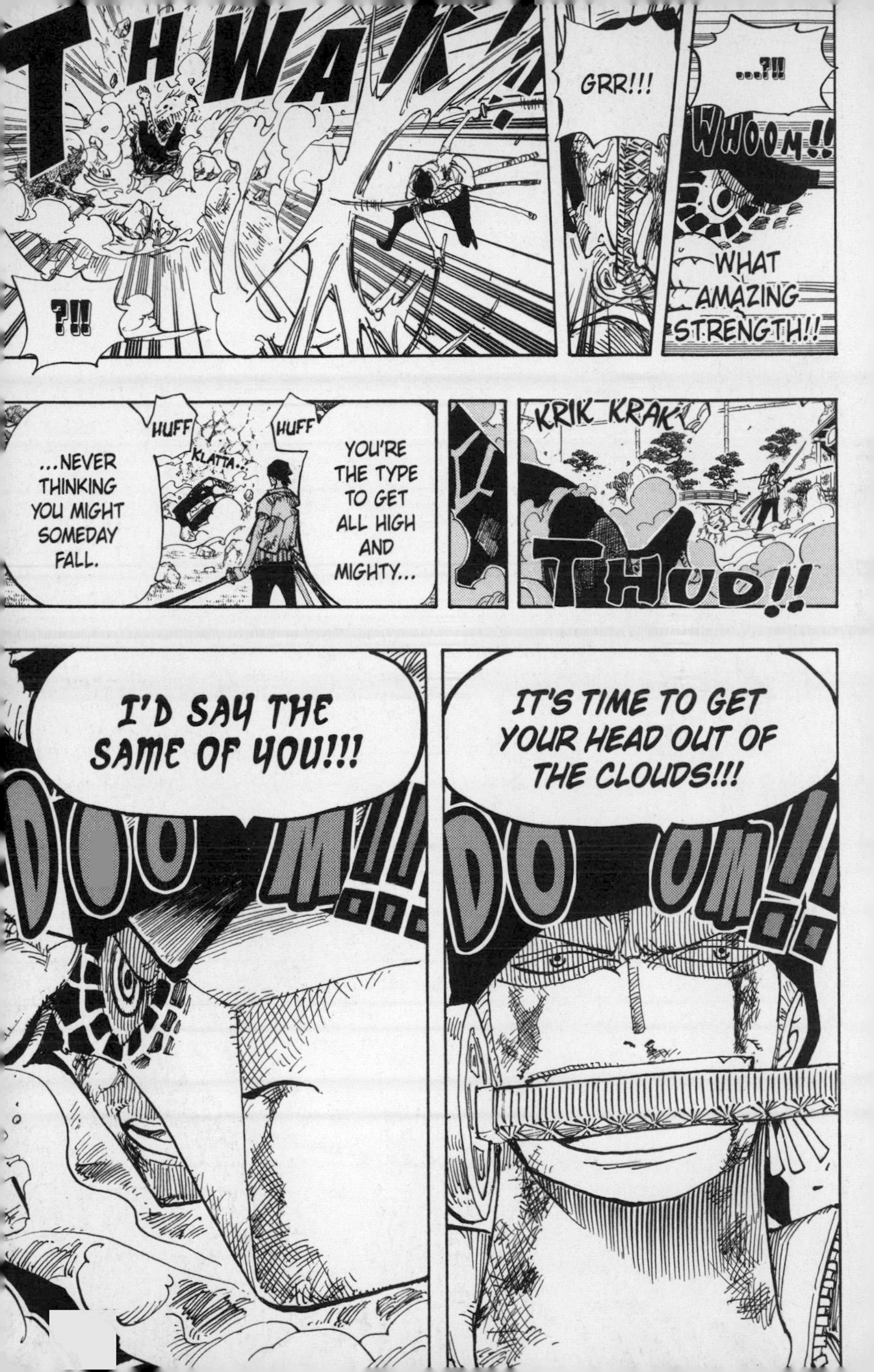
...?!!
WHOOM!!
WHAT AMAZING STRENGTH!!
GRR!!!
THWAK!!
?!!
KRIK KRAK
THUD!!
HUFF
YOU'RE THE TYPE TO GET ALL HIGH AND MIGHTY...
HUFF
KLATTA..
...NEVER THINKING YOU MIGHT SOMEDAY FALL.
IT'S TIME TO GET YOUR HEAD OUT OF THE CLOUDS!!!
DOOM!!
I'D SAY THE SAME OF YOU!!!
DOOOM!!

COLORING PAGE

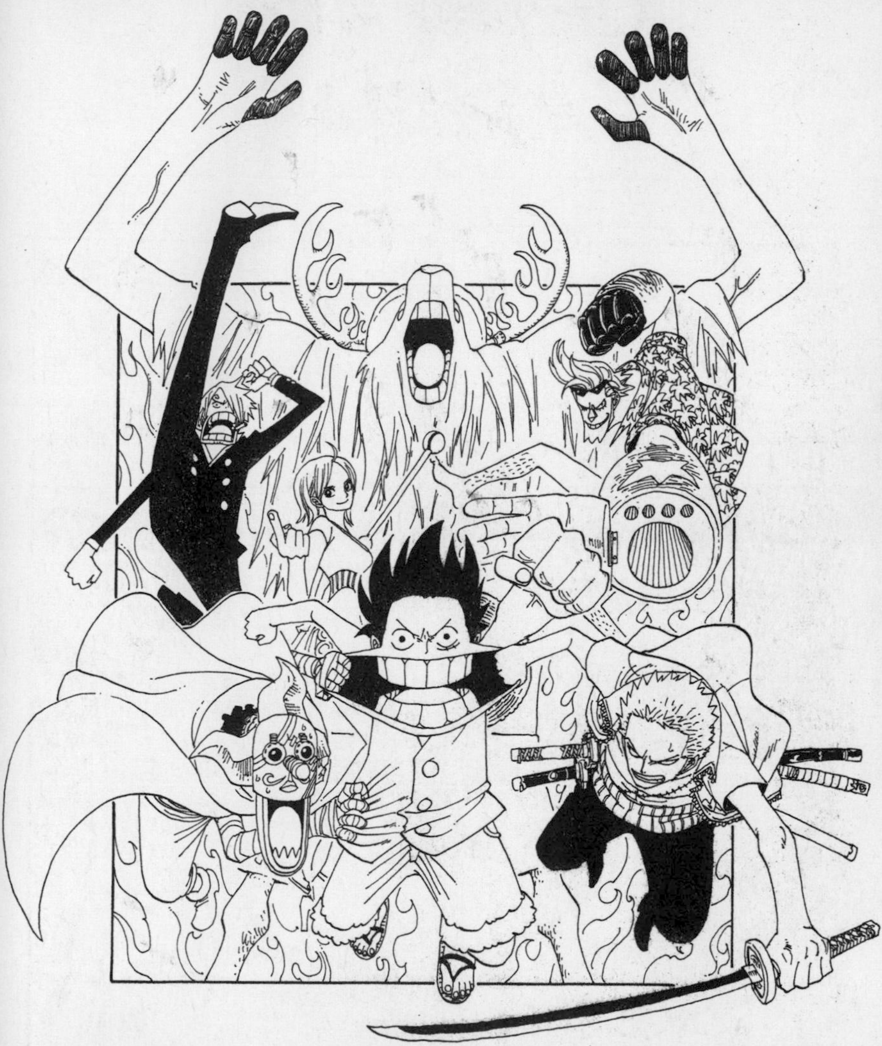

Chapter 417:
ASURA

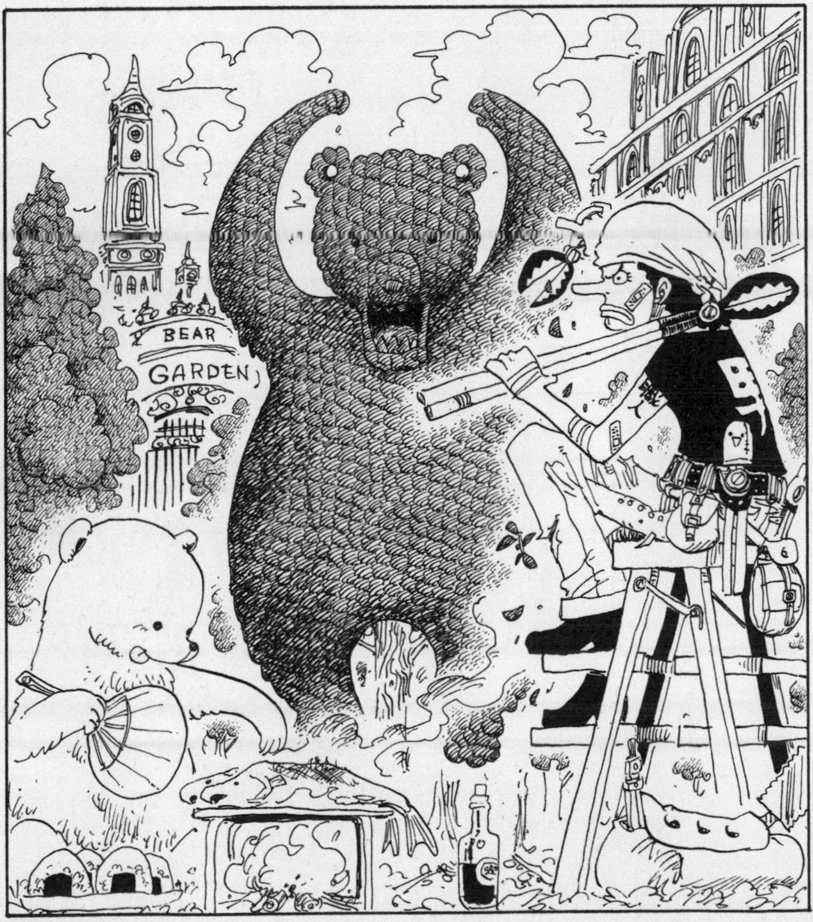
BEAR
GARDEN

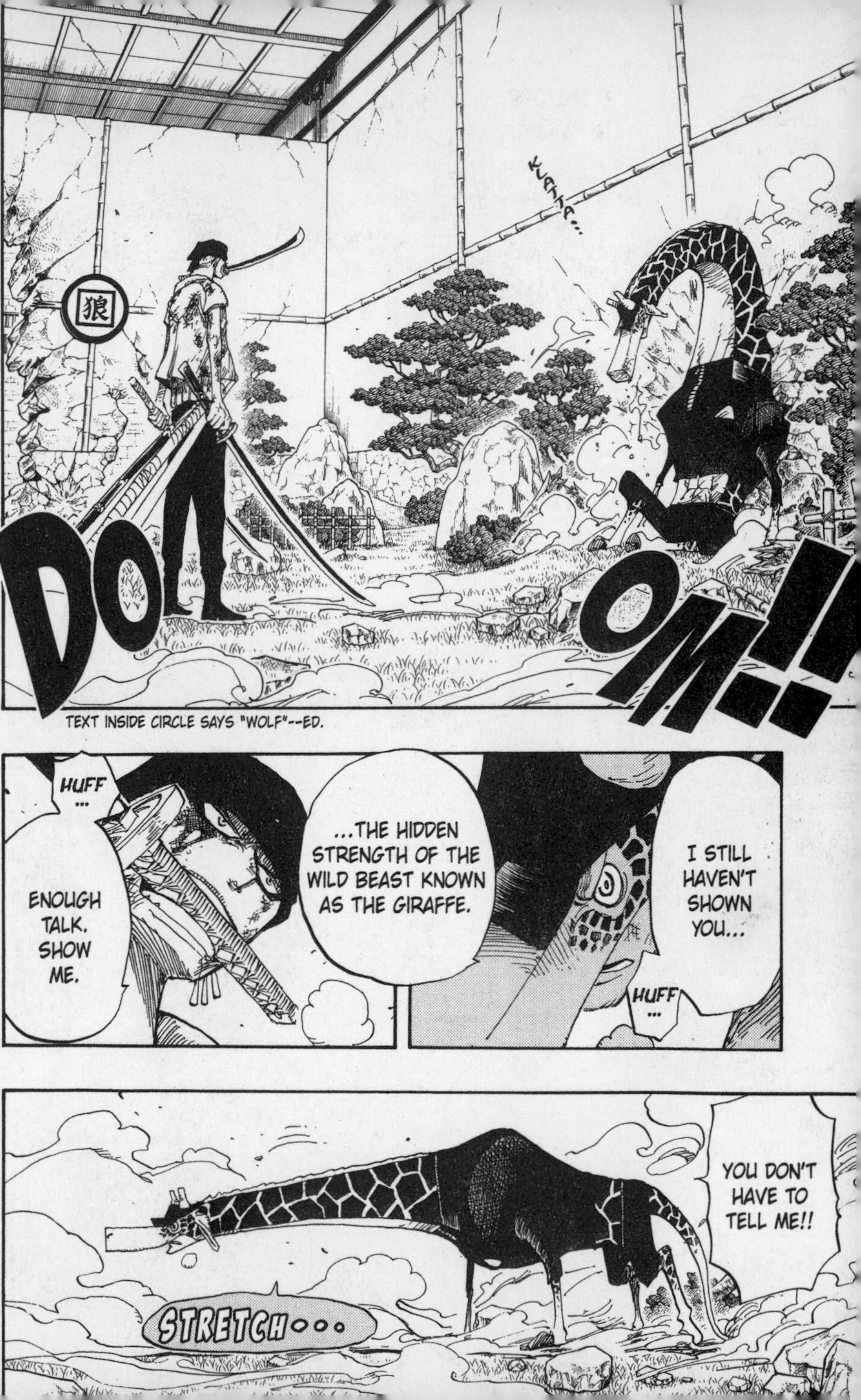
KLATTA...
狼
DOOM!!
I STILL HAVEN'T SHOWN YOU...
HUFF...
...THE HIDDEN STRENGTH OF THE WILD BEAST KNOWN AS THE GIRAFFE.
HUFF...
ENOUGH TALK. SHOW ME.
YOU DON'T HAVE TO TELL ME!!
STRETCH...
TEXT INSIDE CIRCLE SAYS "WOLF"--ED.

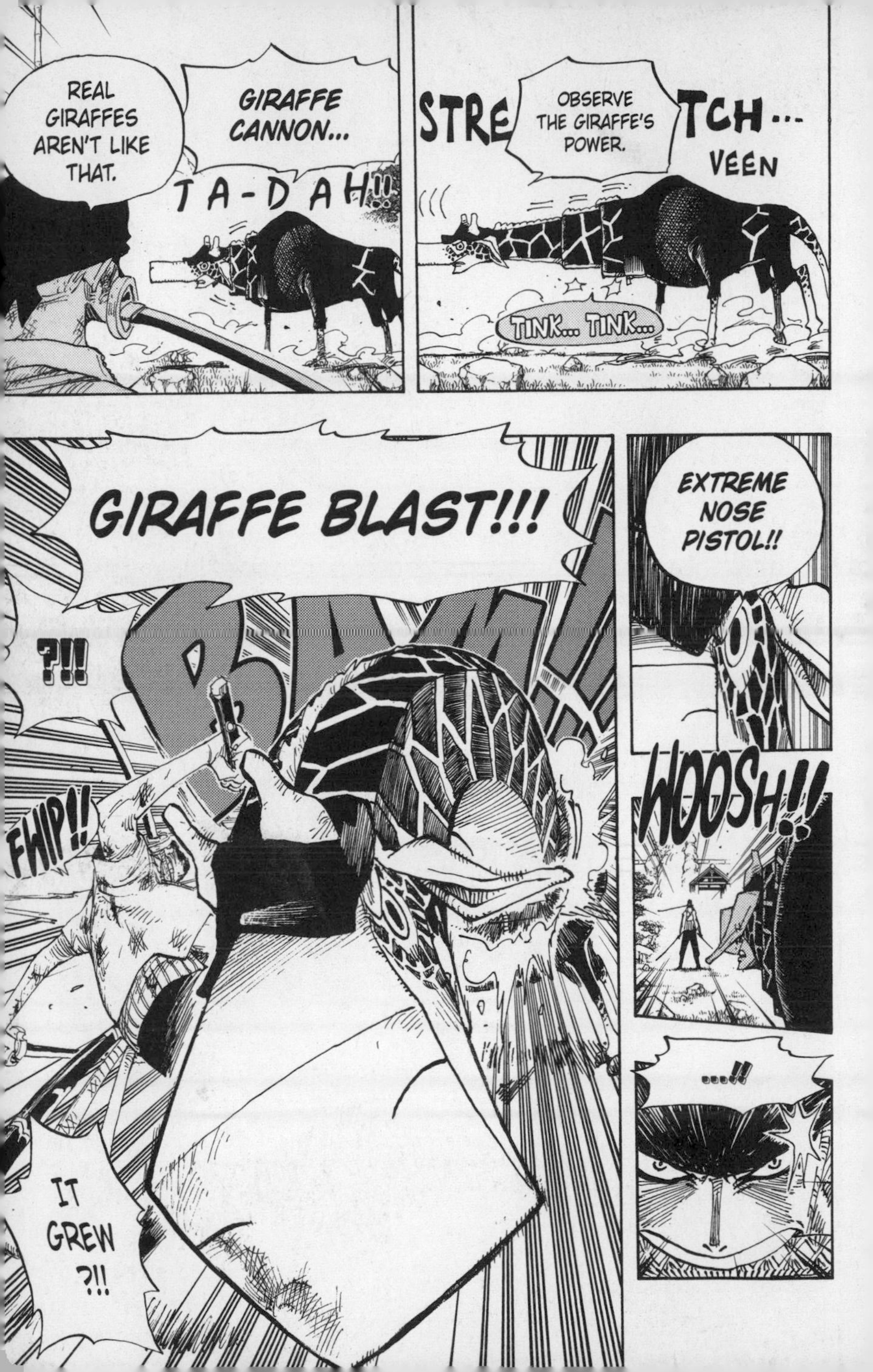
STRE
OBSERVE THE GIRAFFE'S POWER.
TCH...
VEEN
TINK... TINK...
GIRAFFE CANNON...
REAL GIRAFFES AREN'T LIKE THAT.
TA-DAH!!
EXTREME NOSE PISTOL!!
WOOSH!!
...!!
GIRAFFE BLAST!!!
?!!
FWIP!!
IT GREW ?!!

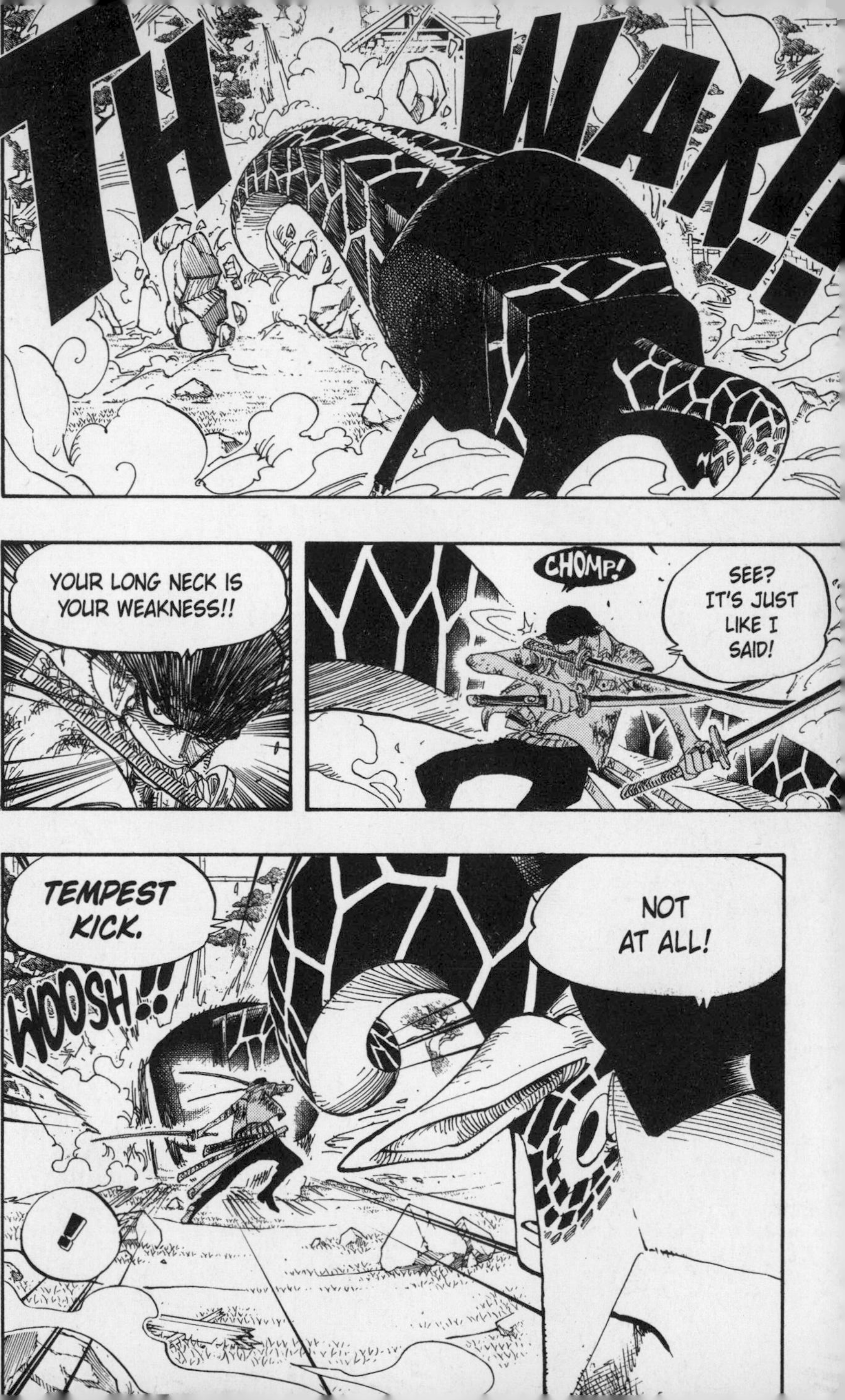
THWAK!!
CHOMP!
SEE? IT'S JUST LIKE I SAID!
YOUR LONG NECK IS YOUR WEAKNESS!!
NOT AT ALL!
TEMPEST KICK.
WOOSH!!
!

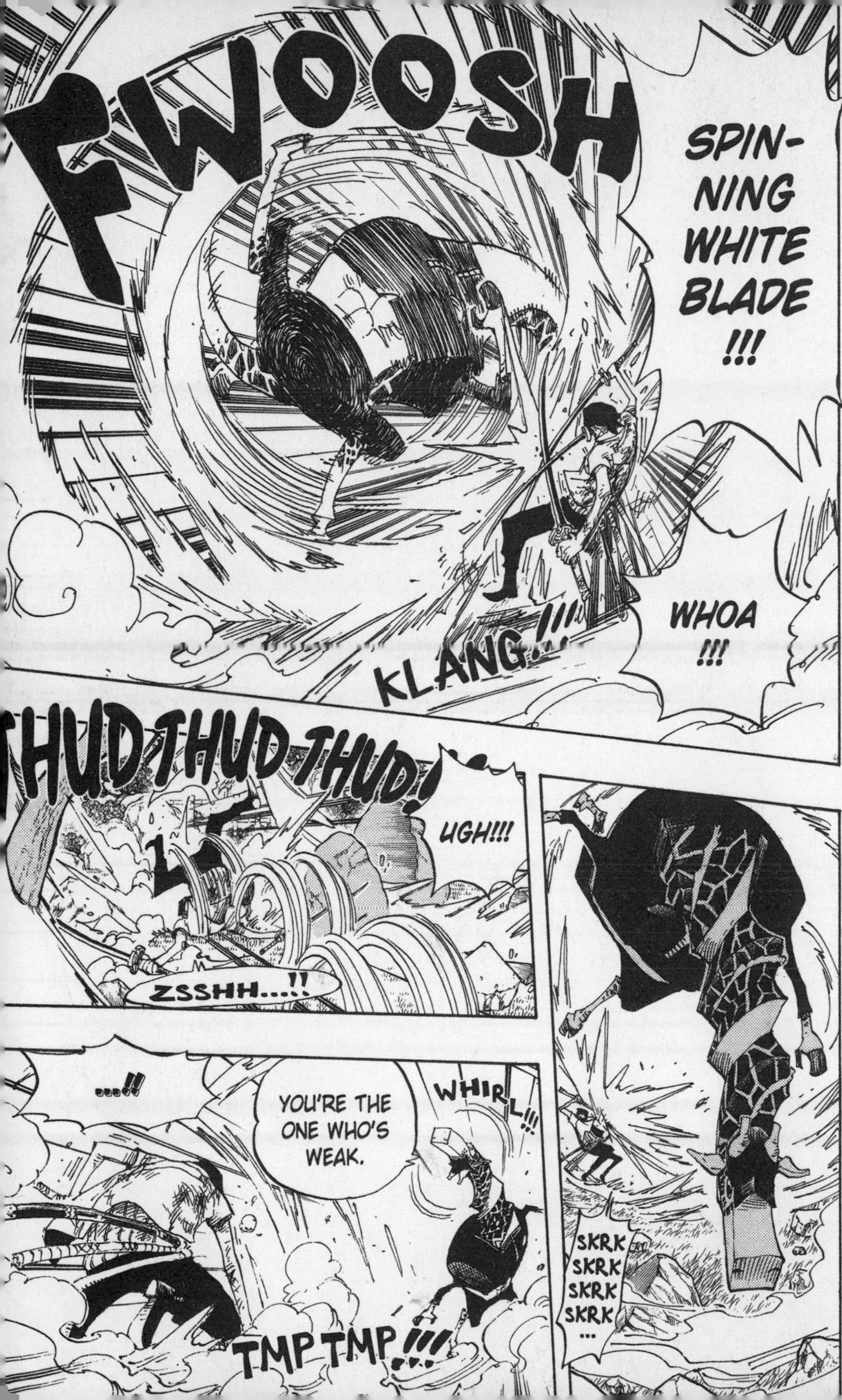
SPIN-
NING
WHITE
BLADE
!!!
FWOOSH
WHOA
!!!
KLANG!!!
SKRK
SKRK
SKRK
SKRK
...
THUD THUD THUD!
UGH!!!
ZSSHH...!!
WHIRL!!!
YOU'RE THE ONE WHO'S WEAK.
...!!
TMP TMP!!!

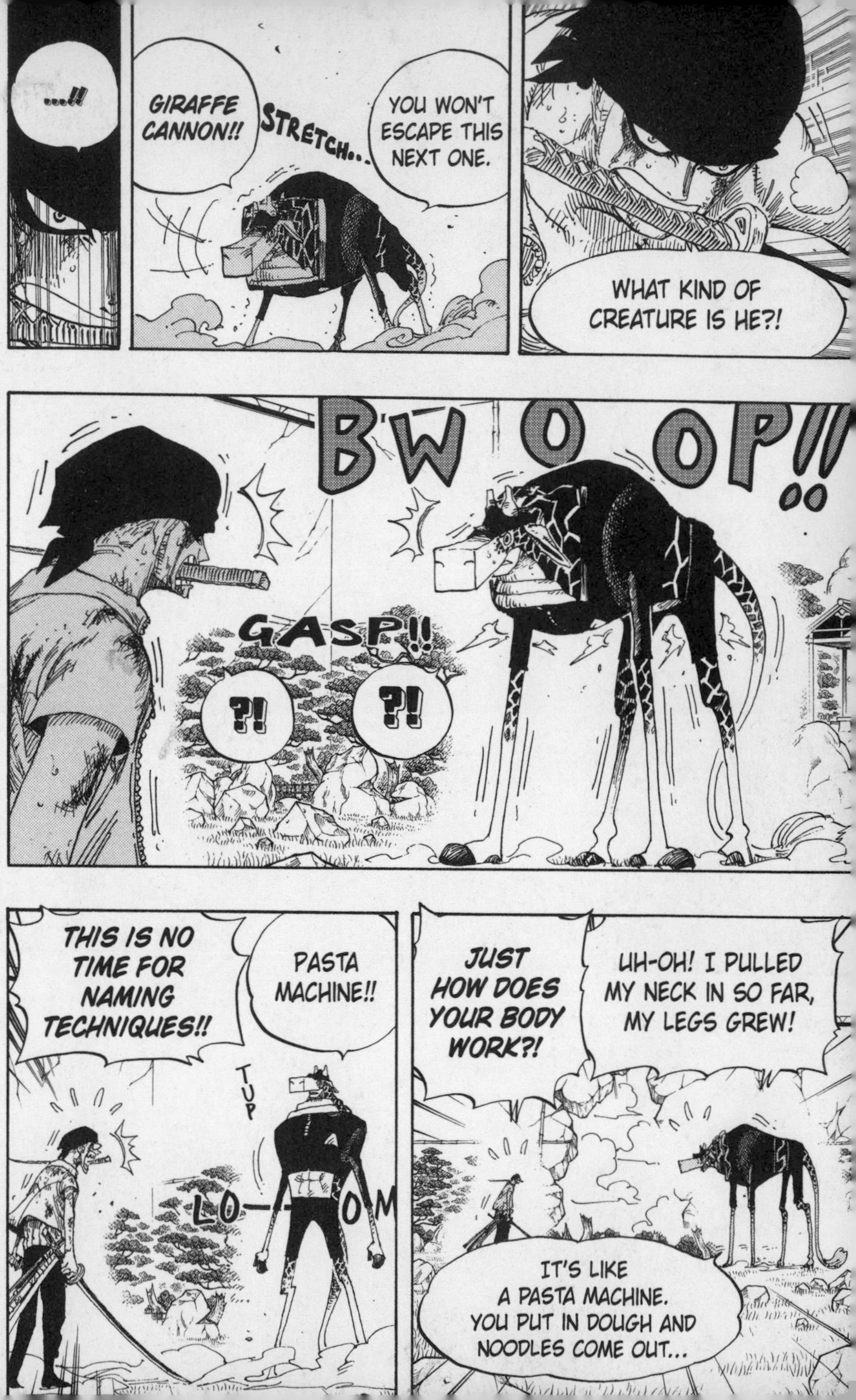
WHAT KIND OF CREATURE IS HE?!
YOU WON'T ESCAPE THIS NEXT ONE.
STRETCH...
GIRAFFE CANNON!!
...!!
BWOOP!!
GASP!!
?!
?!
UH-OH! I PULLED MY NECK IN SO FAR, MY LEGS GREW!
JUST HOW DOES YOUR BODY WORK?!
IT'S LIKE A PASTA MACHINE. YOU PUT IN DOUGH AND NOODLES COME OUT...
PASTA MACHINE!!
THIS IS NO TIME FOR NAMING TECHNIQUES!!
TUP
LO--OM

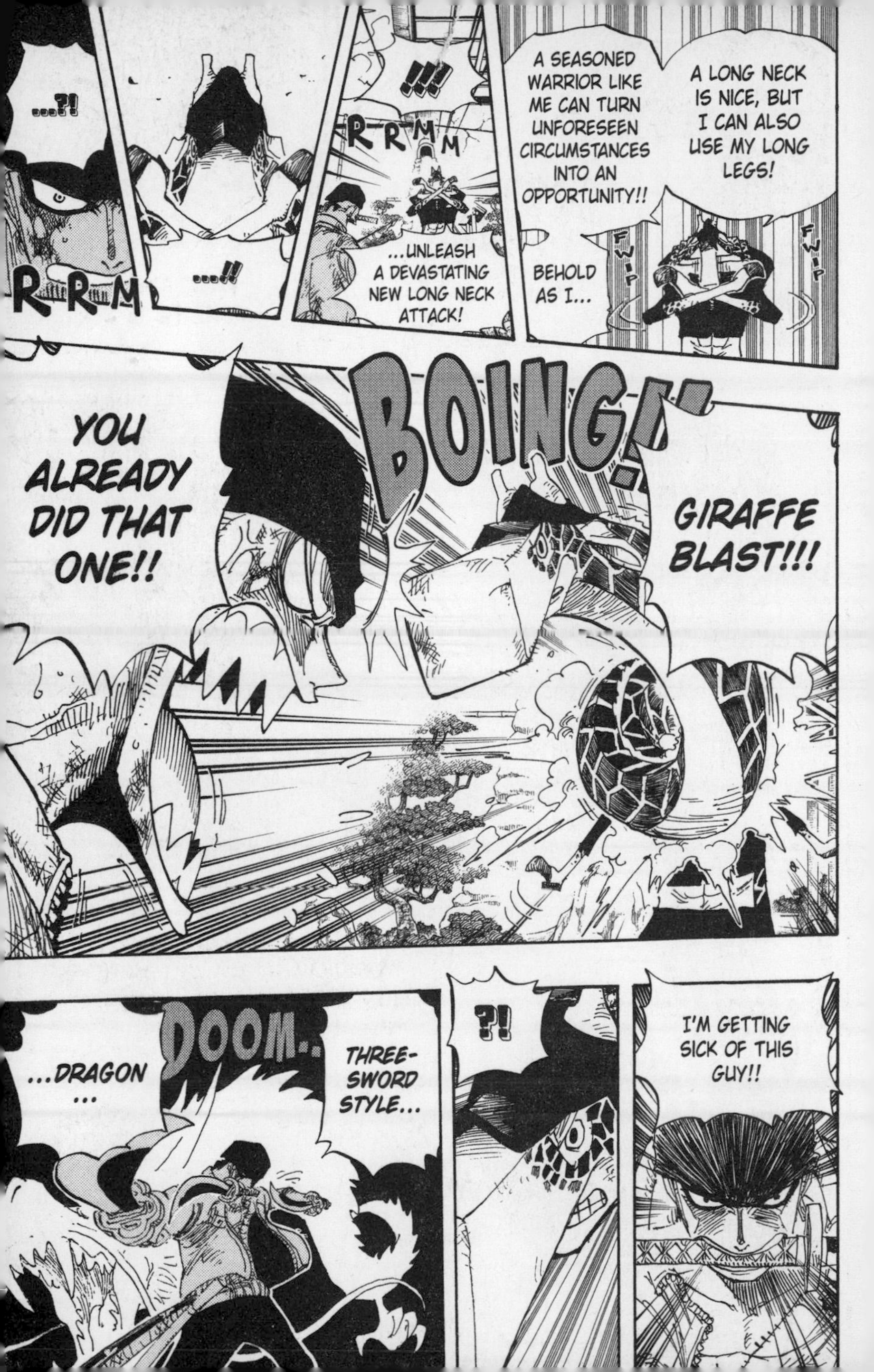
A LONG NECK IS NICE, BUT I CAN ALSO USE MY LONG LEGS!
A SEASONED WARRIOR LIKE ME CAN TURN UNFORESEEN CIRCUMSTANCES INTO AN OPPORTUNITY!!
FWIP
FWIP
BEHOLD AS I...
!!!
RRMM
...UNLEASH A DEVASTATING NEW LONG NECK ATTACK!
...!!
...?!
RRRM
BOING!!
GIRAFFE BLAST!!!
YOU ALREADY DID THAT ONE!!
I'M GETTING SICK OF THIS GUY!!
?!
DOOM..
THREE-SWORD STYLE...
...DRAGON ...

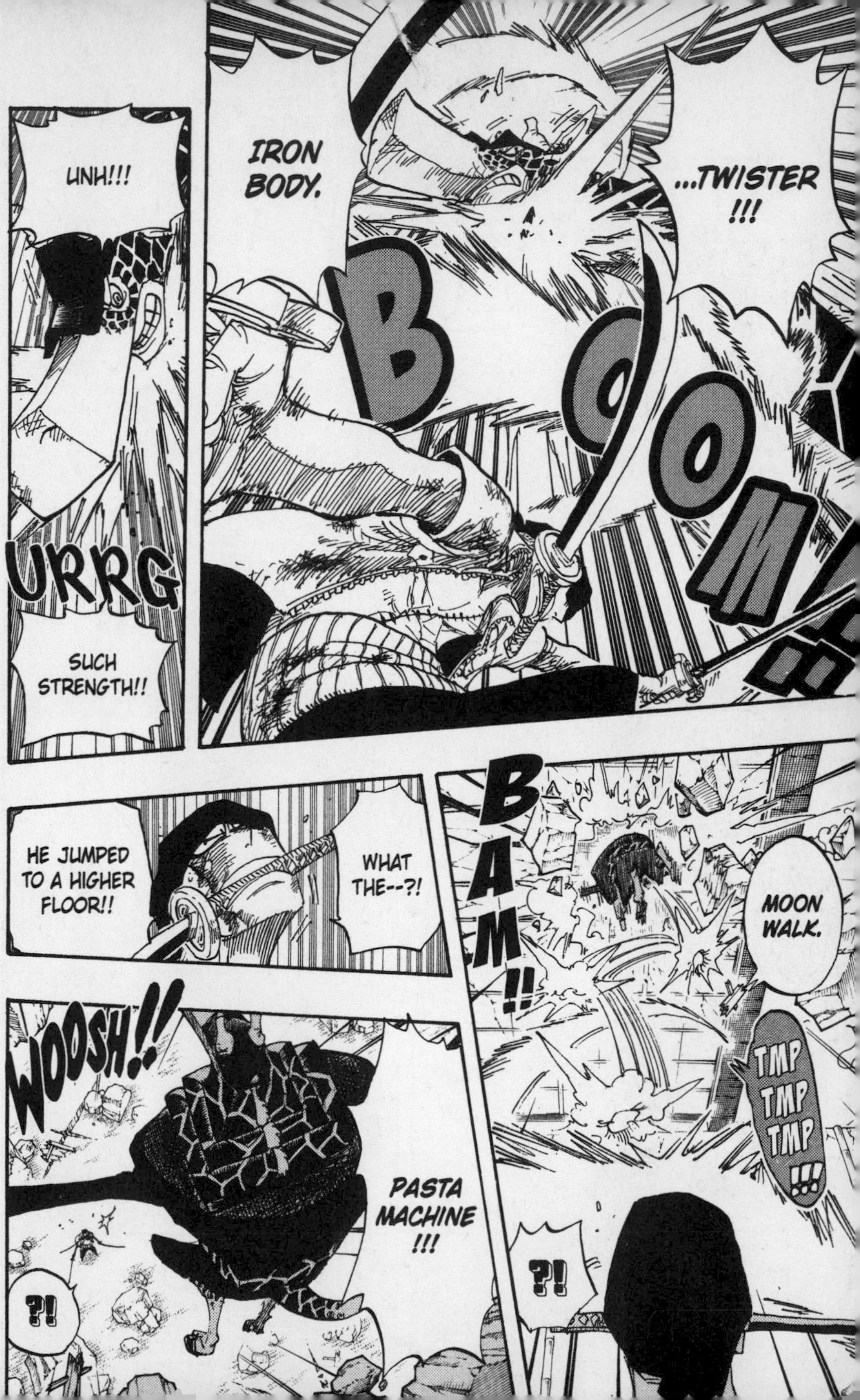
...TWISTER!!!
IRON BODY.
BOOOM!!
UNH!!!
URRG
SUCH STRENGTH!!
BAM!!
MOON WALK.
TMP TMP TMP!!!
?!
WHAT THE--?!
HE JUMPED TO A HIGHER FLOOR!!
PASTA MACHINE!!!
WOOSH!!
?!

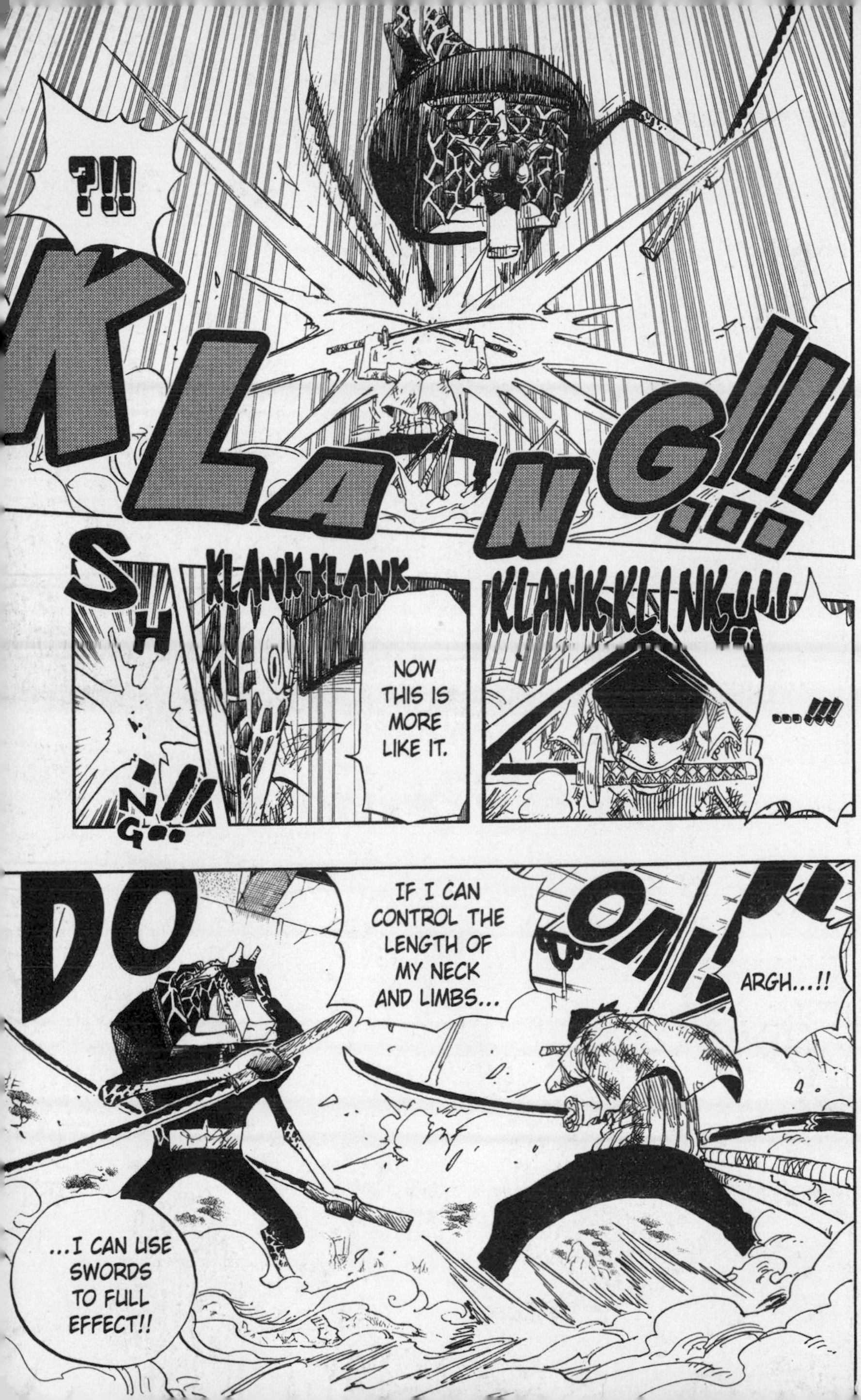
?!!
KLANG!!
KLANK KLINK!!!
...!!!
KLANK KLANK
NOW THIS IS MORE LIKE IT.
SHNG!!
DOON!!
ARGH...!!
IF I CAN CONTROL THE LENGTH OF MY NECK AND LIMBS...
...I CAN USE SWORDS TO FULL EFFECT!!

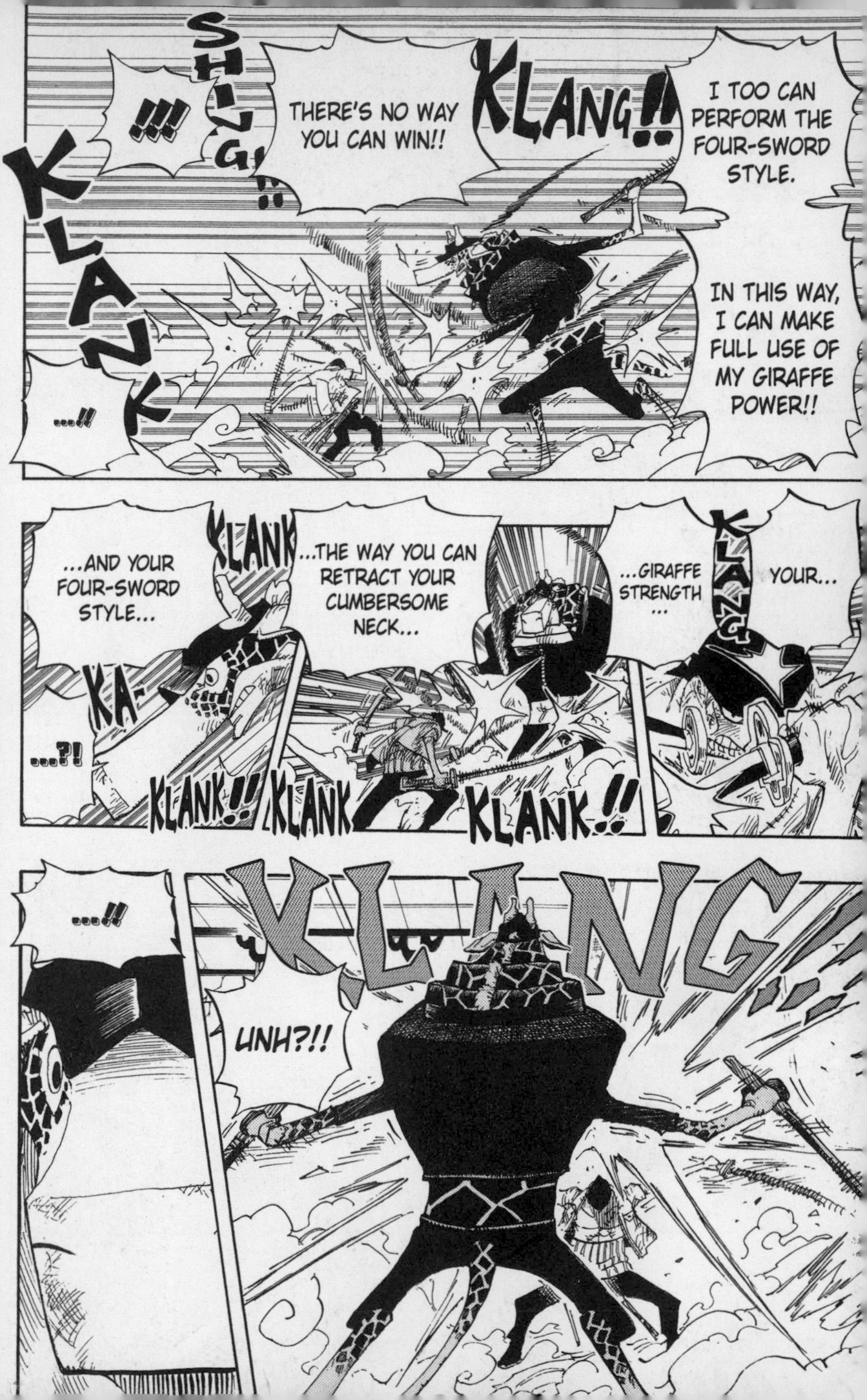
I TOO CAN PERFORM THE FOUR-SWORD STYLE.
IN THIS WAY, I CAN MAKE FULL USE OF MY GIRAFFE POWER!!
KLANG!!
THERE'S NO WAY YOU CAN WIN!!
SHING!!
!!!
KLANK
...!!
YOUR...
KLANG
...GIRAFFE STRENGTH ...
KLANK!!
...THE WAY YOU CAN RETRACT YOUR CUMBERSOME NECK...
KLANK
KLANK
...AND YOUR FOUR-SWORD STYLE...
KA-
...?!
KLANK!!
KLANG!!
UNH?!!
...!!

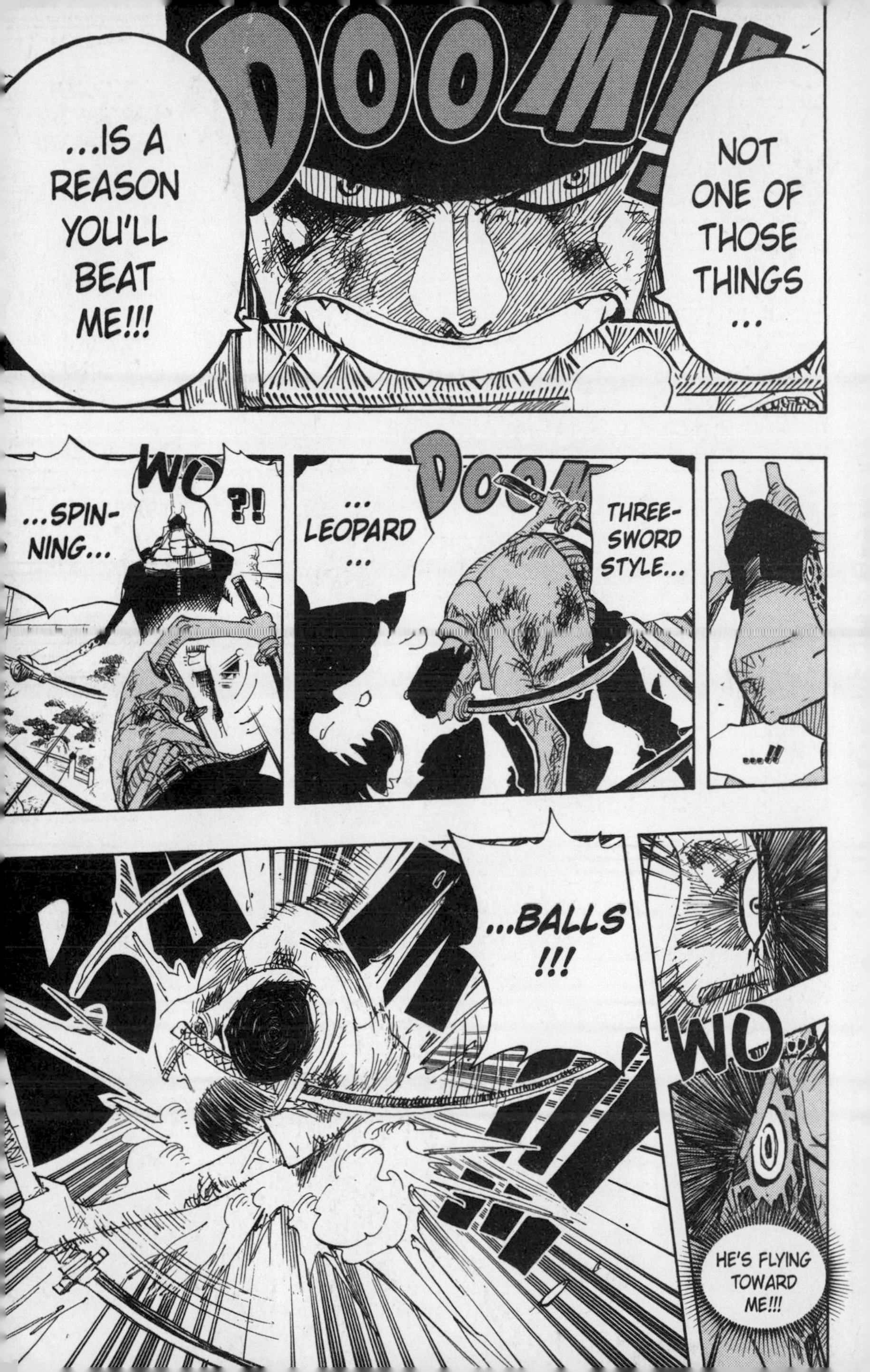
DOOM!!
NOT ONE OF THOSE THINGS ...
...IS A REASON YOU'LL BEAT ME!!!
...!!
DOOM
THREE-SWORD STYLE...
... LEOPARD ...
?!
WO
...SPIN-NING...
WO...
HE'S FLYING TOWARD ME!!!
...BALLS !!!

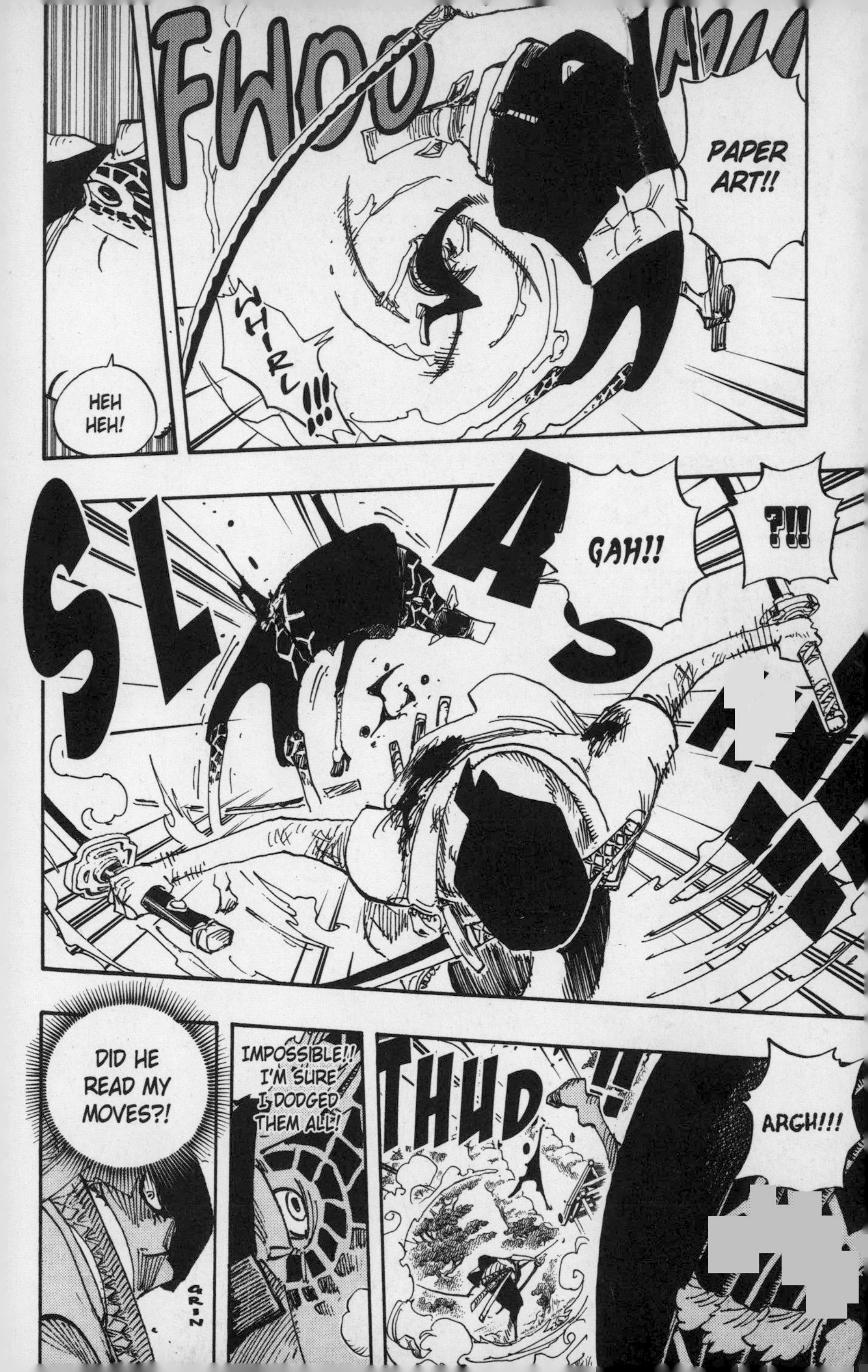
FWOO
PAPER ART!!
WHIRL!!!
HEH HEH!
?!!
GAH!!
SLAS
ARGH!!!
THUD!!
IMPOSSIBLE!! I'M SURE I DODGED THEM ALL!
DID HE READ MY MOVES?!
GRIN

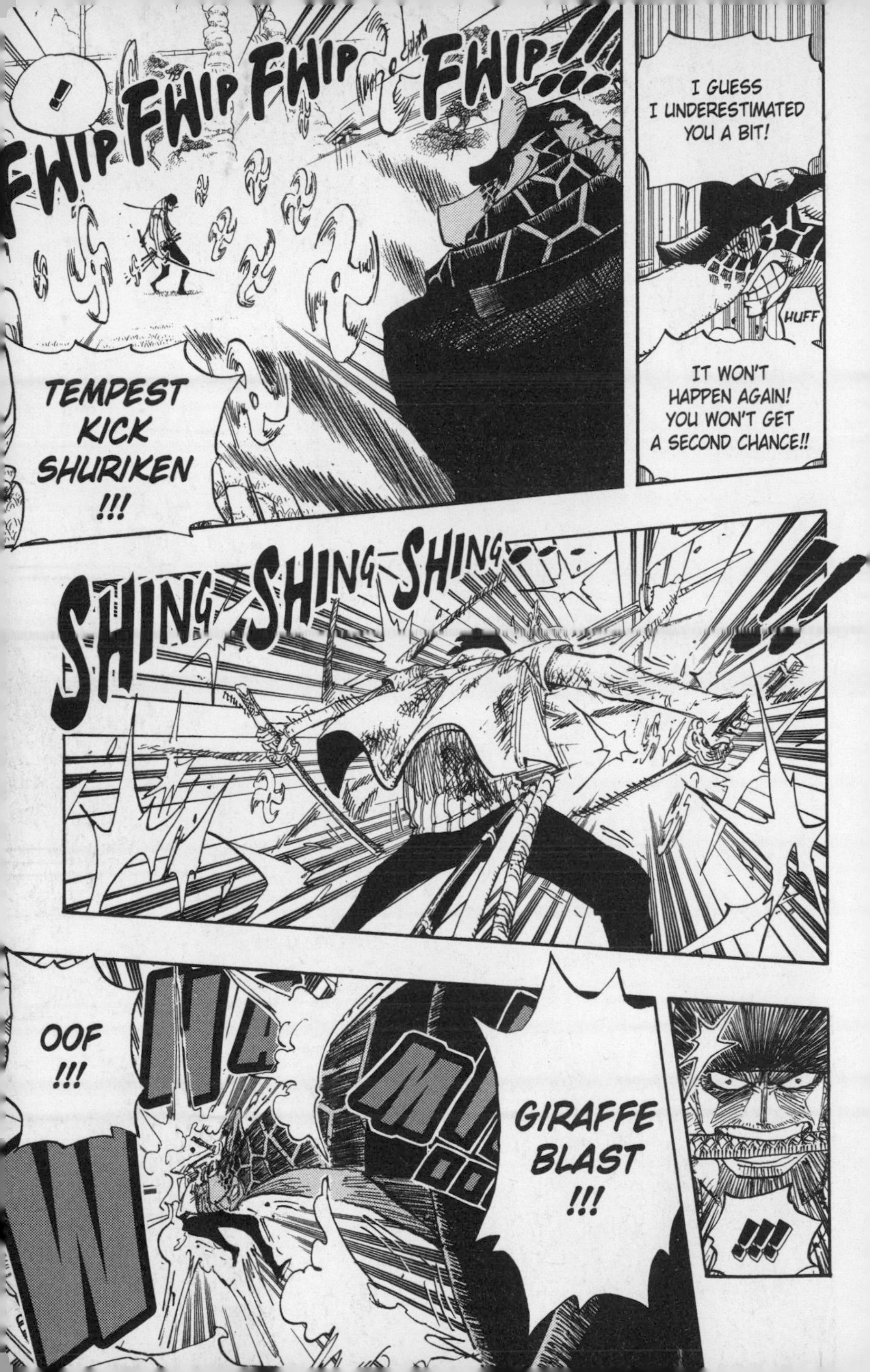
I GUESS I UNDERESTIMATED YOU A BIT!
HUFF
IT WON'T HAPPEN AGAIN! YOU WON'T GET A SECOND CHANCE!!
FWIP FWIP FWIP FWIP!!...
!
TEMPEST KICK SHURIKEN!!!
SHING SHING SHING...!!
!!!
GIRAFFE BLAST!!!
OOF!!!

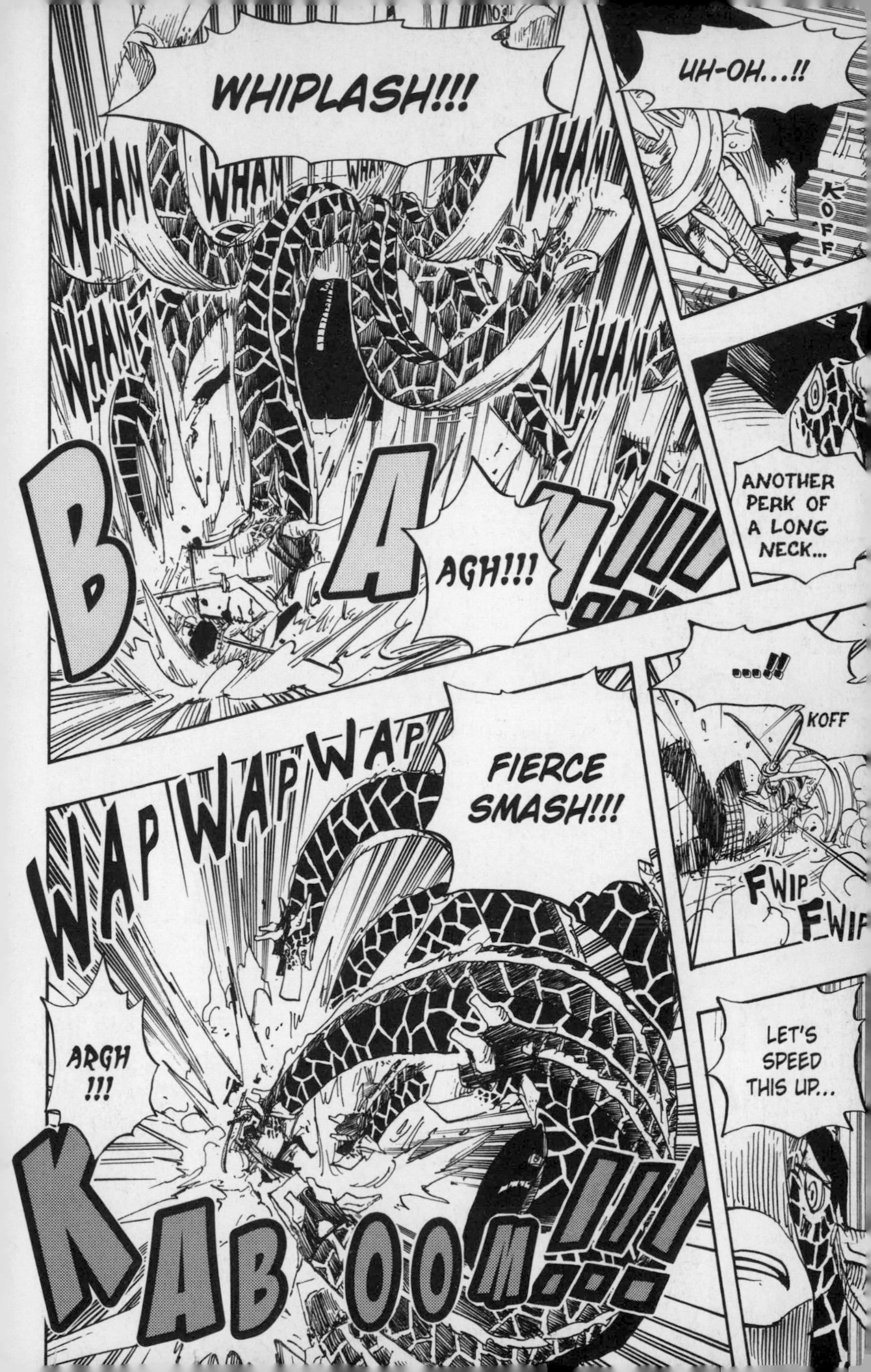
UH-OH...!!
KOFF
ANOTHER PERK OF A LONG NECK...
WHIPLASH!!!
WHAM WHAM WHAM WHAM WHAM WHAM
BAAGH!!!
...!!
KOFF
FWIP FWIP
LET'S SPEED THIS UP...
FIERCE SMASH!!!
WAP WAP WAP
ARGH !!!
KABOOM...!!!

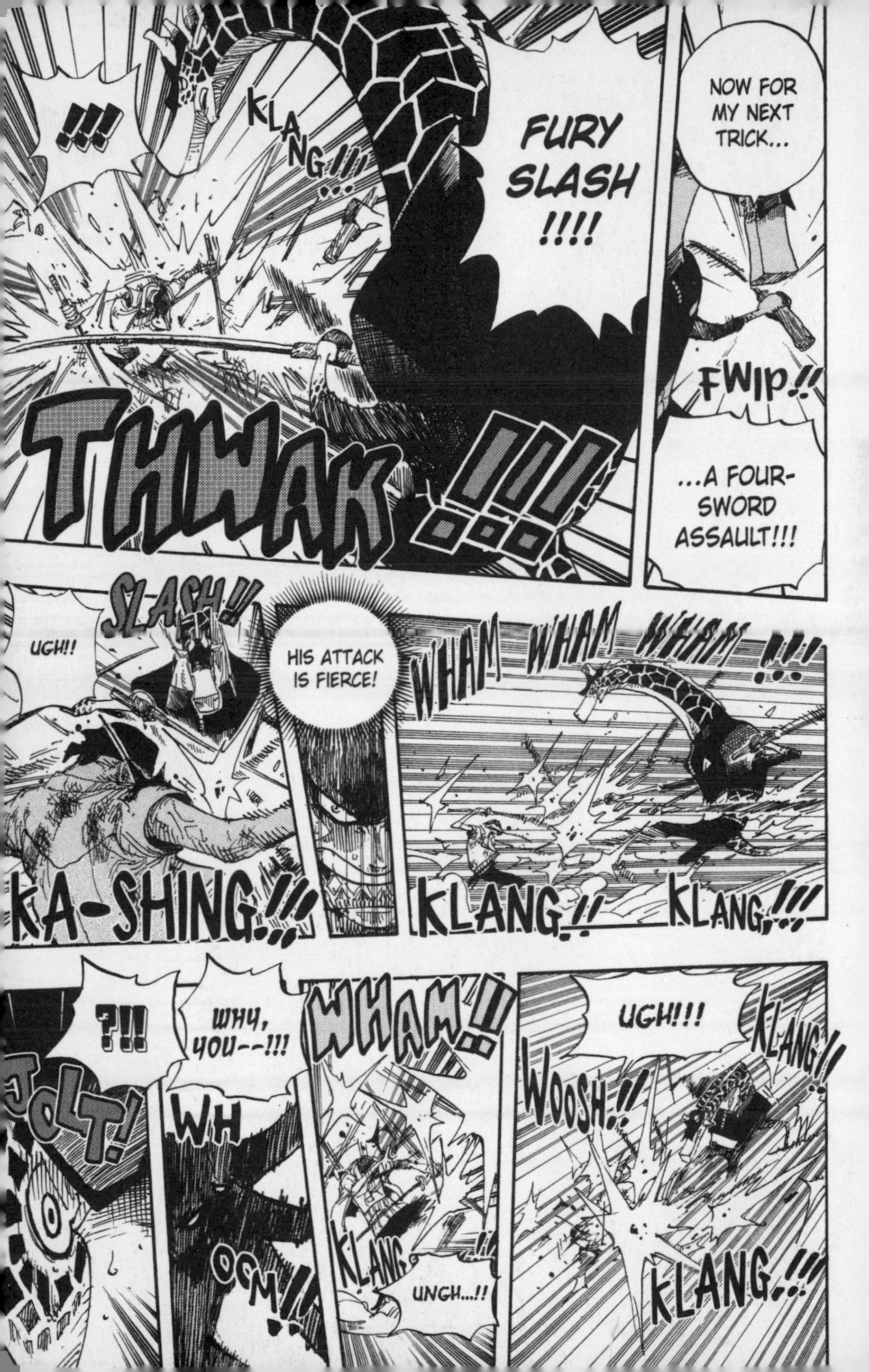
NOW FOR MY NEXT TRICK...
FWIP!!
...A FOUR-SWORD ASSAULT!!!
FURY SLASH !!!!
KLANG!!!
!!!
THWAK!!!!
WHAM WHAM WHAM!!!
KLANG!!
KLANG!!!
HIS ATTACK IS FIERCE!
SLASH!!
UGH!!
KA-SHING!!!
UGH!!!
KLANG!!
WOOSH!!
KLANG!!!
WHAM!!
KLANG
UNGH...!!
WHY, YOU--!!!
WH
OOM!
?!!
JOLT!

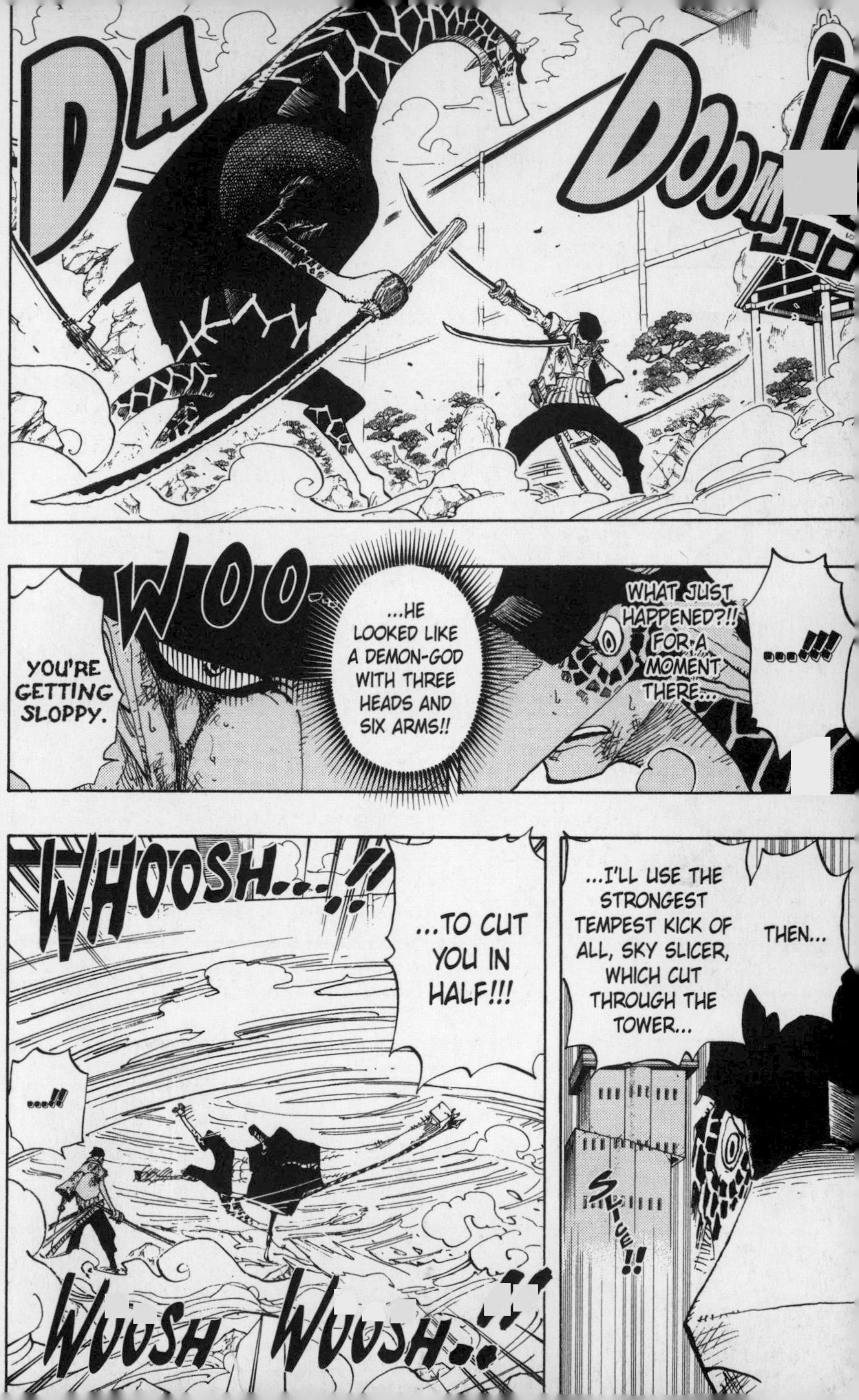
DA
DOOM...
...!!!
WHAT JUST HAPPENED?!! FOR A MOMENT THERE...
...HE LOOKED LIKE A DEMON-GOD WITH THREE HEADS AND SIX ARMS!!
WOO...
YOU'RE GETTING SLOPPY.
THEN...
...I'LL USE THE STRONGEST TEMPEST KICK OF ALL, SKY SLICER, WHICH CUT THROUGH THE TOWER...
SLICE!!
WHOOSH...!!
...TO CUT YOU IN HALF!!!
...!!
WOOSH
WOOSH..!!

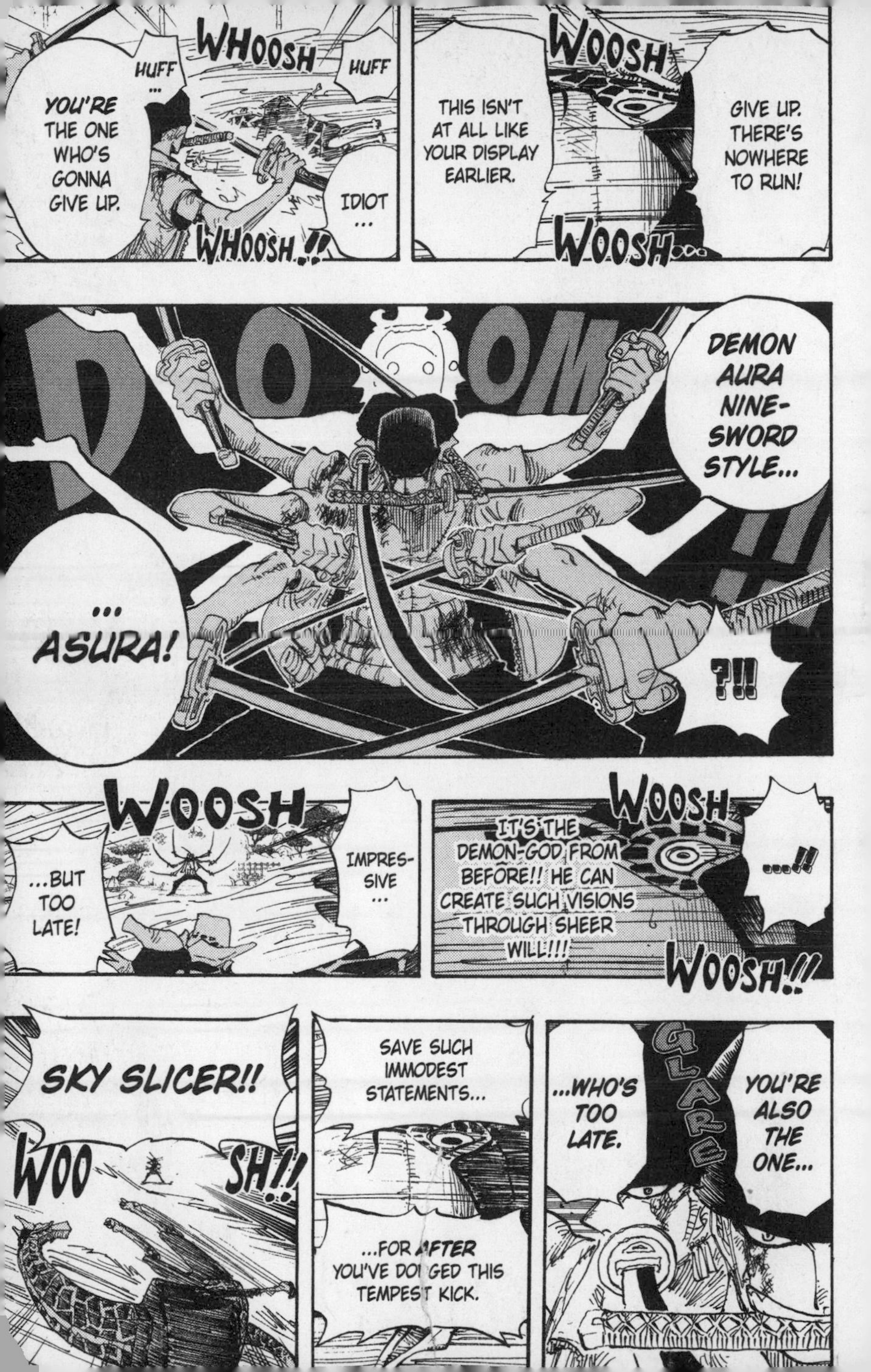
WOOSH
GIVE UP. THERE'S NOWHERE TO RUN!
THIS ISN'T AT ALL LIKE YOUR DISPLAY EARLIER.
WOOSH...
HUFF
WHOOSH
HUFF ...
IDIOT ...
YOU'RE THE ONE WHO'S GONNA GIVE UP.
WHOOSH!!
DOOM
DEMON AURA NINE-SWORD STYLE...
?!!
... ASURA!
WOOSH
...!!
IT'S THE DEMON-GOD FROM BEFORE!! HE CAN CREATE SUCH VISIONS THROUGH SHEER WILL!!!
WOOSH!!
WOOSH
IMPRES-SIVE ...
...BUT TOO LATE!
GLARE
YOU'RE ALSO THE ONE...
...WHO'S TOO LATE.
SAVE SUCH IMMODEST STATEMENTS...
...FOR AFTER YOU'VE DODGED THIS TEMPEST KICK.
SKY SLICER!!
WOOSH!!

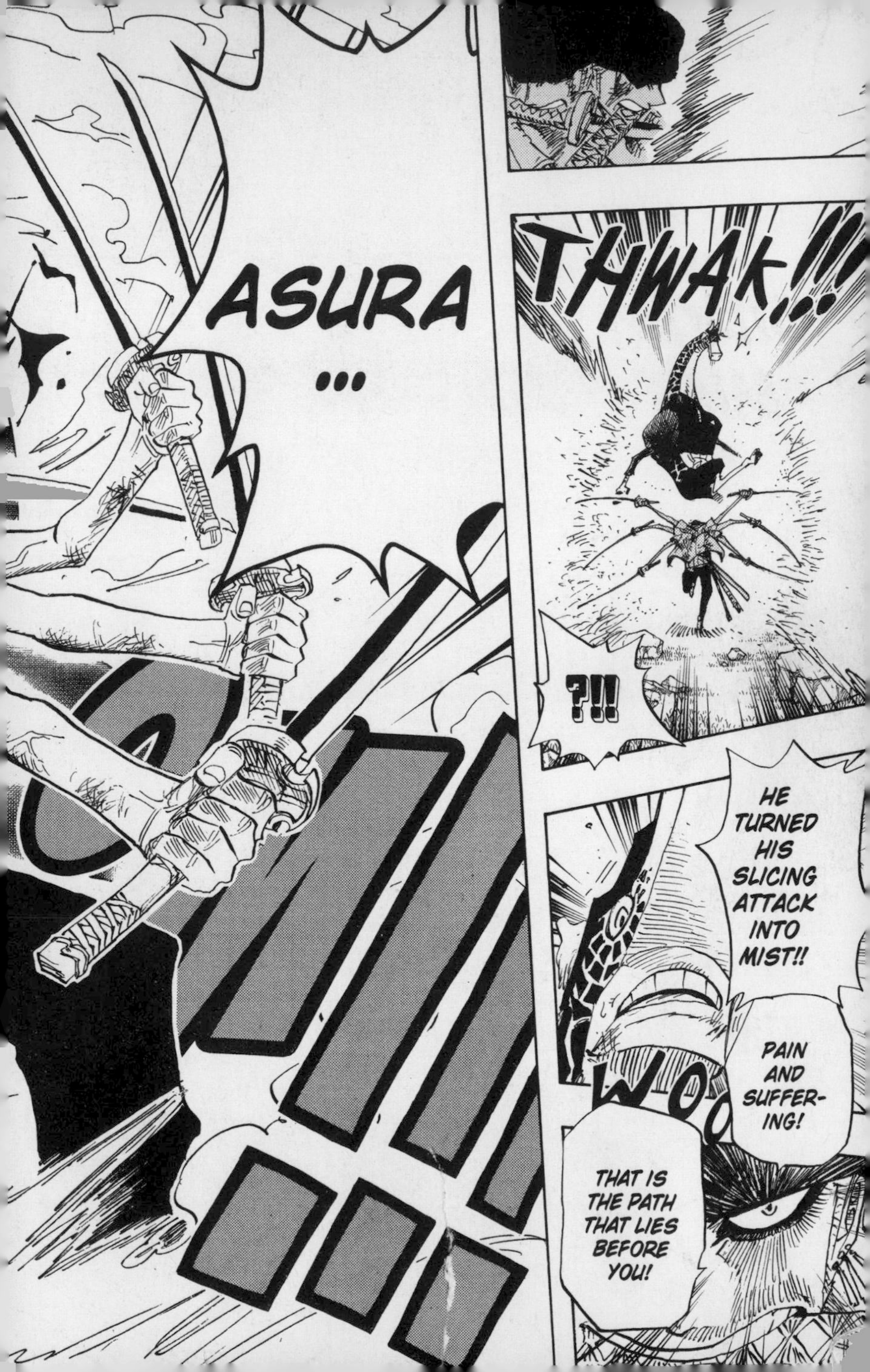
THWAK!!!
?!!
HE TURNED HIS SLICING ATTACK INTO MIST!!
WOO
PAIN AND SUFFER-ING!
THAT IS THE PATH THAT LIES BEFORE YOU!
ASURA
...

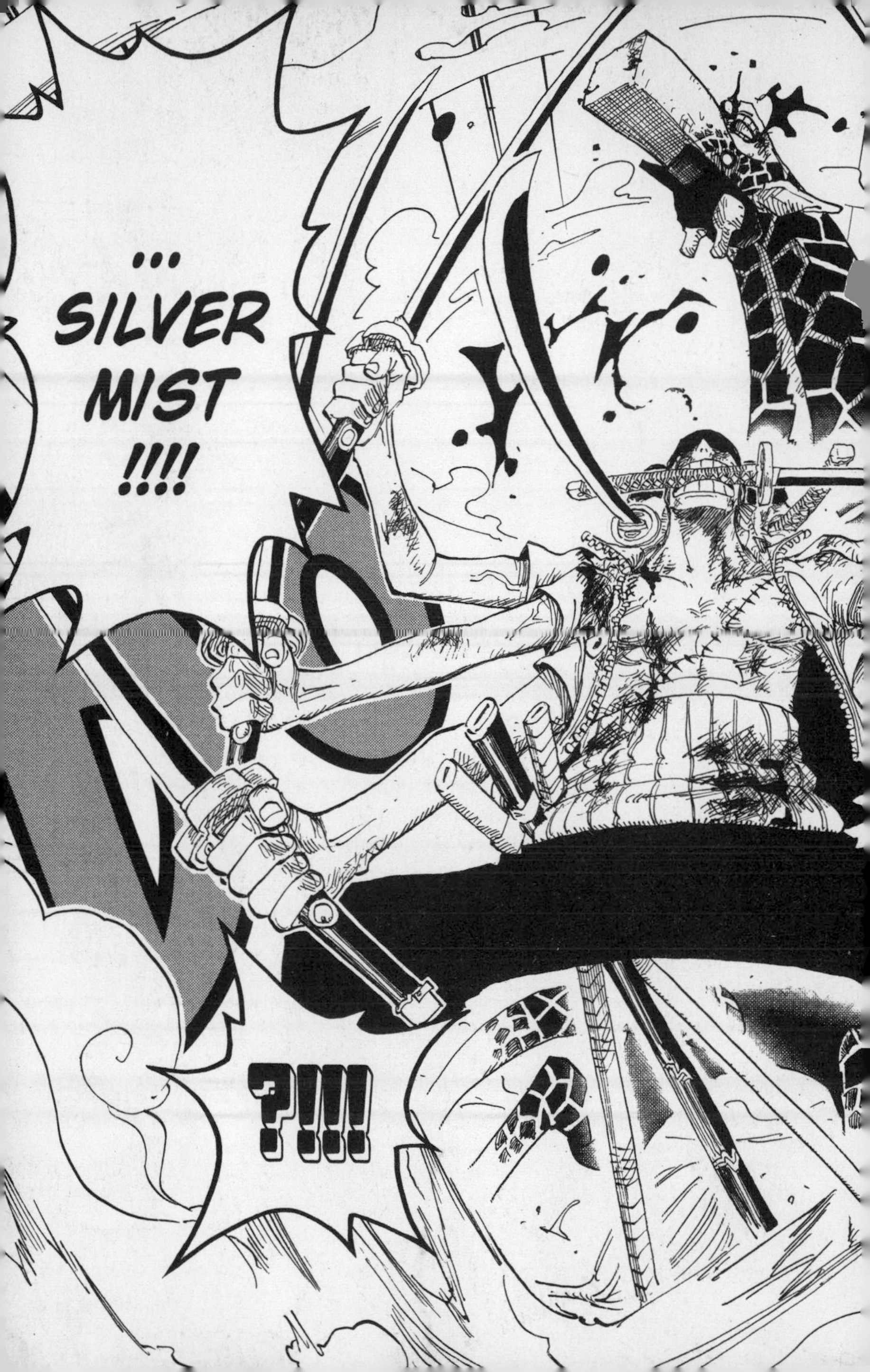

... SILVER MIST !!!!
?!!!

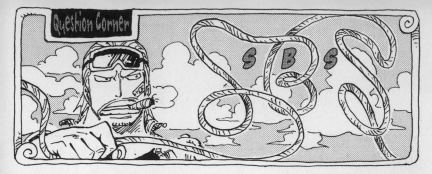

Question Corner
SBS

Q: Whassup? Nice to meet you, Occhin. (At my school, we call you Occhin.) Now here's my question. Please tell me how beautiful a person can get with Sanji's Plastic Surgery Shot, which we saw in volume 39, chapter 372.

--34590

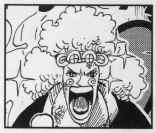

A: Really beautiful. As you can tell from Wanze's example, you can get a beautiful face equal to those of top international movie stars. But there are two drawbacks. First, Sanji can't kick girls. Also, it's only your face that changes. If you're fat, the balance will be off--even if your face improves--so it will look weird.

ONE PIECE
ONE PIECE
ROMANCE DAWN
volume 1

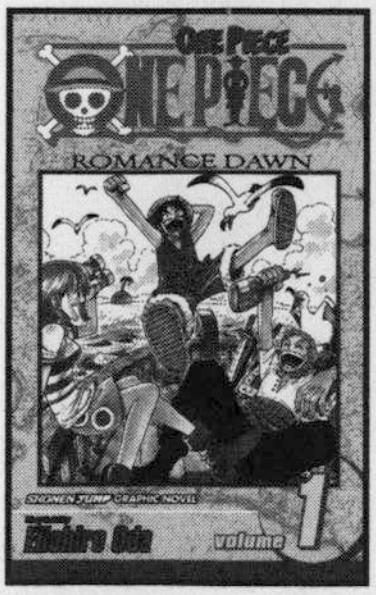

Q: Good work, Mr. Oda! Please answer this unimportant question, which has been bothering me! Manga volumes usually have nine chapters, but *One Piece* sometimes has 10 or 11. Why is that? The books have recently been kind of thick. The story has been intense too!

--John

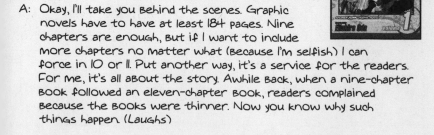

A: Okay, I'll take you behind the scenes. Graphic novels have to have at least 184 pages. Nine chapters are enough, but if I want to include more chapters no matter what (because I'm selfish) I can force in 10 or 11. Put another way, it's a service for the readers. For me, it's all about the story. Awhile back, when a nine-chapter book followed an eleven-chapter book, readers complained because the books were thinner. Now you know why such things happen. (Laughs)

Chapter 418:
LUFFY VS. ROB LUCCI

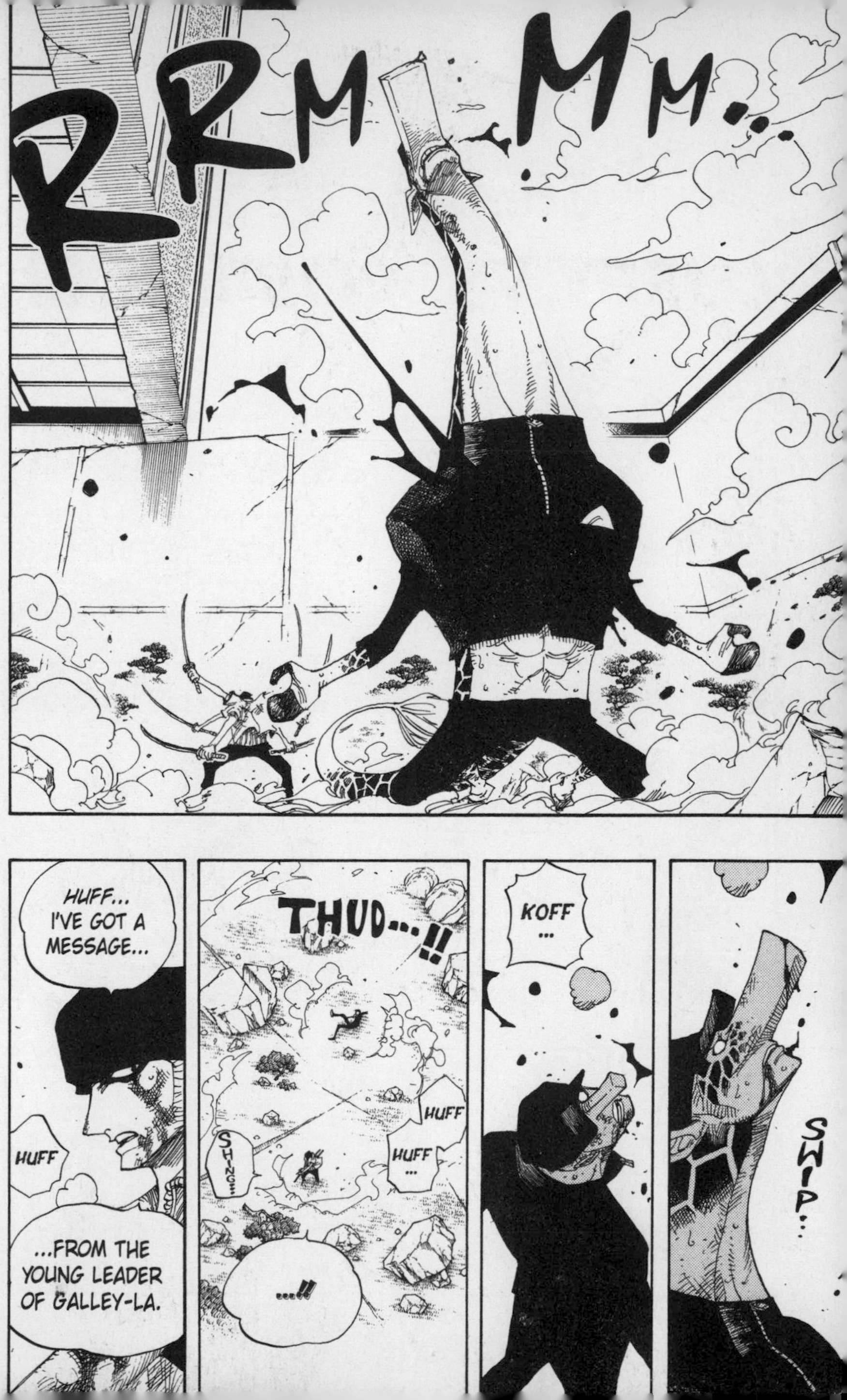
RRMMMM...
SWIP...
KOFF ...
THUD...!!
HUFF
HUFF ...
SHING...
...!!
HUFF... I'VE GOT A MESSAGE...
HUFF
...FROM THE YOUNG LEADER OF GALLEY-LA.

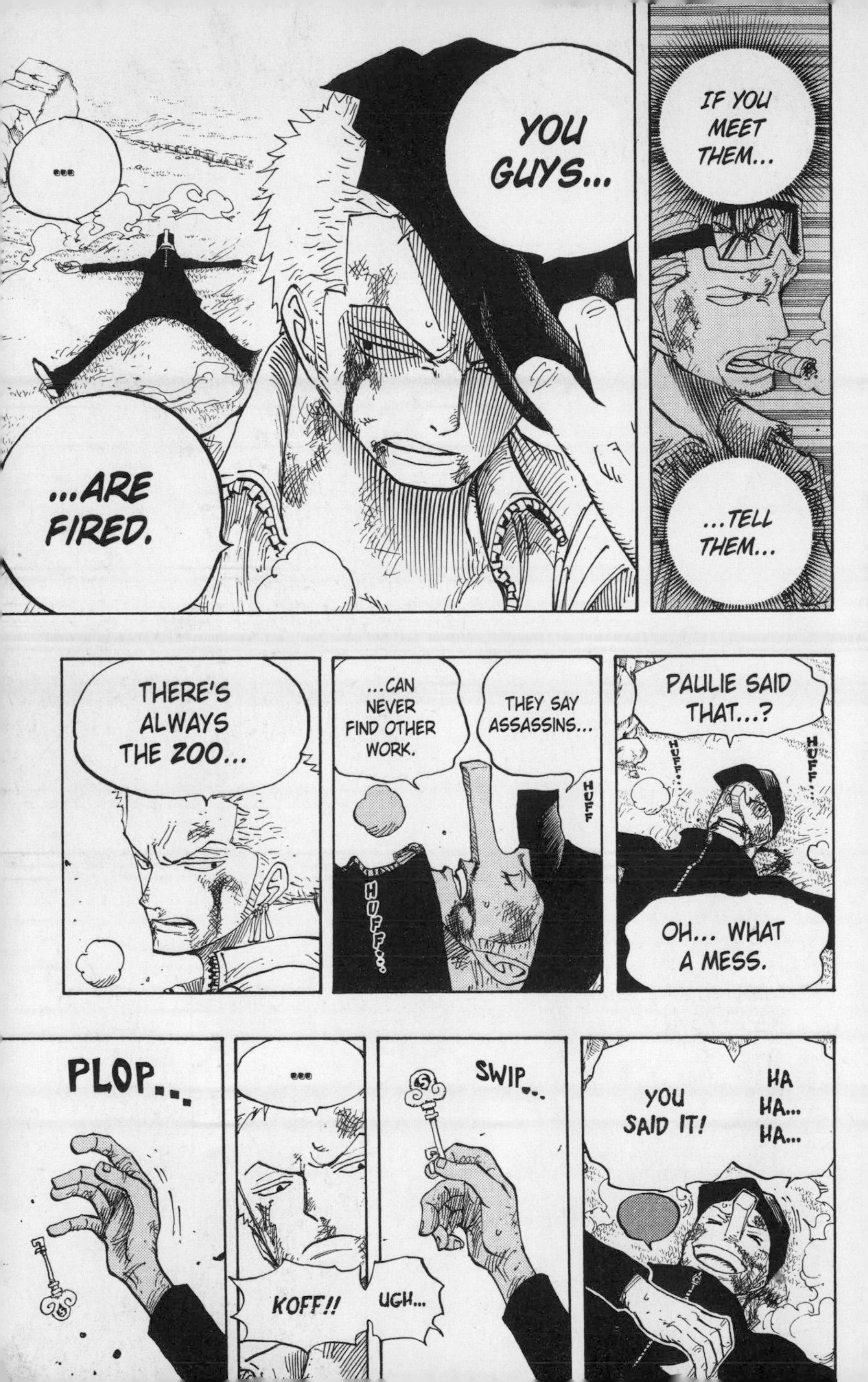
IF YOU MEET THEM...
...TELL THEM...
YOU GUYS...
...ARE FIRED.
...
PAULIE SAID THAT...?
HUFF... HUFF...
OH... WHAT A MESS.
THEY SAY ASSASSINS...
HUFF
...CAN NEVER FIND OTHER WORK.
HUFF...
THERE'S ALWAYS THE ZOO...
YOU SAID IT!
HA HA... HA...
SWIP...
...
KOFF!!
UGH...
PLOP...

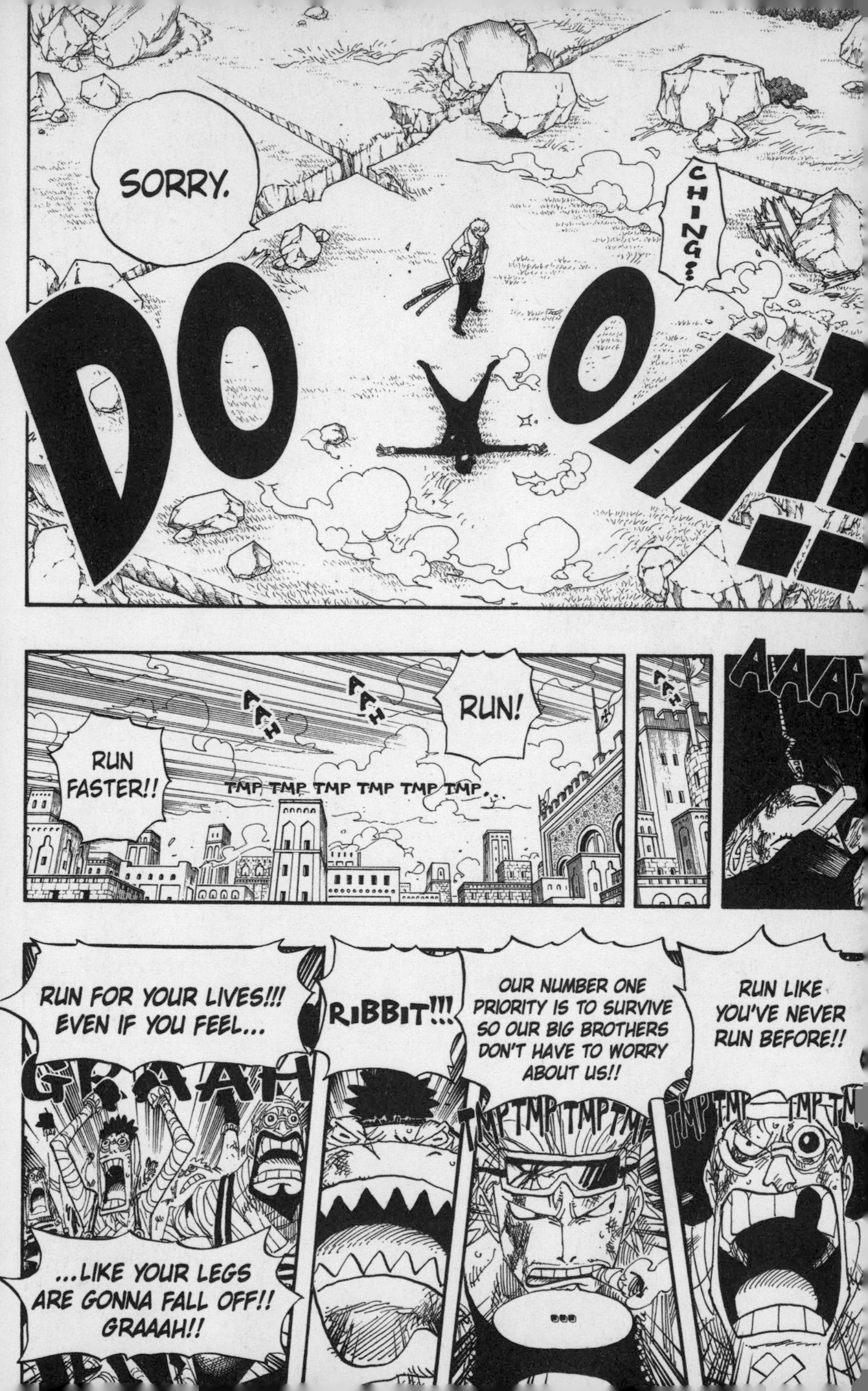
CHING...
SORRY.
DOOM!!
AAAA
FAH
RUN!
FAH
FAH
RUN FASTER!!
TMP TMP TMP TMP TMP TMP...
RUN LIKE YOU'VE NEVER RUN BEFORE!!
TMP TMP TMP TM
OUR NUMBER ONE PRIORITY IS TO SURVIVE SO OUR BIG BROTHERS DON'T HAVE TO WORRY ABOUT US!!
TMP TMP TMP TMP
...
RIBBIT!!!
RUN FOR YOUR LIVES!!! EVEN IF YOU FEEL...
GRAAAH
...LIKE YOUR LEGS ARE GONNA FALL OFF!! GRAAAH!!

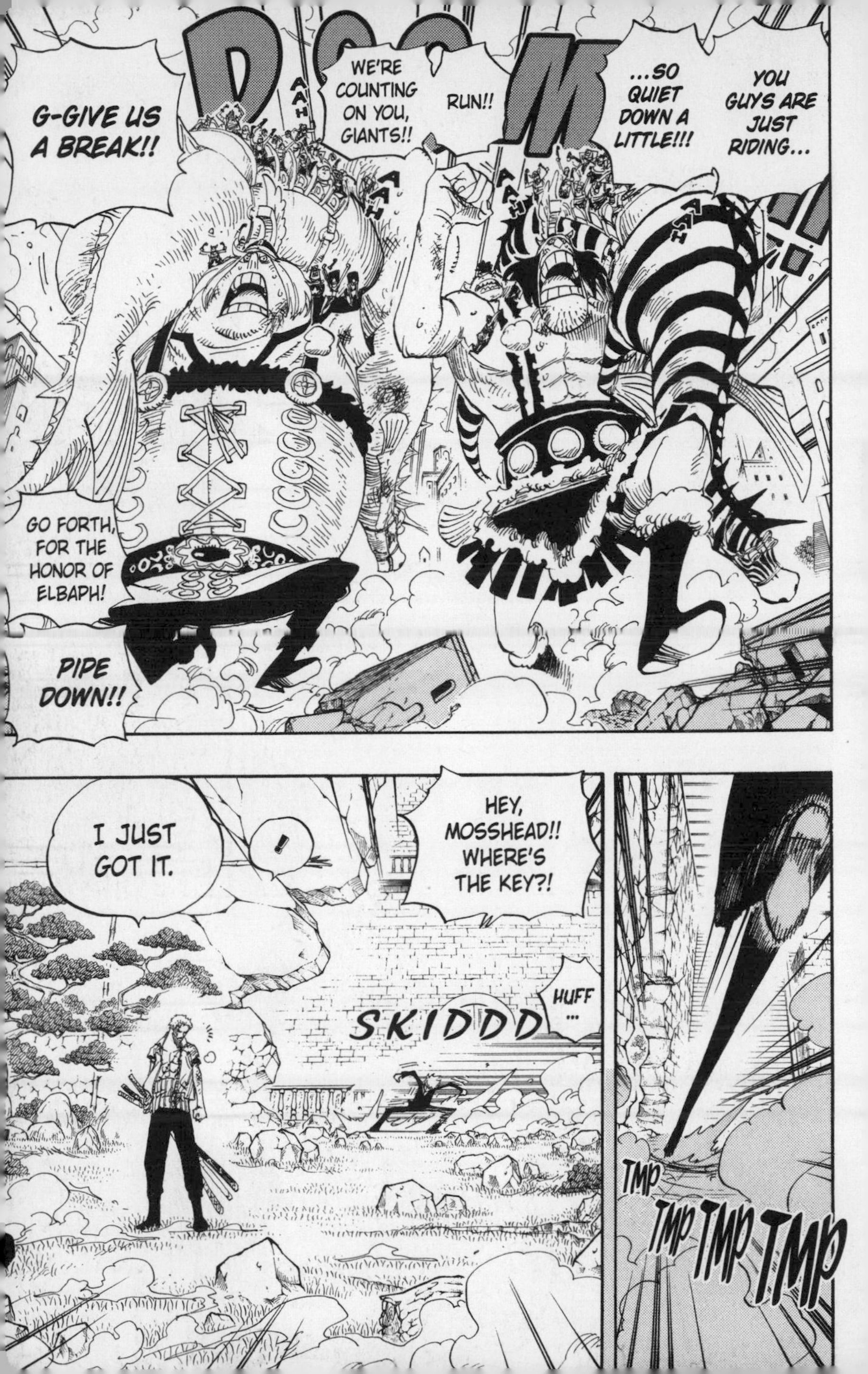

YOU GUYS ARE JUST RIDING...
...SO QUIET DOWN A LITTLE!!!
DOOM
RUN!!
WE'RE COUNTING ON YOU, GIANTS!!
G-GIVE US A BREAK!!
AAAH
GO FORTH, FOR THE HONOR OF ELBAPH!
PIPE DOWN!!
TMP TMP TMP TMP
HEY, MOSSHEAD!! WHERE'S THE KEY?!
HUFF ...
SKIDDD
!
I JUST GOT IT.

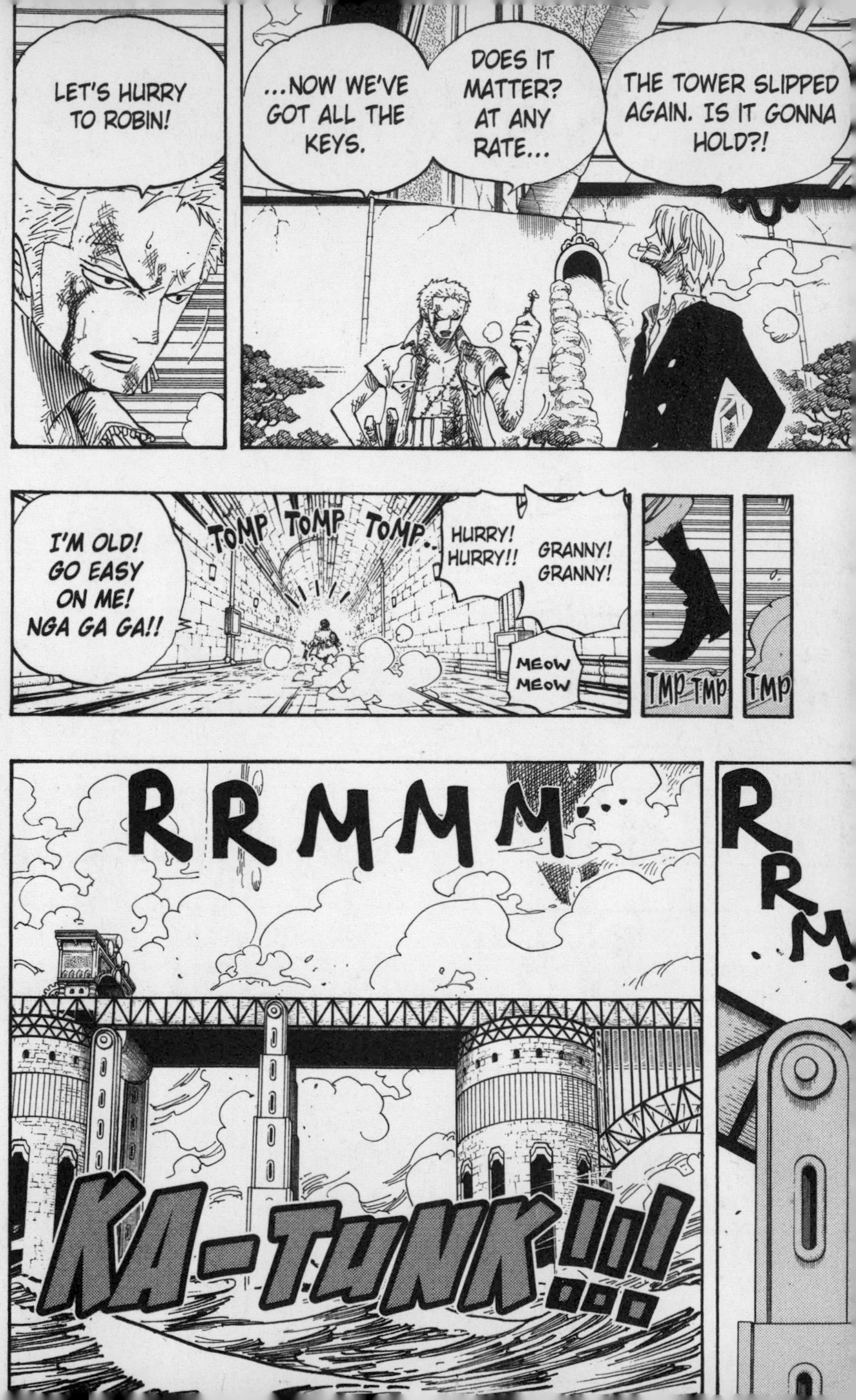
THE TOWER SLIPPED AGAIN. IS IT GONNA HOLD?!
DOES IT MATTER? AT ANY RATE...
...NOW WE'VE GOT ALL THE KEYS.
LET'S HURRY TO ROBIN!
TMP
TMP TMP
GRANNY! GRANNY!
HURRY! HURRY!!
MEOW MEOW
TOMP TOMP TOMP..
I'M OLD! GO EASY ON ME! NGA GA GA!!
RRM..
RRMMM...
KA-TUNK!!!

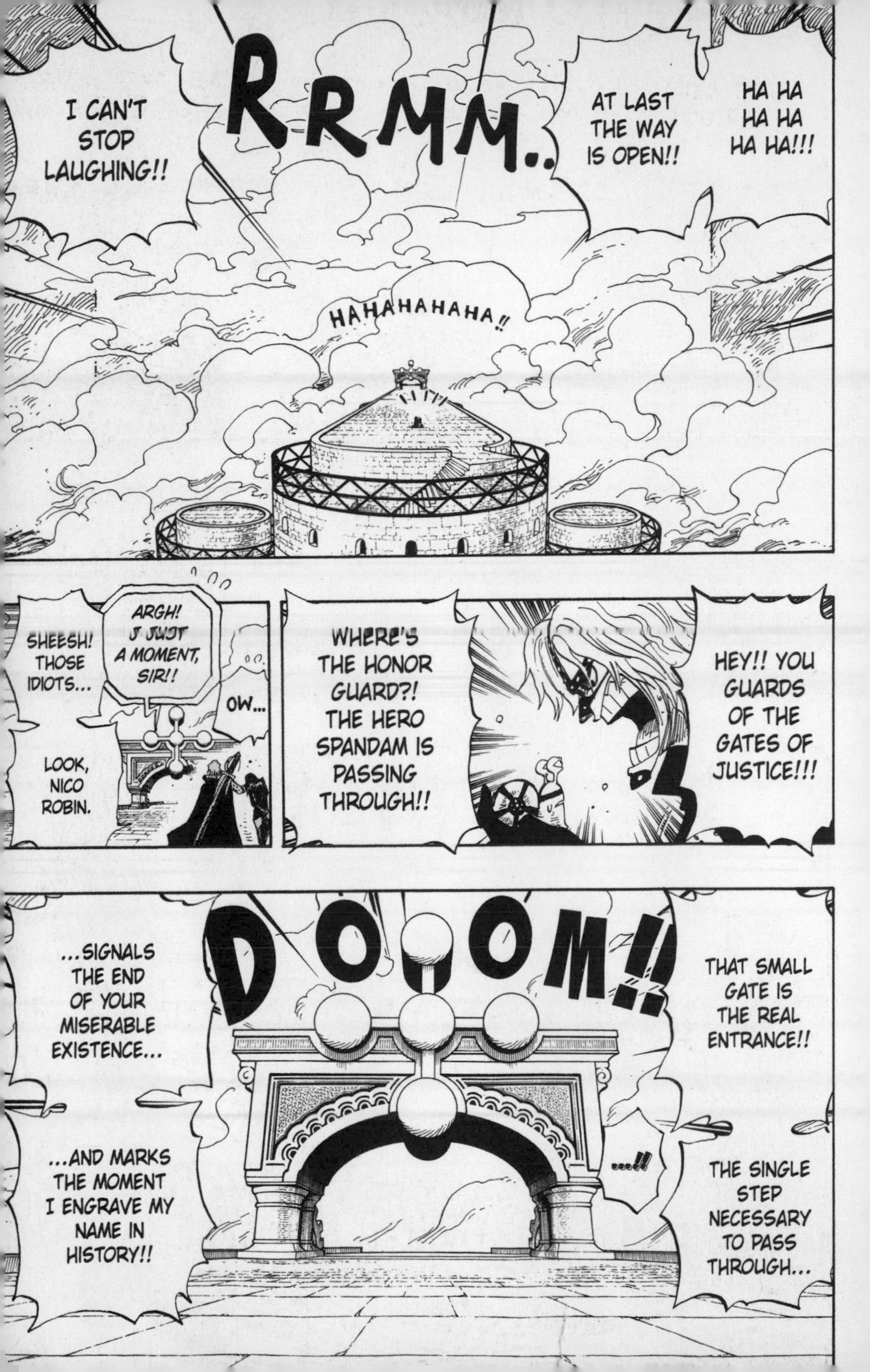
HA HA HA HA HA HA!!!
AT LAST THE WAY IS OPEN!!
RRMM..
I CAN'T STOP LAUGHING!!
HAHAHAHAHA!!
HEY!! YOU GUARDS OF THE GATES OF JUSTICE!!!
WHERE'S THE HONOR GUARD?! THE HERO SPANDAM IS PASSING THROUGH!!
OW...
ARGH! J JUST A MOMENT, SIR!!
SHEESH! THOSE IDIOTS...
LOOK, NICO ROBIN.
THAT SMALL GATE IS THE REAL ENTRANCE!!
THE SINGLE STEP NECESSARY TO PASS THROUGH...
DOOM!!
...SIGNALS THE END OF YOUR MISERABLE EXISTENCE...
...!!
...AND MARKS THE MOMENT I ENGRAVE MY NAME IN HISTORY!!

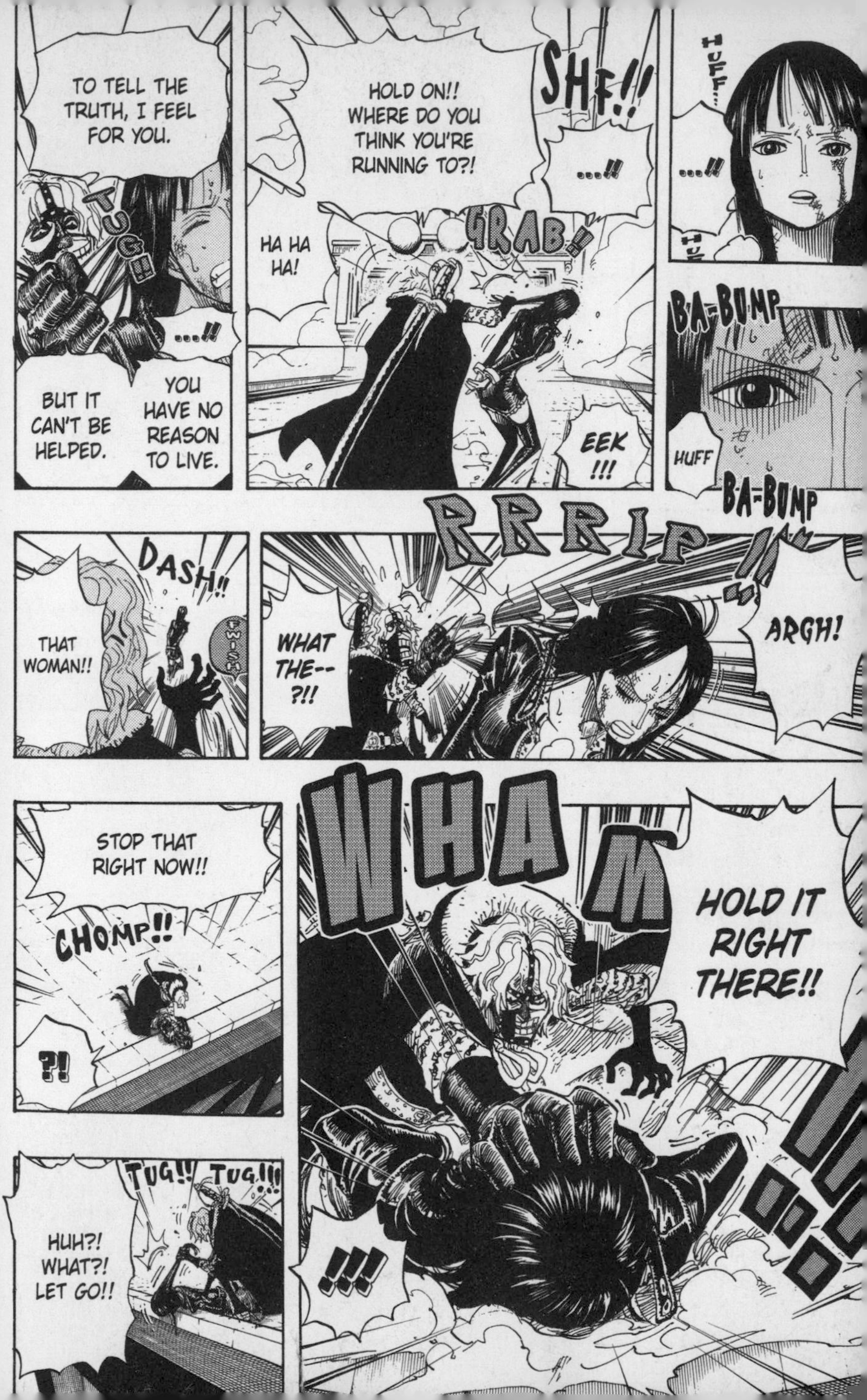
HUFF...
...!!
HU
BA-BUMP
HUFF
BA-BUMP
SHF!!
...!!
HOLD ON!! WHERE DO YOU THINK YOU'RE RUNNING TO?!
GRAB!!
HA HA HA!
EEK!!!
TO TELL THE TRUTH, I FEEL FOR YOU.
TUG!!
...!!
YOU HAVE NO REASON TO LIVE.
BUT IT CAN'T BE HELPED.
RRRIP!!
ARGH!
WHAT THE--?!!
DASH!!
FWISH
THAT WOMAN!!
WHAM
HOLD IT RIGHT THERE!!
!!!
STOP THAT RIGHT NOW!!
CHOMP!!
?!
TUG!! TUG!!!
HUH?! WHAT?! LET GO!!

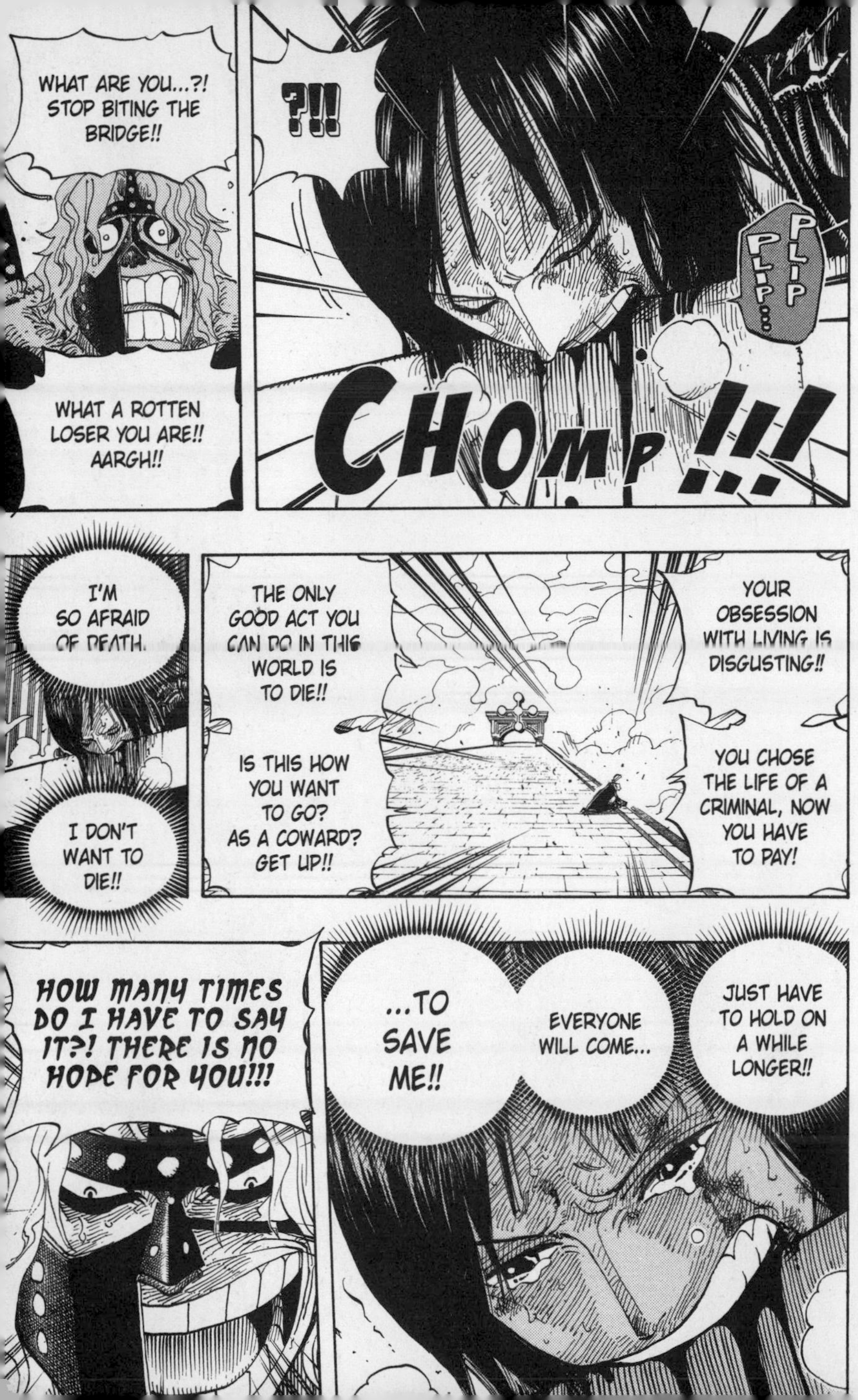
?!!
PLIP PLIP...
CHOMP!!!
WHAT ARE YOU...?! STOP BITING THE BRIDGE!!
WHAT A ROTTEN LOSER YOU ARE!! AARGH!!
YOUR OBSESSION WITH LIVING IS DISGUSTING!!
YOU CHOSE THE LIFE OF A CRIMINAL, NOW YOU HAVE TO PAY!
THE ONLY GOOD ACT YOU CAN DO IN THIS WORLD IS TO DIE!!
IS THIS HOW YOU WANT TO GO? AS A COWARD? GET UP!!
I'M SO AFRAID OF DEATH.
I DON'T WANT TO DIE!!
JUST HAVE TO HOLD ON A WHILE LONGER!!
EVERYONE WILL COME...
...TO SAVE ME!!
HOW MANY TIMES DO I HAVE TO SAY IT?! THERE IS NO HOPE FOR YOU!!!

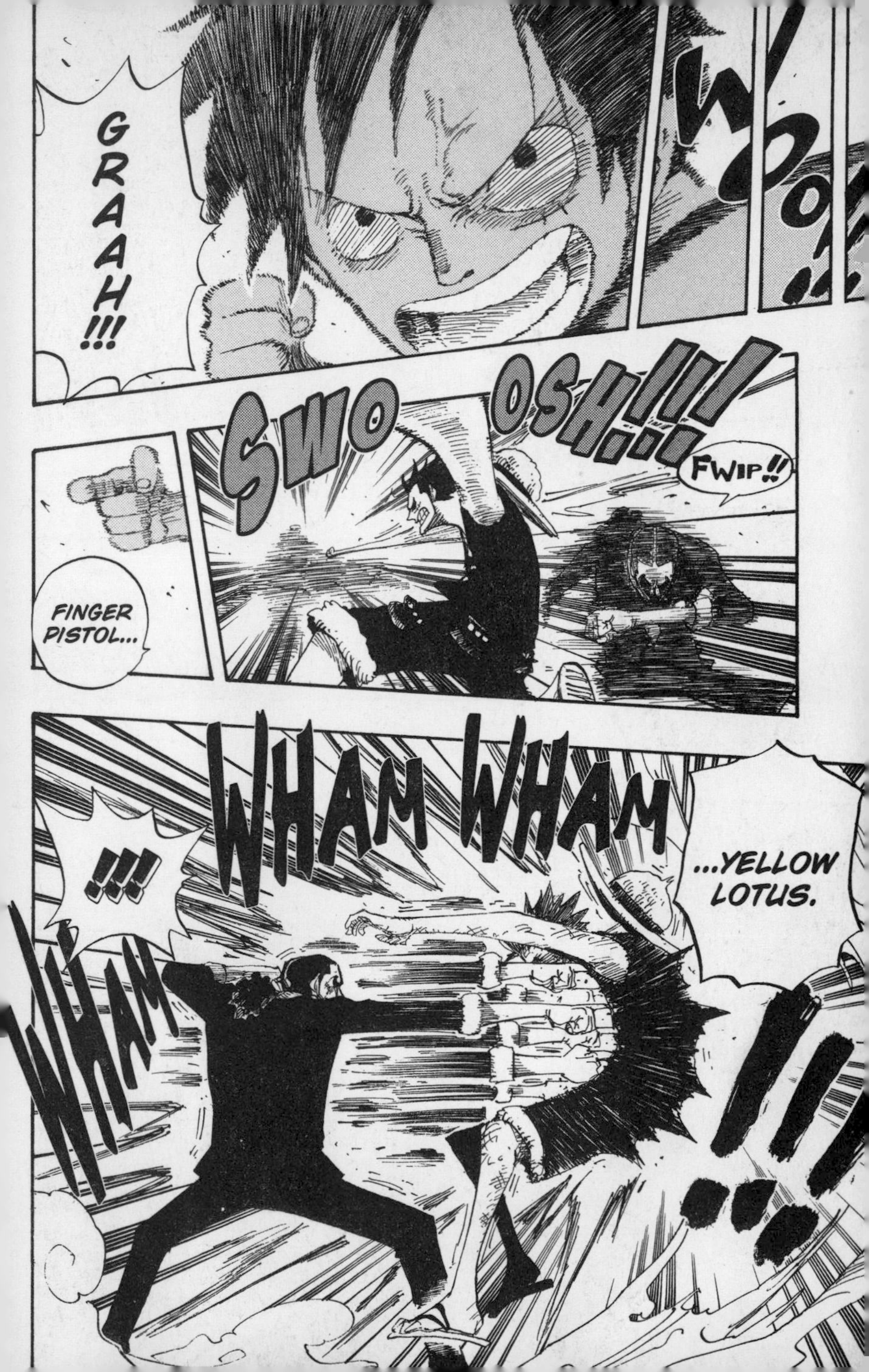
WOO!!!
GRAAH!!!
SWOOSH!!!!
FWIP!!
FINGER PISTOL...
...YELLOW LOTUS.
WHAM WHAM
!!!
!!!
WHAM

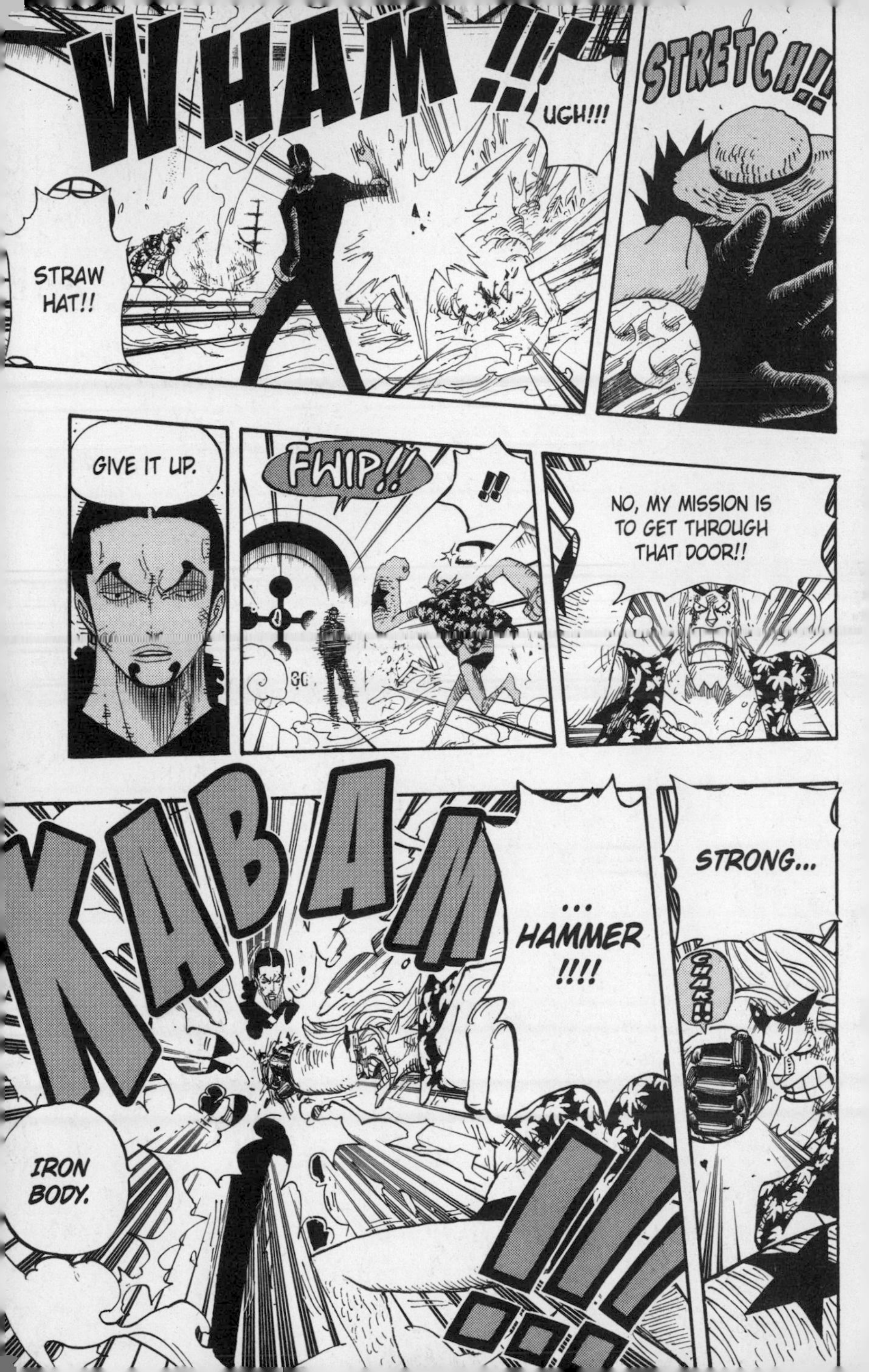
STRETCH!!!
WHAM!!
UGH!!!
STRAW HAT!!
NO, MY MISSION IS TO GET THROUGH THAT DOOR!!
FWIP!!
!!
GIVE IT UP.
STRONG...
KABAM
... HAMMER !!!!
IRON BODY.

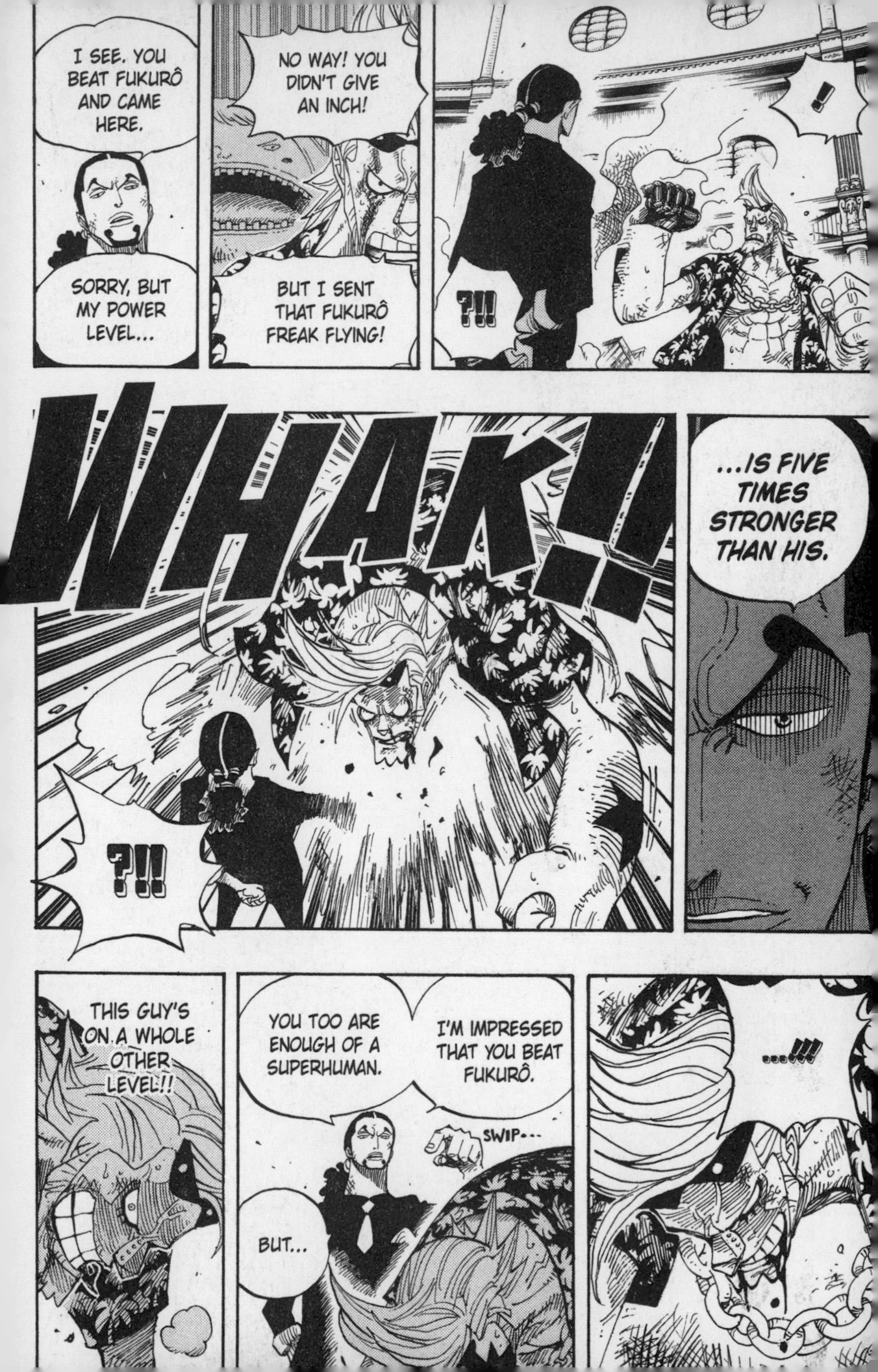
!
?!!
NO WAY! YOU DIDN'T GIVE AN INCH!
BUT I SENT THAT FUKURÔ FREAK FLYING!
I SEE. YOU BEAT FUKURÔ AND CAME HERE.
SORRY, BUT MY POWER LEVEL...
...IS FIVE TIMES STRONGER THAN HIS.
WHAK!!
?!!
...!!!
I'M IMPRESSED THAT YOU BEAT FUKURÔ.
YOU TOO ARE ENOUGH OF A SUPERHUMAN.
SWIP...
BUT...
THIS GUY'S ON A WHOLE OTHER LEVEL!!

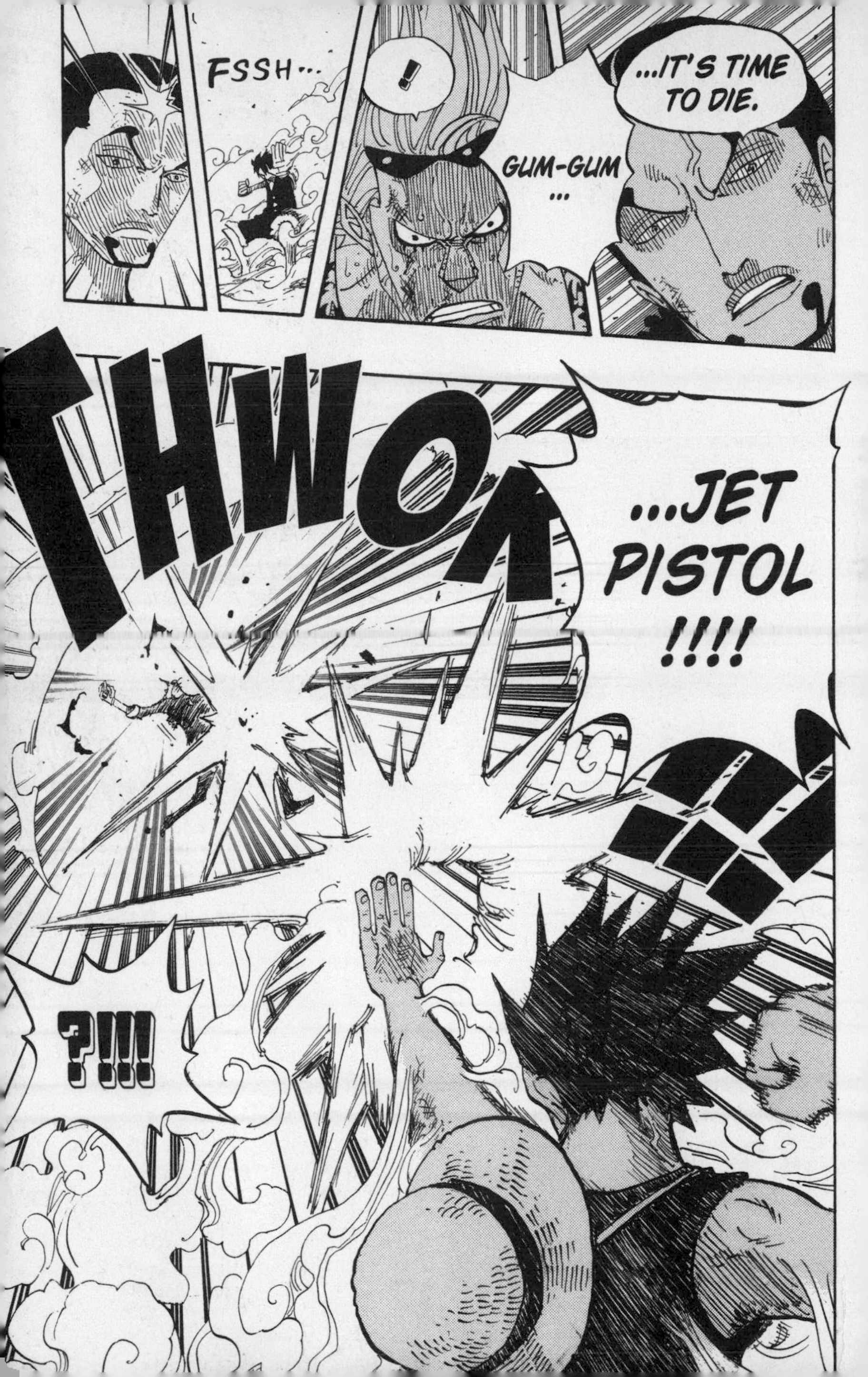
...IT'S TIME TO DIE.
GUM-GUM ...
!
FSSH...
...JET PISTOL !!!!
THWOK
?!!!

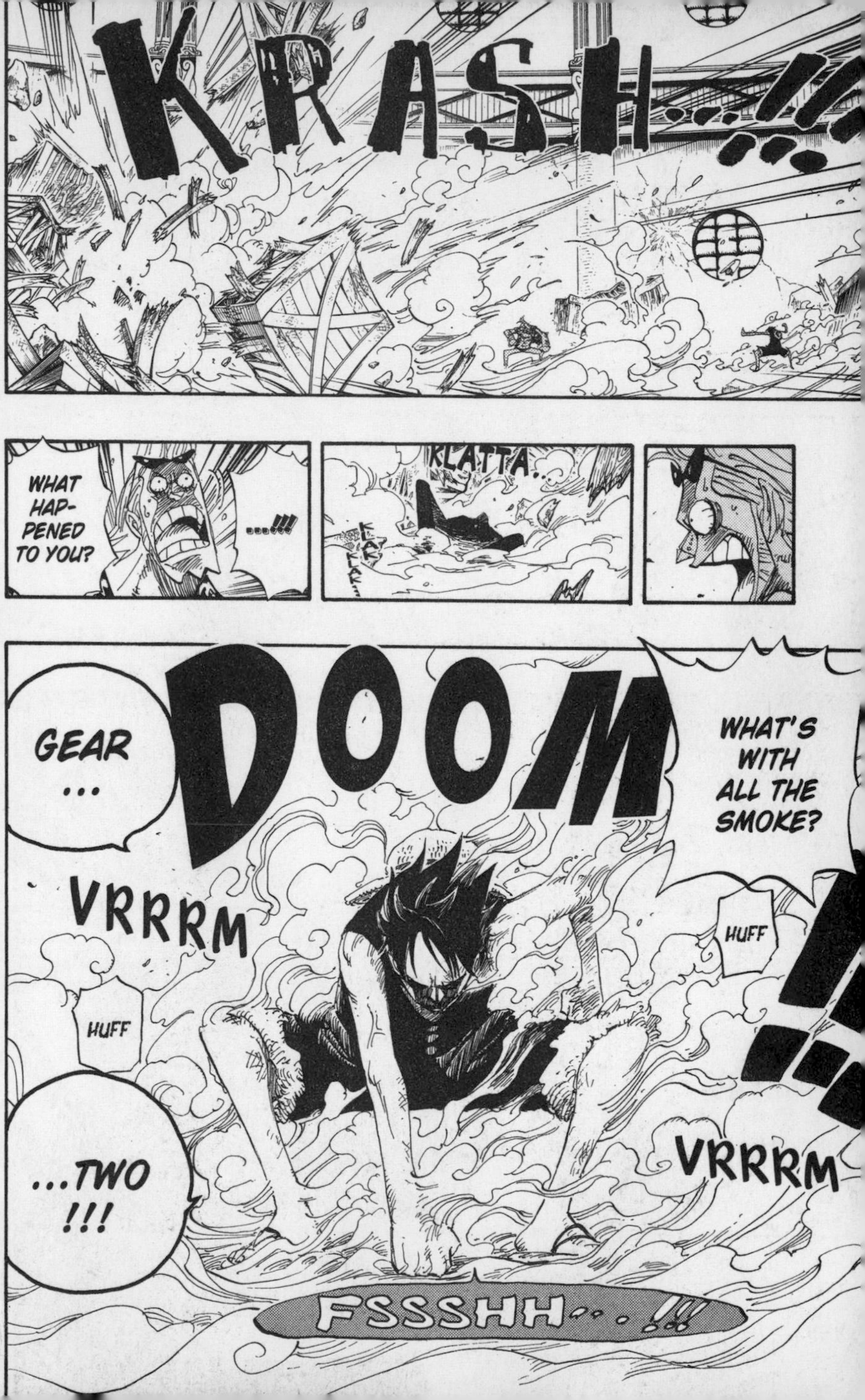
KRASH...!!!
KLATTA...
KLAK KLAK...
WHAT HAP-PENED TO YOU?
...!!!
WHAT'S WITH ALL THE SMOKE?
DOOM
GEAR ...
HUFF
VRRRM
HUFF
VRRRM
...TWO !!!
FSSSHH...!!

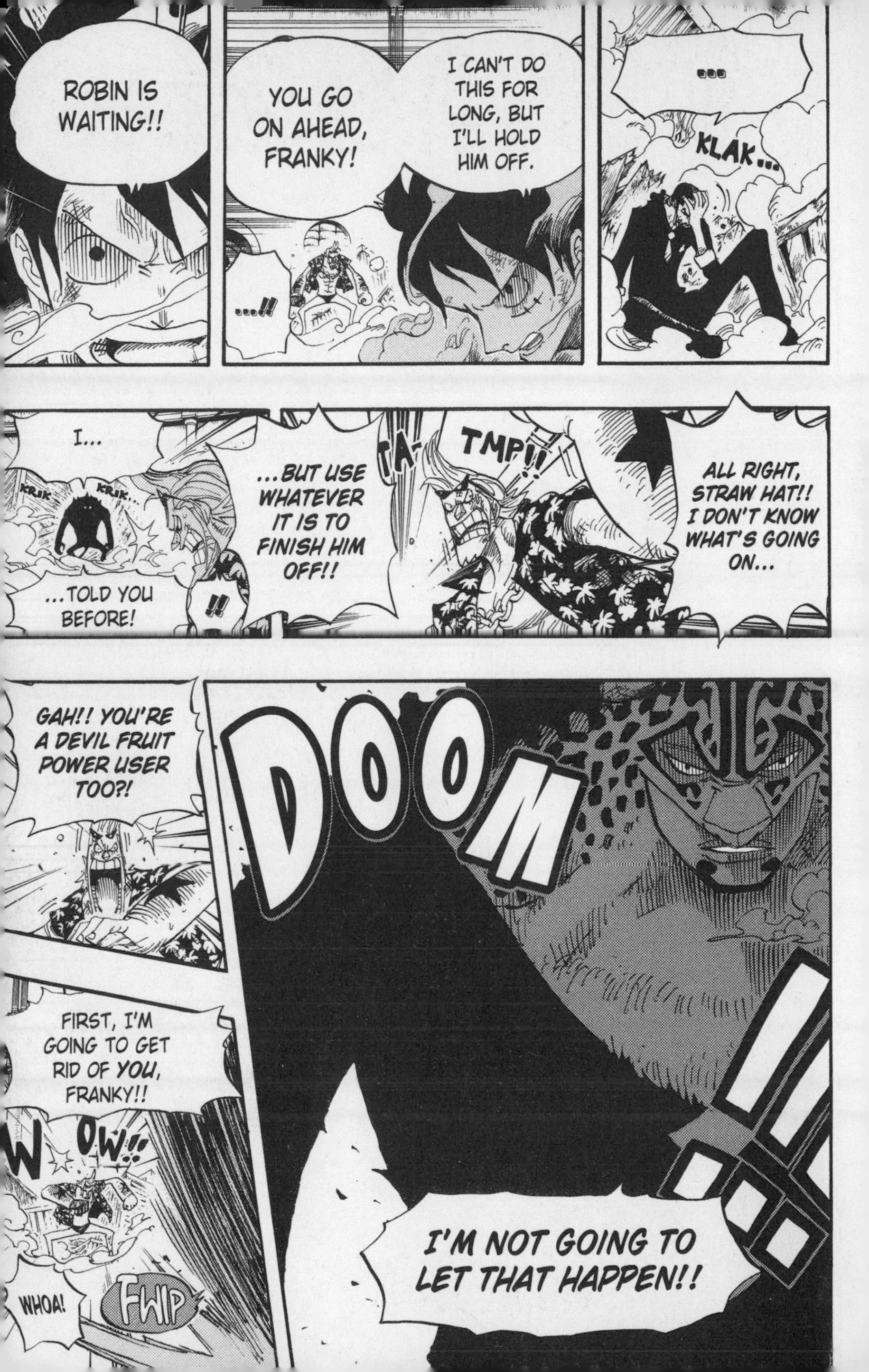
...
KLAK...
I CAN'T DO THIS FOR LONG, BUT I'LL HOLD HIM OFF.
YOU GO ON AHEAD, FRANKY!
...!!
ROBIN IS WAITING!!
ALL RIGHT, STRAW HAT!! I DON'T KNOW WHAT'S GOING ON...
TMP!!
...BUT USE WHATEVER IT IS TO FINISH HIM OFF!!
I...
KRIK
KRIK...
...TOLD YOU BEFORE!
!!
DOOM
I'M NOT GOING TO LET THAT HAPPEN!!
GAH!! YOU'RE A DEVIL FRUIT POWER USER TOO?!
FIRST, I'M GOING TO GET RID OF YOU, FRANKY!!
WOW!!
WHOA!
FWIP

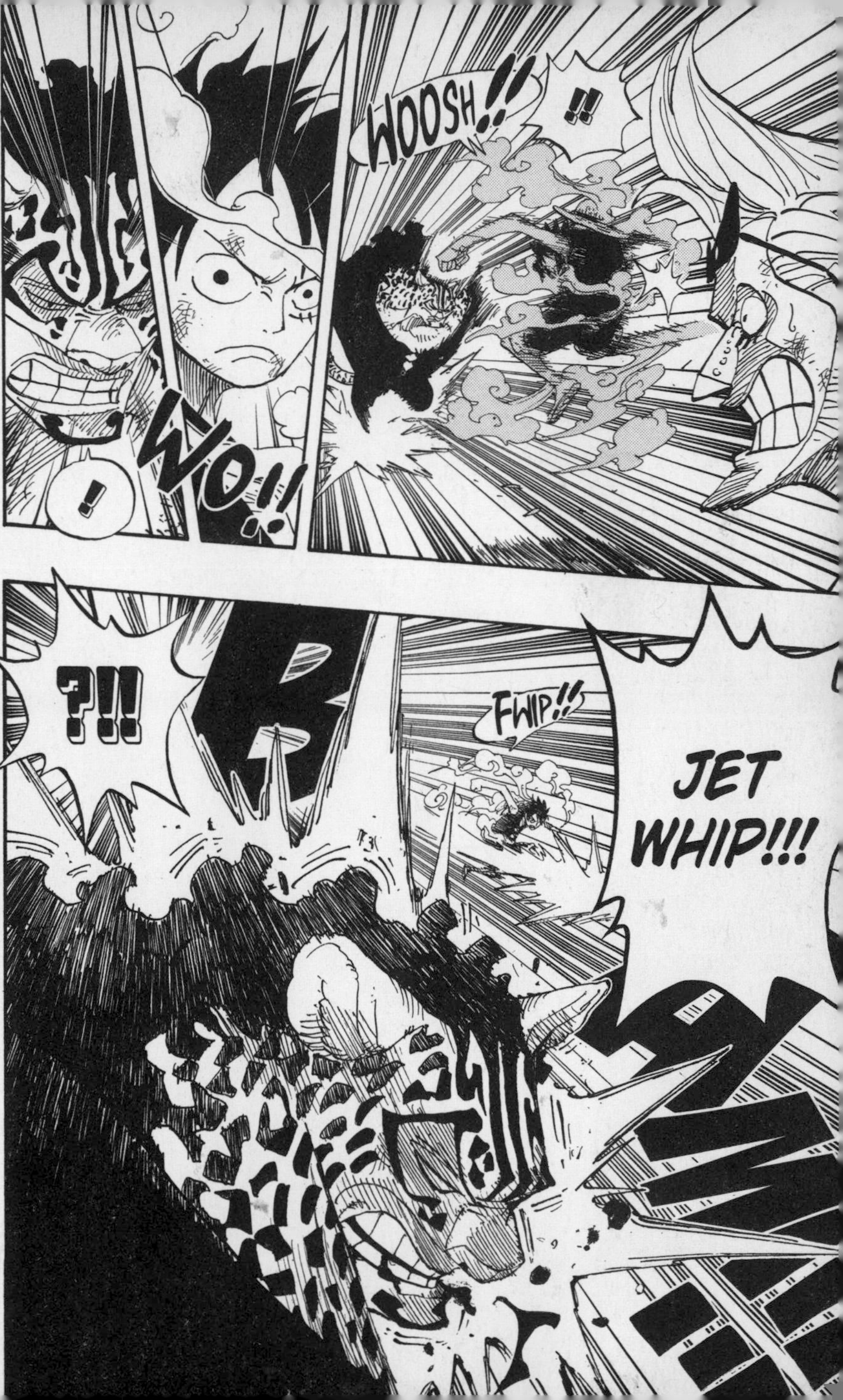
!!
WOOSH!!
WO!!
!
JET WHIP!!!
FWIP!!
?!!

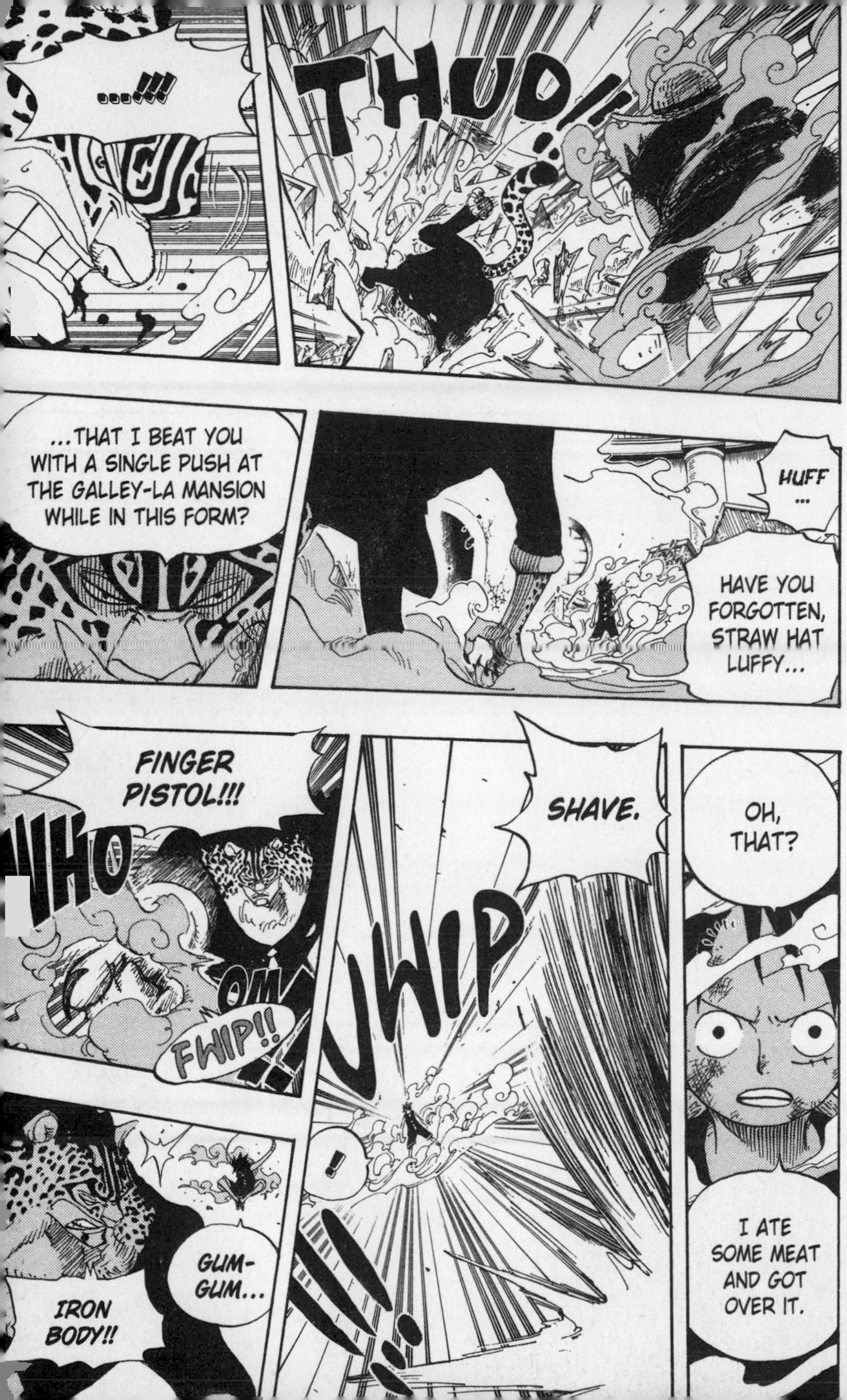
THUD!!
...!!!
HUFF ...
HAVE YOU FORGOTTEN, STRAW HAT LUFFY...
...THAT I BEAT YOU WITH A SINGLE PUSH AT THE GALLEY-LA MANSION WHILE IN THIS FORM?
OH, THAT?
I ATE SOME MEAT AND GOT OVER IT.
SHAVE.
WHIP
!
FINGER PISTOL!!!
WHO
OM
FWIP!!
GUM-GUM...
IRON BODY!!

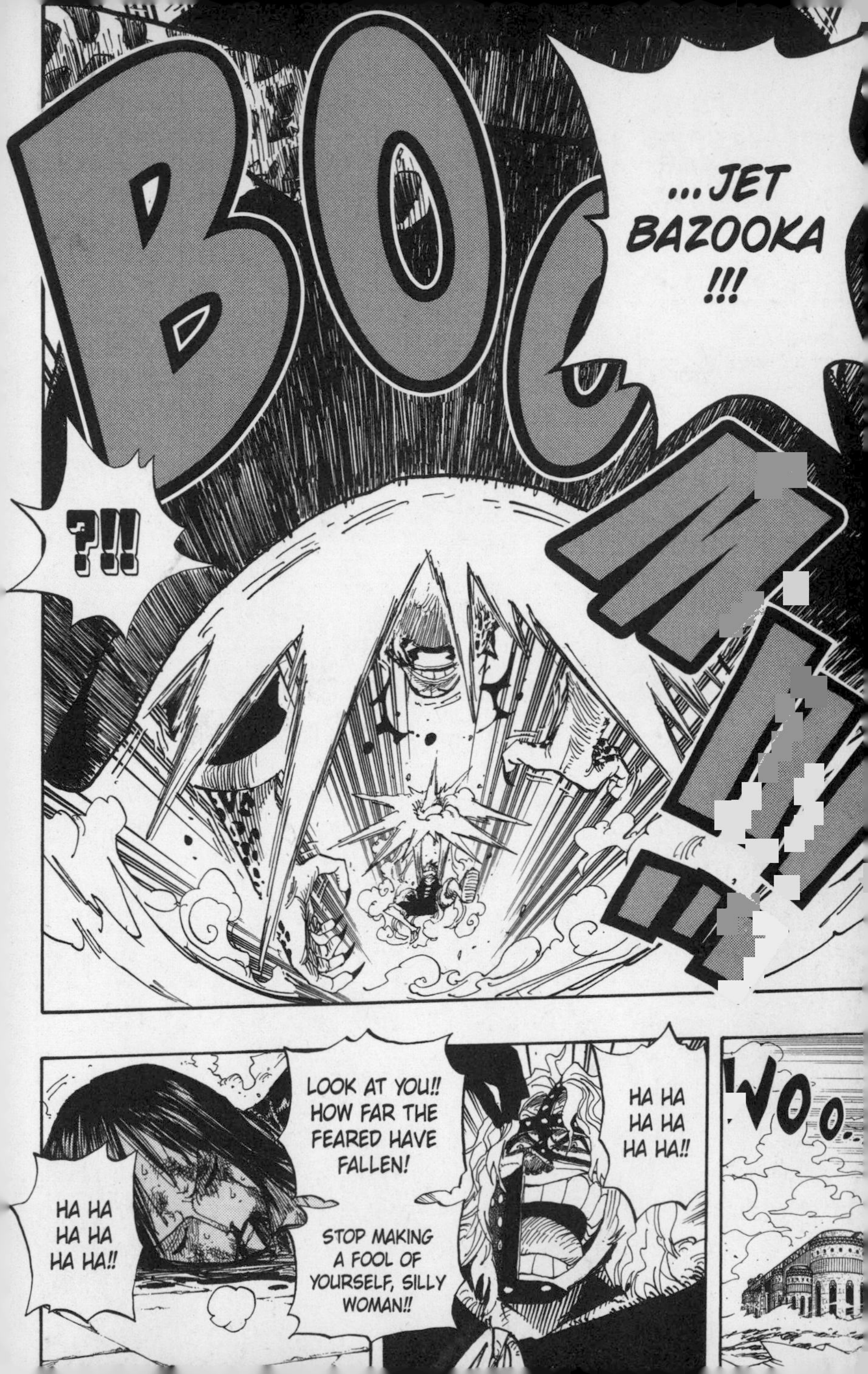
...JET BAZOOKA!!!
BOOM!!
?!!
WOO...
HA HA HA HA HA HA!!
LOOK AT YOU!! HOW FAR THE FEARED HAVE FALLEN!
STOP MAKING A FOOL OF YOURSELF, SILLY WOMAN!!
HA HA HA HA HA HA!!

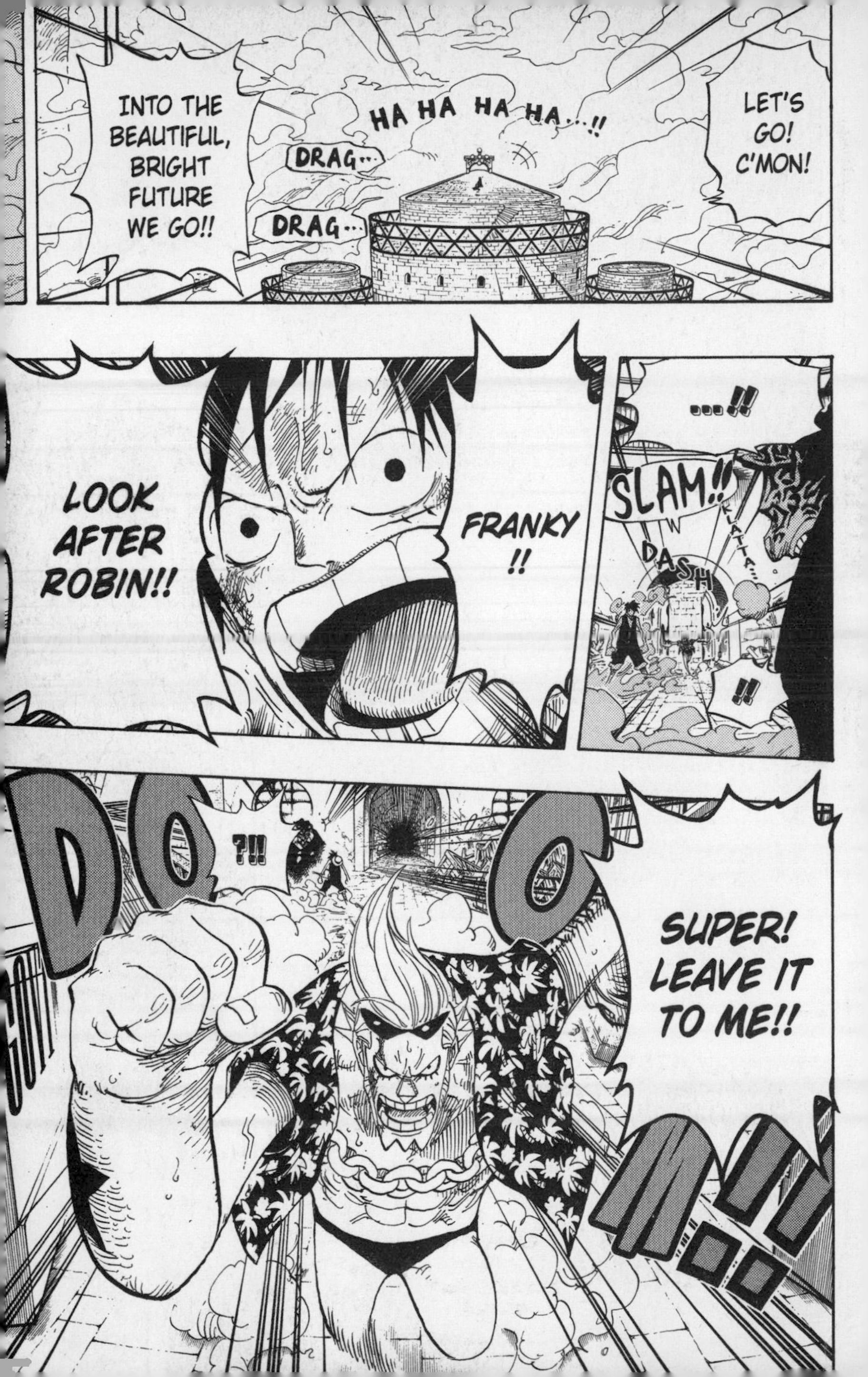
LET'S GO! C'MON!
HA HA HA HA...!!
DRAG...
DRAG...
INTO THE BEAUTIFUL, BRIGHT FUTURE WE GO!!
...!!
SLAM!!
KLATTA...
DASH
!!
FRANKY!!
LOOK AFTER ROBIN!!
SUPER! LEAVE IT TO ME!!
?!!

Question Corner

S B S

Q: I've got a question, Oda Sensei! Did you make up the story about Klabautermann that appears in chapter 351 of volume 37, or does such a story actually exist? Please, tell me.

--Someone Sort of Behind the Luffy Pirate Group

A: Numerous legends around the world tell of a ship's spirit. Klabautermann is spoken of among German sailors. In Japan we call a ship's spirit funadama. Maybe it's easiest to think of it as a guardian spirit of ships. It was once believed that if Klabautermann was on a ship, it would sail safely.

Q: When it comes to square things, Kaku and his long nose come to mind, but there's something even more square! In panel 3 along the left-hand side of page 131 in volume 35, there's a guy whose whole head is square! What is he?! Tell me! Don't be a square!

--A Prince Somewhere

A: Yeah, he's there. And I'll tell you, fair and square! His name is...Blockhead! (Is that too off the top of my head?) Let's see...he's extremely pointy-headed, and I hear he loves getting into four-sided debates. And, uh... he hates being cornered. That's the kind of person he is!! (Is that too off the top of my head?) See you next time in the Question Corner!! (It's over already?!)

Chapter 419:
LEGEND OF A HERO

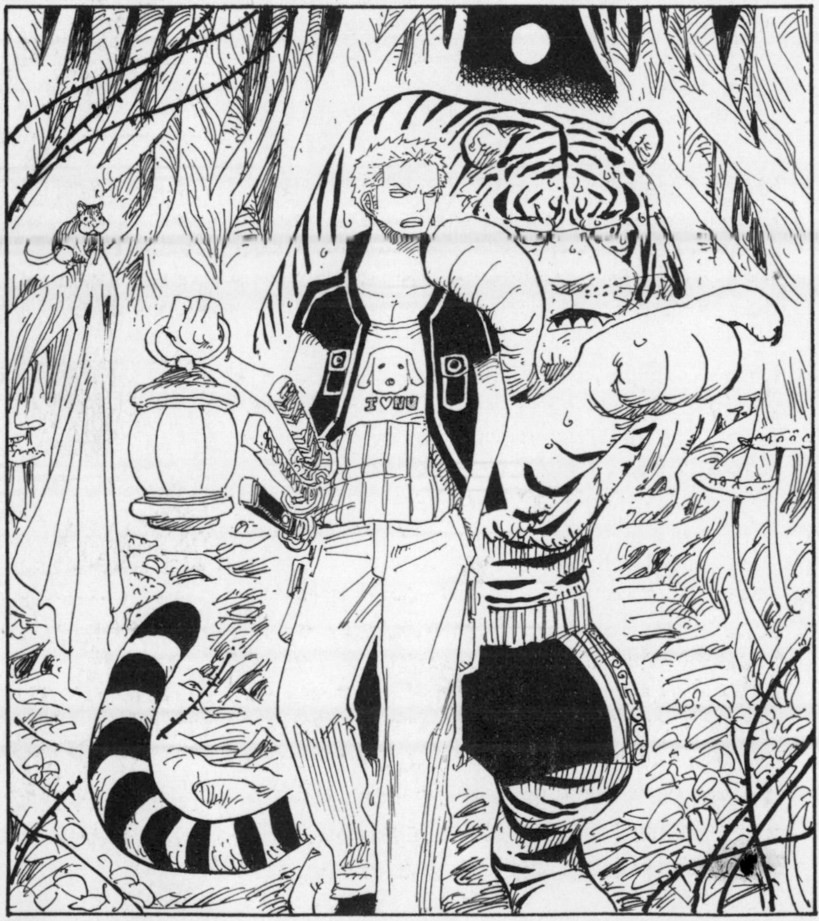

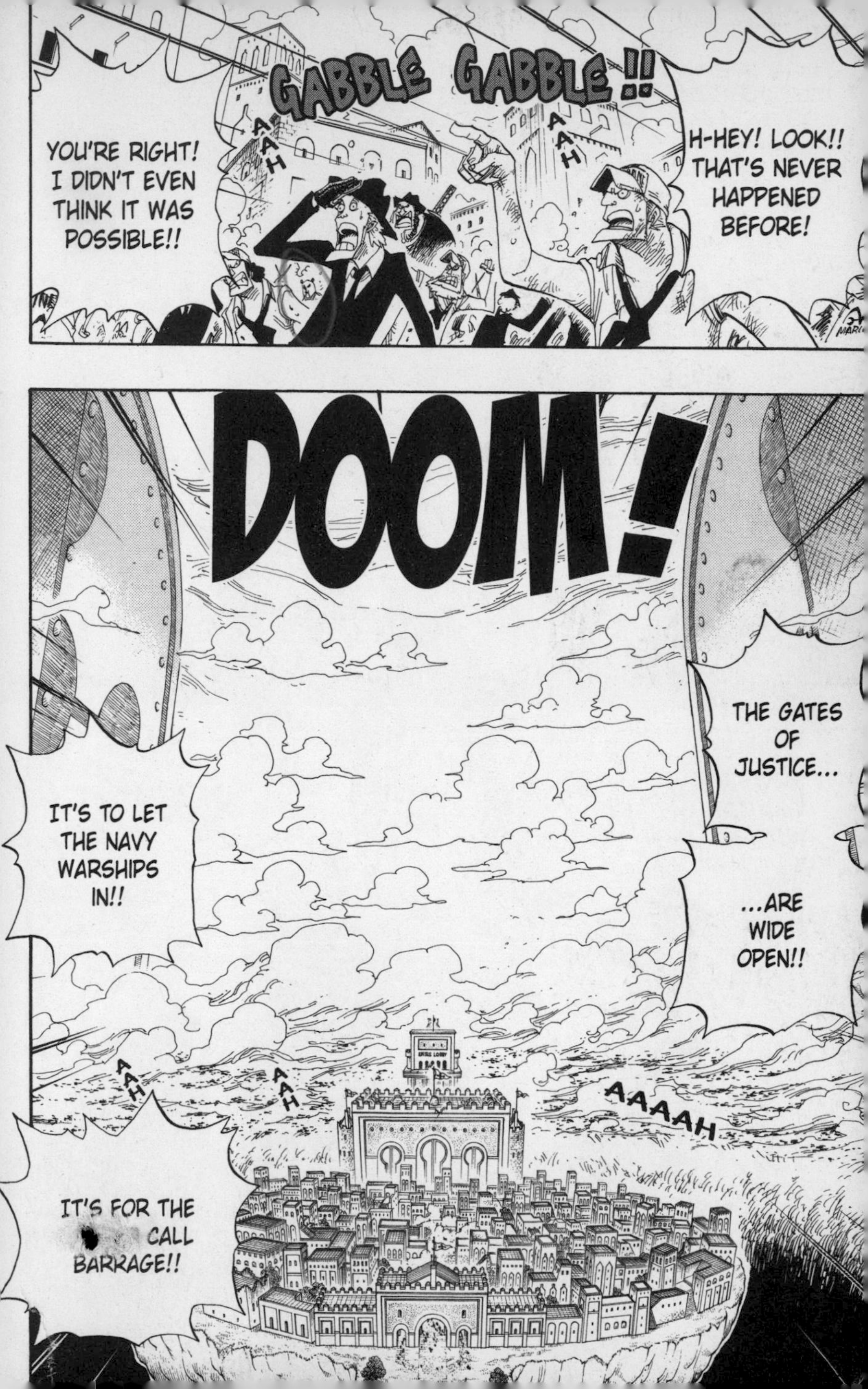
H-HEY! LOOK!! THAT'S NEVER HAPPENED BEFORE!
GABBLE GABBLE!!
AAH
AAH
YOU'RE RIGHT! I DIDN'T EVEN THINK IT WAS POSSIBLE!!
DOOM!
THE GATES OF JUSTICE...
...ARE WIDE OPEN!!
IT'S TO LET THE NAVY WARSHIPS IN!!
AAAAH
AAH
AAH
IT'S FOR THE CALL BARRAGE!!

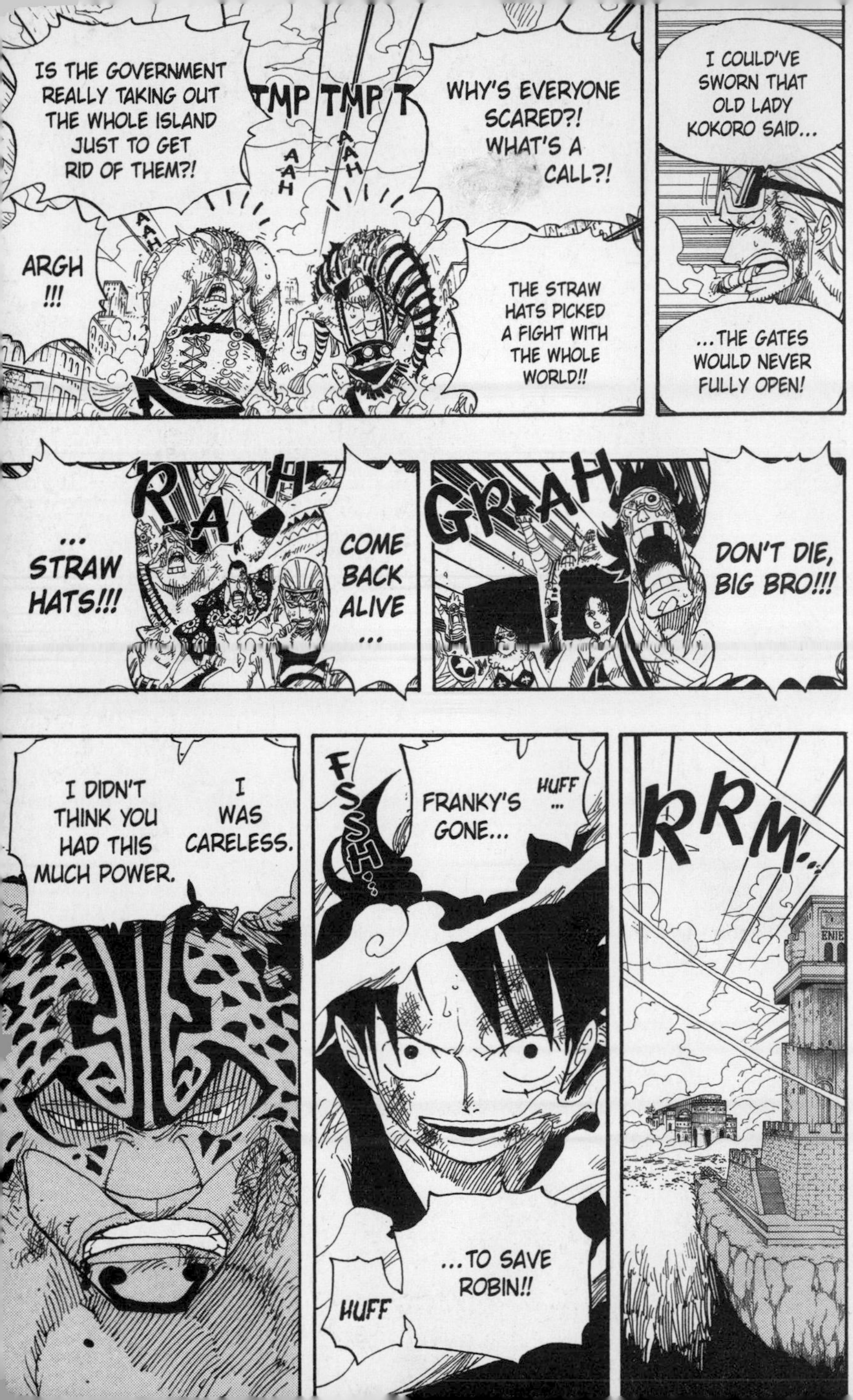
I COULD'VE SWORN THAT OLD LADY KOKORO SAID...
...THE GATES WOULD NEVER FULLY OPEN!
WHY'S EVERYONE SCARED?! WHAT'S A CALL?!
THE STRAW HATS PICKED A FIGHT WITH THE WHOLE WORLD!!
TMP TMP T
AAH
AAH
IS THE GOVERNMENT REALLY TAKING OUT THE WHOLE ISLAND JUST TO GET RID OF THEM?!
AAH
ARGH !!!
GRAH
DON'T DIE, BIG BRO!!!
RAH
COME BACK ALIVE...
...STRAW HATS!!!
RRM..
HUFF ...
FRANKY'S GONE...
FSSH
...TO SAVE ROBIN!!
HUFF
I WAS CARELESS.
I DIDN'T THINK YOU HAD THIS MUCH POWER.

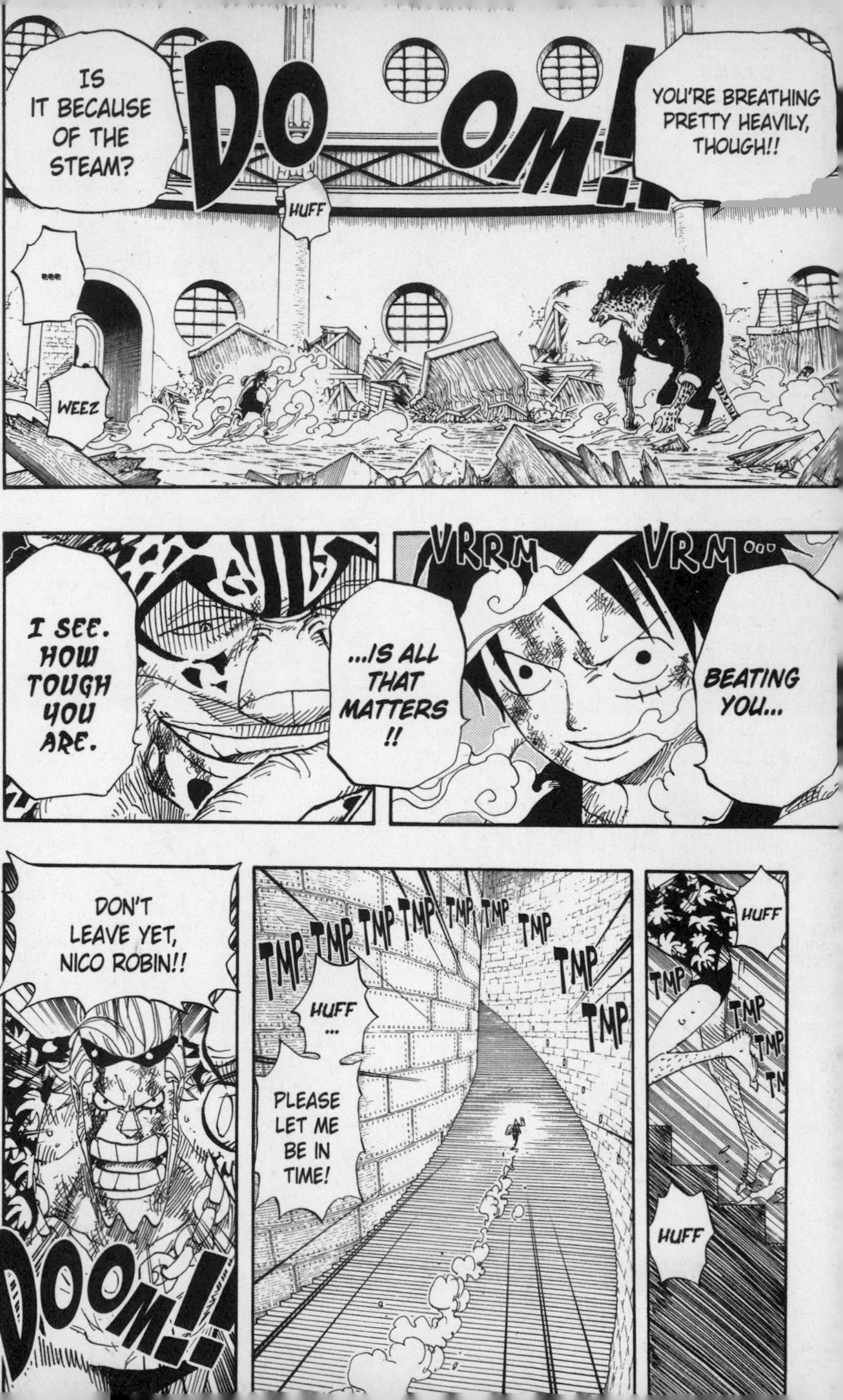
YOU'RE BREATHING PRETTY HEAVILY, THOUGH!!
DO-OM!!
IS IT BECAUSE OF THE STEAM?
HUFF
...
WEEZ
VRRM VRM...
BEATING YOU...
...IS ALL THAT MATTERS!!
I SEE. HOW TOUGH YOU ARE.
HUFF
TMP TMP TMP TM
HUFF
TMP TMP TMP TMP TMP TMP TMP TMP TMP
HUFF...
PLEASE LET ME BE IN TIME!
DON'T LEAVE YET, NICO ROBIN!!
DOOM!!

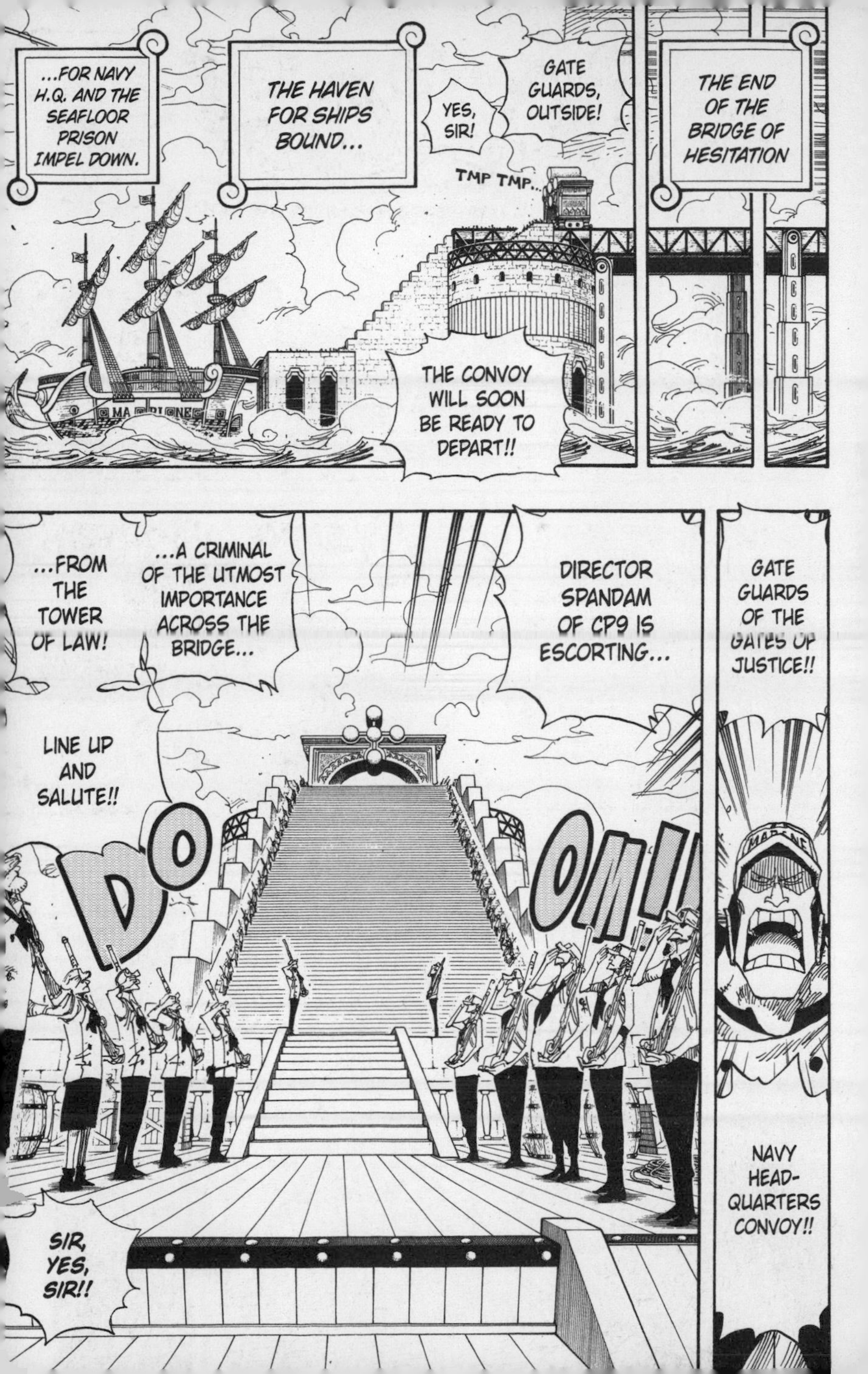
THE END OF THE BRIDGE OF HESITATION
GATE GUARDS, OUTSIDE!
YES, SIR!
THE HAVEN FOR SHIPS BOUND...
...FOR NAVY H.Q. AND THE SEAFLOOR PRISON IMPEL DOWN.
TMP TMP...
THE CONVOY WILL SOON BE READY TO DEPART!!
GATE GUARDS OF THE GATES OF JUSTICE!!
NAVY HEAD-QUARTERS CONVOY!!
DIRECTOR SPANDAM OF CP9 IS ESCORTING...
...A CRIMINAL OF THE UTMOST IMPORTANCE ACROSS THE BRIDGE...
...FROM THE TOWER OF LAW!
LINE UP AND SALUTE!!
DOOM!!
SIR, YES, SIR!!

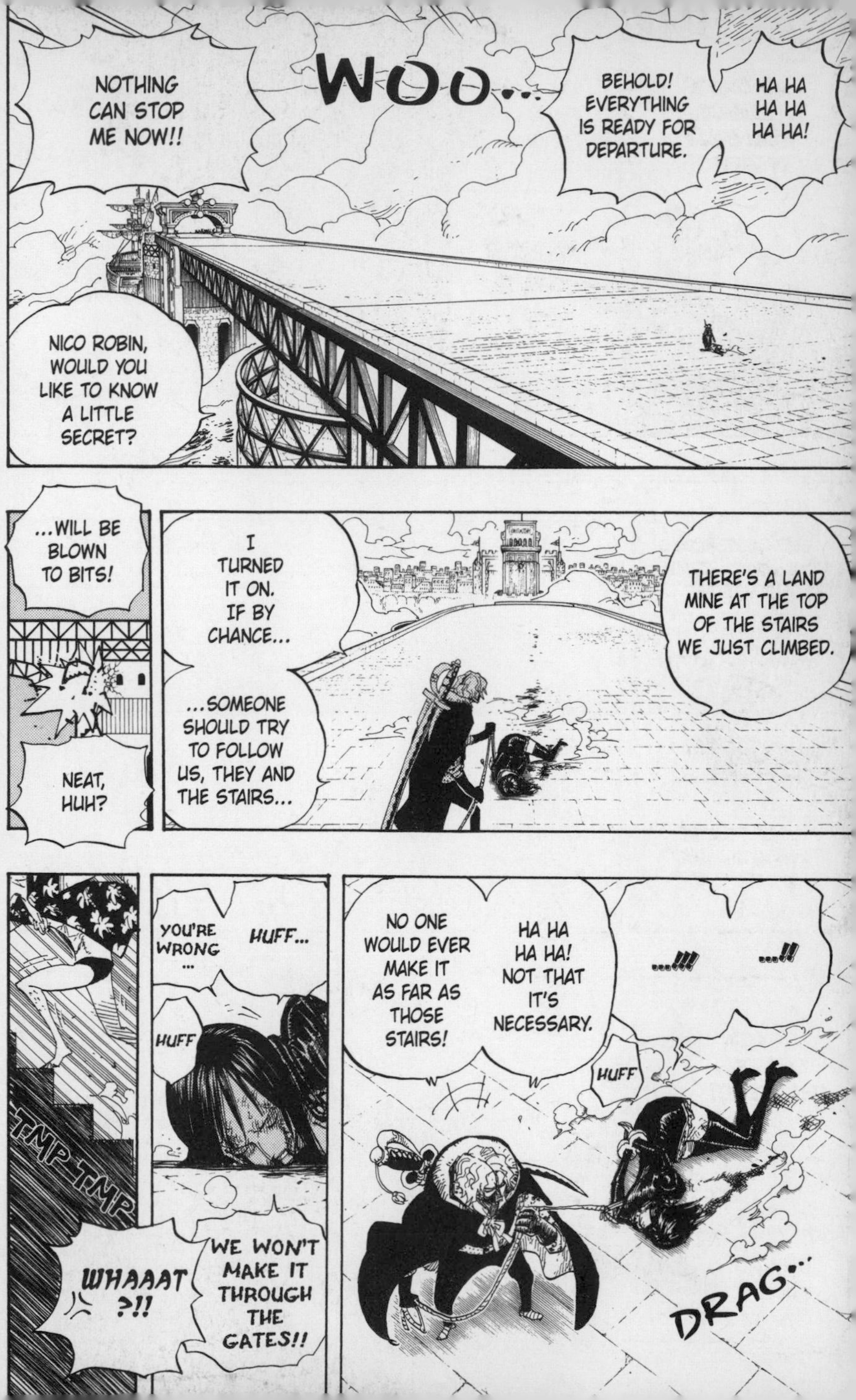

HA HA HA HA HA HA!
BEHOLD! EVERYTHING IS READY FOR DEPARTURE.
WOO...
NOTHING CAN STOP ME NOW!!
NICO ROBIN, WOULD YOU LIKE TO KNOW A LITTLE SECRET?
THERE'S A LAND MINE AT THE TOP OF THE STAIRS WE JUST CLIMBED.
I TURNED IT ON. IF BY CHANCE...
...SOMEONE SHOULD TRY TO FOLLOW US, THEY AND THE STAIRS...
...WILL BE BLOWN TO BITS!
NEAT, HUH?
...!!
...!!
HA HA HA HA! NOT THAT IT'S NECESSARY.
NO ONE WOULD EVER MAKE IT AS FAR AS THOSE STAIRS!
HUFF
DRAG...
HUFF...
YOU'RE WRONG ...
HUFF
WE WON'T MAKE IT THROUGH THE GATES!!
TMP TMP
WHAAAT ?!!

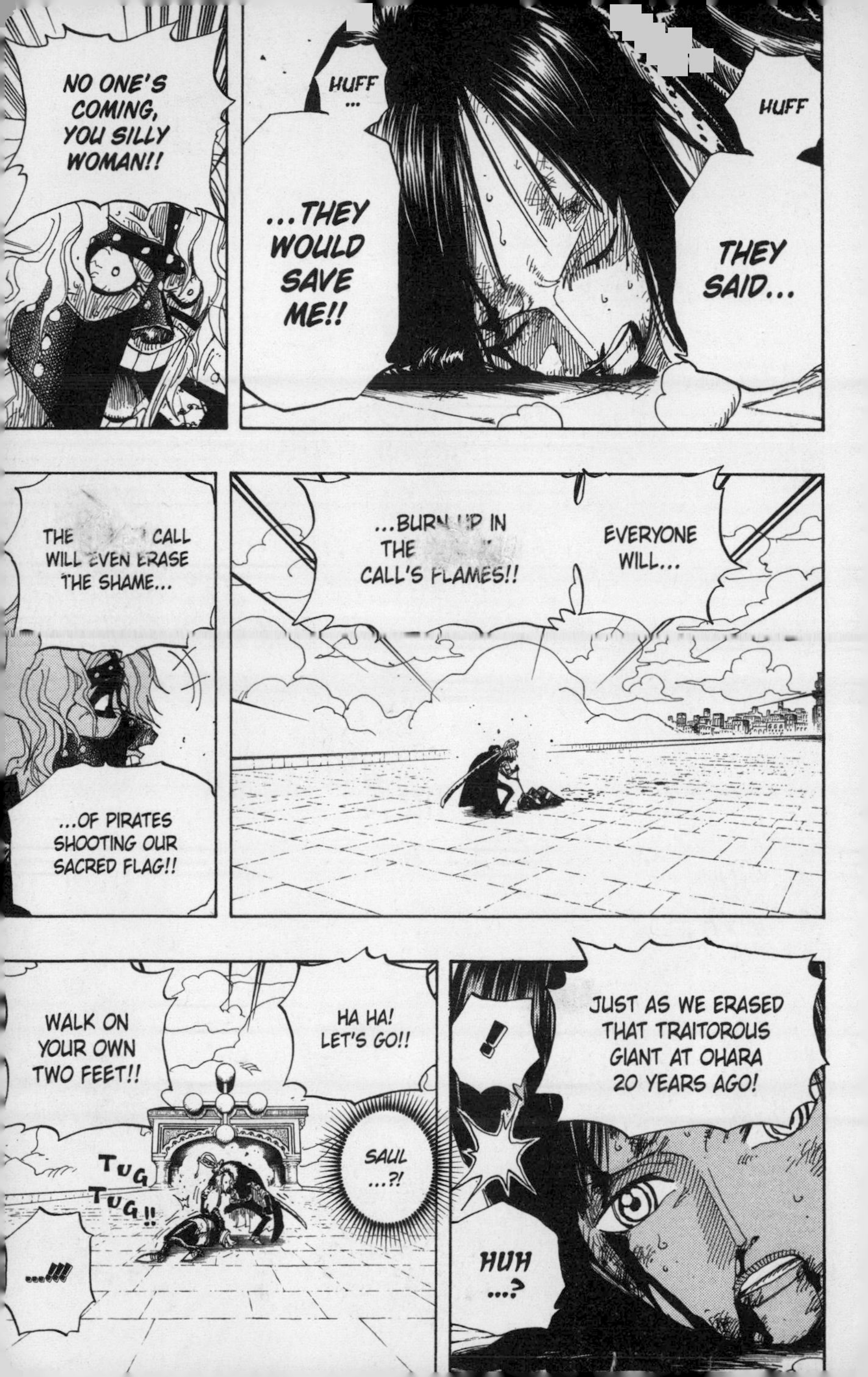
HUFF
THEY SAID...
HUFF ...
...THEY WOULD SAVE ME!!
NO ONE'S COMING, YOU SILLY WOMAN!!
EVERYONE WILL...
...BURN UP IN THE CALL'S FLAMES!!
THE CALL WILL EVEN ERASE THE SHAME...
...OF PIRATES SHOOTING OUR SACRED FLAG!!
JUST AS WE ERASED THAT TRAITOROUS GIANT AT OHARA 20 YEARS AGO!
!
HUH ...?
HA HA! LET'S GO!!
WALK ON YOUR OWN TWO FEET!!
SAUL ...?!
TUG TUG!!
...!!!

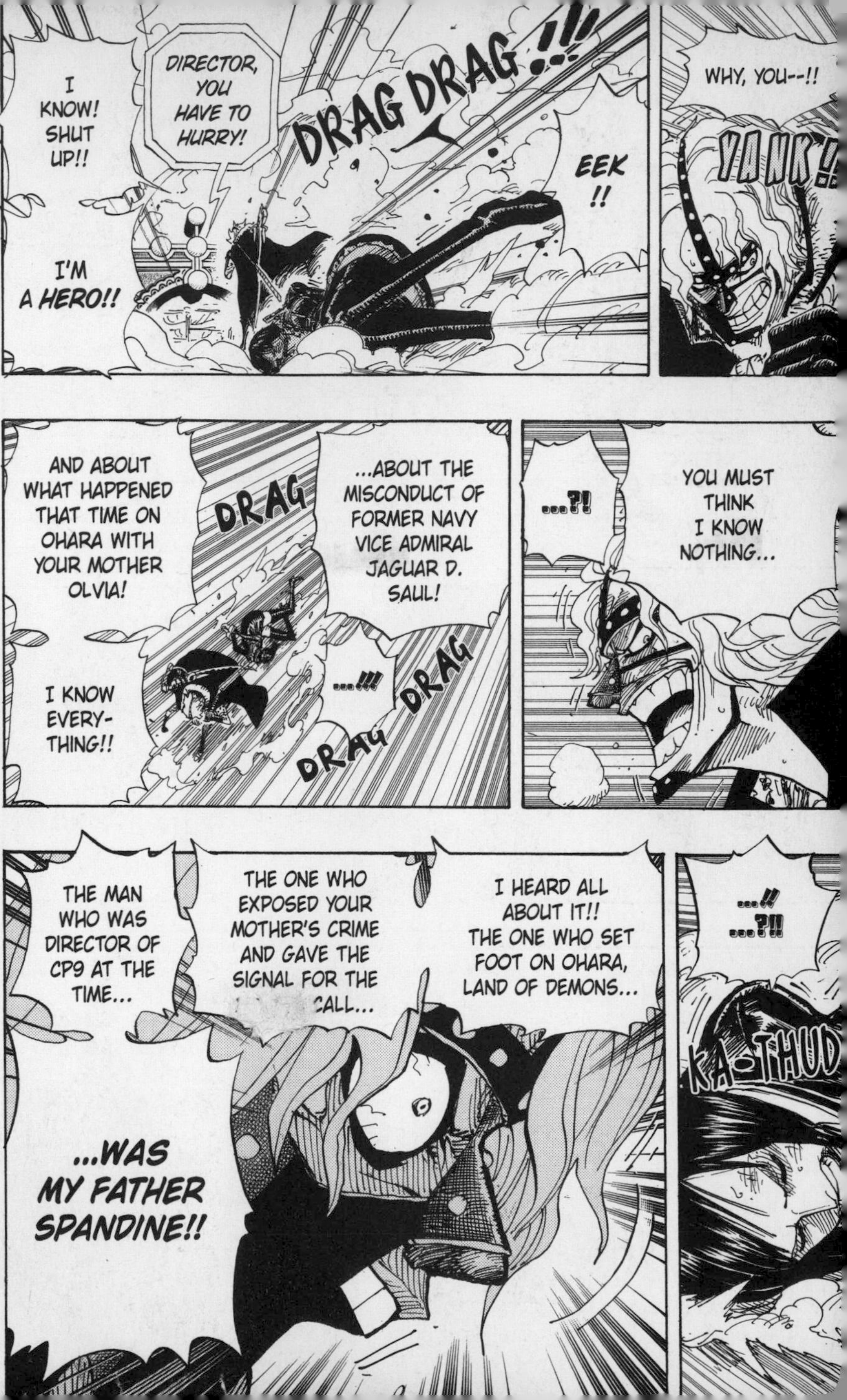
WHY, YOU--!!
YANK!!
DRAG DRAG!!!
EEK !!
DIRECTOR, YOU HAVE TO HURRY!
I KNOW! SHUT UP!!
I'M A HERO!!
YOU MUST THINK I KNOW NOTHING...
...?!
...ABOUT THE MISCONDUCT OF FORMER NAVY VICE ADMIRAL JAGUAR D. SAUL!
DRAG
AND ABOUT WHAT HAPPENED THAT TIME ON OHARA WITH YOUR MOTHER OLVIA!
...!!!
DRAG
DRAG
I KNOW EVERYTHING!!
...!! ...?!!
KA-THUD
I HEARD ALL ABOUT IT!! THE ONE WHO SET FOOT ON OHARA, LAND OF DEMONS...
THE ONE WHO EXPOSED YOUR MOTHER'S CRIME AND GAVE THE SIGNAL FOR THE CALL...
THE MAN WHO WAS DIRECTOR OF CP9 AT THE TIME...
...WAS MY FATHER SPANDINE!!

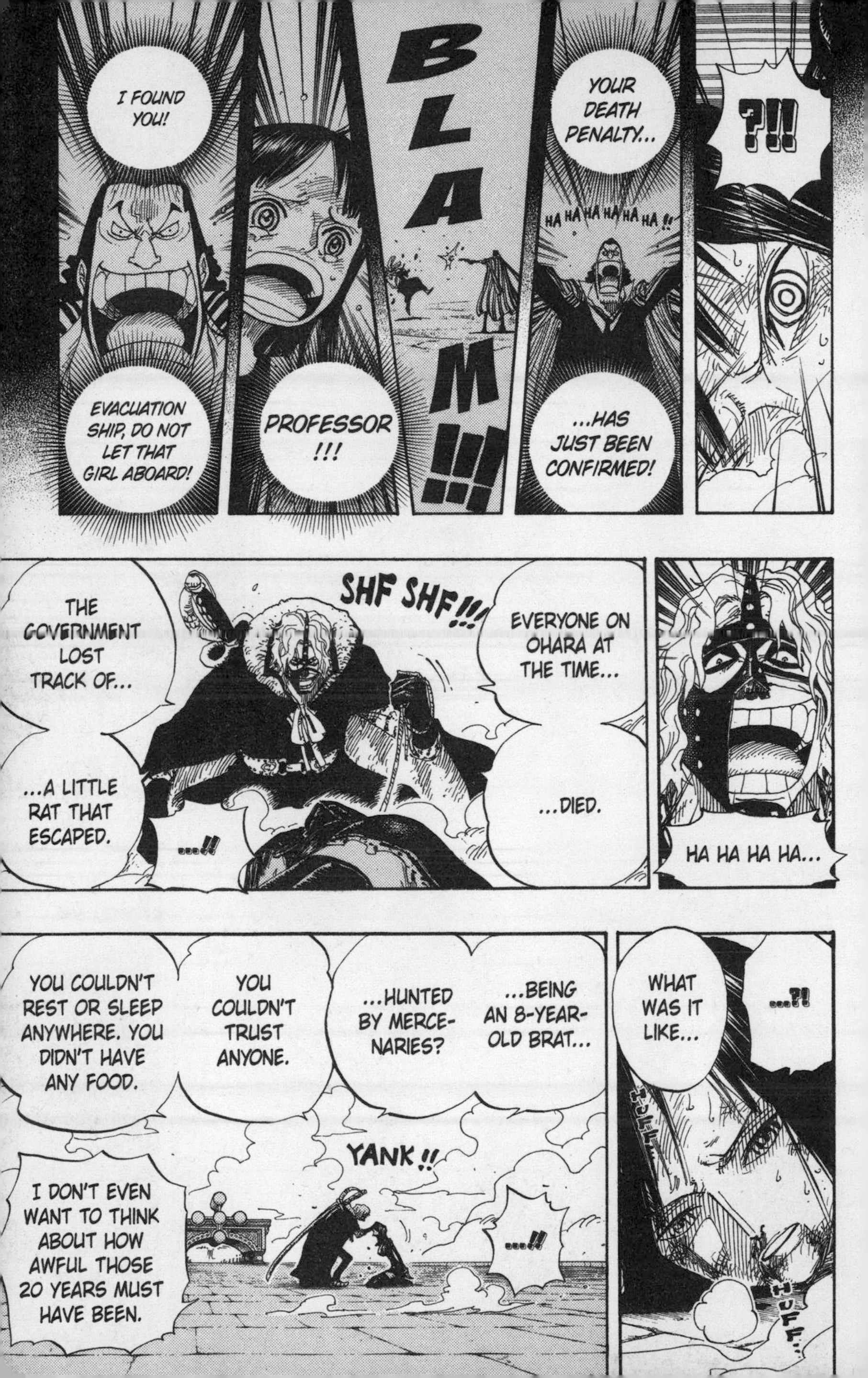
?!!
YOUR DEATH PENALTY...
HA HA HA HA HA HA HA!!
...HAS JUST BEEN CONFIRMED!
BLAM!!!
PROFESSOR!!!
I FOUND YOU!
EVACUATION SHIP, DO NOT LET THAT GIRL ABOARD!
HA HA HA HA...
EVERYONE ON OHARA AT THE TIME...
...DIED.
SHF SHF!!!
THE GOVERNMENT LOST TRACK OF...
...A LITTLE RAT THAT ESCAPED.
...!!
...?!
WHAT WAS IT LIKE...
HUFF
HUFF...
...BEING AN 8-YEAR-OLD BRAT...
...HUNTED BY MERCENARIES?
YOU COULDN'T TRUST ANYONE.
YOU COULDN'T REST OR SLEEP ANYWHERE. YOU DIDN'T HAVE ANY FOOD.
YANK!!
...!!
I DON'T EVEN WANT TO THINK ABOUT HOW AWFUL THOSE 20 YEARS MUST HAVE BEEN.

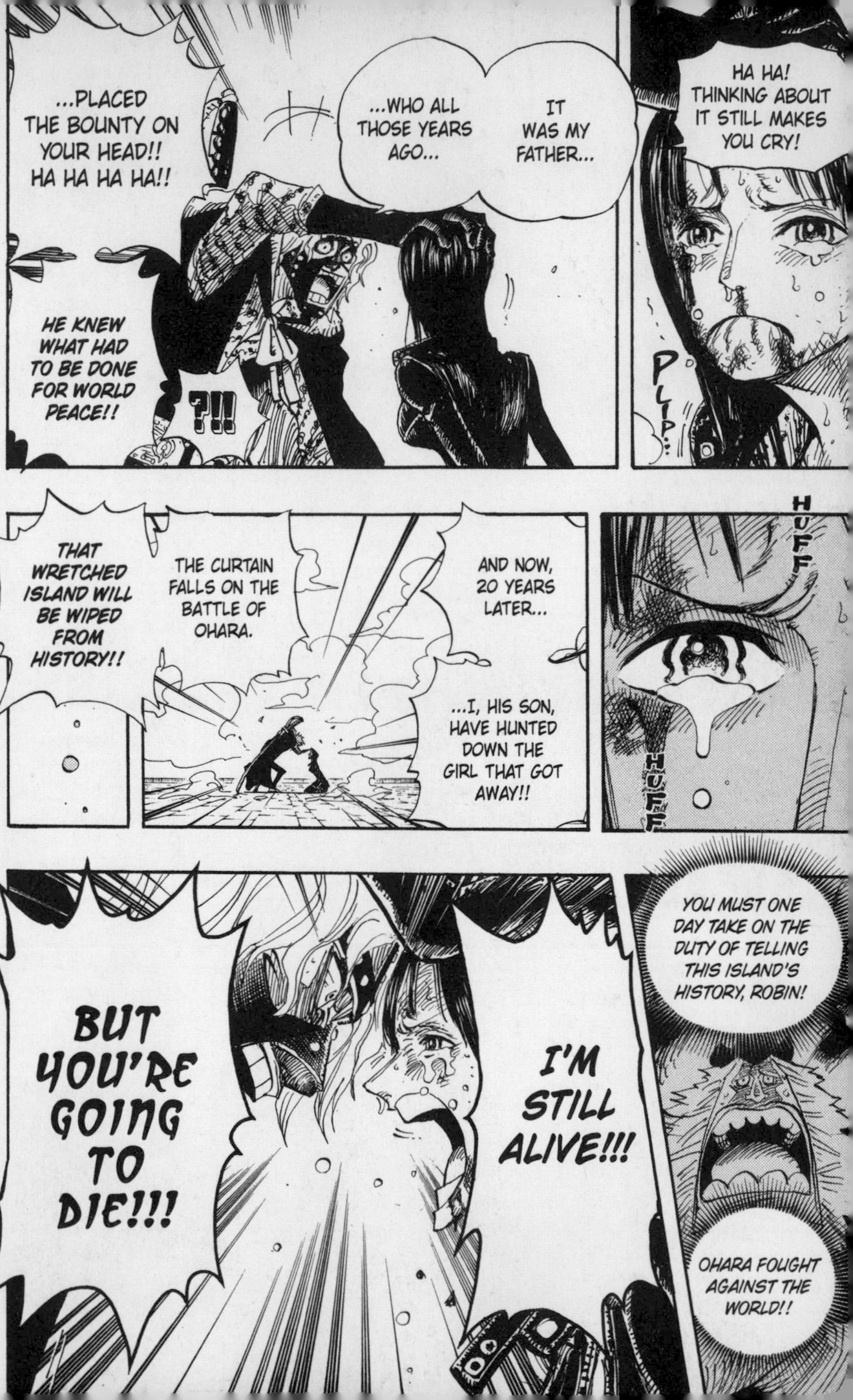
HA HA! THINKING ABOUT IT STILL MAKES YOU CRY!
PLIP...
IT WAS MY FATHER...
...WHO ALL THOSE YEARS AGO...
...PLACED THE BOUNTY ON YOUR HEAD!! HA HA HA HA!!
HE KNEW WHAT HAD TO BE DONE FOR WORLD PEACE!!
?!!
HUFF
HUFF
AND NOW, 20 YEARS LATER...
...I, HIS SON, HAVE HUNTED DOWN THE GIRL THAT GOT AWAY!!
THE CURTAIN FALLS ON THE BATTLE OF OHARA.
THAT WRETCHED ISLAND WILL BE WIPED FROM HISTORY!!
YOU MUST ONE DAY TAKE ON THE DUTY OF TELLING THIS ISLAND'S HISTORY, ROBIN!
OHARA FOUGHT AGAINST THE WORLD!!
I'M STILL ALIVE!!!
BUT YOU'RE GOING TO DIE!!!

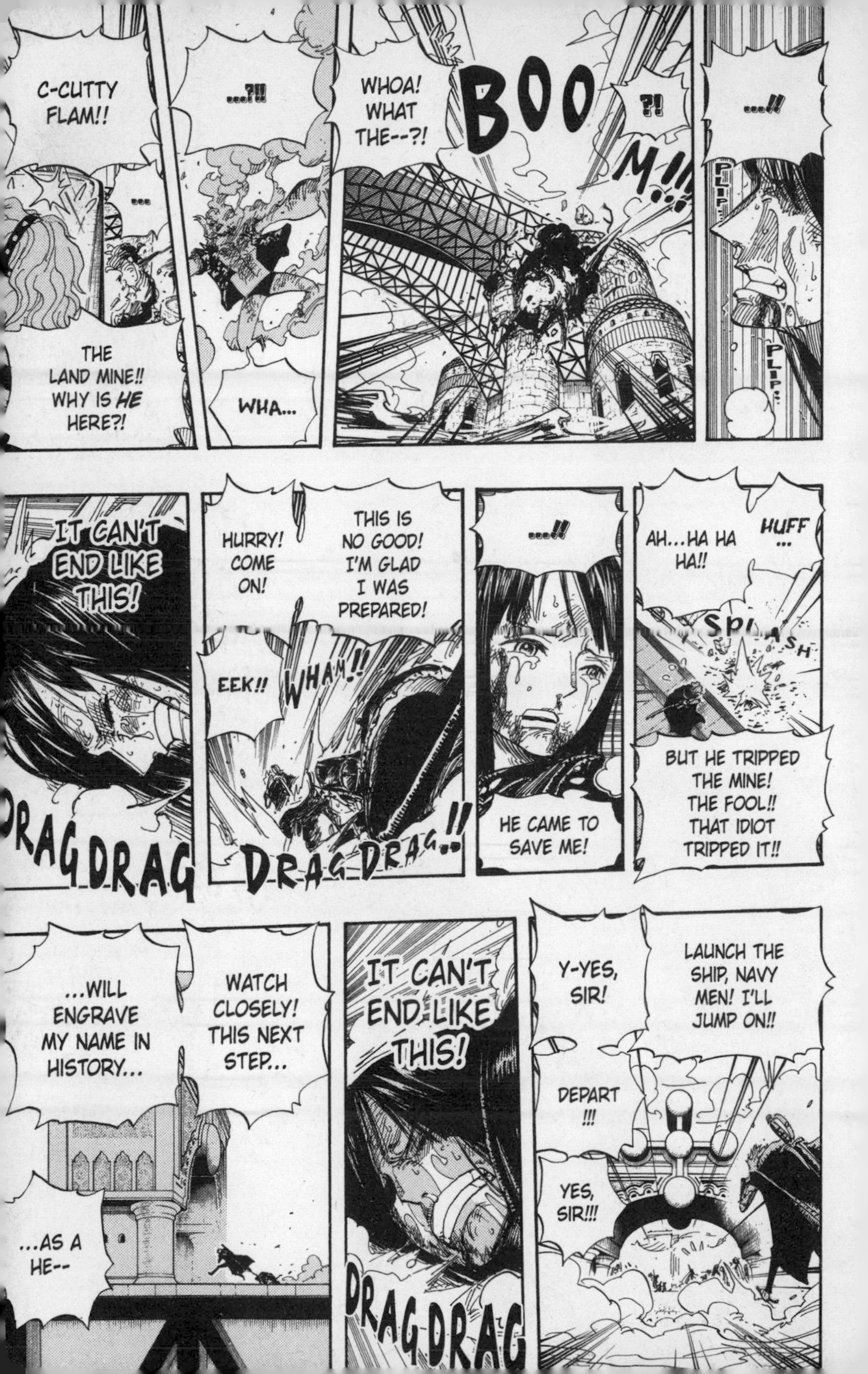
...!!
PLIP
PLIP
?!
BOOM!!!
WHOA! WHAT THE--?!
...?!!
WHA...
C-CUTTY FLAM!!
...
THE LAND MINE!! WHY IS HE HERE?!
HUFF...
AH...HA HA HA!!
SPLASH
BUT HE TRIPPED THE MINE! THE FOOL!! THAT IDIOT TRIPPED IT!!
...!!
HE CAME TO SAVE ME!
THIS IS NO GOOD! I'M GLAD I WAS PREPARED!
HURRY! COME ON!
WHAM!!
EEK!!
DRAG DRAG!!
IT CAN'T END LIKE THIS!
DRAG DRAG
LAUNCH THE SHIP, NAVY MEN! I'LL JUMP ON!!
Y-YES, SIR!
DEPART!!!
YES, SIR!!!
IT CAN'T END LIKE THIS!
DRAG DRAG
WATCH CLOSELY! THIS NEXT STEP...
...WILL ENGRAVE MY NAME IN HISTORY...
...AS A HE--

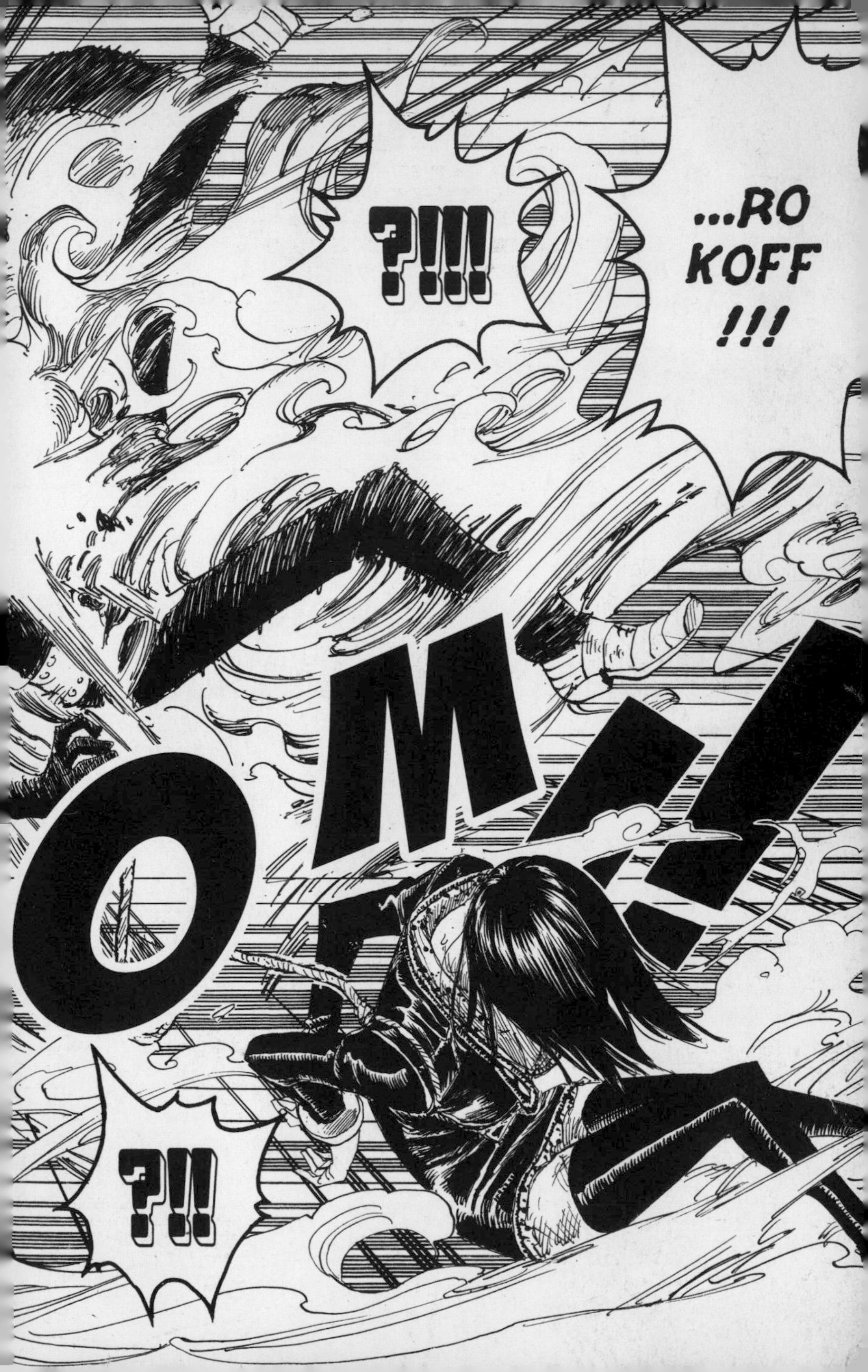
...RO KOFF !!!
?!!!
?!!

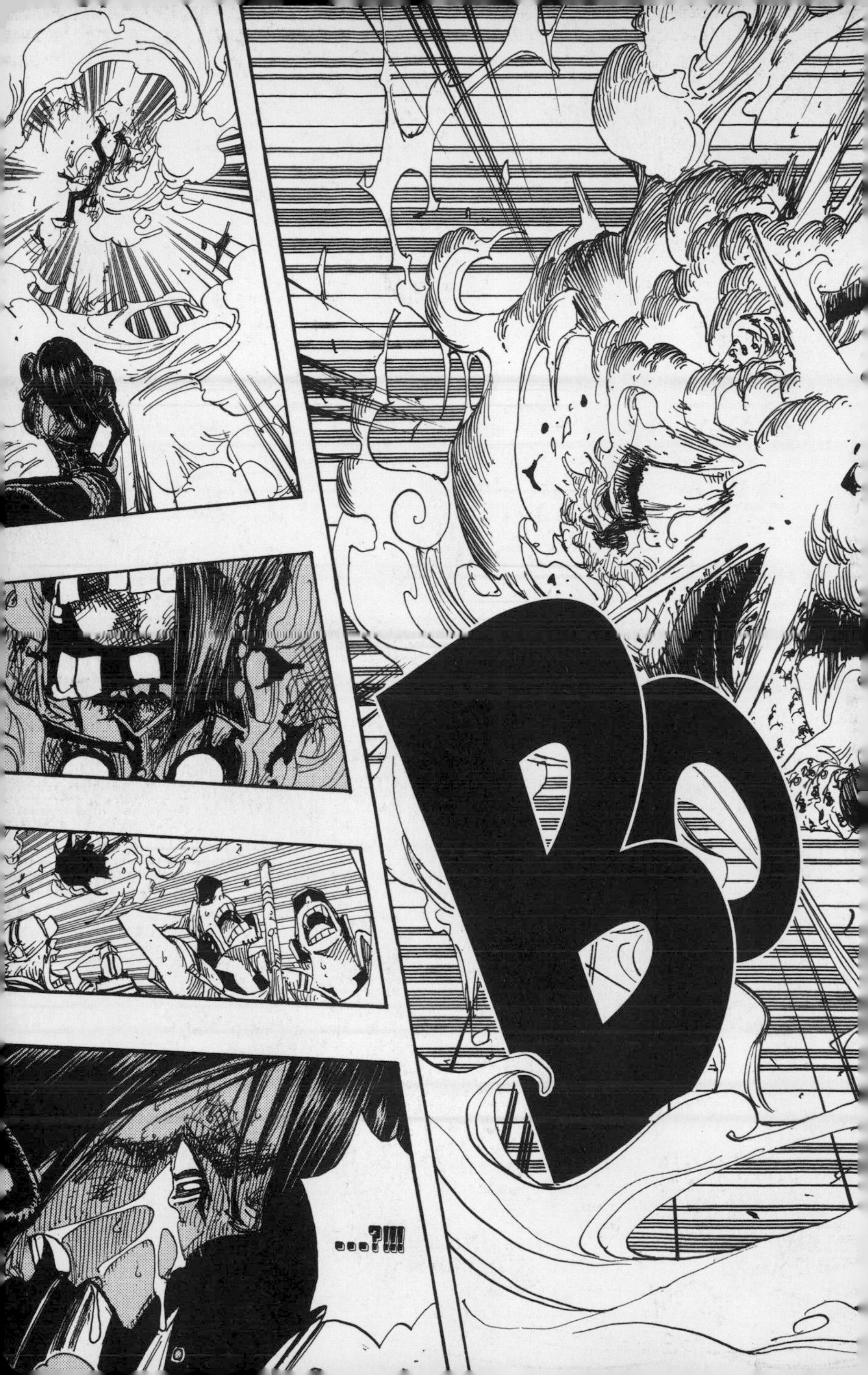

...?!!

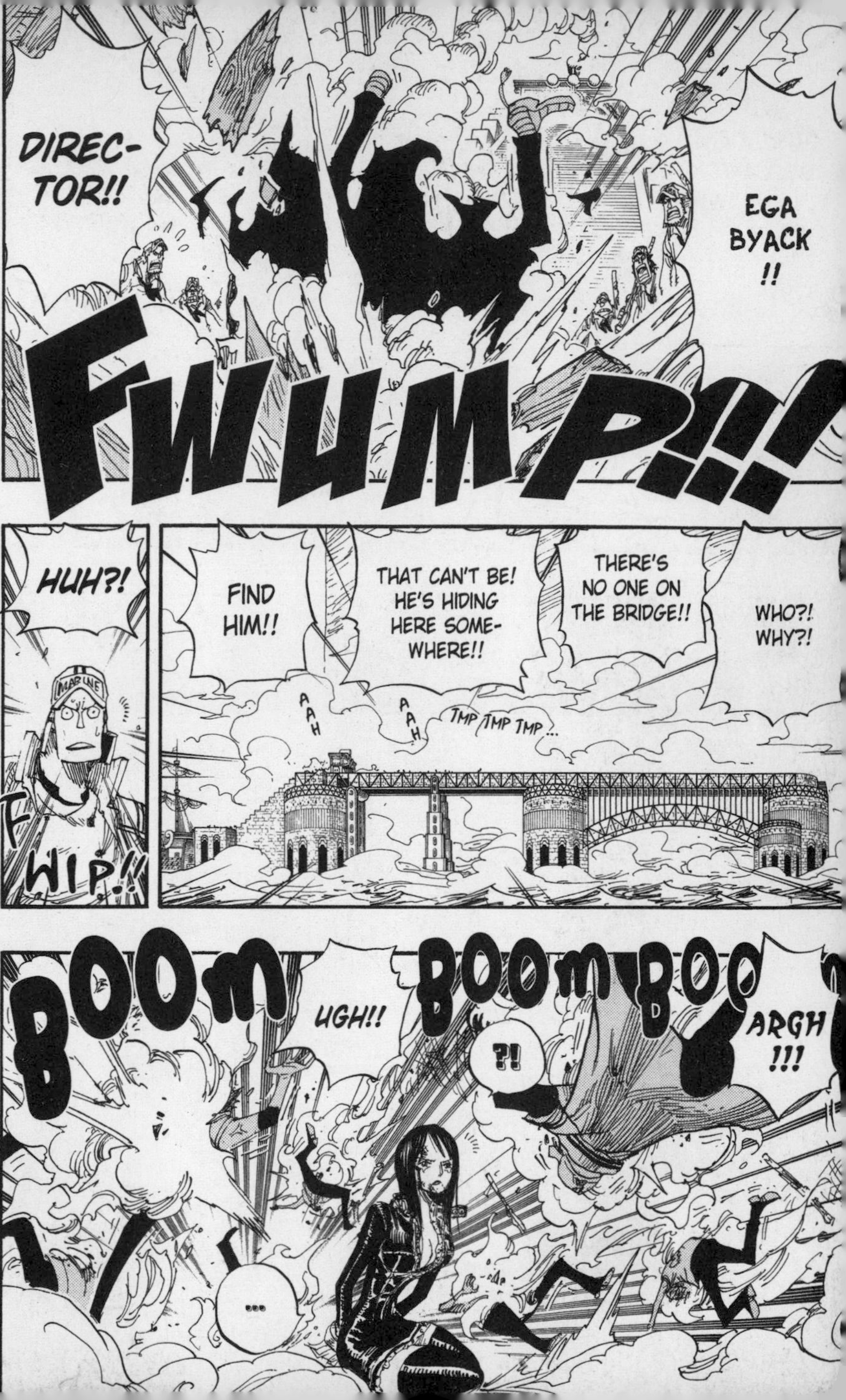
EGA BYACK !!
DIRECTOR!!
FWUMP!!!
WHO?! WHY?!
THERE'S NO ONE ON THE BRIDGE!!
THAT CAN'T BE! HE'S HIDING HERE SOMEWHERE!!
FIND HIM!!
AAH
AAH
TMP TMP TMP...
HUH?!
FWIP!!
ARGH !!!
BOOM BOO
?!
BOOM
UGH!!
BOOM
...

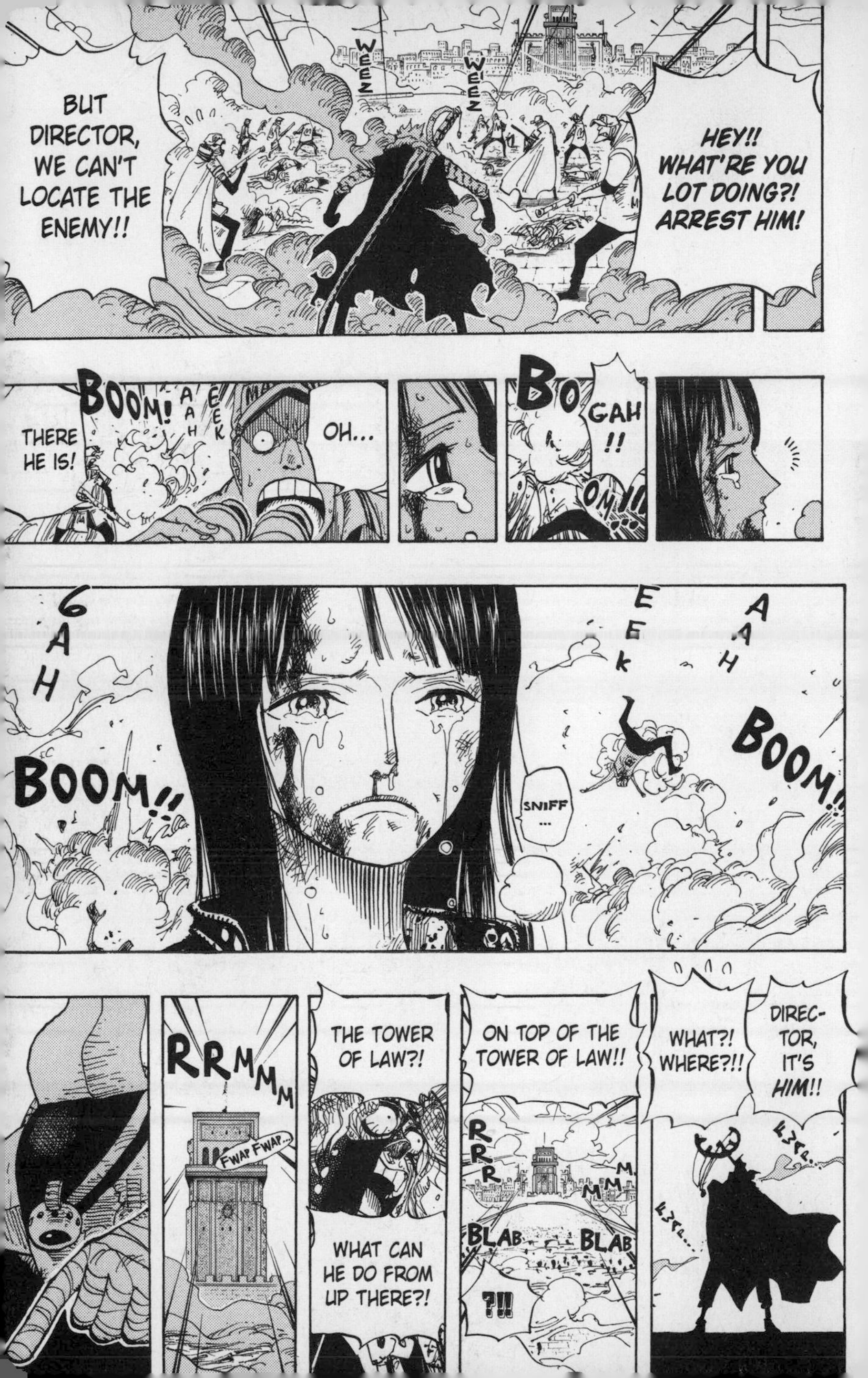
HEY!! WHAT'RE YOU LOT DOING?! ARREST HIM!
WEEZ
WEEZ
BUT DIRECTOR, WE CAN'T LOCATE THE ENEMY!!
GAH!!
BOOM!!
BOOM!
EEK
AAH
OH...
THERE HE IS!
AAH
EEK
BOOM!!
SNIFF...
AAH
BOOM!!
DIREC-TOR, IT'S HIM!!
WHAT?! WHERE?!!
ON TOP OF THE TOWER OF LAW!!
RRRMMMM
BLAB
BLAB
?!!
THE TOWER OF LAW?!
WHAT CAN HE DO FROM UP THERE?!
RRMMMM
FWAP FWAP...

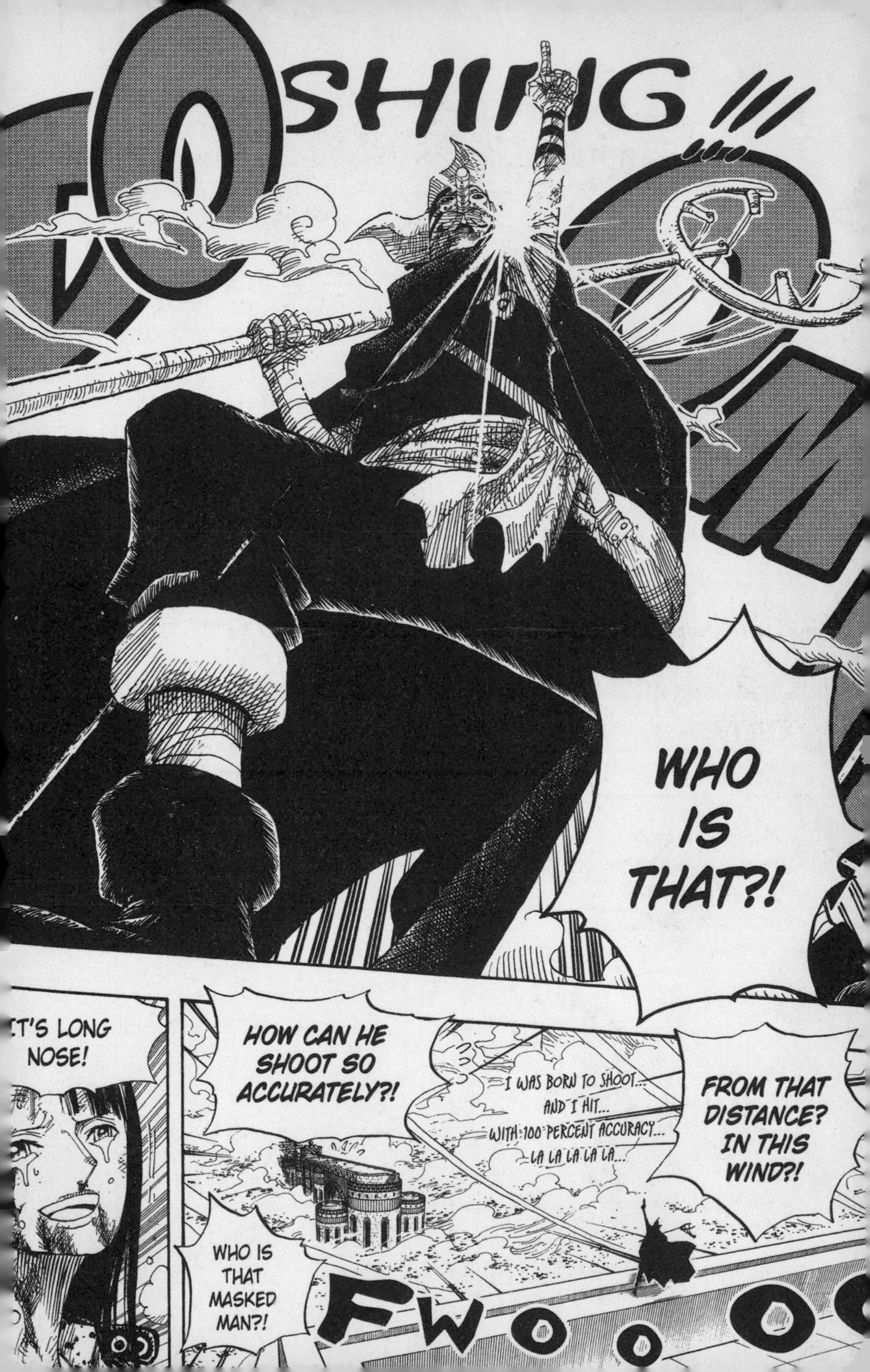
SHING!!!
WHO IS THAT?!
FROM THAT DISTANCE? IN THIS WIND?!
I WAS BORN TO SHOOT... AND I HIT... WITH 100 PERCENT ACCURACY... LA LA LA LA LA...
HOW CAN HE SHOOT SO ACCURATELY?!
WHO IS THAT MASKED MAN?!
FWO...O
IT'S LONG NOSE!

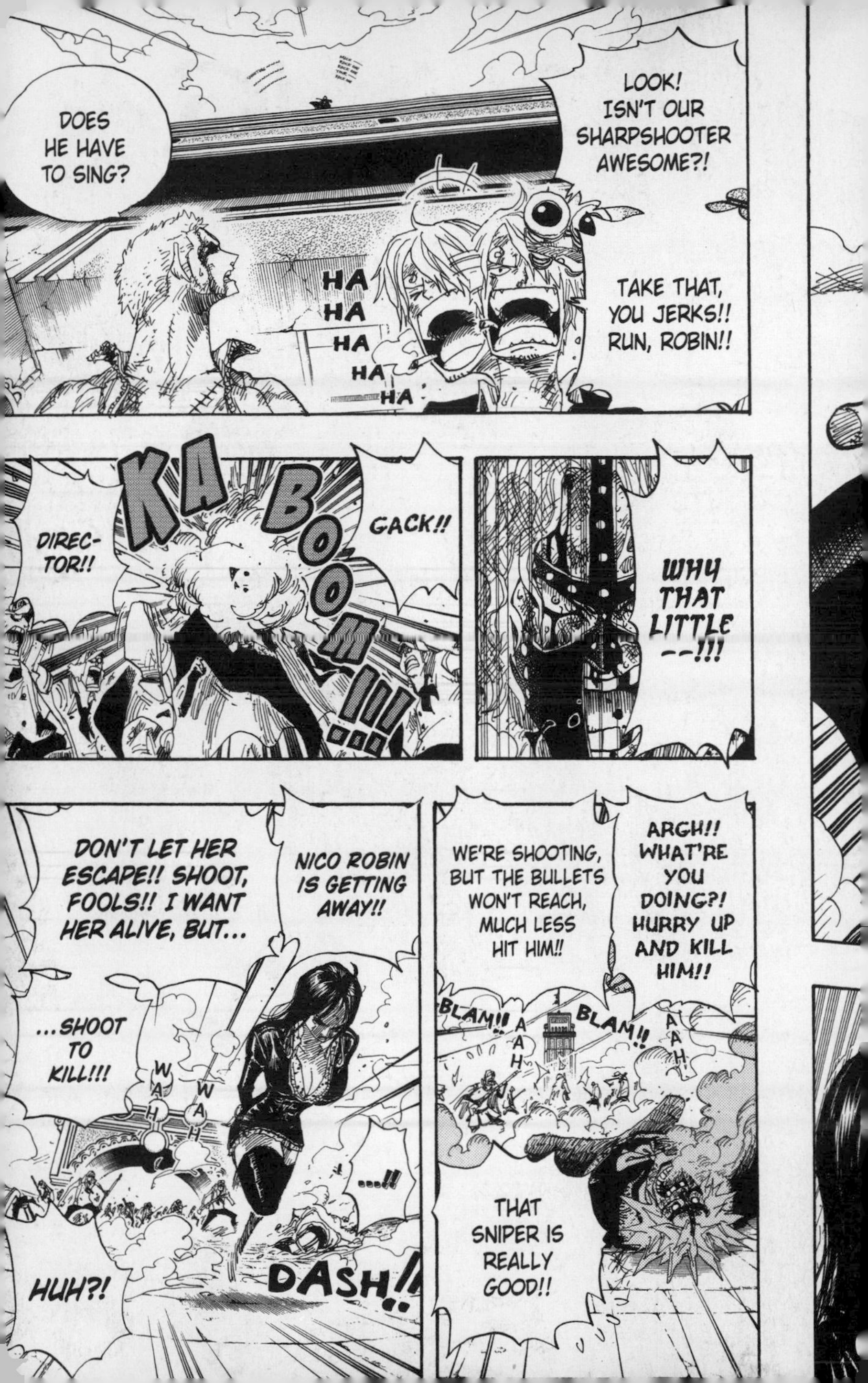
LOOK! ISN'T OUR SHARPSHOOTER AWESOME?!
TAKE THAT, YOU JERKS!! RUN, ROBIN!!
HA HA HA HA HA
DOES HE HAVE TO SING?
WHY THAT LITTLE --!!!
GACK!!
KABOOM!!!
DIRECTOR!!
ARGH!! WHAT'RE YOU DOING?! HURRY UP AND KILL HIM!!
WE'RE SHOOTING, BUT THE BULLETS WON'T REACH, MUCH LESS HIT HIM!!
BLAM!!
AAH
BLAM!!
AAH
THAT SNIPER IS REALLY GOOD!!
NICO ROBIN IS GETTING AWAY!!
DON'T LET HER ESCAPE!! SHOOT, FOOLS!! I WANT HER ALIVE, BUT...
...SHOOT TO KILL!!!
WAAH
WAAH
...!!
DASH!!
HUH?!

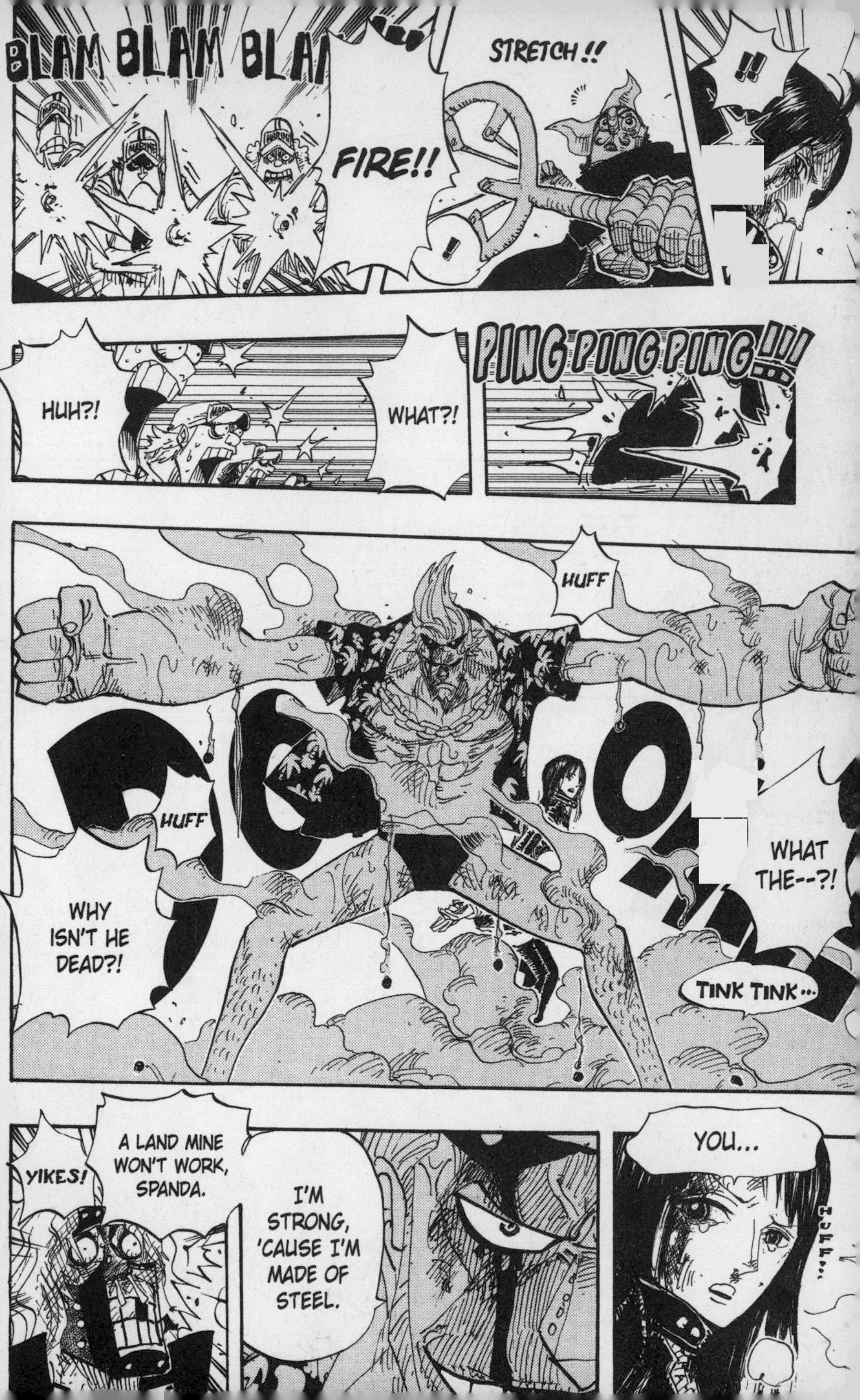
!!
STRETCH!!
!
FIRE!!
BLAM BLAM BLA
PING PING PING!!!
WHAT?!
HUH?!
HUFF
WHAT THE--?!
TINK TINK...
HUFF
WHY ISN'T HE DEAD?!
YOU...
HUFF...
A LAND MINE WON'T WORK, SPANDA.
I'M STRONG, 'CAUSE I'M MADE OF STEEL.
YIKES!

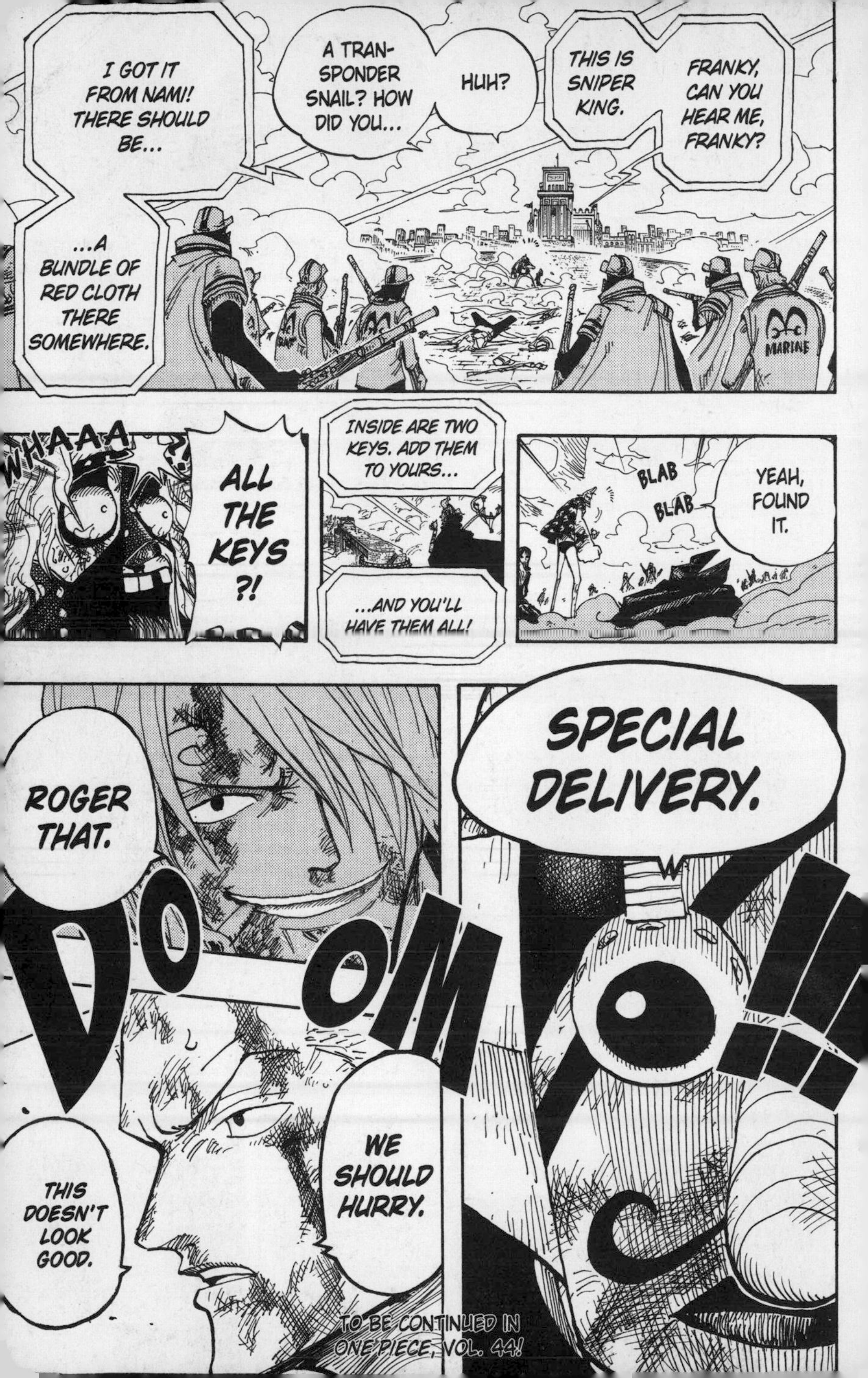
FRANKY, CAN YOU HEAR ME, FRANKY?
THIS IS SNIPER KING.
HUH?
A TRAN-SPONDER SNAIL? HOW DID YOU...
I GOT IT FROM NAMI! THERE SHOULD BE...
...A BUNDLE OF RED CLOTH THERE SOMEWHERE.
MARINE
BLAB
BLAB
YEAH, FOUND IT.
INSIDE ARE TWO KEYS. ADD THEM TO YOURS...
...AND YOU'LL HAVE THEM ALL!
WHAAA
ALL THE KEYS?!
SPECIAL DELIVERY.
DOOM!!!
ROGER THAT.
WE SHOULD HURRY.
THIS DOESN'T LOOK GOOD.
TO BE CONTINUED IN ONE PIECE, VOL. 44!

THIS POLL WAS CONDUCTED IN JAPAN.

TOTAL VOTES: 50,604

1ST PLACE MONKEY D. LUFFY

12,844 VOTES

HE TRULY IS KING!!

DATA

GROUP STRAW HATS: CAPTAIN (BOUNTY: 100 MILLION BERRIES)

POWER GUM-GUM FRUIT

TRAITS FOOLISHLY OPTIMISTIC, ENERGETIC

REASONS

"HE'S CLUELESS BUT MANLY WHEN IT COMES TO HIS SHIPMATES." "EVERYTHING DEPENDS ON LUFFY! HE'S LIKE THE SUN!" "HE DOESN'T EVEN FEAR THE GODS! I ADMIRE HIS COURAGE! HE'S COOL!" ETC. AS THE CAPTAIN, HE IS POPULAR! AS A HERO, YOU HAVE TO LOVE HIM!

2ND PLACE RORONOA ZOLO

8,225 VOTES

HE LIVES BY THE BLADE!!

DATA

GROUP STRAW HATS: SWORDSMAN (BOUNTY: 60 MILLION BERRIES)

ABILITY THREE-SWORD STYLE

TRAITS GETS LOST EASILY. SLEEPS A LOT. DISCIPLINED.

REASONS

"HIS COURAGE IS COOL!" "NEAT SWORDSMANSHIP!" "LOOKS SCARY BUT HE'S ATTRACTIVE WHEN HE SMILES!" ETC. POPULAR AS A SWORDSMAN AND AS A PERSON! NO. 2 TWICE IN A ROW!

3RD PLACE SANJI

6,235 VOTES

A REAL LADIES' MAN!!

DATA

GROUP STRAW HATS: COOK

ABILITY FOOT TECHNIQUES

TRAITS HAS A WEAKNESS FOR WOMEN.

REASONS

"TO SAVE HIS HANDS FOR COOKING, HE FIGHTS WITH HIS FEET." "COOL EYEBROWS!" ETC. NO. 3 FOR ELEGANT FOOTWORK AND DEBONAIR STYLE!

3RD ONE PIECE CHARAC

THANKS TO EVERYONE WHO VOTED! EXTREMELY POWERFUL CHARACTERS TOOK THE TOP PLACES! HOW DID YOUR FAVORITES DO?

4TH PLACE TONY TONY CHOPPER

2,725 VOTES

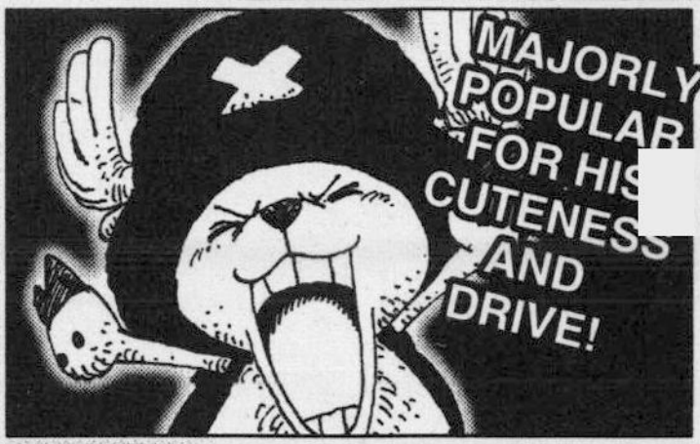
MAJORLY POPULAR FOR HIS CUTENESS AND DRIVE!

DATA

GROUP	STRAW HATS: DOCTOR
ABILITY	RUMBLE BALL
TRAITS	DOCILE, TIMID

REASONS

"HE SOOO CUTE!" "HE'LL BELIEVE ANYTHING!" ETC. BURSTING WITH CUTENESS AT NO. 4!

5TH PLACE NICO ROBIN

2,644 VOTES

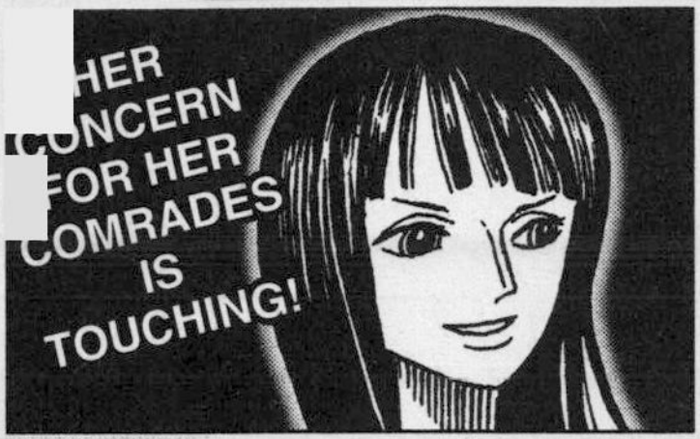
HER CONCERN FOR HER COMRADES IS TOUCHING!

DATA

GROUP	STRAW HATS: ARCHAEOLOGIST (BOUNTY: 79 MILLION BERRIES)
POWER	FLOWER-FLOWER FRUIT
TRAITS	COOL AND COLLECTED

REASONS

"I'M MOVED BY HER AFFECTION FOR HER FRIENDS!" FEEDBACK LIKE THAT POURED IN! SHE'S KIND AND INTELLIGENT, THE IDEAL WOMAN!

6TH PLACE USOPP (SNIPER KING)

2,621 VOTES

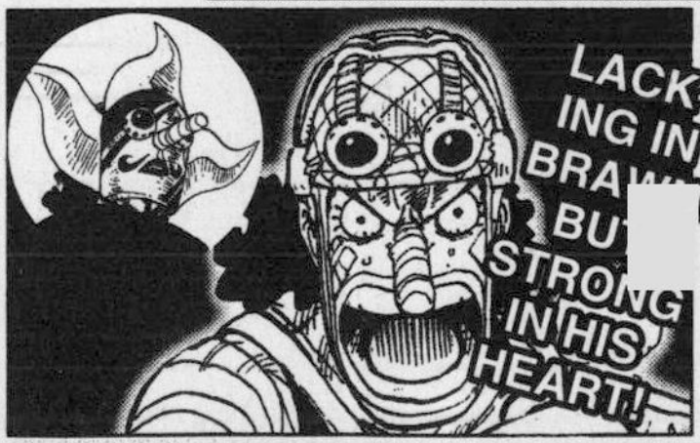
LACKING IN BRAWN BUT STRONG IN HIS HEART!

DATA

GROUP	STRAW HATS: SHARPSHOOTER
ABILITY	LONG-RANGE WEAPONS
TRAITS	TENDS TO LIE

REASONS

"A PERFECT BALANCE OF FOOL AND STRAIGHT MAN!" "HE WON MY HEART AGAIN AS SNIPER KING!" ETC. ONE MAN IN TWO ROLES AT NO. 6!

7TH PLACE NAMI

1,983 VOTES

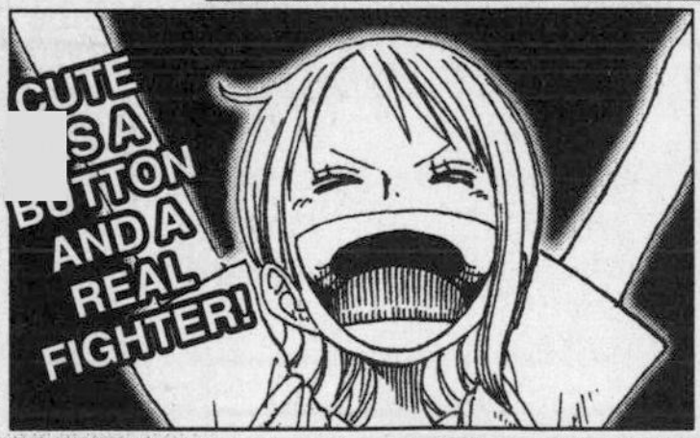
CUTE AS A BUTTON AND A REAL FIGHTER!

DATA

GROUP	STRAW HATS: NAVIGATOR
WEAPON	CLIMATE BATON
TRAITS	LOVES MONEY

REASONS

"SHE'S SMART AND SEXY-COOL!" "SHE'S VERY DETERMINED," ETC. SHE'S ATTRACTIVE FOR HER FEMININITY AND STRENGTH!

THE STRAW HATS DOMINATE 1ST THROUGH 7TH PLACE!

TURN THE PAGE FOR 8TH–30TH PLACES!

RESULTS OF THE 3RD *ONE PIECE* CHARACTER POPULARITY POLL!! (8-30)

8TH PLACE DRACULE MIHAWK

1,744 VOTES

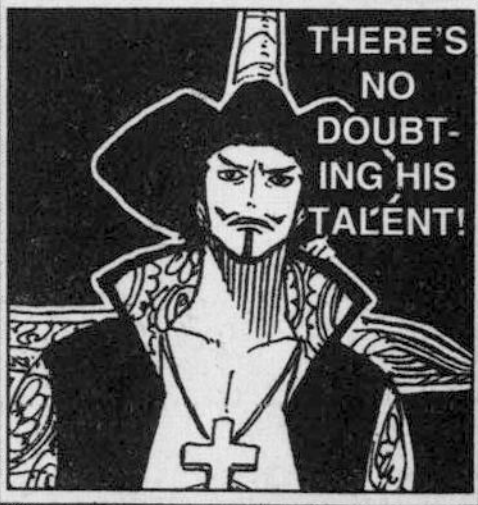
THERE'S NO DOUBT-ING HIS TALENT!

REASONS
"HE'S AMAZING FOR PICKING ZOLO AS HIS TARGET," ETC. HE HASN'T APPEARED MUCH BUT MIRACULOUSLY HE RANKS HIGH!!

9TH PLACE KAKU

1,044 VOTES

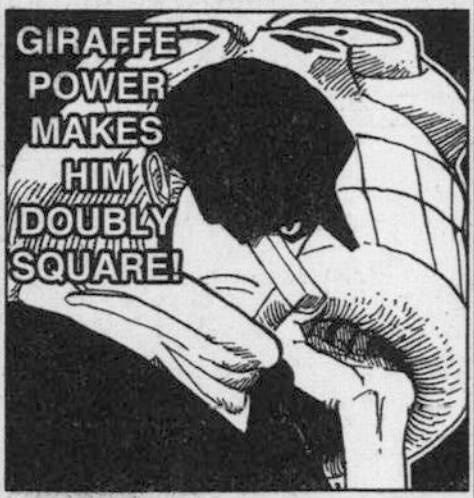
GIRAFFE POWER MAKES HIM DOUBLY SQUARE!

REASONS
AN ENEMY IN 9TH PLACE! "HIS EYES AND EYELASHES ARE COOL!" ETC. MOST POPULAR CP9 AGENT! HIS STRENGTH IS APPEALING!

10TH PLACE PORTGAZ D. ACE

827 VOTES

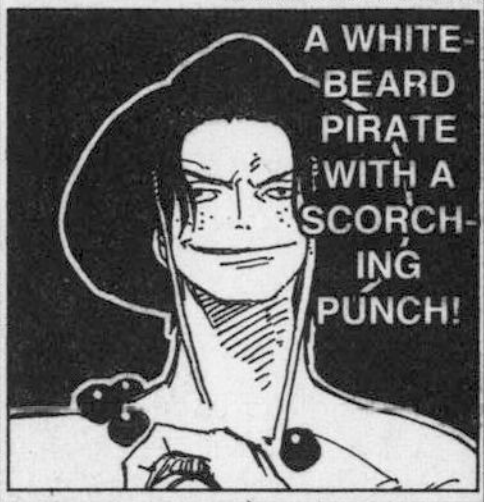
A WHITE-BEARD PIRATE WITH A SCORCH-ING PUNCH!

REASONS
"HE'S LUFFY'S OLDER BROTHER, BUT HE'S POLITE," ETC. IS THAT WHY HE'S POPULAR?! DOESN'T SHOW UP MUCH BUT RANKS HIGH.

11TH PLACE SHANKS

726 VOTES

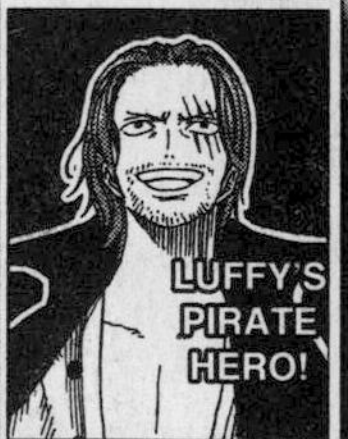
LUFFY'S PIRATE HERO!

12TH PLACE ROB LUCCI

647 VOTES

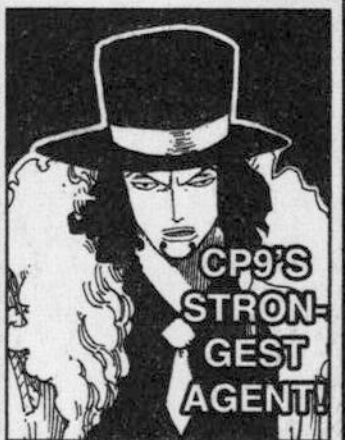
CP9'S STRON-GEST AGENT!

13TH PLACE FRANKY

600 VOTES

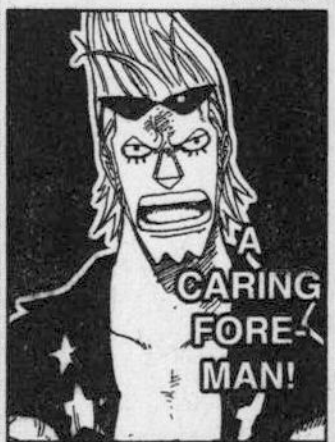
A CARING FORE-MAN!

14TH PLACE CAPTAIN SMOKER

572 VOTES

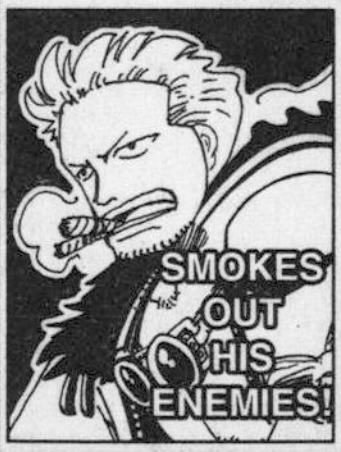
SMOKES OUT HIS ENEMIES!

15TH PLACE NEFELTARI VIVI

529 VOTES

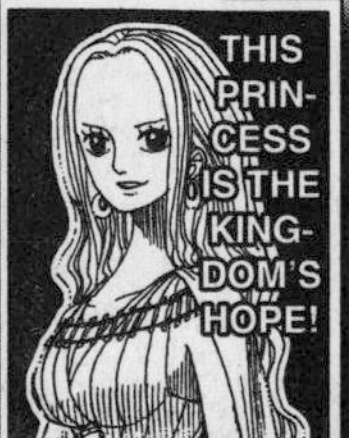
THIS PRIN-CESS IS THE KING-DOM'S HOPE!

16TH PLACE VICE ADMIRAL KUZAN

483 VOTES

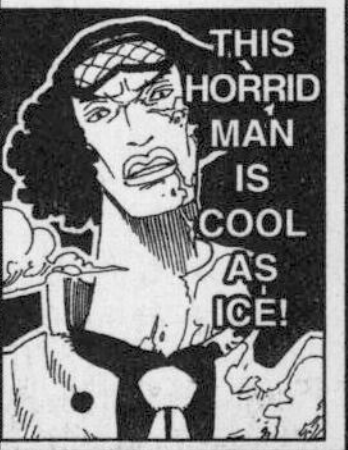
THIS HORRID MAN IS COOL AS ICE!

17TH PLACE JABRA

461 VOTES

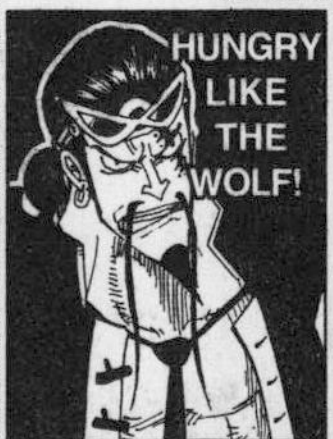
HUNGRY LIKE THE WOLF!

18TH PLACE PAULIE

460 VOTES

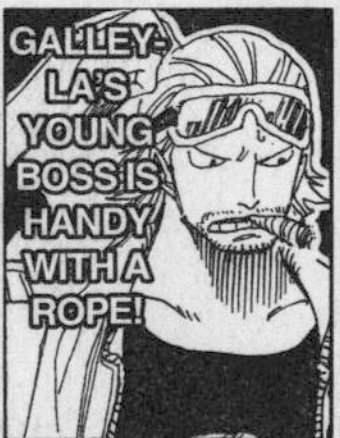
GALLEY-LA'S YOUNG BOSS IS HANDY WITH A ROPE!

THE 2ND POPULARITY RANKING TURNED OUT LIKE THIS!! (ONE PIECE, VOL. 24)

1ST: MONKEY D. LUFFY
2ND: RORONOA ZOLO
3RD: SANJI
4TH: TONY TONY CHOPPER
5TH: NAMI
6TH: USOPP
7TH: SHANKS
8TH: PORTGAZ D. ACE
9TH: MR. 2 BON CLAY
10TH: NEFELTARI VIVI

19TH PLACE
ICEBERG
401 VOTES

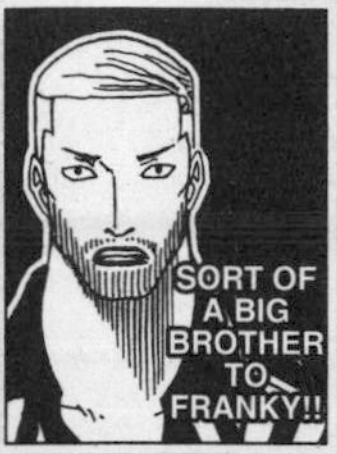
SORT OF A BIG BROTHER TO FRANKY!!

20TH PLACE
TASHIGI
380 VOTES

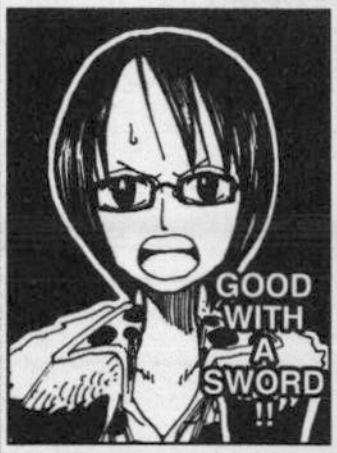
GOOD WITH A SWORD!!

21ST PLACE
MR. 2 BON CLAY
368 VOTES

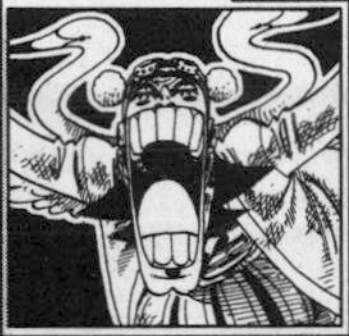

22ND PLACE
ENERU
351 VOTES

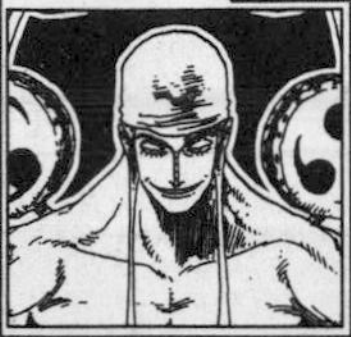

23RD PLACE
KALIFA
346 VOTES

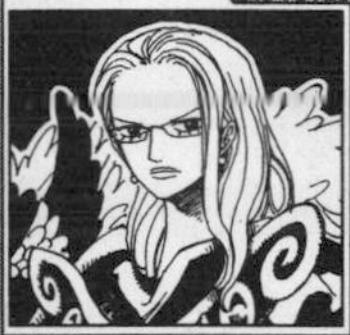

24TH PLACE
CAPTAIN KURO
302 VOTES

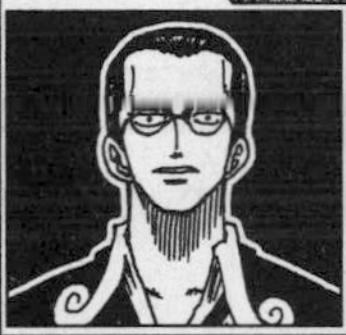

25TH PLACE
SIR CROCODILE
277 VOTES

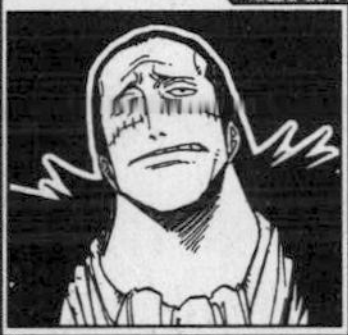

26TH PLACE
FUKURÔ
202 VOTES

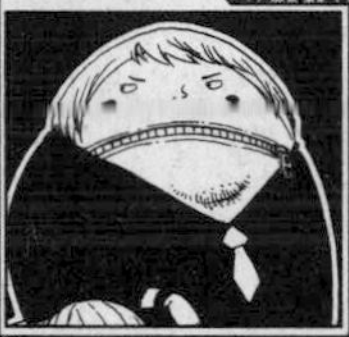

27TH PLACE
PELL THE FALCON
200 VOTES

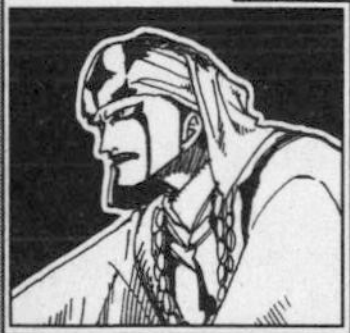

28TH PLACE
SPANDAM
179 VOTES

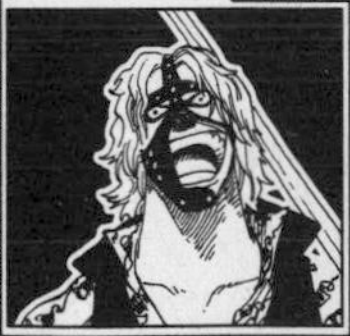

29TH PLACE
RED-SHOES ZEFF
173 VOTES

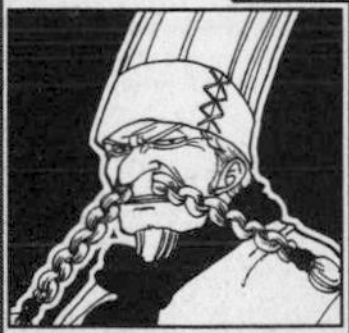

30TH PLACE
BUGGY THE CLOWN
152 VOTES

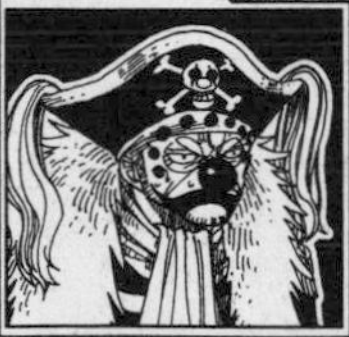

GENERAL COMMENTS FROM SNIPER KING

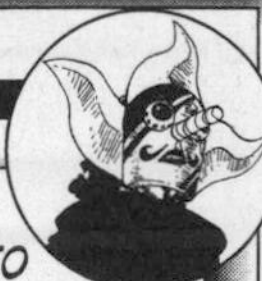

COMMENTS

I'LL BE MAKING REMARKS THIS TIME IN USOPP'S PLACE. THREE MEMBERS OF THE NEW RIVALS, CP9, HAVE MADE IT INTO THE TOP 20. BUT THE STRAW HATS, CENTERED ON USOPP, HAVE RANKED AT THE TOP! WHAT ELSE WOULD YOU EXPECT FROM USOPP'S GANG? YOU WON'T BE ABLE TO TAKE YOUR EYES OFF THE STRAW HATS FROM NOW ON EITHER!

THE RANKINGS CONTINUE! TURN THE PAGE FOR 31ST-50TH PLACE, PLUS A RUNDOWN OF 51ST-99TH PLACE THAT WEREN'T ANNOUNCED IN *WEEKLY SHONEN JUMP*!

RESULTS OF THE 3RD *ONE PIECE* CHARACTER POPULARITY POLL!! (31–99)

31ST PLACE
PANDAMAN
149 VOTES

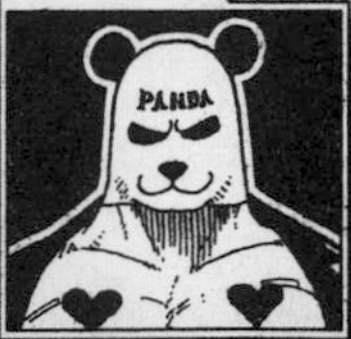
PANDA

32ND PLACE
BELLE-MÈRE
144 VOTES

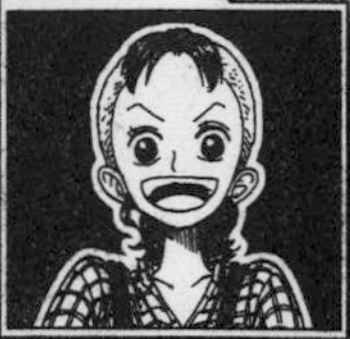

33RD PLACE
BENN BECKMAN
143 VOTES

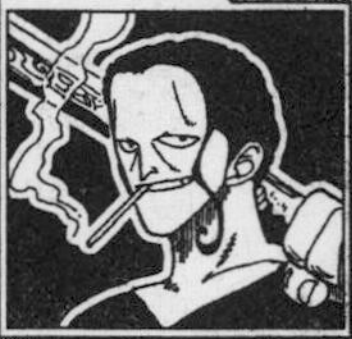

34TH PLACE
DR. KUREHA
128 VOTES

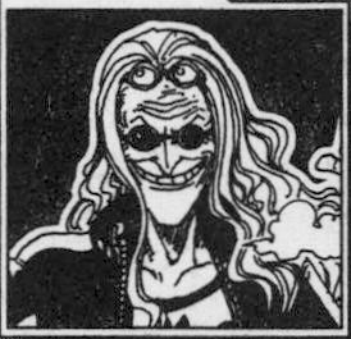

35TH PLACE
GEDATSU
120 VOTES

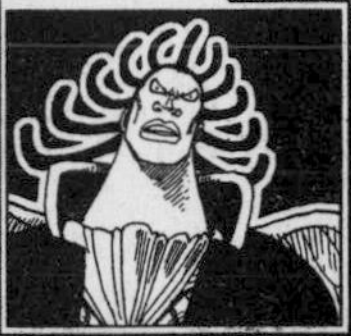

36TH PLACE
HINA THE BLACK CAGE
115 VOTES

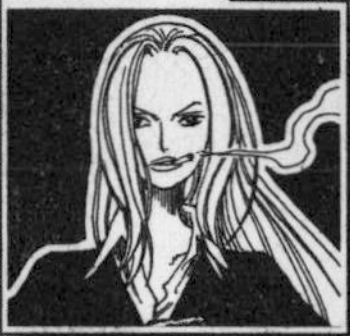

37TH PLACE
WYPER
96 VOTES

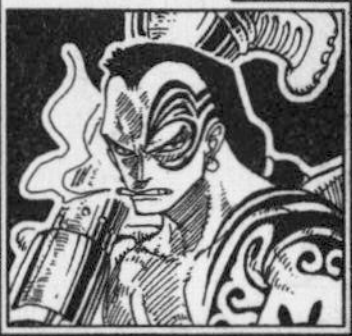

38TH PLACE
KIWI & MOZU
84 VOTES

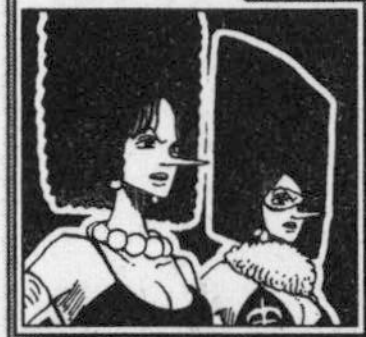

39TH PLACE
DR. HIRILUK
81 VOTES

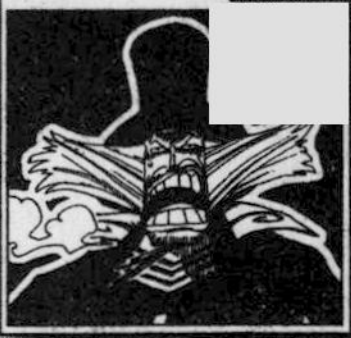

40TH PLACE
COLONEL T-BONE
76 VOTES

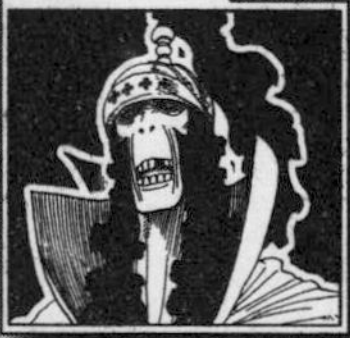

41ST PLACE
TOM
71 VOTES

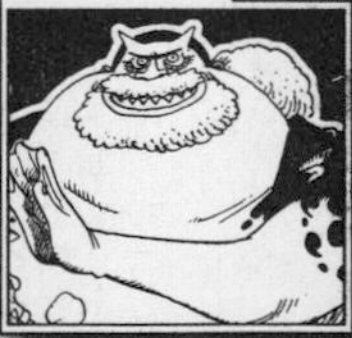

42ND PLACE
MR. 9
66 VOTES

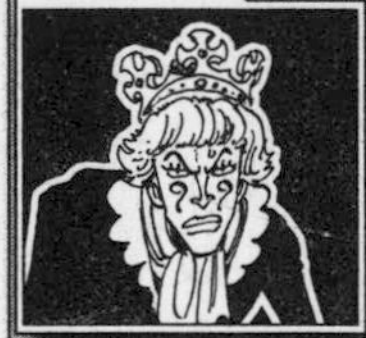

43RD PLACE
EDWARD NEWGATE
65 VOTES

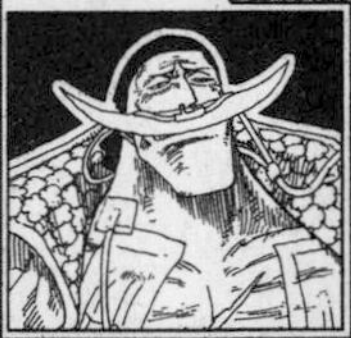

44TH PLACE
NICO OLVIA
60 VOTES

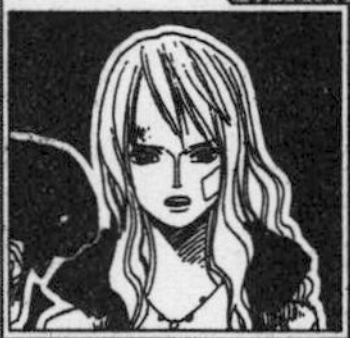

45TH PLACE
KAMAKIRI
53 VOTES

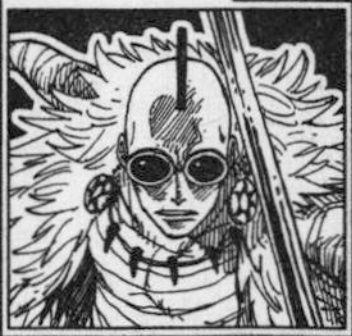

46TH PLACE
KAYA
52 VOTES

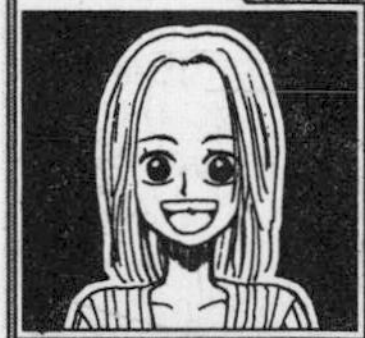

47TH PLACE
KAROO
50 VOTES

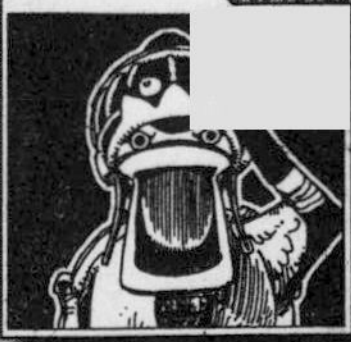

48TH PLACE
EIICHIRO ODA
48 VOTES

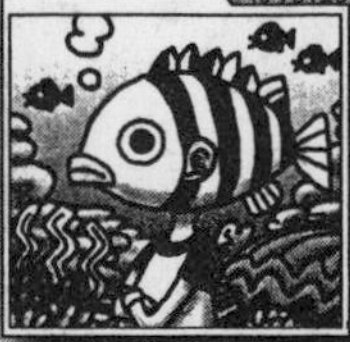

49TH PLACE
KLABAUTERMANN
46 VOTES

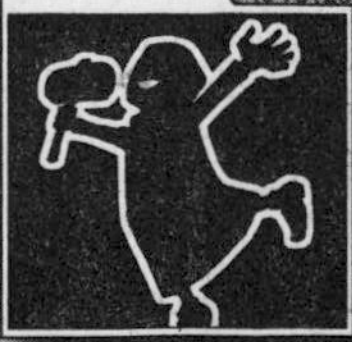

50TH PLACE
MERRY GO
44 VOTES

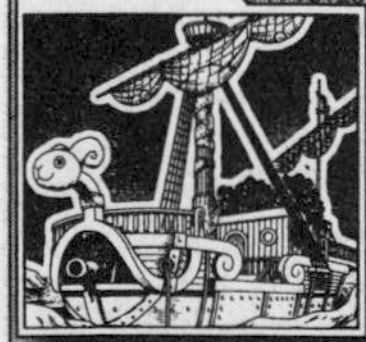

RESULTS OF THE 3RD *ONE PIECE* CHARACTER POPULARITY POLL!! (31–99)

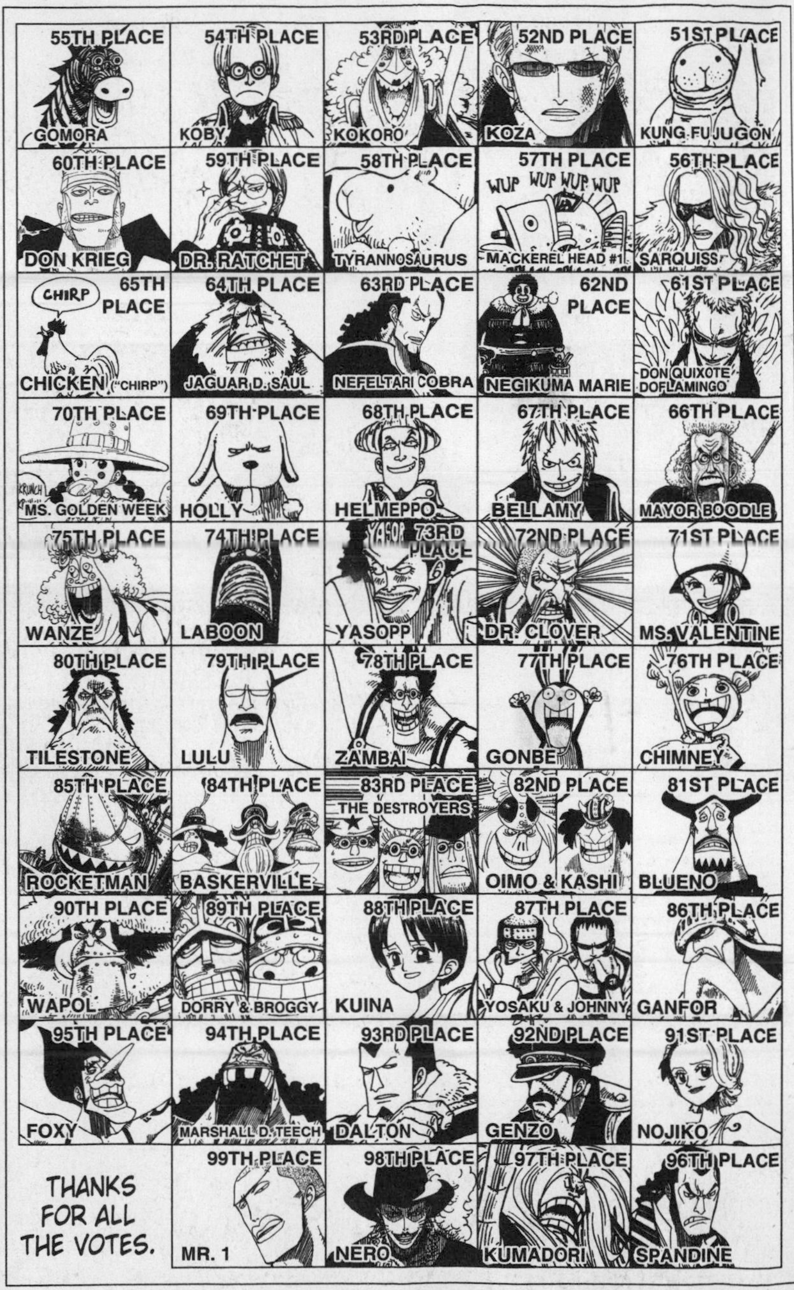
51ST PLACE
KUNG FU JUGON
52ND PLACE
KOZA
53RD PLACE
KOKORO
54TH PLACE
KOBY
55TH PLACE
GOMORA
56TH PLACE
SARQUISS
57TH PLACE
WUP WUP WUP WUP
MACKEREL HEAD #1
58TH PLACE
TYRANNOSAURUS
59TH PLACE
DR. RATCHET
60TH PLACE
DON KRIEG
61ST PLACE
DON QUIXOTE DOFLAMINGO
62ND PLACE
NEGIKUMA MARIE
63RD PLACE
NEFELTARI COBRA
64TH PLACE
JAGUAR D. SAUL
65TH PLACE
CHIRP
CHICKEN ("CHIRP")
66TH PLACE
MAYOR BOODLE
67TH PLACE
BELLAMY
68TH PLACE
HELMEPPO
69TH PLACE
HOLLY
70TH PLACE
CRUNCH
MS. GOLDEN WEEK
71ST PLACE
MS. VALENTINE
72ND PLACE
DR. CLOVER
73RD PLACE
YASOPP
74TH PLACE
LABOON
75TH PLACE
WANZE
76TH PLACE
CHIMNEY
77TH PLACE
GONBE
78TH PLACE
ZAMBAI
79TH PLACE
LULU
80TH PLACE
TILESTONE
81ST PLACE
BLUENO
82ND PLACE
OIMO & KASHI
83RD PLACE
THE DESTROYERS
84TH PLACE
BASKERVILLE
85TH PLACE
ROCKETMAN
86TH PLACE
GANFOR
87TH PLACE
YOSAKU & JOHNNY
88TH PLACE
KUINA
89TH PLACE
DORRY & BROGGY
90TH PLACE
WAPOL
91ST PLACE
NOJIKO
92ND PLACE
GENZO
93RD PLACE
DALTON
94TH PLACE
MARSHALL D. TEECH
95TH PLACE
FOXY
96TH PLACE
SPANDINE
97TH PLACE
KUMADORI
98TH PLACE
NERO
99TH PLACE
MR. 1
THANKS FOR ALL THE VOTES.

COMING NEXT VOLUME:

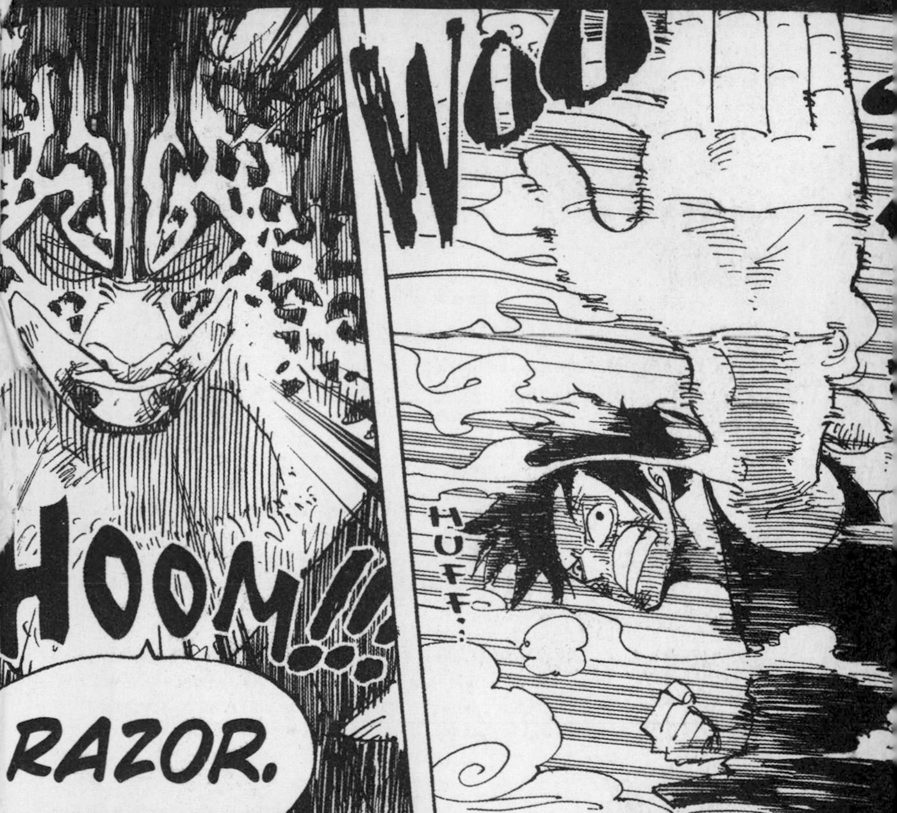
WO
HUFF...
HOOM!!
RAZOR.

As cannonballs begin to fall on Enies Lobby, Luffy squares off against CP9's Rob Lucci in a battle of earthshaking proportions. The clock is ticking now that the dreaded Buster Call is underway. Will anyone (or anything) be left when the dust finally settles?!

ON SALE MAY 2010!

Set Sail with

Read all about **MONKEY D. LUFFY**'s adventures as he sails around the world assembling a motley crew to join him on his search for the legendary treasure "**ONE PIECE.**" For more information, check out **onepiece.viz.com**

EAST BLUE
(Vols. 1-12)
Available now!

See where it all began! One man, a dinghy and a dream. Or rather... a rubber man who can't swim, setting out in a tiny boat on the vast seas without any navigational skills. What are the odds that his dream of becoming King of the Pirates will ever come true?

BAROQUE WORKS
(Vols. 12-24)
Available now!

Friend or foe? Ms. Wednesday is part of a group of bounty hunters—or isn't she? The Straw Hats get caught up in a civil war when they find a princess in their midst. But can they help her stop the revolution in her home country before the evil Crocodile gets his way?!

SKYPIEA
(Vols. 24-32)
Available now!

Luffy's quest to become King of the Pirates and find the elusive treasure known as "One Piece" continues...in the sky! The Straw Hats sail to Skypiea, an airborne island in the midst of a territorial war and ruled by a short-fused megalomaniac!

WATER SEVEN
(Vols. 32-46)
Available from February 2010!

The *Merry Go* has been a stalwart for the Straw Hats since the beginning, but countless battles have taken their toll on the ship. Luckily, their next stop is Water Seven, where a rough-and-tumble crew of shipwrights awaits their arrival!

THRILLER BARK
(Vols. 46-50)
Available from May 2010!

Luffy and crew get more than they bargained for when their ship is drawn toward haunted Thriller Bark. When Gecko Moria, one of the Warlords of the Sea, steals the crew's shadows, they'll have to get them back before the sun rises or else they'll all turn into zombies!

SABAODY
(Vols. 50-54)
Available from June 2010!

On the way to Fish-Man Island, the Straw Hats disembark on the Sabaody archipelago to get soaped up for their undersea adventure! But it's not too long before they get caught up in trouble! Luffy's made an enemy of an exalted World Noble when he saves Camie the mermaid from being sold on the slave market, and now he's got the Navy after him too!

IMPEL DOWN
(from Vol. 54)
Available from July 2010!

Luffy's brother Ace is about to be executed! Held in the Navy's maximum security prison Impel Down, Luffy needs to find a way to break in to help Ace escape. But with murderous fiends for guards inside, the notorious prisoners start to seem not so bad. Some are even friendly enough to give Luffy a helping hand!

SHONEN JUMP

THE WORLD'S MOST POPULAR MANGA

BLEACH
STORY AND ART BY
TITE KUBO

ONE PIECE
STORY AND ART BY
EIICHIRO ODA

Tegami Bachi
LETTER · BEE
STORY AND ART BY
HIROYUKI ASADA

JUMP INTO THE ACTION BY TELLING US WHAT YOU LOVE (AND WHAT YOU DON'T)

LET YOUR VOICE BE HEARD!

SHONENJUMP.VIZ.COM/MANGASURVEY

HELP US MAKE MORE OF THE WORLD'S MOST POPULAR MANGA!

RATED
TEEN
ratings.viz.com

VIZ
media
www.viz.com